# SEALAND

# SEALAND

THE TRUE STORY OF THE
WORLD'S MOST STUBBORN
MICRONATION AND ITS
ECCENTRIC ROYAL FAMILY

## DYLAN TAYLOR-LEHMAN

DIVERSION
BOOKS

For more information, email info@diversionbooks.com

Diversion Books
A division of Diversion Publishing Corp.
443 Park Avenue South, suite 1004
New York, NY 10016
www.diversionbooks.com

First Diversion Books edition, June 2020

Paperback ISBN: 978-1-63576-726-1
eBook ISBN: 978-1-63576-636-3

Printed in The United States of America

Library of Congress cataloging-in-publication data is available on file.

*To Pamela, wild royalty*

# CONTENTS

*Introduction:* The Old Man and the Sea (Fort)                          1

PART I: The Making of a North Sea Kingdom (1921–1967)          7

1       The War Hero and the Beauty Queen                      9

2       Fort Madness                                          19

3       Rock 'n' Roll Rebellion                               33

4       The Battle for Roughs Tower                           45

5       A Most Eventful Fall                                  55

6       *E Mare Libertas*                                     65


PART II: Guns, Germans, and the Defense of a Dynasty
        (1967–2000)                                           81

7       Belasco, Buoys, and the Chelmsford Court
        of Assizes                                            83

8       Behold the Trappings of Statehood                     93

9       Arrival of *die Deutschen*                           101

10      The Coup: World War Sealand                          109

11      The Dynasty Expands                                  127

12      Shots Fired, Forged Passports,
        and Outrageous Criminality                           145

**PART III**: Surviving the Cyber Age (2000–present)     159

13    Cypherpunks and Offshore Data Storage     161

14    Sealand in the New Millennium     181

15    *Athleta Principalitas*     197

16    Two Moments of Profound Silence     209

17    A Dark Mirror     219

18    Crew Change     231

19    Prince of the Cockles     243

20    King of the Micronations     253

*Epilogue:* All Hail the Stubborn Kingdom     265

*Appendix:* Precedent, Justification, and Scholarly
         Opinion on Sealand as a Sovereign Nation     273

*Notes*     287

*Bibliography & Sources*     305

*Acknowledgments*     327

*Index*     331

# INTRODUCTION

# THE OLD MAN AND THE SEA (FORT)

---

*"It's no good having weapons if you're not prepared to use them."*
—Michael Bates

Michael Bates, a fifteen-year-old from a fishing town in southeastern England, stood shivering with excitement and fear on top of an old naval platform seven miles out in the roiling North Sea. It was the middle of the night in late summer 1967, and he had in his hands a beer bottle filled with gasoline and stuffed with a strip of old cloth. The chance to throw a Molotov cocktail at something was any young boy's dream come true, but in this case it was actually necessary: A small boat bobbing in the sea below was full of men looking to invade his family's fortress, and Michael alone was tasked with defending it.

The Bates family knew that invasion was likely at any time, and this is why Michael had stashed numerous firebombs along the perimeter wall of the fort he called home. The bombs sat next to chunks of metal and wood to be used for pelting, and there was even a homemade shotgun if things got especially hairy. The invaders had strength in numbers, but Michael had the literal higher ground, from which he could drop the bombs.

The fort was a simple but improbable structure, comprised of a metal deck spanning two massive concrete pillars that rose out of the open ocean. When it was light, Michael could see all the way to the horizon and could easily spot any approaching vessel. He was asleep when the boats puttered over, but, attuned to the sonorous murmurings of the sea, he jumped up from his slumber at the disturbance and ran crouching to the perimeter of the fort.

*Oh shit*, he thought. *Here we go again.*

This was at least the sixth time that summer that someone had tried to take over the fort. Originally called Roughs Tower, it was built during World War II to protect the Thames channel from Axis bombers. Following the war, the fort sat abandoned in international waters for twenty years until competing groups of pirate radio broadcasters realized how perfect it was for broadcasting outside the UK's restrictive radio laws. Thanks to subterfuge and straight-up physical force, it was Michael's family that currently held the reins to this extraterritorial kingdom. Michael's father—a businessman, war hero, and raconteur named Roy Bates—was the man in charge, and he had indeed launched his own pirate radio station and stashed Michael on the fort to keep it secure.

And so, on that summer night, young Michael stayed low and hidden as the boats puttered in the darkness closer to the huge pillars. He fumbled with a lighter, flicking the flint until he finally ignited the rag in the bottle full of gas.

"It's no good having weapons if you're not prepared to use them," he later said. "Freedom is a very fragile thing."

As the small yellow dinghy got into a strategic position alongside one of the pillars, Michael smiled a sadistic smile like Kevin in *Home Alone* and dropped the bomb directly onto the front of the inflatable craft. Tiny points of light were reflected in the occupants' eyes as the bottle fell in slow motion. Bullseye!

The bottle exploded, the roar of the flames echoing under the fort, the choppy waves illuminated by the glorious orange clouds. The men on the boat yelped and dove into the water as the raft shriveled in the flames, spun in a few circles, and then sunk limply into the abyss. The smell of burned plastic hung in the air, and the trespassers clung helplessly to the rough concrete pillars, trying to protect their heads from the chunks of metal and wood raining down from above.

As the waterlogged invaders were picked up by their comrades and taken back to shore, Michael smiled a huge smile. He was prince of the sea. He had kicked their asses, and he couldn't wait to tell his dad.

**A BURNING BOAT** is only the prelude to the adventure, intrigue, and family togetherness that would play out on Roughs Tower for a half century. Michael defended the fort with the same fervor one might a homeland, and that's because it eventually was. Roy Bates saw opportunity in the fort when he took it over, and he realized the scope of that opportunity would be even greater with the authority of statehood. And so, on September 2, 1967, Roughs Tower became the "Principality of Sealand," the world's newest and smallest country. Roy became Prince Roy, his wife Princess Joan, and Michael and his sister Penelope, prince and princess. The normal trappings of statehood soon followed, including coins, stamps, passports, a flag, and a constitution. The Sealanders would be joined by many proud citizens over the years—a cast of adventurers, rogues, conmen, and cypherpunks all happy to call the principality home and go head-to-head with the British government.

Sealand has now been around for more than fifty years, "longer than Dubai has been in existence," as Prince Michael points out. This book is a chronicle of the principality's storied history, from its pre-Sealand days as a claustrophobic military readout to an experiment in nation-building that has inspired micronations on every continent.

"Our life has always been rich in adventure. You cannot imagine all that took place on Sealand," Princess Joan said. For starters, there have been weddings, battles, attempted coups, and a half-marathon run on the fort. The principality served as an offshore data haven, challenging internet laws that had yet to be written. The principality's legal claims have delighted scholars of international law, while others view Sealand as a social experiment on how we might conduct ourselves when climate change forces us to live at sea in *Waterworld*-ian floating enclaves. Athletes have been proud to compete in the principality's name, and a Sealand flag even made it to the summit of Mount Everest. But like any nation, there have been numerous challenges to the principality's leadership: Forged Sealand passports have been used in crimes all over the world, and, lurking in the shadows is a bizarre exile government of quasi-Nazi mystics vying to harness a mystical energy called Vril.

Maintaining Sealand introduced enormous amounts of stress and financial hardship to the family and led many to wonder why anyone would hold onto the rusting maritime heap. But the endeavor has been a unique cause to rally around—one that has drawn the Bates family closer together. The story of Roy and Joan Bates is one of storybook devotion, a powerful romance filled with ups and downs and schemes and theatrics. The family now boasts a fourth generation of Sealandic royalty: youngsters that have yet to throw firebombs at invading boats but whose lives will no doubt harken the example set by their feisty forebears.

At its very core, the story of Sealand is an inspiring tale of daring and self-determination in a world of homogeneity, a quixotic adventure that has accomplished more than even Roy Bates thought possible. Defending themselves from imperial governments and rapscallion usurpers, Sealanders have always managed to come out on top, and the tiny nation's motto encapsulates this rogue spirit.

*E Mare Libertas*: "From the sea, freedom."

Indeed.

Hunker down in the comfortable surroundings of your own kingdom, and we'll set sail into the astonishing story of Sealand, the world's foremost micronation.*

### A NOTE ON THE USE OF
### THE TERM *MICRONATION*

The term *micronation* is distinct from "microstate," which is a tiny country recognized worldwide with membership in international organizations such as the United Nations. Examples of microstates include Andorra, Lichtenstein, and Niue.

A "micronation" is generally defined as an invented country within the territory of an established nation whose boundaries typically go unrecognized on the world stage. Micronations have been declared for reasons serious and tongue-in-cheek alike. Some are a hobby, whose participants roleplay affairs of state, while others are born from arguable claims to disputed lands. Micronations are also called "ministates," "ephemeral states," and "counter-countries," although these terms are less commonly used.

---

* The Principality of Sealand is unrelated to the "SeaLand" often seen on the side of shipping containers. SeaLand is a subsidiary business of Danish shipping giant Maersk and not an economic arm of the principality.

   "Sealand" also refers to a region of Wales and a Babylonian dynasty, but these entities are unrelated to the story that follows.

The Principality of Sealand is often called a micronation and is a respected grandparent of these entities for obvious reasons. However, some argue that the term *micronation* isn't serious enough to do the principality justice—Sealand was founded on territory that was in genuinely international waters and has endured since 1967. All the while, the Sealanders have fought to keep these claims alive in ways unmatched by most other micronations.

I will use the term *micronation* throughout this book when referring to Sealand for reasons of convenience, but the reader can rest assured that I imbue the term with the gravitas the principality is due, as its history can hold its own alongside that of any macrostate.

PART I

# THE MAKING OF A NORTH SEA KINGDOM

(1921–1967)

# CHAPTER 1

# THE WAR HERO AND THE BEAUTY QUEEN

*"I fought for both sides. I didn't care, I just wanted to fight."*

—Roy Bates

For months on end in winter and spring 1944, the men of the British Army's 8th Indian Infantry Division stared up at a monastery in central Italy that hovered over the sodden soldiers like the sigil of a cruel god. The monastery sat atop a promontory of a 5,000-foot-tall mountain, overlooking the Liri Valley and a small town called Cassino. The Nazis occupied the hill and guarded it fiercely with machine gun nests and mines, as it gave them a commanding view of the landscape in every direction and thus control of the resupply route to Rome.

Built in 652 by Benedictine monks, the monastery was preposterously well endowed. With concrete walls 10 feet thick and 150 feet tall, the readout offered a genuinely impenetrable vantage point. A consortium of Allied troops, representing countries as far-flung as Poland, New Zealand, and Nepal, were tasked with wresting control from the Nazis.

The four major attacks on Monte Cassino were legendary in their wretchedness. The only way up the mountain was a path comprised of hairpin turns and jagged, rocky terrain. The first assault was launched in January in the midst of remarkably harsh winter conditions. In the spring the flooded Gari and Rapido Rivers turned the roads into a morass of mud. Frostbite and trench foot were common, and in many cases the "venomous outbursts" of fighting at Monte Cassino amounted to slaughter. Fighting was so concentrated in the ruined town of Cassino below that individual buildings were sometimes occupied by troops from both sides.

Standing straight-backed and proud among this rank agglomera-
tion of violence and miserable weather was Roy Bates,* age twenty-three,
who hailed from Essex, an industrial county in southeastern England
studded with shipping warehouses and fishing boats. Roy was a soldier
with the Royal Fusiliers, an infantry division attached to the 8th Indian
Regiment, and he had been fighting in battles across the world since
1939. Roy had black, slicked-back hair and a slight underbite. Over
six feet in height, he also was noticeably tall among the forces in the
valley.

Roy was a seasoned fighter, having joined the military as soon as
he turned eighteen. In fact, by the time he was fighting at Monte
Cassino, he had fought in two wars on three sides. When he was fifteen
he dropped out of boarding school to fight in the Spanish Civil War.
It was a wrenching ideological conflict for control of the Spanish state,
pitting the ultimately successful fascists against united leftists, anarchists, and communists, but Bates's interests were less political and
more visceral. "I fought for both sides," he said. "I didn't care, I just
wanted to fight."

That ambition for adventure called again during the Second World
War, though this time Roy had a more vested interest in the conflict,
fighting in defense of his beloved England. Roy "was a throwback,"
said a friend and colleague named Bob Le-Roi. "He should have been
born in the time of the first Queen Elizabeth and sailed with Drake.
If ever there was a true buccaneer, it was Roy."

Winter slowly turned into summer in the Liri Valley, and on a
muggy day in May 1944, Roy and his fellow Fusiliers were briefed on
an upcoming assault just south of the town of Cassino. He and two
other soldiers were carrying supplies for the attack to be launched the
next day, in which the Fusiliers would paddle rubber boats across the
river and wipe out the German defenses on the other side. Following
the briefing, Roy crouched as he ran with his Bren gun to a bank of
trees to prepare for the assault. Suddenly, the ground below him
erupted in a geyser of fire and dirt. One of the thousands of mines laid
by German troops had exploded under foot, sending rock and shrapnel

---

* Press accounts of Sealand often refer to Roy as "Paddy Roy Bates." Paddy was his first
name according to his birth certificate but he almost always went by Roy.

ripping through trees and human flesh. Roy was in and out of consciousness, his breathing heavy in his own brain, as he was rushed away from the battlefield by expeditious medics.

Roy missed out on the upcoming assault on account of the explosion, but it turned out to be another battle of indeterminate importance. The Fusiliers had crossed the river but were unable to get much farther, pinned down by machine gun fire until Canadian tanks made their way to the front line and gave the Fusiliers the chance to pull themselves out of their holes. Nevertheless, it burned Roy that he couldn't be there, and he lay in the field hospital willing his wounds to heal.

Roy recuperated enough to rejoin his men in July, who by that point had excised the Germans from Monte Cassino and were pushing their way further north. Roy had already been stabbed, shot, and crippled by frostbite and disease, and being blown up by a mine was merely an inconvenient setback to the horrendous and wildly exciting duty of being a Royal Fusilier. "I rather enjoyed the war," Roy was known to say throughout his life, and he always maintained he'd do it all over again as soon as he was called.

Fittingly, this was the man who would go on to found a kingdom in the North Sea and reign for decades as its prince. Roy was indeed a buccaneer from times of yore, and he would put his blood, sweat, tears, and family savings into a singular experiment whose reverberations would endure well into the next century.

## BIRTH OF A SCALAWAG

Roy's preternatural bravery and knack for survival came from tragic circumstances. He was born on August 29, 1921, to Harry and Lilyan Bates in the west London suburb of Ealing,* the lone surviving child of six brothers and sisters, who had himself overcome a severe bowel obstruction when he was a baby.

Harry Bates, a butcher, had earned a Military Cross for bravery in World War I and was by many accounts a fairly severe and demanding figure. Lilyan, a nurse during both World Wars, was a force to be

---

* As it would happen, a studio in Ealing produced the 1949 movie *Passport to Pimlico*, in which the London suburb Pimlico technically becomes an independent enclave of a French dukedom, thereby separating itself from British jurisdiction.

reckoned with herself. Things could get so volatile that at one point young Roy was accidentally knocked into the fireplace when his parents were fighting, and to toughen Roy up, his father used to draw bathwater in the evening, let it freeze overnight in the unheated bathroom, and then break the ice in the morning and throw Roy in.

The family moved to Southend-on-Sea in Essex when Roy was a few months old because of his father's lung condition. Harry had been gassed in the war and had difficulty breathing; at one point he had been given no more than a year to live on account of the damage. Southend, built along the north shore of the River Thames where it empties into the North Sea, was popular at the time as a resort city. With its ample seaside air and mud said to contain healing properties, Harry had fond memories of Southend from when he was stationed there during his tenure in the army. (The "on-Sea" suffix was added to many area towns to make them more attractive to tourists.)

When Roy was a boy, Southend had become a midsized, bustling city, characterized by winding thoroughfares and residential streets lined with rows of tightly packed townhouses and apartments. With a shopping district and esplanade filled with arcades along the shore, Southend sits atop steep hills that slope down to the Thames, treating residents and visitors to incredible views of the river that seems oceanic in its vastness. Far off in the distance lies the Isle of Sheppey and the county of Kent forming the opposite shore, with numerous islands in between separating the river into channels that flow out to sea. Extending more than a mile into the estuary is the Southend Pier, the longest pleasure pier in the world, which is serviced by its own train.

The Bates family settled into a home in the upscale Thorpe Bay neighborhood in eastern Southend, but imposing trees gave the property a despairing aura. Grim foliage notwithstanding, the climate suited Harry, and he lived very actively until he died at age seventy-nine. Meanwhile, Lilyan continued as a practicing nurse well into her late seventies.

Young Roy was a day boy at a boarding school but was not engaged by the experience. He was expelled a few times, though typically allowed to resume his studies at the start of the next term. "It was a quite nice school and they were quite efficient, except what they wanted to teach me and what I wanted to learn were quite different," he said. "The only examination I ever passed in my life was my medical."

Roy dropped out of boarding school to fight in Spain, and when he was deported back to England, he began apprenticing with thirty other young men as a rancher for Lord Edmund Vestey, whose family owned a meat processing empire that spanned three continents. There was a big map behind Vestey's desk, and the Lord asked young Roy where he wanted to be stationed. "All the same to me," Roy said as he pointed to a random area of South America. Vestey told him that was Argentina. "Great," Roy replied.

Roy's Argentinean escapade was scrapped when Britain declared war on Germany in September 1939. The chance to travel and fight once again beckoned, so Roy tried to extricate himself from his responsibility to Lord Vestey in order to fight against the Nazis. But the Vestey outfit had already booked him a ticket to Brazil, and, try as he might, Roy couldn't get himself fired. As a "controlled job," his was necessary for war production, and his country needed him to tend to his post. So Roy simply stopped going to work, and after sending a series of telegrams trying to persuade him to return, they finally cut him loose.*

Meanwhile, the military didn't immediately accept Roy's enlistment because the war wasn't projected to last longer than six months. But it quickly became apparent that the world would be mired in another hideous conflict, so Roy was accepted into the Coastal Battalion. To Roy, this was not a suitable option, however, since a home front defense force assignment meant that he wouldn't be sent overseas for combat. Roy successfully worked his way into the army, where he was put into the Essex Regiment and then commissioned into the Royal Fusiliers.

The British line infantry regiment Roy was assigned to got its start in 1685 as a unit of weapons' bearers who carried special rifles that could be lit with a less caustic spark, thereby providing cover for the artillery without accidentally blowing up barrels of gunpowder. Since

---

* For their part, the Vestey family was enormously wealthy but would later raise some eyebrows for their complex but legal tax avoidance schemes, whose workings one official described as being so hard to understand that it was "like trying to squeeze rice pudding."

that time the Fusiliers had been dispatched to conflicts all over the globe, including the American War of Independence and the slaughterhouse that was World War I's Battle of Passchendaele. During the Second World War, they were attached to the 8th Indian Division, fighting in Iraq, Syria, and Iran. In 1943, the 8th Indian Division was moved to Europe, traveling north through Italy, where Roy and his fellow soldiers would engage in the four battles of Monte Cassino. "As fighting men they were of one piece—the warp and woof of an unsurpassed military fabric," recalled one historian.

Roy was officially discharged in 1946, when he was barely twenty-five, as the only surviving officer from his battalion. He had entered the army as a private but came out as A2 Major—a company commander in charge of up to two hundred people. At one point the youngest Major in the British Army, Roy "would've gone further up the rank in the war had he not kicked an officer for rebuking him for doing things the way he wanted to do them," his son Michael later said.

In addition to the numerous injuries he sustained during the war, at one point a German grenade exploded right in front of Roy's face, shattering his jaw and shredding the skin on his rubicund visage. The damage was so severe that a doctor told him that no woman would ever be able to love him again. A born contrarian, Roy defied the words of the doctor and met Joan, the woman who would be his partner in crime—sometimes literally—for the rest of their lives.

## WHEN ROY MET JOAN

As Roy recalled, sometime in late December 1948, he went to the famed Kursaal dancehall on the Southend shore simply "to drink." There he caught sight of Joan Collins, just eighteen years old at the time. She was laughing with friends and trying to look at Roy without looking at him at the same time. The scene was one of classic romance, where the room darkens, a spotlight shines on two people on opposite sides of the room, and the music becomes fuzzy as they stare at each other through the swaying of an indistinct mass of people. Roy floated across the room, looked at her tenderly, and asked her to dance.

"It was stunning, like what you read in a book," Joan recalled. "He was tall, dark, and handsome. There was no question in my mind that we would always be together from the first minute."

Joan was a striking woman with a radiant smile and long, blonde hair, her aura shining as brightly as any actress of the time. She did a good bit of modeling, lending her face to a variety of ad campaigns, magazines, and fashion shows organized for charitable purposes. Her modeling career continued throughout the 1970s. In fact, Michael would take his girlfriends to a club in town where a picture of his mother, donning fur, hung in the foyer.

Roy and Joan were seemingly fated to be together. Joan herself was from a military family whose forebears were coalminers from northern England and Ireland. She was born in the Aldershot Barracks on September 2, 1929, to Elizabeth and Albert Collins—a relatively quiet, normal family as compared to Roy's—but there were some odd coincidences between them. For example, Roy and Joan's fathers had served together at the Battle of the Somme, both were in the Royal Horse Artillery, both were stationed at the same barracks, and both even had the same toe blown off the same foot.

Joan grew up with her younger brother in Wakering, a small town just east of Southend housing various military installations. Eight years younger than Roy, she was too young to work in munitions factories during the war years, so she took jobs like theater usherette or chocolate biscuit factory employee that were perennially staffed by teens. Joan's parents sometimes kept her out of school to help around the house, which had water pumps in front and back that straddled the line between the Victorian era and the modern day.

Technically Roy was already engaged when they met (and to Joan's friend, at that), but it was one of those situations in which the direction he had to take was clear. It took Roy three days to propose, Joan said, "and I thought he was taking a hell of a long time." The two were married at the Caxton Hall registry office in Westminster in February 1949. They would stay married for more than six decades. "After all these years we never need anyone else around. We're never bored together," Joan said later in life. "I met Roy at eighteen and married him after six weeks. I admired him then, and still do."

Roy initially embarked on the dutiful responsibilities of a husband, putting on a tie and commuting to work at a company that imported poultry by the trainload from Southern Ireland to the rationed North. "There was rationing in the country then, and I found the only thing that wasn't rationed that people could really eat plenty of was poultry," he said. But Roy found that this endeavor involved a lot of dreary deskwork, and he soon had an *Office Space* moment about the horrors of the nine-to-five.

"I found myself sitting in a train one day at Leigh station and there were five [businessmen] sitting on my side with blue suits and briefcases and bowler hats, and five sitting on the other side," Roy said. "So I got up at Leigh and threw my bowler hat and my briefcase in the water and phoned up my lawyer and said 'Get rid of everything. I'm not going to do this any longer.' And I went and bought a fishing boat."

While the couple had friends who sailed or fished, neither of the Bateses had any practical experience working in the commercial fishing industry. Fortunately, cheap boats were in ready supply on account of the surplus of vessels built for the war, and the Bateses bought an old military harbor launch that he called the *Mizzy Gel*. The thirty-six-foot boat was previously used to shuttle troops between ship and shore, and the couple outfitted it with other bits of military surplus. B&B Fisheries, the family's fishing business, would grow to become a decent-sized operation with around a half-dozen boats, but Roy and Joan began looking into additional business options once they discovered that fishing did not bring in significant money. "As they used to say in Leigh, 'every fisherman's got his backside hanging out of his trousers,'" Roy said.

In early 1946, the couple set up Airfern, Ltd., a business that would harvest and export "white weed" or "air fern," a living colony of polyps related to coral that, when taken out of the water and dried, looks like a plant and doesn't require any water or maintenance. The North Sea is one of the only places in the world where air fern grows in commercial quantities, and Roy got to work learning how to harvest and dry it. He bought one of the very first Scuba outfits and had to spend a week in the Scuba factory undergoing pressure tests to make sure he knew what he was doing. Once he had a handle on diving, he dove down to investigate where the air fern was growing along the bottom of the sea. He soon developed a process in which he would dive down and load the air fern onto giant metal rakes being dragged by a retrofitted boat from his fleet. The business was tough to get off the ground, but eventually it flourished, with air fern being sold to fancy florists in New York for use in bouquets and floral arrangements. A horrific flood in 1953 swamped the coastal region, killing dozens of people and wiping out the fern beds, but the business was able to make a comeback, and the family maintained the operation into the 1980s.

Roy was willing to try anything, and his ambition led to increasingly grandiose plans. Later ventures included a chain of butcher shops, a real estate agency, and Decor, Ltd., which imported latex from Malaysia to manufacture swim fins. The only time Joan reportedly put her foot down was when Roy suggested they move to Kenya and buy a farm during the Mau-Mau uprising. "These things attract me like a madman," Roy admitted. "She puts a little caution into me and makes me think about things. She taught me so much with patience and understanding."

Besides, there was the family to think about. Penelope "Penny" Bates was born on March 19, 1949, and then came Michael Roy Bates on August 2, 1952. The family moved around Southend, eventually settling into an apartment on the corner of Avenue Road and Avenue Terrace in a Southend neighborhood called Westcliff, where they inhabited a second-floor apartment reached by ascending a half-walled flight of stairs.

Joan was a devoted mother, taking care of the kids as Roy worked and engaging them in society activities such as horseback riding. Her demeanor contrasted somewhat with Roy's, who, like his own father, was said to sometimes run the home like it was his army barracks. He expected the same level of old-school toughness out of his children that allowed him to live life on his own terms, and he wasn't afraid to allow his children to get a little banged up in the process. Michael recalled being thumped by his dad for falling out of a tree instead of successfully climbing it. "It's difficult to relate to—my father's reasonably Victorian," Michael recalled.

But Michael often witnessed his father's remarkable daring and compassion. When he was around ten years old, they were relaxing at the family's beach hut at Thorpe Bay when Michael heard the cries of two teenage girls who were being pulled out to sea, bobbing up and down in the insurmountable current. Suddenly, Roy sprang into action and ran down the beach, pushing his way through beachgoers, flinging off his sunglasses and sandals, and leaping into the water. Another man followed him, and they dragged the girls ashore. A nurse attempted artificial respiration on the seemingly lifeless girls laid out on the sand to no avail. "Get out of the way!" Roy shouted. He picked up one of girls from behind, pushed his fists into her stomach, and shook her like a ragdoll.

"Unbelievably, what seemed like a gallon of water gushed from her mouth onto the beach," and the girl began coughing and breathing again. "I have never before or since seen such an unconventional and successful resuscitation," Michael recalled.

The Bates children were ultimately sent off to separate boarding schools, where Roy's reputation preceded them. The headmaster of Michael's school initially wouldn't accept him as a student because he said he was too old to take on another pupil like Roy. Michael was prone to fighting in the schoolyard, but he eventually settled into a groove in an all-boys school in Wales while Penny was dispatched to an all-girls school. At home on holiday, they were driven to horse-riding lessons in the family Bentley, and the family was by then known as always well-dressed and glamorous.

Even so, the comforts of a prosperous life were not fully satisfying for the Bateses. Though he had forgone the bowler hat and briefcase, Roy—always on the lookout for the next adventure—felt that even his series of unusual yet lucrative pursuits were just another version of the daily grind. Some strange military structures were faintly visible on the horizon from the shores of Essex—ungainly silhouettes just begging to be explored.

# CHAPTER 2

# FORT MADNESS

---

*"It was like a watery bus in the sea, stripped of all its fillings."*
—Roy Bates

At 220,000 square miles, the North Sea is a little smaller than the state of Texas. The funnel-shaped, relatively young body of water stretches from Scotland to Norway and is bound in the east by the shores of Germany, Holland, and Belgium and in the west by Great Britain. Above France it becomes the English Channel, which in turn empties into the Atlantic Ocean. Previously a stretch of earth called Doggerland that connected the British Isles to mainland Europe until about 6500 BCE, the North Sea formed after ice sheets of the most recent ice age melted, isolating what would become the United Kingdom as a series of islands. It is also a fairly shallow—though frigid—sea, only around three hundred feet deep on average and just twenty-one miles wide at its narrowest point between Dover in the UK and Calais in France.

The North Sea region is known for its commercial fishing and oil production industries. It boasts some of the busiest ports in the world, in particular those around the Thames Estuary, around thirty-five miles east of London. Overlooking that estuary and the river that feeds it, Southend-on-Sea has been an important fishing area for hundreds of years and a nexus of human activity since the first communities were established there around 40,000 years ago. Twice a day, the waters of the Thames recede and leave a mile of mudflats in their wake, stranding boats in the muck until the waters return. Beyond the mud, channels of water flow between the various islands and sandbanks.

The Bates family had their boat the *Mizzy Gel* docked on the River Roach, around six miles north of their home in Southend. From there they would take it past Foulness Island and up into the River Crouch, which in turn flows into the North Sea. Roy sailed for business and pleasure, with his son Michael often accompanying him. As the first generation of the family to make a living from the water, the father and son would sail past docks and container ships and lighthouses on their jaunts to sea, but the huge sea forts peppering the estuary escaped their notice until a fateful day in early 1965.

The fort that would become the Principality of Sealand is an altogether perplexing presence whose use isn't immediately apparent. Attached to a sturdy concrete base, two immense concrete "legs" rise sixty feet out of the water, with a thin metal platform measuring 120 by 50 feet—about the size of two tennis courts—laid across the top. In the middle of the platform, positioned above the gap between the legs, is the fort's command center. In its original incarnation, there was another room on top of the first that held radar equipment, giving it a tiered look not unlike a pagoda.

The forts are dwarfed by the humongous container and cruise ships that pass them by, but they seem immense when approached by small boat. In the same way a building seems to move as you look up from below, so too does the fort seem to "loom drunkenly from the waves." The structures vibrate deep, unsettling tones when pounded by stormy seas, but on calm days the water gurgles playfully as it sucks and slaps the concrete.

Fortifications have been built along the water at strategic points for over one thousand years, given the ease of access the Thames gives to mainland England, and they represent the struggles endured by various dynasties and kingdoms. Sturdily built to withstand combat, the Maunsell Naval Forts are named for their designer, Guy Anson Maunsell, a British engineer who is most famous for his unconventional but utilitarian concrete structures. Four of these duoliths were put into place in 1942 to defend the Thames Estuary from Nazi fighters dropping bombs and magnetic mines, since it was said that German pilots didn't need maps when going on bombing runs to London as they could just follow the river to their target like a highway. The forts—Sunk Head, Tongue Sands, Knock John, and Roughs Tower—were set roughly six miles apart from each other and stretched twenty-six miles from the north near Clacton-on-Sea in Essex down south to

Margate in Kent. By the early 1960s, the forts had been left to decay into the sea. The government briefly considered demolishing them or turning them into lighthouses, but ultimately decided that the expense wasn't worth it.

## A GIANT LEAP FOR MICRO-KIND

January 30, 1965, was a day that would change everything—not just for the Bates family but the world map as we know it—as Michael and Roy made their approach to Fort Knock John. Located about three miles out in the Thames Estuary from Southend, it was clear that twenty years of no maintenance had taken its toll. Bits of concrete fell into the sea, and rust was apparent even from far off. Nevertheless, Roy began looking for a way to hoist himself up to the top of the platform to see the fort close up.

The *Mizzy Gel* did a puttering circle around the legs and stopped near a remarkably dangerous-looking cage that seemed moments away from rusting apart. Maunsell had apparently forgotten to include a way to resupply the fort, and so a scaffolding-like platform was built between the concrete base and the metal platform. A zigzag of ladders led to a small platform under the superstructure, which in turn led to the fort above. Piece by piece it had begun to fall apart over the years, but enough beams and ladders were intact to provide a direct—if hazardous—way of accessing the top. Roy Bates steadied himself on the gunwale of the boat, leapt onto the cage, and shimmied his way up to the underside of the fort. Michael looked up at him, not content to remain on the boat.

Warm currents from the North Atlantic generally keep the North Sea free of ice, but it is a notoriously tempestuous ocean that can make boats bounce "like a champagne cork in a pan of boiling water." Even Roy second-guessed putting his son up to the treacherous task of jumping from the boat to the cage. But Michael swore he could do it and, swallowing his fear, he leaped to his destiny.

It was one small step for Michael and one giant leap for micro-kind.

Roy stooped under the hatch that led to the deck proper and rammed his shoulder against the door until it finally wrenched loose. He emerged triumphantly into the sunlight. Roy could see for miles in every direction, spotting soaring birds, distant boats, and the buildings lining the shore. It was the first time he was able to see the familiar environs from such a unique vantage point. "The sea, once it casts its spell, holds one in its net of wonder forever," as Jacques Cousteau put it. Twelve-year-old Michael scuttled up the hatch right behind him, practically kissing the deck when he stood on its stable surface. Michael took a few deep breaths, and the pair got to exploring.

The fort was a time capsule full of old machinery beset with rust and the infinite shit of countless birds. The forts were approximately 5,920 square feet—about that of a large house—but the square footage is divvied up among cramped concrete rooms in the towers and the superstructure's workspaces. The metal superstructure was bisected by a narrow hallway that led to three large rooms on one side and four smaller rooms on the other. The hallway led from the south deck to the north, both of which boasted heavy antiaircraft guns and other pieces of wartime equipment. The walls were big sheets of steel held together with large metal rivets, lending the fort an obvious maritime appearance.

Each leg of the fort was divided into seven floors, the majority of which are located under the water's surface. Steep, narrow ladders extended down from tiny openings on each floor. The doors seemed to reveal only a depthless, yawning chasm, but beyond the darkness lay the marines' quarters and storerooms. The fort's other leg was filled with two 5,000-gallon tanks for fresh water and gigantic pieces of machinery that supplied the fort with electricity and a nominal amount of heat. An elevator in one of the legs had long since fallen apart, leaving a huge shaft that seemed to go straight down to hell. The bottommost floor was about as spooky as could be imagined, and in time the Bateses would find that it served very well as a prison cell.

Michael and Roy walked into what used to be the control room in the middle of the fort. Window coverings were creaked open to let in sunlight, revealing officers' quarters, workbenches, and ancient privies. There was no human presence, but they felt they were being watched. Cormorants "sat with hunched shoulders and look[ed] at us from under hooded eyes like the boatman from Hades that carried souls across the River Styx," Michael writes in his autobiography *Holding the Fort*.

All in all, it was a desolate and postapocalyptic environment, and even the entrepreneurial Roy's first impression was not great. "It was like a watery bus in the sea, stripped of all its fillings," he said. Nevertheless, the fort held promise, and the trip hadn't been undertaken for mere curiosity's sake. Roy could sense the connection between the abandoned sea forts and a roguish new fad sweeping across the UK. He thought deeply about how he was going to claim the territory for himself, like an explorer who had just set foot on a distant land.

## THE CONCRETE ATLANTIS

If Roy Bates was Sealand's founder, then Guy Anson Maunsell was its unwitting architect. It was thanks to the exigencies of global conflict that an idea for mid-ocean forts was taken seriously and would come to make up an unconventional part of England's seascape.

Maunsell was born in India to British parents in 1884. His father was a strict military man "with little interest in anything other than the men and horses in his command," but young Guy found himself much more drawn to the challenges of civil engineering than mortal combat. He graduated from university at the top of his class and spent a year traveling and painting before returning in 1908 to work for a construction firm that specialized in concrete. It was a propitious landing, as Maunsell took to the material and would use it in almost all his work.

During World War I, Maunsell worked for the firm that built the largest explosives factory in the world. Maunsell was conscripted into service and served on the front lines before being placed as an engineer in government offices at Westminster, where he was tasked with designing concrete-hulled boats and shipyards. Twelve of the tugs he designed were built, and he designed what is probably one of the most claustrophobic apparatuses ever conceived: a manned concrete fort smaller than a car and tethered to the ocean floor to monitor enemy ships that could be quickly sunk to the bottom of the ocean if spotted. But most importantly, he uncovered plans for a series of seaborne bulwarks developed during previous wars, and these plans would influence the creations for which he is most known.

Concrete forts were a fixture along the British coast, with some of

Sealand's forebears standing since the Napoleonic Wars, when the government built almost 150 brick towers up and down the coast from Sussex to Scotland. They were called Martello towers after the region in Spain from which they originated, and many of them are still standing throughout England today. Maunsell also found that someone had designed a 10,000-ton structure resembling a giant buoy that was intended to be built onshore and dropped to the ocean floor, with its tower and weapons left sticking far above the waves like a well-armed lighthouse. Because the war was over before full-scale production could begin on the tower project, only two were ever built, one of which was scrapped, and the other of which was turned into a lighthouse.

During World War II, Maunsell worked for the British government in much the same capacity as he did during World War I. He was tasked with coming up with some way to protect the British coastline, particularly the Thames Estuary, which was a vital throughway for supplies. The batteries along the shore and the steamboats outfitted with antiaircraft guns just weren't cutting it defense-wise, and Maunsell drew inspiration from the earlier towers when considering how to prevent further German raids. He designed an updated version of the mid-ocean tower-fort that employed two concrete pillars instead of one, topped with a metal superstructure that guns could lay across. The towers would also provide the element of surprise to German pilots not expecting gunfire so far from the coast.

According to Maunsell's designs, the forts would measure 110 feet from the base to the top of the radar apparatuses, with the deck level standing approximately 60 feet above the seabed once sunk, depending on the tides and water depth at the different locations. The pillars initially boasted a blue, black, and gray camouflage intended to help blend the forts in with the horizon while the structures' odd profiles were meant to be difficult to hit with bombs. At 4,500 tons each, their sturdy construction was meant to withstand significant impact.

Given the profusion of mines dropped into the water and the seriousness of the German attacks—bomb raids necessitated a lights-out policy on shore with the onset of dusk—the idea was to get the fort project up and into production as efficiently as possible. One selling point was the efficient method of construction. The forts were to be built in their entirety on huge, hollow pontoons, which would be towed out to sea. Once above the predetermined location, the concrete base would be flooded and sunk so that it came to rest firmly on the ocean floor, with the metal command center and gun decks high above the water. Five hundred tons of brick rubble would be dumped around the base to keep the Maunsell Forts—built at a cost of £40,000 (around £2,100,000 today)—in place.

But the plan did not catch on with the Admiralty's top brass. The forts were simply too unusual and were regarded, as Maunsell put it, "as a wild cat scheme." Maunsell, a "strong character with immense confidence in his own judgment," was incredibly annoyed by the seeming shortsightedness. As the war raged on, however, the plans for the forts got bumped up to the right person and the project was greenlit in March 1941. Construction began early that summer in the shipyards at Gravesend,* a port city on the Thames a few miles in from the estuary. Huge sections of the shore were dredged to make room for the construction sites. The towers were built by stacking massive reinforced concrete circles called "biscuits" on top of tubular walls, whose rebar insides looked like tremendous cages. Pre-built wooden interiors were lowered into place in the cylindrical towers wholesale, giant rings fit snugly into tubes. Civilians living nearby saw the giant structures taking shape but were in the dark as far as what they were looking at, given the secrecy of the project.

The forts were technically known as "Thames Estuary Special Defense Units" (or TESDUs) and were given the Ministry of Defence code "Uncle," a number 1 through 4, and the name of the sandbanks on which they were placed. Roughs Tower, which would eventually become the Principality of Sealand, was U1. Knock John, which Michael and Roy explored in 1965, was U4.

Roughs Tower was towed out to sea by three tugs on a frigid February 9, 1942. Moveable objects like tables and chairs were lashed down for the ride. The tower was to be positioned at 51° 53' 40.8" latitude north, 1° 28' 56.7" longitude east, the farthest of the

---

* So named for the graveyards holding the remains of those who died at sea, so pestilence wouldn't make its way into London.

forts from the coast and technically outside of British territorial waters for the next forty-five years. This extraterritorial positioning would prove crucial to the birth of Sealand and its longevity to the present day.

Bad weather caused a delay in sinking the fort, but conditions improved enough that the operation could take place on February 11. At 4:30 p.m., Maunsell himself opened the gates on one end of the pontoon to flood the base of the fort. He noted politely that sinking the forts did not "constitute a definitely controlled operation in the sense that the movement once started can be arrested or altered." Sure enough, the sinking of Roughs Tower was almost a complete calamity.

A crazy gurgling sounded from underneath the pontoon as the water filled the succession of chambers in the base. One of the stopcocks wasn't working, so the chambers were filling unevenly. Any weight imbalance from the incoming water could tip the fort onto whatever lay in its path, or at the very least straight into the ocean. Troops were on deck and in the radar station surrounded by sharp-edged objects and extremely heavy pieces of equipment as Roughs Tower leaned at a more and more unsettling angle. They closed their eyes and gritted their teeth, a steady *"ohshitohshitohshit"* running through their minds, hoping against hope that the engineer's calculations were correct.

It took an eons-long, white-knuckle forty-five seconds for the first pillar to hit the bottom. The troops let out a communal sigh of relief at the resounding thud. The other pillar took only fifteen seconds to sink, putting the fort on an even keel on the bottom and bringing the process to a close.* The mix of concrete and steel in the middle of the sea would later be described as an "industrial-era Stonehenge," a "Blade Runner-style metallurgical building," and a "grotesque marine oasis."

---

* Louis Mountbatten, Supreme Allied Commander in Southeast Asia during World War II, observed the placement of Roughs Tower from a nearby boat and ordered that crewmembers were not to be aboard the other forts when they were sunk. The next day, he met with other Allied commanders to plan D-Day. D-Day would prominently feature another Maunsell design—this time for portable concrete harbors that allowed Allies to land on the Normandy beaches.

But in that moment, the fort stood triumphant, as eager and strapping as a fresh-faced recruit to join the fray.

"It was successful," Maunsell told one reporter laconically.

## A WATERY TOMB

A crew of approximately 120 men was stationed on each fort: ninety marines, thirty sailors, and three officers. Forts were linked by a telephone cable that came ashore at Felixstowe, with radar dishes and radar antennae lining the top of the superstructure. Each fort was outfitted with two 94mm Vickers heavy antiaircraft guns and two 40mm Bofors light antiaircraft guns. The Vickers guns were able to fire a 28-pound shell more than 20,600 yards up to 25 times per minute while the smaller Bofors guns could fire a two-pound shell more than 10,800 yards. Numerous other small machine guns were aboard the fort, and the troops were even given lances with sharpened hooks to fend off any invaders.

A Navy grunt could be expected to be on the fort for around six weeks at a stretch, after which they were given ten days leave and three days of duty at the base on the shore. The officers lived in relative comfort in the top floors of the towers, but the crew, who slept below the surface of the water, had inadequate light and heating. The lapping of the waves on the sides of the pillars could be soporific, but, as journalist Simon Sellars recently recalled, the sensation was also like sleeping in an underwater tomb.

"The room has no windows. It is dank, pitch-black, and deathly still. I've lost all spatial coordinates," Sellars wrote. "I hear a distant, dull hissing, like soil leaking through a coffin lid…I fall asleep, letting the blackness suffocate me. The dark is so heavy, it's like I'm buried alive." So unusual is the feeling that one of the caretakers on Sealand said he was surprised when Sellars didn't wake up screaming.

Living on the fort did in fact provoke psychological issues in many of the marines, manifesting itself in a condition called "fort madness." Recruits were required to take up knitting, painting, model building, egg decorating, or any other activity they could to keep their minds occupied. Marines were reportedly not allowed on leave until they showed the fruits of their labor, and the best project was awarded a carton of cigarettes. Nevertheless, a medical orderly stationed on the fort reported troops often coming to him in tears. At least one soldier jumped to his death in despair, preferring to drown in the North Sea than stay another moment on the fort. Eerily enough, he took his cigarettes with him over the edge but left his clothes folded neatly on his bunk.

"The story I heard, the guys that were actually out here were people that had been on shore-based gun emplacements and disappeared with the local girls and got drunk and god knows what else, and so they sent them out here as punishment," said Sealand's longtime caretaker Mike Barrington, whose association with the Bates family goes back more than thirty years. "It's like Alcatraz—there's no escape. Aside from jumping over the side, but you'll break your neck when you hit the water and end up somewhere in France or something if you're lucky."

The vulnerability to attack could be maddening as well. At one point a magnetic mine was floating on the surface of the water toward the fort. Marines began shooting at it trying to blow it up, but the mine remained unharmed as it floated closer and closer. The men all plugged their ears and braced themselves for the blast, but miraculously, it passed under the tower without exploding, and a nearby ship eventually blew it up after making fun of the people on the fort for being such bad shots.

The four naval forts weren't the only unusual Maunsell structures off the coast of England. He also designed 11-by-11-square-meter buildings that sat atop four narrow concrete legs for the army. Seven of these structures together comprised one complete fort, with catwalks connecting the individual units. The control tower with radar equipment at the center of the arrangement was surrounded by towers full of antiaircraft guns and powerful spotlights. The army forts were placed in the Mersey Estuary in northwestern England, and three more were built in the Thames in 1943. The towers took eight weeks to build on the pontoons but were battle-ready in the middle of the ocean in less than eight hours. Interestingly, the closest fort to the Bates family home is one of the army forts, and to this day it can be seen with the naked eye on a clear day from the shores of Southend.

Both sets of Maunsell's forts did their duty throughout the war, blasting away at incoming German planes and watching them crash and explode in the water miles away. By the time the forts were all up and running, blitzkrieg-style air raids were on the decline, though, as the Germans concentrated their diminished airpower elsewhere in Europe. The forts were ultimately responsible for the destruction of twenty-two planes, one German submarine, and thirty-three "Doodle-bugs"—jet-powered missiles that presaged the ballistic missiles used in later wars. The number was not tremendous, but the men were always happy to paint another swastika on the tower to celebrate the planes they shot down. The forts are credited with greatly reducing the number of mines dropped into the estuary, thereby facilitating the vital movement of people and supplies.*

The British government left the forts to the elements following the end of the war. Some remained occupied by a bare-bones crew, but by 1958 the forts were abandoned completely. A few of the forts were used intermittently for British military training exercises, and in 1968 the "Fury from the Deep" episode of *Doctor Who* was filmed at the Red Sands army forts.

Maunsell once said the forts were designed to last two hundred years, but some didn't fare that well. On March 1, 1953, a Swedish freighter called the *Baalbek* crashed into the Nore Army Forts, in the Thames Estuary between the Isle of Sheppey and Southend-on-Sea, during a heavy bout of fog. Two of the forts were destroyed, and four of the forts' maintenance crew died in the collision.** The Nore towers were removed and scrapped in 1959. Other forts were built on a shifting sandbar that eventually pulled them into the sea.

---

* Mines and bombs still occasionally wash up along the shore or are caught in fishing nets. The three masts of the USS *Montgomery*, which sank in the Thames Estuary with more than 6,000 *tons* of explosives on board, still stick up from the water, and nobody is quite sure what would happen if the munitions exploded. It would either send a tremendous geyser of water into the air or a catastrophic tidal wave toward the populated Southend shore.

** The Red Sands army forts in the Thames Estuary are still standing today, albeit quite precariously. No doubt influenced by the numerous plans for developing Sealand, a developer put forth plans in 2015 to turn the army forts into a forty-four-room luxury hotel, replete with glass walkways, sundecks and terraces, a helipad, and a landing jetty for hovercrafts.

As for the naval forts, Tongue Sands became unstable because it hadn't settled properly. In 1947 it had started shaking and falling apart, and the crew had to be rescued. Not long after, one of the fort's legs was severely damaged in a storm, and the fort started leaning fifteen degrees. An intense storm broke the rest of Tongue Sands apart in 1996 and left only a macabre eighteen-foot stump of the southern leg. Knock John Fort is broken but still standing, while Sunk Head was eventually blown up to teach Sealand a lesson (see chapter 5). Roughs Tower, the bastion of power that it is, was resurrected as Sealand in 1967 and appears to be in good health into the present day.

Maunsell is known in industry circles for his other contributions to the war effort and for his "undeviating professional integrity." He was said to be a parsimonious boss who paid his employees less than scale, as well as a family man who based his family vacations around trips to inspect engineering projects, but G. Maunsell & Partners, the firm he founded following World War II, would come to be known for its economical but quality engineers and methods of construction. Many of Maunsell's extant projects are remembered today for their functional designs, such as bridges in Australia and Denmark that are known among engineering enthusiasts to be modern classics.* G. Maunsell & Partners merged with the engineering consultant firm Oscar Faber in 2001, becoming Faber Maunsell, and then with global engineering firm AECOM in 2002. The group officially changed its name to AECOM in 2009.

"Engineers have always been society's unsung heroes yet they have played a pivotal role in the success of civilization," Maunsell biographers Frank Turner and Nigel Watson write. In Maunsell's case, he played a pivotal role not only in safeguarding England from invading fascists but also in the development of a new, unorthodox type of statehood.

---

* The firm, however, had a crisis on its hands when a bridge they partnered in constructing in Australia collapsed in 1970, killing thirty-five people in the worst industrial accident in the country's history up to that time.

ON THE WAY back from Knock John in January 1965, Roy felt a kinship with the old structure, as both had served king and country with pride and aplomb. As it would turn out, in just over two short years, Roy would be king of his own country. Until then, however, he was going to don a different crown. The 1960s brought an endearing kind of piracy to Britain's shores, and from atop the glorious heights of Knock John, Roy Bates was going to hoist a Jolly Roger of his own.

# CHAPTER 3

# ROCK 'N' ROLL REBELLION

*"Yes, it's the cheapest, but by God it's the best!"*
—Roy Bates

In the 1950s and 1960s, rock 'n' roll was taking the world by storm. Like youth everywhere, young Brits were keen to cut loose, and a flourishing postwar economy provided them with the time and money to do so. But while bands sprung up in every town and millions of young people went to dance every weekend, there was hardly any pop music on the air.

The British Broadcasting Corporation was Britain's only licensed broadcaster, and since its inception the mission had been to provide highbrow, culturally enriching programming for its listeners that was free from political influence and the "extreme intrusions of advertising" heard on commercial radio in places like the United States. Listeners paid an annual fee to listen to BBC programming through BBC-licensed transmitters. The BBC did make an effort to include a wide variety of features, including soap operas, coverage of obscure sports, and readings of the classics, but pop music's dubious intellectual value relegated it to the occasional weekend program.[*]

In response, groups of rogue broadcasters developed a remarkable way to combat the stale content of the airwaves: ships, outfitted as radio stations, would broadcast from the freedom of international waters. The "radio pirates," as they'd come to be called, often operated with cobbled-together equipment and minimal broadcasting experience, but their activities would prove invaluable to the pop sensibility of the nation. The pirate stations drew millions of listeners, challenged

---

[*] The station did occasionally have a pop hits hour. But the BBC employed house bands to cover original songs as a way around the licensing fees, and these versions felt woefully inauthentic.

governmental norms, and became one of the UK's most endearing criminal legacies. And when Roy set foot on the fort Knock John, this maverick enterprise was precisely what he had in mind.

Enter Radio Essex, and enter the family Bates.

## THE RISE OF THE RADIO PIRATES

Playing fast and loose with radio regulations wasn't a new phenomenon. People had been building their own receivers since the advent of radio in the UK. It was fairly easy to buy parts and construct one's own transmitter, but home broadcasting produced some interference in nearby radios and made it easy to trace illegal broadcasts back to the source. Remarkably, listeners' agreements with the BBC gave the company's agents permission to search their homes for unlicensed equipment. As such, enterprising DJs needed to figure out a way to broadcast from somewhere beyond the reach of the BBC—which meant beyond the UK's territorial reach.*

At the time, the territorial claims of most countries extended three miles from shore, a measurement said to be just beyond the distance a cannonball could be shot and still damage the wood of a ship. The idea wasn't entirely new. The first modern pirate radio station was a ship calling itself Radio Mercur, which transmitted pop music into Denmark from the North Sea starting in 1958, though one British group had attempted seaborne tuneage as early as 1928. When its equipment wouldn't work, the ship simply put loudspeakers on the deck and blasted music toward shore at top volume. Scandinavian countries eventually passed laws that allowed for multiple radio stations, obviating the need for pirate stations, which meant the owners were eager to unload their equipment and ships.

---

* On the international scene, nations were trying to work out an equitable way to broadcast in a way that would minimize interference to and from other countries. An eighty-nation conference held in 1965 attempted to outline some kind of international wavelength agreement. Ultimately, a group operating under the aegis of the United Nations developed a master frequency register board and attempted to allocate wavelengths accordingly. Written into the "European Agreement for the Prevention of Broadcasts Transmitted from Stations outside National Territories" were statutes against pirate radio broadcasters, and the onus was on national governments to address their respective countries' pirate problems.

Sea-based broadcasting began in the UK thanks to an enterprising group calling itself Radio Atlanta. Radio Atlanta was started by an Australian music publisher named Allan Crawford, along with a stage actress and courtesan "contemptuous of government intervention in the arts" named Kitty Black. Crawford and Black went to speak with a man with the very British name of Oliver Smedley to get the project off the ground. Smedley was a twice-wounded British war hero who had no compunction about putting himself in danger. A radio operator during the war, Smedley won a Military Cross for running behind German lines to get better reception for radioing in coordinates for artillery fire.

Smedley considered the BBC a form of government overreach that foreshadowed nothing less than a "future of humiliation, tyranny, and death." In early 1964, with Smedley's backing, Radio Atlanta purchased a ship previously used by Swedish pirates, renamed it the *Mi Amigo*, and scheduled some repairs to make it fully operational.* However, the son of the owner of the shipyard they took it to realized what Radio Atlanta was trying to do and held up repairs until he could kit out his own vessel: an old ferry he called the *Caroline*. The two stations took up positions in the Thames Estuary and raced to begin broadcasting.

Other ships and stations followed suit. A "professional freak" and proto shock-rocker named Screamin' Lord Sutch founded "Radio Sutch" in 1964, announcing his presence by appearing in front of the press in pirate garb with a group of cohorts dressed in leopard skins. Radio London was started by a Texas businessman, Radio 390 played "romantic music popular with Kent housewives," and Reg Calvert, a guy who owned a school that trained young men to be in bands, founded his own miniature radio empire and would later play a huge but unwitting role in the clampdown on pirate radio by accidentally getting himself killed.

---

* Radio Atlanta created a series of companies within companies in order to fund their station. The financial situations of many stations were, to "varying extents, intentionally obscure," explains Adrian Johns in *Death of a Pirate*, a history of the pirate radio era. "It certainly helped if one's financial expert held a conviction that offshore financial havens were not only prudent in general but morally necessary."

The ships were quite a sight to behold. They were substantial vessels, if not a bit creaky, and they were outfitted with incredibly tall antennas. The *Mi Amigo* had an antenna easily the length of the ship perched at a slight angle sticking up from its stern, held (ideally) in place with guy wires. Ships put into place increasingly larger antennas to out-broadcast their rivals.*

The public now had a variety of radio stations to choose from, and they tuned in in droves. Importantly, with an audience reaching into the millions, the stations attracted no end of advertisers. Not only did local businesses advertise but so did airlines and governmental entities like the National Egg Board, which gave a sense of legitimacy to the operation. A number of stations even stayed afloat by featuring religious broadcasts paid for by American evangelicals. At its peak, the pirate stations were earning millions per year in advertising revenue; some stations were said to individually bring in upwards of £20,000 each month (no less than £368,000 in 2019). The enterprise also became so popular that the pirate radio was said to influence the outcomes of local elections, and the Beatles even recorded Christmas greetings for Radio London and Radio Caroline.

In an attempt to underscore the radio stations' menace, the British government deemed them "radio pirates." The name obviously had the opposite effect. "The public instantly loved it," recalled Michael Bates, "and the press took to the exciting new phenomenon with glee." Far from being a menace, broadcasters became folk heroes and celebrities.

"Pirate broadcasting became definitive of popular culture," wrote one historian. "The stations claimed that their audience was larger than the BBC's; and if that claim was hard to verify, nobody doubted that it was at least plausible."

## RADIO ESSEX, ON 222 METERS 24 HOURS A DAY

Pirate radio was not foreign to the Bates household. Michael and Penny, then teenagers, were hip to the spotty broadcasts of Radio Luxembourg, a quasi-legal station in operation since the 1930s

---

* Call signals such as "You're in heaven on 187" did not refer to the height of antennae but rather the frequencies on which they broadcast, which were denoted in meters.

(though the station was known to play only half of a song as induce-
ment for listeners to buy the record). Like most parents, Roy didn't
care much for the caterwauling of pop artists, preferring crooners
like Dean Martin and Frank Sinatra, but he recognized an opportunity when he saw one, and he had also witnessed firsthand the
lucrative possibilities of commercial radio during his many business
travels to the United States. Over the summer of 1965, Bates final-
ized plans to establish a radio station on Knock John, the fort that
had occupied Roy's thoughts so profoundly after he and Michael
explored it earlier that year.

"I was tinkering with the idea to see if it could be done," Roy said.
"It was always in my mind a little bit, but when I heard the first thing
of Caroline going on the air, that did it. I decided to set one up myself."

Bates was not the only person who had his sights set on the
abandoned forts. The forts were a hot commodity among the
pirates, as there were only a finite amount of freestanding, unclaimed
structures in the waters around the UK. Indeed, almost every fort
in the Thames would come to host a radio station. So valuable were
the platforms that when one group took over a fort, a competing
group was almost certain to try to eject them. Thus, almost as soon
as Roy entered the world of radio piracy, he found himself embroiled
in conflict.

Radio City, home of the "Sophisticated Pirates" because they
broadcast on two frequencies, was going after Knock John Fort
around the same time Bates was. Radio City owner Reg Calvert sent
some of his engineers to clean the fort and ready it for occupation,
but Bates had already commissioned an antenna and had no intention of slowing his plans.

In late October, Bates—"6'3" tall and tough with it"—set out to
take the fort from Radio City with the help of some local ruffians. He
and his men clambered up the towers, manhandled a few of Calvert's
men, and left two teenagers on the fort like a flag stuck in the dirt.
But then Radio City got together their own crew, ejected the teenagers,
and re-staked their claim. Roy was incensed. This could only go on
for so long, and Roy drew on his adventures as a soldier to get the
upper hand.

"The old man was by now getting himself a bit of a reputation as an unstoppable nutter, which under the circumstances was quite a useful reputation," Michael said.

Seeing that the ladders hanging from the platform had all been retracted, Roy threw a specially made ladder onto the rickety landing platform and climbed up a rusty derrick to the deck while dodging a barrage of wood and metal projectiles. He stood on deck in a spotless suit, appearing to be nothing short of a secret agent. "We mean to stay on Knock John. Possession is nine-tenths of the law," Roy declared.

The move was so brazen and executed with so little regard for his own well-being that the Radio City folks applauded Bates as they turned over the fort. Bates was a sporting chap and shuttled the stunned Radio City crew back to shore, leaving them without a fort but no worse for the wear. "A disc jockey has to be many things—but a prizefighter isn't one of them," said one displaced DJ.

Calvert conceded defeat.

"As far as I am concerned, we are withdrawing from the fight," he said. "We have decided Knock John is too small for our purposes."

Though the Bates crew was in possession of the fort, it did not mean anyone knew what they were doing. Bates had to learn the ropes of running a radio station—he had to hire DJs, coordinate supplies, and figure out a way to fund the station. Ads for more DJs were placed in area papers, offering £12 per week.[*]

Bates made no bones about the fortitude required for the job. The trip from the shore to the fort took at least three hours (often accompanied by copious vomiting by those who hadn't yet gotten their sea legs), and the DJs could expect to be out there for weeks at a time. Simply getting onto the fort was a tremendous ordeal that entailed a treacherous climb up a ladder to get to the rickety landing stage and then being pulled up by "spotty pale teenage DJs, whose only physical exercise was dragging on a cigarette or opening a can of beans." When DJs weren't helping to get the equipment up and running, they were expected to clean, peel potatoes, and haul fuel.

---

[*] One DJ recalled knocking on Roy's door in pursuit of a job. "A huge guy called Roy Bates was standing there and looking at me." 'What the fuck do you want?' Roy asked. "I want to be a DJ, sir," he stammered.

"No frills here, you'll have to work bloody hard," Roy said.

The first transmitter was an old US Air Force beacon, and the crew slept on old army cots. Roy purchased in bulk red wool blankets left over from the war, which, according to Michael, were probably rejected by charity for being too uncomfortable. The blankets were also cut up and used to soundproof the steel walls in the studios and to make turntable slipmats. The toilet—a hole in the deck with a toilet seat on top of it—was nicknamed the "squat box." There were no functioning taps or showers, and it was reportedly impossible to convince Bates to repair them. Fortunately, Dick Palmer, "one of the more sensible lads out there," cobbled together parts for the diesel generators already on the fort and got them working again, providing, however erratically, heat and electricity.

Lunchtime and dinner meals were typically a variation of Spam, potatoes, and beans. A crewmember recalled eating the same food for months at a time depending on what Roy could get a deal on. "Yes, it's the cheapest, but by God it's the best!" he was known to say. The crew found old WWII rations in the bottom level of the fort but they didn't tell Roy because they knew he would have made them eat it instead of buying fresh supplies. The station had an electric teakettle, but it couldn't be turned on during the day. "If the kettle was used, the record decks slowed down," recalled pirate Bob Le-Roi. The DJs would sometimes make jokes on air about the quality of the food on the fort, which resulted in the Coast Guard coming to the fort to make sure nobody was actually starving. However, their grumbling also resulted in packages of chocolate and cigarettes sent to the station by sympathetic listeners.

Bates called his station "Radio Essex" after the nearby county. Radio pirate historians never fail to mention that Bates's operation was a thoroughly—though lovably—ramshackle enterprise characterized by an "air of jovial amateurism" and a "pleasantly anarchic tang." The station's first test signal was broadcast on October 27, 1965, using an impressive 222-meter homemade antenna, part of which was an "incredibly lethal" wire strung between masts above the fort's deck.

The first transmission was made by seventeen-year-old Mark Wesley: "This is Radio Essex, the voice of Essex on 222 meters and this is a test transmission." Wesley suggested they add the phrases "Phase 1" and "Phase 2" into the test broadcasts to make it sound like the station had really complicated equipment.

Commercials and call signs were made by tape recording someone talking with a gramophone being played in the background, the music turned up and down manually for effect. Roy himself read and recorded much of the advertisement copy in his living room, and greetings and call signs were recorded in several languages for the fun of it. Program continuity was assured by splicing recordings together with Scotch Tape. Bates knew he couldn't compete with the larger stations and their fancy equipment, but he was content to launch a regional station with the expectation that his enterprise would expand. "We're doing a job that's needed; the public wants us to do the job, and so do businesses. I think while this demand is here, we'll remain in business," he said.

Within a few weeks, Radio Essex had a full schedule of programming, playing all day, every day. They employed a total of fifteen DJs—each of whom had an area of musical expertise and would bring crates of their own records to the station—over the course of the radio's existence. Radio Essex was known for its inoffensive "middle of the road" programming, with pop programs and slightly edgier selections later in the evening. Bates initially had his DJs doing a rotating schedule of one-hour programs, but they were able to talk him into a more reasonable schedule of three- or four-hour blocks of music at a time. Either way, Radio Essex was the first station in Europe to run around the clock, and it quickly attracted a listenership. "Radio Essex on 222 meters 24 hours a day," announced the DJs over the airwaves at regular intervals. The station received frequent inquiries from young bands interested in having their music played on air. Lore has it that at one point a fledgling rock group called the Rolling Stones paid a visit to the Bates home to play a tape of their music for on-air consideration. "What a load of bloody crap," Roy said after giving the tape a listen.

The station was notorious for its spottiness, but the Essex-specific programming, news, and advertisements ensured a steady listenership in the area. As Joan explained, Radio Essex was the only local commercial station with programming and advertisements specific to the area. Most pirate stations were financed with American or Canadian money, and some featured DJs from abroad, but the Bateses kept the operation deliberately local. "The only American newsman we had was a salesman, he was as Yank as Yank can get, but he was the only one," Joan recalled.

Roy often traveled to tend to his other non-radio businesses, and this left Joan in charge of the radio enterprise. She worked as a station manager and caretaker to the DJs, balancing the expense accounts and coordinating the shipments of supplies. Joan also listened intently to the programs and provided constructive criticism to the presenters and undertook the PR work for radio, TV, and newsprint. She also acted as a liaison between the DJs and Roy, who could sometimes be quite prickly.

"Between the two of us, we had to do it all. We had to teach ourselves by listening and learning and reading. We knew what we wanted and what we thought was the best programs to put out, and we trained them to do it," Joan said. "Given that I had not been in any way in business before, the entire operation Essex was a revelation. The children had reached an age to go to high school, so I had my hands free. I have to say that I did it with a lot of pleasure."

Many of the more professional stations were poised to hit the ground running when the stations inevitably transitioned to legitimate enterprises, but aside from a general hope to make some money, Bates's motivations for starting his station are harder to determine. Roy said as much himself. "I'm not introspective really—I never really look for the reasons I do what I do," he said. "I suppose if I was introspective, I wouldn't do anything, [considering] some of the wild ideas I get and the things I do. Those sort of things attract me like a magnet, and I just have to do them, that's all."

On the one hand, Bates was an experienced businessman, and the variety of his endeavors spoke for a man who was willing to try his hand at anything. The pirate radio years were basically a grand adventure—the undertaking of an ornery, self-made millionaire, happy to combat needless governmental regulation. But other accounts speak for a different side of Bates. Far from being a millionaire, one pirate said Bates was always broke but adept at smooth-talking creditors. He was allegedly always with a ready excuse for why wages couldn't be paid for weeks on end. "There is some mystery about Bates' continuing source of income, and even his solicitor says he does not know where Roy Bates gets his money," as one article later put it.

Bates also had the reputation of being as ruthless as he was brave. He was known to plunder abandoned platforms for usable supplies, but he also targeted functioning radio stations as well, nabbing their equipment and even stealing light fixtures. Roy applied the same pressure to advertisers: If a business wasn't sure about the efficacy of advertising on Radio Essex, Roy would announce the business's phone number on air, leading to a barrage of telephone calls that tied up the phones for hours.[*] "That is how a mythology about Roy Bates and how he was a real pirate started," Mark Wesley said. "I think we got painted pretty black by other radio stations."

The DJs had a secret code in which they would play certain music or speak certain phrases to let their comrades back on shore know they were running out of supplies, but Roy was known to leave his crew stranded out on the fort. In one harrowing incident, his men were stranded for seventeen days with only four days of provisions. "We'd long ago eaten the [Radio City] food, we'd eaten the contents of the dustbin—the potato peelings and such, and we were reduced to a huge drum of Heinz salad cream and another huge drum of Maxwell House coffee," Dick Palmer said. The crewmembers were "starving, emaciated, [with] the beginnings of scurvy" when they were taken to shore, but Roy upbraided them for leaving the fort open to invasion.

Nevertheless, despite the "week-long storms, antennas collapsing, intermittent starvation, dehydration, and the possibility of fairly severe electrocution," building Radio Essex was revolutionary fun. The music, the camaraderie, and the pranks made for an environment in which making a living was secondary to the joy of the enterprise. Penny and Michael would often come out to the fort on breaks from school, and they were in awe of the operation, which was also the envy of their

---

* Roy also tried less inconvenient methods to lure advertisers, such as offering to run an ad for free for a week. Businesses saw a marked increase in business after advertising with Radio Essex, which in turn led to a longer-term advertising contract.

friends, who listened to pirate radio and could scarcely believe that their family was engaged in such a winsome crusade.

Whether crafty shark or lovable rogue, Roy Bates had joined the ranks of the pirates by forging a radio station out of an old, crumbling fort. But the stakes were growing increasingly serious for the radio pirates. The flagrant violations of copyright law and streams of untaxed revenue rankled government officials, who, up to that point, hadn't yet made any serious moves to confront them. It would take a shocking event in the summer of 1966 to force the government's hand. Consequently, Roy Bates would make an even bigger splash on the scene.

# CHAPTER 4

## THE BATTLE FOR ROUGHS TOWER

*"When things are going smoothly, I lose interest."*

—Roy Bates

Pirate station bosses Reg Calvert and Oliver Smedley had been butting heads over the payment for a new transmitter and squabbling over possession of a different fort. After "having threatened to remove [Smedley] with means up to and including nerve gas," Calvert paid a visit to Smedley's home on the evening of June 21, 1966. Hearing the commotion of Calvert yelling at the housekeeper, Smedley grabbed a shotgun, snuck out the back door, and crept around to the front of the house. Fearing that Calvert was going to hit the housekeeper with a small statue, Smedley shot him point-blank in the chest, killing him on the spot. Radio piracy, once a nuisance, was now officially deadly.*

Prodded by the shock of Calvert's murder, the Marine Broadcasting (Offences) Act was introduced to the House of Commons on July 27 and was expected to be passed into law by royal assent in the near future. The MBOA aimed to criminalize practically every aspect of unlicensed broadcasting.

---

* It turned out Calvert was in fact armed with a pen filled with poison gas. Smedley was ultimately acquitted of murder, as he was found to have fired in self-defense. After the verdict, he said he was tuning out of radio until it became totally legal.

Police also investigated the forts for an unrelated incident in which a suitcase packed with the dismembered remains of a Japanese man washed up on a beach in Amsterdam. Investigators heard a rumor that the rest of the man's body was in a tower of one of the Maunsell Forts, but this proved to be totally unfounded. Roy Bates said this was news to him. "I have never heard anyone talk about this matter and since the fishermen here always tell everyone everything, it would have come to my attention," he said. The murder was never solved, though another Japanese man in Belgium who was questioned in the case died in a car accident that investigators suspected was a suicide.

According to the act, all broadcasting to the UK from ships and aircraft was prohibited. This included anyone who operated or participated in a pirate broadcast, anyone broadcasting from a marine platform, and the broadcast of any British subjects of any kind into the UK from outside of it. Furnishing a ship with broadcast equipment, supplying food or fuel to a pirate station, advertising on illegal programs, and writing or performing a work for illegal broadcast were all an offense. Violators could expect substantial fines and prison sentences as high as two years.

Pirate stations began preparing to evade the bill, which only applied to stations operating in British jurisdiction. Broadcasters looked for international advertisers, organized resupply ships, and set up offices in Holland. One station run by an Irishman named Ronan O'Rahilly reportedly asked its staff to renounce their British citizenship in order to continue broadcasting. Two British members of his staff offered to go through with it, with one saying he couldn't stand to remain a citizen of a country with such restrictive laws. O'Rahilly also said he would deliberately broadcast the very day the bill was passed into law, and when his DJs were arrested he would take their case to the Court of Human Rights. "It wasn't easy asking these people to make up their mind on an issue as important as this, but we must look to the future," O'Rahilly said. "I am morally right in this. [Prime Minister] Harold Wilson is morally wrong."

However, while the MBOA was being worked on, the government began going after the pirates under the aegis of an older law. The Post Office, which had authority over the airwaves, deftly wielded the 1949 Wireless Telegraphy Act. Slowly but surely, summonses were issued and radio pirates were hauled into court. On September 28, Roy Bates received a summons of his own: He was charged with unlawful use of an "apparatus for wireless telegraphy," which the government alleged was interrupting the emergency signals of other ships and radio transmissions as far away as Hungary.

Roy vowed to fight the charge. "I might be sticking my neck out, but we who believe in commercial radio can't just sit back and be steamrollered," he said. "My plan is to carry on. There is a future for commercial radio in this country and I plan to stay a part of it."

Bates represented himself when he appeared in court on November 30. In order to prosecute, the government had to demonstrate that these offenses were taking place within British territory, where British law applied. John Newey, prosecuting for the Post Office, followed the same tactic he used to make cases against other pirates. While the forts were not incontrovertibly under British jurisdiction, Newey argued that the territorial boundary line could start from a sandbank that appeared at low tide. If extended from this "seldom drying sand," Knock John Fort was within British territory, and thus Radio Essex was broadcasting illegally.

DJs decried the "dubious hydrographic data" used to define the boundary line, with one DJ sarcastically noting that the government could have only come up with the measurement using black magic. "Sacrificing chickens under a full moon would influence the tide to retreat to a point that, when multiplied by the number of affairs the Prime Minister had with his secretary, showed the forts were inside territorial waters," the DJ cracked.

Black magic or no, Bates was found guilty of illegal broadcasting since he was within territorial waters. He was fined £100 (which came to around £200 with court costs) and was told he would be fined every day he continued to broadcast. It was not the first time a boundary dispute had not worked out in the Bateses' favor. Joan was elected Southend Carnival Queen eighteen years earlier but was ultimately disqualified because she lived one hundred yards beyond the county line.

"I'll continue to transmit even if my solicitors advise me to the contrary," Roy said. And if Knock John Fort was within British territory, then he'd move to another platform—one that was unquestionably beyond the reach of the law. "No war is won until the last battle is fought," he declared.

To the boss of a seat-of-the-pants radio station and a man tasked with providing for his family, the £200 (£3680 in 2019) fine was a gargantuan unforeseen expense. According to a report from the Solicitor's Department, Roy tried to buy time by saying that, while he was unable to pay anything at the moment, he was developing some ideas that would allow him to pay back the fine in six months. An official told him this was unacceptable, and an agreement was worked out that he should pay £5 per month until February 1968.

Roy Bates was said to be a millionaire at the time he became a radio pirate, but within a short time he was reduced to selling pieces of furniture to keep things going for another week. He skirted the line of total insolvency but would stick by the pirate radio endeavor with perplexing, even maddening vigor. Was it madness, or was it a winning strategy? Those close to him could never be sure, but he exuded the kind of winning confidence to which one couldn't help but to be drawn.

Fortunately, there was another Maunsell Fort that would take the place of Knock John, and setting up shop there was the first step to getting back on his feet: Roughs Tower, located 24 nautical miles (27.6 land miles) away from Knock John and at least six miles away from British shores. No matter how it was measured, from shoreline or sandbank, it was more than far enough from the contested territorial border. Roy dropped the Radio Essex moniker and announced a new endeavor: "Britain's Better Music Station," or BBMS, based on Roughs Tower.

## STORMING ROUGHS TOWER

Roughs Tower, like the other Maunsell Forts, had already been the object of significant broadcaster interest. In August 1965, investors (rumored to include George Harrison and Mick Jagger) expressed interest in turning the tower into a sort of health resort and pleasure den or using its damp concrete caissons as mushroom farms. The plans never came to fruition, so Radio Caroline claimed the fort as a resupply station for its ship *Mi Amigo*. Caroline crewmembers began preparing the fort for habitation, using acetylene torches to cut off the top of the structure in order to make way for a helicopter landing pad.

Thanks to their earlier battles, Roy and his crew had cultivated a certain infamy as the "hard bastards of the North Sea," a group whose resolve bordered on entitlement. If the previous back-and-forth was a battle, the struggle for Roughs Tower would be nothing less than war.

Bates and his crew dismantled and packed up everything on Knock John Fort at the end of December 1966, and made plans to establish themselves on Roughs Tower. The transmitter, records, living supplies, and recording equipment were all laboriously lowered down to the waiting *Mizzy Gel*. The crew had no easy go of maneuvering the heavy cargo as it swung on ropes, to say nothing of doing so with hands, bodies, and equipment coated in freezing ocean spray. Much was lost overboard when the boat suddenly pitched and bounced in the troublesome sea, but finally, after an excruciating amount of work, Knock John was cleared out. All the Essex crew had left to do was putter over to Roughs Tower, conquer it, and hoist the equipment fifty feet up onto their new home.

Around 10:00 p.m. on Christmas Day—an "extremely black and bitterly cold night that would change [their lives] forever"—Roy, Michael, and company pulled their boat alongside Roughs Tower, gliding as silently as they could through the icy sea. The Caroline DJs were just about to cut the roast turkey when the Bates crew thudded themselves onto the deck, armed with iron bars, illuminated only by the candles and the light of a small stove.

The Radio Caroline crew quickly acquiesced to their demands.

In the weeks following the raid, an uneasy truce was brokered between BBMS and Caroline. They each stationed a few people on the fort at a time, working together to make Roughs Tower inhabitable.

Michael, aged fourteen, was used to the hustle of radio piratedom, as he had helped his dad with Radio Essex as often as he could when he was home from school. His alternate life as a radio pirate made the stuffy boarding school seem all the more oppressive. When Michael came home for Easter in spring 1967, he begged his parents not to make him return. "What will I remember of this ancient scholastic place of learning…this vast Gothic pile?" he said poetically. "What will I recall when I'm an old man?" Incredibly, Roy and Joan agreed, and young Michael soon became a fixture on Roughs Tower, working with the two radio crews to get the fort into shape for the new endeavor.*

---

* It was possible that Roy would have yanked him out of school eventually anyway. "There was absolutely no consideration that you might want to get a job or go to university and lead what most would consider a normal life," Michael said. His dad "had plans, and everyone else was expected to back him up."

On April 19, 1967, a horrible though fortuitous accident happened on the fort. One of the Caroline men suffered a traumatic hand injury when another man let go of a rope being used to lower oxygen cylinders onto a barge below. The cargo went into freefall, with the rope shearing a man's fingers to the bone. Michael recalled thinking that the incredible friction of the rope likely cauterized the wound, but moments later blood started pouring from the man's hand and onto the deck. The man stood dumbfounded, looking back and forth from his hand to the gore on the ground, but the crew leapt into action and wrapped greasy rags tightly around his hand.

"I was mortified and the bloke was a tough lad to not pass out," Michael said, impressed.

The injured man was lowered onto the boat to be taken ashore, accompanied by the other Caroline crew member, who had decided he'd had enough.* Their exodus was a critical mistake for Radio Caroline: The Bates crew used the injured man's misfortune to claim once and for all the fort as their own.

Over the next few weeks, Radio Caroline made a few token gestures to retake the fort. But Michael, by this point a "hard bastard" himself, could sense a larger attack was imminent and pushed the crew to solidify the defenses. The crew placed old tanks and bits of metal on the edge of the fort, ready to be pushed down onto any threatening boats. Fuel and supplies were stockpiled, and Michael made a substantial stash of Molotov cocktails. Some local reporters were shown the fort's arsenal: six shotguns, a flamethrower, and two air rifles. The crew even wrote "DANGER ELECTRIC FENCE 10,000 VOLTS" on the side of the fort—a false claim that nobody was willing to test.

## ENTER: MIKE THUNDERSTICK

All was quiet on the Roughs Tower Fort until June 27, 1967, when all hell finally broke loose.

The Radio Caroline crew, backed by a former police inspector and a "mob of Gravesend Dockers and local heavies recruited from pubs,"

---

* There were whispers that the rope accident was orchestrated as a way to force the Carolinians to leave; this suspicion caused at least one of Bates's crew to leave with the Caroline men, dismayed by the apparent ruthlessness.

sailed out to the fort on a boat called the *Offshore II*. As the ship drew closer, those on board shouted that they were sent by Roy to relieve the crew. Michael laughed at the pathetic attempt at subterfuge, and the two sides "exchanged much swearing and death threats" when the ruse was exposed. Michael and a twenty-three-year-old crewman and former radio pirate named David Belasco—the only two on the fort— took strategic positions and warned the boat to stay back. Michael made the first move, lobbing a warning bomb at the concrete pillar, where it exploded but was quickly extinguished by the lapping waves. The *Offshore II* didn't take the hint.

"Well, I gave it a shot," Michael reasoned.

A barrage of petrol bombs and gas cylinders were lobbed from atop the fort, and they shot at the invaders with an air rifle. One man on the *Offshore II* was knocked overboard in the process while another had to hit the deck and roll when his coat caught on fire. Projectiles were launched from the bores of the old antiaircraft guns like fireworks launched out of their tubes.

If this were a movie, the scene would pause here in a freeze-frame. Imagine Michael frozen with wide eyes and his arm raised in a throwing motion, his mouth open mid-shout. Debris flies through the air all around him, with Belasco caught midstride and preparing to launch a piece of metal.

Michael was amazed at the turn his life had taken. Not more than a few weeks before he was away at school, dressed in uniform in a wood-paneled jail. Now, "Mike Thunderstick," as Belasco called him, was bedecked in an old sailor's sweater and shooting at people, vowing and fully intending to defend his father's territory to the end.

And this is what was *expected* of him: Roy kept him out of school for a reason, and that reason was to defend the fort. Roy would want to know the tactical defenses Michael had mounted and wouldn't hesitate to take his son to task if he blundered. Michael knew of his dad's exploits in the war, and he vied for his approval. Throwing a flaming bottle of gas was one way to do it, and Michael found for himself that the heat of the battle was a world unto itself. It was dangerous, it was violent, and it was terribly exciting.

And with that, the scene lurches back into action with the

projectiles resuming their trajectories and the piercing war cries echoing from above and below.

The *Offshore II* got close enough that a man named John Hoiles was able to jump onto the ladder dangling from the bottom of the fort, but by the time he had climbed halfway up, the rain of bombs had caught the deck of the ship on fire. The ship was carrying five tons of fuel oil, so the captain retreated with extreme haste as they rushed to put out the blaze. Hoiles was left dangling on the ladder, caught between the fearsome characters above and the merciless sea below.

"I'm afraid we overdid it a bit," Belasco later admitted. "We let the boat have it with petrol bombs. We tried to hit everyone we could and the whole boat went up."

Depending on who is telling the story, Hoiles hung on the ladder for two, three, or four more hours, since the *Offshore II*'s captain refused to come any closer to the fort. In the meantime, Michael and Belasco offered him some relief, lowering down a crate for him to sit in and a cup of tea. A neutral lifeboat eventually came to retrieve him, and the *Offshore II* retreated back to shore. "We arrived just in time," said one of the rescuers. "The man was numb, cramped, and suffering from exposure."

There was more to come. The June 27 raid was said to be one of at least eight attempts on the fort that summer, with one raid allegedly involving thirty men. They came "in foreign-looking boats, rather like Dutchmen, armed with guns and knives. Some tried to swim with snorkels but they were spotted and given short shrift with a flame thrower," Roy said.

The final attempt on the fort during the golden age of radio piracy took place a few weeks later. Michael was awoken by the sound of an inflatable boat puttering up to the fort in the middle of the night. He knew how to man the defenses without alerting the enemy. Opening a hatch, he calmly lit a Molotov cocktail and dropped it straight down onto the boat. The boat erupted in flames and forced the would-be raiders to jump overboard. When the parent vessel pulled up to retrieve the men, Michael peppered the captain with air pistol fire, making the deck slick with blood. "If you're your own defense, you've got nobody to bleat to," Michael said.*

Having made his point, Michael finally allowed the boat to throw out some rope and pull the men back aboard. As usual, the boat retreated. Michael lay back down on the deck, high on adrenaline and shaking with battleborne excitement. Such was life on the heap, and so went holding the fort.

The raucous warfare inspired directly by Roy Bates did not escape the eyes of government officials. The House of Commons had done a second reading of the Marine Broadcast (Offences) Act in February 1967, but other plans were in the works to reclaim the Maunsell Fort for the British government, up to and including storming the fort and taking it by force. It was a challenge Roy gladly accepted.

"When things are going smoothly," he said, "I lose interest."

---

* Lore has it that the two men in the water were Reggie and Ronald Kray, a pair of infamously ruthless twins who ruled the British criminal underworld in the 1960s.

# CHAPTER 5

# A MOST EVENTFUL FALL

*"I'd rather die than surrender!"*

—Roy Bates

As Michael and Roy battled for control of the fort throughout the spring of 1967, discussion about how to address the occupation of Roughs Tower was taking place at the highest levels of the British government. Memos about Roughs Tower flew back and forth between no less than nine separate departments, including the Ministry of Defence, the Post Office, and the Home Office, a department overseeing police, fire, security, and immigration needs for the UK government.* Concern about the situation on Roughs Tower reached all the way up to Prime Minister Harold Wilson, who was being kept abreast of the developments by his own request. The department heads got together in a top-secret meeting in April to find a way to go after Roy Bates.

Exactly how they should close down his "squalid operation" posed a genuinely vexing problem. Unlike the last time Bates had been prosecuted, which was successful because Radio Essex was based on a fort clearly inside territorial waters, Bates's new location was "unambiguously" outside UK territory. It was uncertain if the government was even legally allowed to approach Bates on Roughs Tower without contravening international agreement. "The position with regard to present legal title, if any, is obscure," wrote one official. But then the petrol-bomb-and-man-hanging-from-a-ladder incident happened,

---

* The names of government officials mentioned in these documents seem almost parodic. Among others, the UK at one point employed PP Groat, HP Lillicrap, PE Turl, MS Igglesden, CP Bone, Mr. Dredge, Lord Justice Diplock, and the author's personal favorite, Dingle Foot. A consistently used abbreviation for the Permanent Undersecretary of the Army is "PUS ARMY."

and the more truculent cabinet members couldn't stand to see Bates "cock a snook" at the British government. Calls to remove the people from the fort began getting louder, and this directive became the default position of every department.

"A controlled scientific destruction would be preferable to something as haphazard as bombing," wrote one official, but there was still the question of how to get everyone off the fort before it could be destroyed. On top of the issue with the fort's location, they could be sure that the fort would remain staffed 24/7. The government could shout at the occupants all they wanted—literally, one of the ways they proposed telling Bates he was violating the law was to yell at him from a boat with a bullhorn—but the officials all knew that Bates would only leave by his own accord. As they strategized on how to compel the intransigent former war hero to vacate the fort, no angle was left overturned.

Officials discussed blockading Roughs Tower, nabbing the *Mizzy Gel* on customs technicalities, and taking the "Al Capone approach," which is to say going after Roy for something unrelated to broadcasting, such as keeping Michael out of school. They looked into the Continental Shelf Act for relevant statutes and discussed making the legal claim that Roughs Tower, like a lighthouse, was a "freehold property" that the government inherently controls forever. Officials even considered legislation that would expand Britain's territorial waters specifically to encompass the fort, but they decided that such a huge undertaking for a relatively small purpose would be "a ponderous move, inviting ridicule."

There was some hope in the toothy Marine Broadcasting (Offences) Act, which the ministers were confident would be written into law later that year, but Roy Bates soon realized that Roughs Tower was too small to mount the enormous antenna needed to broadcast effectively. He made a few test broadcasts but nothing further and cancelled plans for Britain's Better Music Station, thereby squelching the government's plans to go after him with the MBOA.

The Ministry of Defence ultimately agreed to the "doubtful privilege" of retaking the fort, provided the other cabinet ministers "not automatically assume [the cost] will come from the Defence budget."

In order to do so, the cabinet officials came up with a remarkably low-key plot that did justice to the codename it was given: "Operation Callow."

Essentially, Operation Callow called for a government agent to drop in on Bates at home, reason with him like a gentleman, and get him to agree to hand over the fort. The agent was even authorized to offer Bates a little bit of cash for moving expenses and to assure him that no rival radio stations would take over the tower. Then, once Bates gave up possession, Royal Marines would helicopter out to the platform, rig it with explosives, and destroy it.

Problem solved.

All in all, it was to be a thoroughly nonviolent affair: firearms were explicitly disallowed in every part of the operation. In fact, it was so nonviolent that the mission would be called off if Bates even became uncooperative. Prime Minister Wilson signed off on Operation Callow on August 3, expecting that nobody could turn down money for something that wasn't his in the first place.

Two days later, the mission was put into play. It did not go as planned.

## A CALLOW PROPOSAL

Just before 9:00 a.m. on August 5, 1967, a man named William Sweby strolled down the street to the Bateses' apartment in Southend-on-Sea, walking around to the back of the building to the concrete stairs that led to the front door. He wove his way around the oil drums and miscellaneous engine parts that littered the walkway and noted the unpainted and neglected state of the Bates domicile.

Sweby, an avid bicyclist who served as a pilot during World War II, was the land agent with the Ministry of Defence tasked with talking Bates into giving up the fort. Lines of argument running through his head, he took a deep breath as he raised his knuckles to the door.

*Rap! Rap! Rap!*

Nothing. Sweby knocked again and rocked on his feet, trying to see past the curtain in the window. Still nothing.

He heard some children yelling in the distance and the rumble of a passing car.

Agents watching the home had assured him that Bates's car had been in the driveway since the previous evening, but still nobody answered. Scratching his head, Sweby turned on his heels and walked away. He knocked again every ten minutes for the next hour. Each time, Roy Bates peeked from behind a curtain and watched him leave.

A few hours later, Sweby walked back to the house and was pleased to see a van parked in the driveway. This time Bates answered on the first knock, greeted Sweby officiously, and invited him into a large, "untidily and shabbily furnished" room. The Defense agent took off his hat and they got down to business.

Bates sat agitatedly on the couch as Sweby made his case for why Bates should hand over the fort.

"I know I'm sound in law!" Roy exclaimed, jumping up suddenly. "I'd rather die than surrender!"

Then Roy sat back down and the conversation softened. Bates spoke of the difficulty of maintaining the fort and the serious amounts of money he'd already sunk into the project. Sweby realized Bates was hinting at being bought out. Having "established by this time an informality which enabled complete frankness," the conversation veered toward the topic of payment.

"I'll hand over the fort this instant for £100,000," Bates said.

"That figure," Sweby said, "is totally unrelated to facts."

Bates "once again reverted to the 'over my dead body' line," and, rubbing his temples, Sweby suggested that Bates call his lawyer and meet him at a pub for a beer later that evening. Bates agreed. Sweby walked back down the concrete stairs and headed back to the street. When he reached his car, he found he had a flat tire.

A few hours later, Bates arrived at the pub as arranged but told Sweby his lawyer was playing cricket. Sweby hung out with Bates and his "electrician friend," shied away from talking business, and had a surprisingly good time. They were to reconvene the next morning at 10:30, the earliest Bates would agree to meet.

Burnished by his lawyer's presence, Bates resumed his claims of ownership the next morning and told Sweby he was doing him a favor by requesting only £100,000. "It's easily worth double that," he said. Sweby, saying they had to be mindful of the taxpayer, came back with an offer of £5,000. Bates countered with £90,000. Negotiations came to a halt shortly thereafter. Sweby walked away fortless, bringing to an end the first phase of Operation Callow.

"The Ministry hasn't got enough money to get me off Sealand," Roy proclaimed.

Meanwhile, perhaps anticipating that little would come from meeting with Bates, a contingent of Royal Marines stood by to carry out Part 2 of Operation Callow: sailing out to the fort itself. They knew Joan and Michael were on the fort while Sweby was meeting with Roy, and they felt they might have better luck convincing the mother and son to give up the fort than the hardheaded father.

In the late afternoon of August 6, Michael quietly loaded a pistol as he watched a trawler called the HMS *Bembridge* creep its way slowly toward the platform. The *Bembridge* came to rest right below the fort, and Michael saw a phalanx of uniformed officials standing solemnly on the deck. The men eyed the fort warily, noticing the warning messages painted on the side of Roughs Tower and the heavy, hanging gas cylinders ready to be dropped onto the waiting boat.

The men yelled up to Michael and Joan that Roy had officially sold the platform to the government and that the marines were simply there to occupy the fort while it changed hands. Mother and son rolled their eyes. *No way in hell.* The police asked Michael and Joan to throw down a ladder so they could come up and talk. Michael shrugged and tossed it down.

Michael recalls with relish the authorities' complete inability to scale the dangling rope ladder. They didn't get the trick—if you try to climb it like a normal ladder, your weight will make you swing like a pendulum; the correct way is to climb it on one side, with the rungs pointing straight out in front of you. One official after another gave it a shot, only to end up swinging helplessly a few feet above the boat. A hat even flew off comically in the struggle. "The James Bonds, the would-be 007s," Michael snorted. "It had never occurred to me that a simple skill that I had learnt could be such a hard thing to do for the uninitiated."

Once it was clear nobody was going to be coming up (and having made his point), Michael did them a favor and came down to the boat.

"His manner was very friendly, and he was quite talkative," recalled the excursion's duty commander, but he "made it very clear that no-one was going to be allowed on the fort at any time without the direct permission of his father." Detaining Michael any further was discouraged when Joan waved a pistol at them from atop the platform. Michael climbed back up to the fort, and the *Bembridge* disembarked.

Operation Callow had not only failed but it also succeeded in embarrassing the government. Roy Bates, once referred to as a "grandmaster of the preemptive press strike," quickly alerted the media that helicopters and marines were waiting nearby to ambush his wife and son. Newspaper headlines like "Commandoes Set to Seize Fort" quickly followed.

Meanwhile, the family was also dealing intermittently with the Customs and Excise Department. Their primary offensive tactic was to get on Roy's case for his boat not having a valid load-line certificate* authorizing him to travel to and from Roughs Tower, which from time to time they treated like a foreign port. The thinking was that Bates's boat was in such poor shape that it would never pass official muster and would thus be declared unusable. Customs officials were also known to board the *Mizzy Gel* while in port in Harwich and puncture and dump out their tins of food in a manner Michael Bates said was reminiscent of Prohibition-era booze raids. The dispute seemed personal, and Customs in particular would continually ask for stronger language in departmental opinions against Roughs Tower. "It seems absurd that Bates comes and goes whenever he likes and just laughs when Customs are mentioned," sniffed one official.

The tête-à-tête with Customs came to a head one evening when Roy was loading the boat with supplies to take to Michael and Penny on Roughs Tower. Officials came down hard on the still-lacking load-line certificate and adamantly refused to let Bates sail out to the fort. Roy walked away in an extreme huff, cursing every human cog in the bureaucracy, but instead of avenging himself on some hapless bureaucrat, he went straight to the press and told reporters that Customs officials were keeping his kids from eating.

---

* A load-line certificate certified that a ship had been surveyed to mark the safety limit of its load.

The reaction was explosive. The *Daily Mail* first sent out a plane to take shots of Roughs Tower and the kids from the air, the next day publishing photos showing pitiable kids waving up at the pilots. The paper then chartered a tug, with a photographer obviously on board, to take Roy and Joan back out to the fort and "rescue" his kids. "Look at their starving faces," the headline read. Customs fruitlessly tried to explain that all Bates had to do was get the certificate or charter a different boat, but the public rushed to the cause of the "Children on the Tower."

To their credit, Penny said they weren't scared or lonely while by themselves on the fort. The family would take turns serving shifts, and the siblings were often stationed out there together. The days went by quickly on account of the time it took to do basic tasks, and giving up or calling for help was never discussed. Only in instances where things were extremely dire were they to light a bonfire on deck to alert the Coast Guard. "We listen to the radio and there is plenty of work to be done," Penny said.

Roy expected them to be tough, and Penny made a point to show off her hardiness, subsisting for stretches at a time on biscuits made from flour and distilled sea water, Marmite, and whatever fish they could catch off the deck of the fort. (A healthy supply of worms was provided by a sympathetic local fisherman.) A famous photo of seventeen-year-old Penny shows her posing in a beret with two guns in her hand on the deck of Roughs Tower, a couple of Molotov cocktails visible on the railing behind her, looking not unlike Patty Hearst. She recalled being called downstairs by her father after a huge reproduction of the photo accompanied a story about the fort in a Sunday paper. Roy wasn't upset about Penny showing off the family's weapons, but she was holding the pistols with her fingers on the triggers. "How many times have I told you, you don't hold a gun like that?" he said.

"It was normal to us, we didn't know anything different," Penny said later in life. "Bit weird of an upbringing, isn't it?"

Nevertheless, that Customs was apparently so forthright in disregarding the well-being of children so incensed area Minister of Parliament Paul Channon that he wrote to Customs to inquire about what was going on. "If the rules are to be interpreted strictly, I imagine it is technically illegal to take one tin of beans on a small yacht," he said snidely. Customs backed off.

After all this, the failure of Operation Callow Parts 1 and 2 and the debacles in the press, government officials finally concluded that Roughs Tower should be left alone. "Nobody can feel this is satisfactory," wrote one official, but they must accept the situation for what it was "in the expectation that Mr. Bates will probably abandon his uncomfortable perch eventually of his own accord." Bates hadn't really won, but he had forced a stalemate.

## SUNK HEAD: SACRIFICIAL LAMB

Perhaps because they couldn't destroy Roughs Tower, the Royal Marines took out their irritation on another Maunsell Fort, Sunk Head, which was south of Roughs Tower and visible in the distance. On August 21, 1967, Royal Engineers planted 3,200 pounds of explosives that, when detonated, created an explosion whose sound was heard more than twelve miles away and whose shockwaves could be felt on shore. One slightly embellished account reported that the "explosions sent the huge structures cartwheeling hundreds of feet in the air.* Helicopters carrying explosives buzzed over Roughs Tower, and from a Navy tug carrying a demolition squad came shouts of "You're next!" at whoever was on the fort.

Roy was in England and Michael was on the fort when news of the destruction hit the papers. Reporters got the name of the fort wrong so that the headline read "Navy Blows Up Roughs Tower"; Roy had no way of contacting Michael and freaked out for a bit until he was assured that it was in fact Sunk Head that was destroyed and not Roughs Tower along with his son.

Despite the frustrations, the government did have some reason to celebrate. The Marine Broadcasting (Offences) Act had been officially passed into law on August 14, 1967, and the government used the law to go after every facet of pirate radio they could. DJs and station managers got nervous, advertisers soon began falling off as the stakes grew higher, and the whole stack of cards began to tremble. One captain

---

* The Sunk Head explosion, a highly entertaining blast, can be viewed on YouTube.

was even given a nine-month prison sentence for simply delivering diesel to a Radio Caroline station.

But the most effective pirate-fighting tactic came in the form of doing what likely would have made the most sense in the first place: playing pop music on licensed radio. The government began reworking copyright law and negotiating with musician's unions to make playing music on the radio amenable to all parties. The BBC restructured its operations and split into four new radio stations in September, called, logically, BBC Radio One, Two, Three, and Four. Three channels maintained the "enlightening" programming the BBC prided itself on, while Radio One played the pop music that was previously relegated to the domain of pirates.

As the end grew extremely nigh, pirate DJs bid their listeners emotional farewells or gave political harangues against the government's policies. One radio station reportedly threw its entire record collection into the sea in protest, though many of the radio pirates ended up working for the much better-paying BBC, which had been recruiting them as the pirate stations fell apart. One by one, the pirate radio frequencies disappeared—their transmissions only a memory in the vast ether. The radio pirate era had made for an incredible few years, but for those who simply wanted to listen to music, the BBC was the most convenient choice.

Not long after, a leaky old boat could be seen once again making its way out into the North Sea. The sun was high in the sky, and Roy Bates stood at the stern of the *Mizzy Gel*, straight-backed and feeling the sun through the glassless windows. After the nerve-wracking events of the past few months, a nice, leisurely sail relaxed him and helped him think.

Getting another radio station up and running again was not in the cards, and this was actually quite a relief. The most important part was that he had ended up with a fort that was far outside British jurisdiction.

Roy squinted into the horizon, savoring the implications of this most auspicious location. He had been dreaming of an unprecedented way to one-up the conflict that had been going on for years, and it was time to put this plan into action.

# CHAPTER 6

## E Mare Libertas

---

*"I remember my father sitting myself, my mother, and my sister down and saying those immortal words: 'I have an idea to declare independence from the UK. A separate country. An independent state. It might take some time...'"*

—Michael Bates

Sometime in late August 1967, Roy and Joan Bates were out at the pub at the Railway Hotel for their customary predinner pint. The couple sat under the dim lights amid the bustle of conversation. All the locals, of course, knew of Roy's adventures, and he featured prominently in area news. His platform was a frequent topic of conversation. He was used to receiving advice about how to fix it up or what he could turn it into, but that particular evening, Roy and Joan were out with one Lionel Conway, a childhood friend of Roy's who also happened to be his legal counsel. They had some big ideas to discuss.

Since Roy had taken over Roughs Tower, Joan had taken to referring to the fort as the family's own private island. And while it didn't necessarily have the trappings of a traditional tropical retreat—the fort was "hardly a dream getaway [without] a pot plant in sight, let alone palm tree," as one reporter later commented—it was fun toying with such a symbol of grandeur. Plus, the island was captured and won by her partner, adding a sense of valor that no amount of money could buy. Joan's characterization, while somewhat tongue-in-cheek, was inspiring.

Roy turned to Conway and asked him straight up how he could declare Roughs Tower his own country.

Conway sputtered on his drink. Although an experienced lawyer, he'd never dealt with such a request. But Roy had given it some thought, and he was serious. The fort's theoretical sovereignty was key to what he wanted to do next.

"I wasn't surprised," Joan said. "I've learned not to be surprised at anything my husband does."

It was a logical question. Being the citizen of a new nation would help Roy get around laws like the UK's Marine Broadcasting (Offences) Act that only applied to British citizens, but he also knew that a fort in international waters could have many commercial applications similarly unbound by British law. There was also a matter of pride: Staying out on the fort and having justification to do so that would hold up in international court was a way to continue cocking a snook at the British government who had tried so hard to shut him down. In essence, if he ruled his own country, he could dictate all the rules.

But Conway said there was no way the Crown would stand for it. They simply couldn't. The precedent it would set could be disastrous. "You might be tossed in a dungeon for treason, and maybe even beheaded," the lawyer said. But Bates pressed him to check into the basis for sovereignty and promised he would do the same. Roy even offered to double Conway's research fees if he could find any reason he couldn't do it.

Sure enough, after that night at the pub, Roy "burned the midnight oil looking at all sort of law books we had lying around," Joan said, and Conway did the same. The group reconvened a few days later and shared their startling conclusion: declaring Roughs Tower his own country was not only theoretically possible but technically doable.

Among other reasons, their preliminary research revealed a few legal principles that seemed to justify their claims:

- **Britain violated the law when it built the fort in international waters:** The fort was possibly illegal in the first place, and thus Britain couldn't lay claim to it. Moreover, Britain had neglected to take it down, which was also a contravention of international law.
- *Res derelicta/Terra nullius:* The UK had relinquished its claim to the territory by abandoning it after the war and leaving it to rust. According to international law, territories that didn't

have defined ownership became *terra nullius*, or "no man's land." "It's called dereliction of sovereignty. We took over the sovereignty that the British government had derelicted," Michael said.

• **The Montevideo Convention on the Rights and Duties of States**: A 1933 treaty signed by sixteen nations declared the following: "The state as a person of international law should possess the following qualifications: (a) a permanent population; (b) a defined territory; (c) government; and (d) capacity to enter into relations with the other states." A country based on Roughs Tower could arguably fulfill these qualifications once it got up and running.

But what would the new country look like? How would it operate? Roy decided the fort would be a principality: a sovereign territory ruled by a prince or princess whose word is unilateral law.* This meant, of course, Roy and Joan would be the prince and princess, but the idea of making it a principality wasn't for vanity—there was simply no time, manpower, or energy to develop a political infrastructure. "Unless you make it a principality, you have to write a pile of law books, you see. It becomes very, very complicated," Joan said.

## SEALAND'S MICRONATIONAL FOREBEARS

Sealand is not the first or last territory to make experimental claims for sovereignty; neither is it the first or last to make claims based on the Montevideo Convention. The powers-that-be ensured that none of these proto-nations were able get off the ground, but their existence, however brief, is worth noting for the examples they set. The existence of these crypto-countries also likely influenced how the UK interacted with Sealand, as each one set an example that could be seized upon and furthered by

---

* Principalities are primarily a thing of the past, but some principalities currently exist. Lichtenstein and San Marino, for example, are functionally equivalent to principalities, and they are often cited as countries that operate much like micronations.

the burgeoning principality as it made the case for its own nationality.*

The Indian Stream Republic and the Republic of Madawaska were established in North America in the early 1800s in areas not yet claimed by any European nation. They existed for significant amounts of time with their own constitution and government and demonstrated that belonging to an enormous nation-state was not necessary to flourish. The United States' Guano Islands Act of 1856 specifically allowed US citizens to take possession of islands with guano deposits anywhere in the world so long as they are not occupied by or within the jurisdiction of other governments.** The act led to random islands around the world suddenly being legally colonized by turd-harvesting operations, suggesting that, if unclaimed, any random piece of territory could suddenly be seized by a country on the other side of the world.

The Nation of Celestial Space, headed by Chicagoan James Mangan, claimed dominion over the moon in 1949 in an effort to prevent it from being carved up into private territories by Terran nations. The notion that a breakaway nation could claim a territory and prohibit the use of its resources by other nations was of concern to the UK, specifically if Sealand lay claim to the oil reserves in the North Sea.

The Principality of Outer Baldonia also came into being in 1949, and it showed that a micronation, no matter how tongue-in-cheek, could cause a diplomatic crisis. Baldonia was established on an island off of Nova Scotia purchased by a wealthy American fisherman and Pepsi lobbyist named Russell Arundel. Arundel crowned himself "Prince of Princes" and he and his fishing buddies developed a parodic constitution whose Western imperialism was so decadent that it was the subject of a withering critique in

---

* These situations of course took no heed of the indigenous people who preceded European settlement, and today's society is predicated on the Western notion that one can "own" land, drawing precious little influence or guidance from the people who have inhabited areas for millennia without the need for specific delimitation.

** Guano was a hot commodity used to make gunpowder and fertilizer.

a prominent literary gazette in the USSR. In response, Baldonia declared war on Russia in 1953, with an area yacht club and its "eight-star" Baldonian admirals pledging their vessels as the Baldonian Navy. War never broke out, fortunately, and the would-be prince sold the island to the Nova Scotia Bird Society, who eventually turned the island into an avian sanctuary named after the putative former ruler.*

Closer to home, the UK had to deal with the Rockall situation. Rockall is a large granite rock sticking out of the ocean off the coast of Scotland, about sixty feet tall and completely uninhabitable. Its only vegetation was a small patch on the island's summit, meaning that there historically hadn't been many people interested in claiming it. However, Rockall was officially claimed by the UK in 1955 to prevent the USSR from taking over the island to spy on Britain's first nuclear missile test. A British flag was stuck in the ground and a plaque was affixed to the rock, and the islet eventually became an official part of Scotland. The Rockall situation was especially relevant to what was going on with the principality, for the UK, as Michael put it, "did not want a Cuba off the east coast of England."

And there were many more experiments in nationhood that tried other novel tactics to establish themselves, such as the Kingdom of Humanity and the Republic of Morac-Songhrati-Meads, which both attempted to dredge up sand and establish acreage on reefs in international waters. Expanding one's territory artificially has long been done everywhere from Denmark to China to the famously opulent Palm Jumeirah in the United Arab Emirates. There is no question that these artificial expansions are the valid territory of the country they're connected

---

* Most people who have written about Outer Baldonia note that the constitution was an obvious joke, and the "hyperbolic" nature of the Russian article criticizing the micronation's constitution is itself a parody of stuffy statesmanship. All in all, the dispute seems like a farce enjoyed by both sides—a moment of levity and perspective during the height of the Cold War. Though it should also be noted that Baldonia's founder was caught in a minor political scandal when he attempted to curry favor with Senator Joe McCarthy with an offer of $20,000 to help alleviate the senator's debts. This form of statesmanship suggests the truly decadent practices of Baldonia's government.

to, and Sealand could use this as a reason to expand its own footprint.

In an effort to bring some semblance of consistency to conduct in the high seas, representatives from around the globe began revamping agreements in the 1950s on how boundaries should be delineated in international waters. Later we'll explore one of these major agreements to show how the rules can work both for and against Sealand's claims of sovereignty.

It happened that Roy and Joan were contemplating independence at a pretty auspicious time in British history. The number of countries in the world tripled following the dissembling of empires after World War II. Many of the Crown's former colonies formally declared independence throughout the 1960s, and it was increasingly impolitic to operate as old-school colonial overlords. The French were making a brutal show of trying to hold onto their colonies in Algeria and Vietnam during the same time, in the process looking remarkably cruel and gauche. The Crown relinquished some claims to distant lands and granted them at least the appearance of operating on their own. At least eighteen other countries divested themselves from the British Empire in the 1960s: Jamaica was granted independence from the Crown in 1962, for example, Kenya in 1963, Barbados and Botswana in 1966, and Yemen in 1967.*

At home, 1967 saw the passage of acts making abortion and contraceptives much more accessible, as well as an act decriminalizing homosexual relationships. The Thames Estuary area in particular was home to numerous experimental communities that thrived under a broadening mindset. As Rachel Lichtenstein writes in *Estuary*, a history of the Thames Estuary, the rivers around Leigh-on-Sea were full of nomadic houseboats made from scavenged material during World War II, while a suffragette boarding house was set up on Canvey Island, and a community for alcoholics and homeless men still in existence today was set up on Hadleigh Farm near the remains of an eponymous castle. With public opinion apparently in favor of the right to live in the

---

* Though love for the Empire was still in effect. In September 1967, Gibraltar voted 12,138 to 44 to remain British rather than become a part of Spain.

community of one's choosing, perhaps Roy's claims weren't that unreasonable. At the time, declaring his own country and gaining acceptance for his nation "shouldn't have been that difficult, really," he said.

Although British society was changing, Roy Bates was not necessarily on the forefront of these progressive shifts, and his principality wasn't intended to be a bastion of hedonistic liberality to go along with the "permissiveness" that was the social climate of the day. Roy, a proud Englishman, stressed that he wasn't seceding or declaring his own country in an attempt to contribute to the decline of Britain. If anything, his nation was a throwback to the Britain of yore—a country of hard-nosed adventurers contrasted against a country that had gone "soft" and "namby-pamby." That he was butting heads with the government and local police was not a critique of the state but rather an assertion of his individual liberty and the right to free enterprise.

But he was also bothered by the way he'd been treated by the British government for his involvement with the radio pirates and felt that he had been targeted specifically and excessively, suggesting that Britain didn't respect individual initiative like it used to. He had been hounded and pursued and pushed into an endeavor that at times put him in genuinely dire financial circumstances. He felt especially let down considering the duty he'd given the country as a proud and brave soldier during World War II. "When they went to hand out [broadcasting] licenses, they should have given them to the entrepreneurs who had the balls to do it and who had the expertise. But they gave licenses to businessmen, like heads of department stores, not people who were in it and enthusiastic about it," Michael Bates later said.

If his declaring his own country started off as an almost sarcastic way of responding to the government's repressiveness, Roy became quite serious about the project when he saw increasing promise in the fort's commercial applications. He couldn't be restricted by any government if *he* was the government. Roy envisioned tax-free company registration, TV stations, a lottery system, the issuing of passports, stamps, and coins, flags of convenience,* and the conferring of titles.

---

* A flag of convenience is when a ship is registered to a country different from that of the vessel's owner. According to legal resource HG.com, "Registering a ship under a flag of convenience is typically done to avoid the regulation, taxes, and fees that might be

The significant financial recompense would be a nice dénouement to years of fines and legal fees. "As in Lichtenstein, Sealand could be used by companies purely as a nameplate," Roy said. The new country could even prove to be charitable. "Our main objects are to make money and to help [charities] such as Freedom from Hunger and Displaced Persons," Joan said.

They decided that the world's newest nation would be called the Principality of Sealand—a simple, catchy toponym that spoke for the fort's present location and suggested its future growth. Further afield, Roy envisioned growing Sealand by linking it with a series of similar forts to expand the national imprint. "It is precisely what it says—'land from the sea,' and we've got to raise land there," he said.

Armed with territory, government, population, and dogged enthusiasm, it was time for a formal declaration of independence. A ceremony was in order to welcome what would at the time be the world's 164th country. "I'm a Royalist, but that didn't mean there wasn't room for a principality off the British coast," Roy said.

## INDEPENDENCE DAY
September 2, 1967, Joan Bates's thirty-eighth birthday, was rainy and cooler than average, but the gloomy weather didn't dampen the celebration. The Bates family and a handful of invited guests were on hand to transform the platform from Roughs Tower into the Principality of Sealand. The group made their way up the metal staircase to the helipad early in the afternoon, where the new Sealandic flag was to be raised. In line with Roy's ambitions, the family had already made a profit from the burgeoning nation. An area newspaper chronicling the event paid the family "handsomely" for the exclusive rights to the story.

Roy was clad in a suit and tie, and Michael wore khakis and a knit shirt. Joan and Penny were bedecked in sleeveless dresses with colorful flower prints. Cohorts who had helped win the fort were dressed in

---

incurred by registering in the home country, and in some cases to provide the ship with a flag of a country welcome in more ports. Flags of convenience also mean that a ship can operate with less regulation and responsibility for the safety of its workers if the country under which it is registered has less stringent labor laws."

classy black and white. The newspaper's helicopter circled around the platform and captured the group gathered on top of the helipad, surrounded on all sides by the grandeur of the North Sea.

The men were smiling, hands in their pockets, beaming manly congratulations at one another while Michael stood alongside Roy and looked up at him with a sense of awe. The triumphant Sealandic national anthem was decades away from being written, but a few solemn words were said for the occasion. "When we came here, everywhere in the world was owned by someone, some country, except this fort," Michael recalled later with pride.

The "unprecedented, 'I'm the king of the castle' claim" was certainly one for the history books, but just as important was the romance behind the gesture. Roy officially crowned Joan princess, thereby outdoing the gift-giving abilities of spouses everywhere. "She had always been his princess but now he was going to tell the world," Michael said.

Princess Joan had the honor of raising Sealand's tricolor flag over the newly founded principality. Like the name Sealand, the standard was simple but effective, red and black halves divided by a slightly off-center white stripe running diagonally from one corner to another. The red stood for Roy, the black for pirate radio, and the white for the "path of purity [they] would endeavor to walk." (The "path of purity" was somewhat tongue-in-cheek, Michael said.) The flag slowly ascended the wire holding the anti-helicopter mast stable, coming to a stop at the top and flapping in the breeze one hundred feet above the waves below. At this height, Sealand's billowing gonfalon could be seen from miles away.

A cheer erupted. They felt the national motto in their bones: *E Mare Libertas* ("From the Sea, Freedom"). And with that, the ceremony was complete. The impressive North Sea winds were the caresses of an approving Fate. Joan was now Princess Joan; Roy was Prince Roy; Michael and Penny were Crown Prince and Princess. Fruitcake, the family cat, was Sealandic royalty as well and purred monarchically aboard the fort. The future was as boundless as the sea and sky of their domain.

"Don't call me King," Roy said. "This is a principality."

## "HELL ON EARTH"

Nowadays residents and workers of Sealand leave for the fort from the quiet port town of Harwich, around sixty miles from where the Bates family still lives in Southend. The nation is overseen by caretakers Mike Barrington and Joe Hamill, who alternate shifts aboard the fort and tend to its many ongoing projects and mechanical needs. They generally hitch a ride with a fishing boat on its way down the channel and past the fort, swapping out equipment and men every two weeks (or as the weather allows). One of the first orders of business is to go over the following weeks' work over numerous cups of tea in the fort's kitchen, a surprisingly cozy room with a table, chairs, modern amenities, and even houseplants in the window. There are davenports, desks, armchairs, and gym equipment in the fort. Electric lights facilitate reading or playing chess. The large storm windows in the kitchen and living room look out across the open sea.

All in all, the fort feels like a comfortable cellar with the giddy adventurousness of a childhood tree fort. Provided there is enough food and water, a stay on the fort can be incredibly peaceful: Sealand is a location where it is almost impossible that you'll be bothered by another soul. Insulated from the elements while nonetheless literally right out in them, a Sealander feels almost untouchable.

"On a clear day, you can see the shore and all the twinkling lights from the city, but it's ridiculous how many stars you can see at night—you can even see all the craters on the moon because there's no light pollution out there," said Michael's son James Bates, the current *charge de affairs* of Sealand's operations who started going out to the fort with his brother Liam when he was around four years old.

But the micronation wasn't always quite so inhabitable. To put it mildly, the first few months on Sealand were rough: freezing cold, sparsely furnished, ransacked of light switches and portholes, and prone to perilous shortages of food and water. "It was like hell on Earth," Joan Bates said. "There were no windows, no doors, the wind howled through, and everything was covered with a thick layer of crumbling rust." The *Mayflower* ship that carried the Pilgrims to North America was said to have departed from Harwich and docked at Leigh-on-Sea in Southend, and that's where the Sealanders based their operations as well. Like these famous explorers, the Bateses embarked on unknown adventure at their own peril.

In fact, simply getting to Sealand was an arduous, almost comically grueling task. All supplies, from food to building materials to drums of heating oil, were taken from the family's home in Southend to a bus stop. There, they caught a bus to Paglesham, close to where the *Mizzy Gel* was tied up. The bus let them off on an unpaved road, where supplies were unloaded and walked more than a mile to a small dinghy, which was in turn rowed to the *Mizzy Gel*. Then the family would sail approximately three miles down the winding River Roach before making a ninety-degree turn northward and exiting onto the River Crouch. It was another few miles before they reached the North Sea, where they only had to go another *forty* miles to reach Sealand. All told, a one-way journey to Sealand took almost five hours, not including the time it took to load and unload the supplies or the problems that invariably popped up on the boat.

"It was hours and hours from Paglesham on the boat going 'chug, chug, chug,'" Penny Bates recalled. "I used to sit there in a blanket and think, 'For God's sake will someone kill me please?' It was horrible, horrible."

But the work was only beginning when they arrived. The tower still didn't have a mechanized winch system, but they were able to cobble together some odds and ends to pull things up from the *Mizzy Gel* in heavy rubble sacks or in a box attached to a rope. The box was built from wood taken from some of the dozens of bunk beds lining the pillars' concrete walls, and the winch and wires were salvaged from defunct pieces of equipment found on other forts. The other method was climbing up the landing platform—an already dangerous task made even more precarious when you had to carry supplies up with you.

Most of the food resembled the diet followed by the Essex radio pirates—i.e., tinned foods and nonperishable victuals—but resupply missions were infrequent and unpredictable. Even on nice days, sudden winds could turn the North Sea into a roiling cauldron that made passage to Sealand extremely dangerous. "Rationing was a way of life on Sealand," Michael shrugged. Thus it was of critical importance that he taught himself to fish from the fort. He used a hook made from a nail he sharpened by scraping it against the cement floor and a piece of synthetic rope he found in one of the pillars. The family would trawl for lobsters with homemade lobster pots. They were so successful at catching lobsters that the delicacy became a nuisance.

"At least you aren't being forced to go to school," Joan said.

Each fort was constructed with cisterns for drinking water, but this was only a useful feature when there was water to fill them. Five-gallon drums of drinking water—weighing approximately forty-five pounds each—were carried up the rope ladder on fifteen-year-old Michael's increasingly hardy back. When imported water ran low, the Sealanders relied on rainwater, much of which was collected from the helipad. After Air Force jets flew by on exercises out at sea, the water on the helipad tasted like jet fuel. At one point, Michael rigged up pieces of sheet metal to make a filtration system that steamed seawater between two kettles through a small bit of rubber hose. "It was a very slow process that didn't produce much water and it certainly didn't taste very nice, but it gave us just enough to survive on," he recalled.

One of the most grotesque tasks was cleaning out the platform's legs, as they were full of dead birds. "They used to fly in and, because there were no doors or windows, couldn't find their way out again. Eventually they starved to death," Joan said. "We shoveled them into an old dustbin and hauled them up to the top on a pulley and dumped them over the side."

Fall was well on its way when independence was declared and conditions quickly became frigid. Although double-glazed glass windows were eventually installed in the living quarters and electric generators (and later wind turbines and solar panels) replaced the coal stoves, concrete and steel are not known for their ability to insulate. The naval forts were originally heated with a complex fan system, and this meant that there were large openings throughout the structure designed to help circulate the air. But the fan system was never repaired, leaving numerous conduits for freezing air. Doorframes were ringed with rubber gaskets, but aside from this minor protection, there was no way to seal the rooms from the cutting wind, which can howl across the North Sea at over sixty-five miles per hour. Consequently, the water tanks often froze. "In winter you would go out with a hammer and chisel to get water," Michael said. When seas were rough, which was frequent, the platform would shake with the crash of every thirty-foot wave.

Unfortunately, heating oil was prone to running out as well. When a supply boat didn't turn up for three weeks in November 1967, all the family could do during an intense cold spell was wrap themselves in blankets, with the occasional hot water bottle buried inside the cloth cocoon with them. "[Y]ou wouldn't believe how cold it was. That first winter I can remember going into the kitchen and trying to prepare just simple food—it was almost impossible. My hands ached so much I didn't know what to do with them," Joan said. More than once she fainted from the cold.

The events of summer 1967 had even altered the family's circadian rhythms. The fort was still under constant threat of being taken over and necessitated round-the-clock watches. Michael and other members of the Bates crew had been trading three-hour sleep schedules for the better part of a year. Michael would sometimes sleep on the deck when the weather was nice, but sleeping outside also gave him the opportunity to confront invaders as soon as they appeared. Michael said he welcomed rough weather because it meant a much-reduced chance of an invasion. "To this day, I find it very reassuring when the windows are rattling and it's blowing a gale," he said. "Because then I know that nobody can reach us—and no one can attack."

Everyone took to guarding their new dominion very seriously. Shoulder holsters were a ubiquitous fashion accessory, and Joan carried a .38 pistol during the day and kept it under her pillow at night. "I got my title the hard way. I had to earn it," she said. "But the thing that made me do it is that I'm just as determined as Roy is." Roy agreed. "She has bottomless courage," he said.

Typically, Michael and one other person stayed out on Sealand at a time. Michael had been out of school for almost a year, and, aside from losing contact with his friends, he didn't care. When he left school, Michael thought he might keep in touch with some of his friends and maybe even take a trip to see them again sometime, but the amount of time he spent on the platform made it impossible to do so. His school dorm was exchanged for a concrete room below sea level. He developed his own curriculum: perfecting his pistol shot, filling his own shotgun shells, and rebuilding bits of machinery.

Despite the unromantic privations of the first months, cleaning and personalizing Roughs Tower breathed new life into the platform, and Sealand began to feel more like a proper home. Once routines were established (and up to three years' worth of food was stockpiled), the family was able to "concentrate upon their lifestyle comforts rather than upon survival," as Michael put it.

Some of the bunks that previously accommodated marines were fitted with frilled bed covers, walls were adorned with framed hunting scenes, and a giant Sealandic flag, specially made by an area sailmaker, covered an entire wall. Couches and chairs were laboriously winched up; rugs and pieces of carpet covered the concrete floor.* Books and games were imported, as were cooking accessories and more tools. Rust was sanded down and walls were given new coats of paint. The words "Sealand" and "Roy Bates" were painted on the outside of the fort. Joan told a reporter that the conditions on Sealand were steadily improving and were "sheer luxury" compared to when they arrived. "[L]uxury is security and being able to do your own thing at your own time," Joan said. That stolid attitude reflected a philosophical life lesson—what good is opulence if you don't have the freedom to enjoy it?

"People always ask, 'But what do you *do* all day?'" Roy said. "But there's always something to be done. Between keeping things shipshape, we fish, tend injured or exhausted migrant birds and racing pigeons, wave to passing ships in the summer, sunbathe."

Sealand's declaration of independence was laughed at by the British government. "This is ludicrous," said a spokesman for the Ministry of Defence. "Mr. Bates is trespassing, and it now looks as if he is being very foolish."** It was the best the Crown could do in the face of

---

* The toilets emptied into the sea. Regarding dumping their waste into the ocean, Michael said the North Sea is the UK, France, Holland, and Belgium's public toilet. "I don't suppose our small contribution will make much of an impact on it!" he said.

** A spokesman for Radio Caroline, the entity from which Bates had wrested the fort, said the company was unimpressed. "[The petrol bomb-throwing ] was bad enough, but this Sealand rubbish is going a bit too far," he said.

continued Sealandic success. Roy's willingness to be a stick in the mud and shrug off the consequences had so far given him the upper hand. "I had seen him make things work that others said wouldn't," Joan Bates said. "It was only crazy to people who didn't understand Roy."

In allowing the Bates family to stay on the fort, however reluctantly, Britain unwittingly set herself up for whatever misadventures would come next. A new kind of fort madness would continue to tax the sanity of the British government into the present day. Even Roy Bates had no way of knowing just how strange the adventure would become, or how others would attempt to piggyback on his achievements for their own, often outright bizarre ends. The history of any country is checkered with unexpected challenges, and the history of Sealand would be no exception.

PART II

# GUNS, GERMANS, AND THE DEFENSE OF A DYNASTY

(1967–2000)

# CHAPTER 7

## BELASCO, BUOYS, AND
## THE CHELMSFORD COURT OF ASSIZES

*"I think the government finally left me alone because I am a decent chap."*

—Roy Bates

November 13, 1967, around 3:00 p.m. A minesweeper from the Royal Navy called the HMS *Egeria* was passing by the Principality of Sealand on a depth-surveying mission of the waters around the fort. When it got within one hundred feet of the micronation, a young boy with a shaggy haircut framing a "round boy's face" popped up from behind the deck. It was apparent that the *Egeria*, with its prominent radar equipment, was not a fishing boat or a hapless pleasure cruiser. Another raid could be imminent, or they could be looking for a sandbank to remeasure Britain's territorial waters. He decided to make the boat go away.

"Clear off!" he yelled down at the boat. "Why don't you clear off!"

Suddenly, the boy raised a pistol. It was—of course—Michael Bates, by now an expert in small arms. He fired some warning shots in the air and then unloaded the rest of the clip in the waters in front of the boat. "I heard the *phut* as the round entered the water," one crewmember reported. The *Egeria* retreated.

Despite the severity of the incident, the Crown declined to prosecute, as the location of the shooting was just too complicated. "I do not think this would be a suitable case with which to test the question of jurisdiction, even if a criminal charge becomes feasible," wrote an official from the Ministry of Defence. The disinclination to press charges could be seen as a suggestion the Sealanders were in control of their territory. The Crown thus began looking into other clandestine options for taking the fort. One plan involved buddying up to a disaffected Bates crewmember and convincing him to flip on his onetime comrades.

On November 2, 1967, William Sweby, the Ministry of Defence land agent who'd attempted to get Bates to hand over the fort as part of Operation Callow, received a letter from a Customs and Excise agent named Brisley, informing him that David Belasco, a former associate of Roy Bates, might be able to "unofficially" take over the fort and hand it over to the Crown.

Twenty-four-year-old Belasco had linked up with Bates during the pirate radio days and worked as a DJ and a deckhand. He fought alongside Michael in the numerous battles on the fort and was on deck with his wife Marjorie when Sealand's flag was raised for the first time. Belasco is also the one who said they "might have overdone it a bit" when they threw petrol bombs onto an invading boat earlier that year.

A fit guy with the mug of a handsome criminal, Belasco earned such a face by serving time in jail for ten charges over the past eleven years. Though a former convict, Roy had given Belasco a chance, remembering that some of the men who'd served under him in the war had similar pasts but proved to be solid under fire. While the other DJs' enthusiasm had waned, Belasco, "out of loyalty or possibly some other reason," had remained a Bates compadre, but the stress of the Sealandic endeavor had finally deteriorated the relationship. It was unclear if the MOD approached the former pirate or vice versa about retaking the fort—both insisted it was the other who initiated contact.

Brisley was dispatched to pay Belasco a visit on November 17 at his home on Manchester Drive in Southend-on-Sea, as Belasco had intimated he would be making an attempt on the fort the following day. "You are not to go alone," Brisley's supervisor instructed, and so Brisley asked land agent Sweby to go with him. The two met in Southend and made their way to the residence.

The agents were shown into the Belasco home—a well-kept, comfortable abode filled with the accouterments of three kids. Sweby noted privately how friendly, neatly dressed, and well spoken the former pirate was, and how much evident regard Belasco had for his wife. Belasco regaled the officials with tales of the fort. "His personality was evident when he said his ambition was to have been a 'stunt man,' and this may in part explain his earlier social failure," Sweby wrote in his notes.

Belasco soon revealed a fairly benign reason for wanting to take over the principality: It was for narrative purposes, he said, as he was writing a book about the pirate radio days and wanted a suitable ending to his tome. Belasco claimed he didn't want any money for his service but certainly wouldn't be opposed to a well-publicized handover of the fort.*

Belasco's criminal record included crimes of violence, and the Crown took this to mean there was a good chance he would try to take the fort by force. For that reason, the Crown said they couldn't in any way encourage what he was going to do. But, as Sweby said on the sly, if Belasco "should at any time obtain sole possession of Roughs Tower and be willing to hand it over to the Ministry, they would be ready to accept possession at short notice."

Belasco assured the officials the takeover would be nonviolent.

"What we're planning to do is—"

Sweby cut him off.

"I think, given the circumstances, I would rather not have that information," he said.

Nevertheless, Belasco was given a letter of introduction that would clear the raid with local police, and the Crown waited anxiously to see what would happen.

But the raid never happened. Despite the official clearance, the financial logistics proved daunting, and Belasco apparently wasn't able to secure a suitable boat. That seemed to be the end of the Belasco plan—at least until the following spring, when a tell-all article was published on May 30 in the *Daily Telegraph* that blew open the government's secret efforts to engage Belasco against Roughs Tower.

The article quoted from Belasco's sworn affidavit, in which he attested that the plan had been concocted by government officials. Belasco provided the newspaper with the phone number he was supposed to call after he took possession of the fort, which the reporter noted did in fact connect to the duty commander in the Naval Operations Room. Sweby, who by this time had retired, admitted that some

---

* Roy Bates had recently sold the rights to an exclusive article to an area newspaper for £750, making it seem that there was some money to be made in recounting their adventures.

of the statements in the affidavit were true, but the article's suggestion that the government was engaging a mercenary to do their dirty work was "totally unjustified."

"It is incorrect to say we approached Belasco," he said. "We said we were not interested in anything to do with violence [and that] we were not prepared to offer any money."*

Michael Bates recalls another side of the story: Belasco hadn't been able to secure a boat for the raid because he was unable to steal one, he said. In fact, his father had interrogated Belasco and found out the scope of the plan. Far from being a nonviolent takeover, Roy said he found Belasco in possession of a bag whose contents read like a serial killer's murder kit: ski masks, tape, a flashlight with tape over the lens to allow only a pinprick of light, and a bottle of chloroform—the latter of which was going to be used to knock out Michael and send him out to sea.** Appalled that this was done with the knowledge of the British government, Roy promptly alerted the *Daily Telegraph* as to what was going on, which prompted the explosive article. Bates also wrote to his Minister of Parliament Paul Channon, expressing concern that his kids could have gotten hurt if the scheme was carried out as planned. Channon in turn admonished the Ministry of Defence.

"I am sure you will agree that any attempt to organize an unofficial landing which will inevitably lead to fighting and possibly bloodshed is an act of highest responsibility," Channon wrote. "I would...appreciate receiving from you an assurance that your Department has no intention of organizing such an attack in the future."

## WARNING SHOTS

With the government/Belasco double-cross thwarted and another round of publicity working in favor of the Bateses, the Sealanders were free to focus on another legal issue playing out around the same time. On May 6, 1968, a ship called the *Vestal* appeared on the horizon and

---

\* Unbeknownst to the officials, Belasco had drilled a hole next to the light fixture hanging in the room and had installed a microphone to record the conversation. Unfortunately, the microphone didn't work, so he couldn't present a recording of the actual conversation.

\*\* Michael recalls it being a chocolate soaked with a sedative.

made for Sealand. The *Vestal* belonged to Trinity House, a private organization based in Harwich, contracted by the British government to maintain the navigational installations in UK waters, including the two buoys near Roughs Tower.* While the forts were no longer being used by the Crown, the buoys were still necessary to guide ships around it. Located about seven hundred feet from Sealand, they were filled with fuel and had to be replenished every few months.

On that day in May, a few Trinity House men were lowered in a small boat from the deck of the *Vestal* to refill a buoy. Michael looked down from Sealand as the boat pulled up close to the fort. The crewmembers noticed Penelope Bates was sunbathing on top of the tower. A barrage of lascivious comments followed. "It was something like, 'I'd like to give you one,'" Michael recalled. Irritated, her brother pulled out a .22 pistol and fired two warning shots in the air, two shots across the bow and then into the water in front of the boat. "One shot actually hit a buoy when Trinity men were on it," one worker later testified, aghast. According to Michael, he was merely defending his realm and the dignity of his family. "They were making indecent comments to my sister," he said.

Trinity House quickly said they wouldn't be going anywhere near Roughs Tower until the safety of their men could be guaranteed. As such, a military escort accompanied the Trinity House ship to the Roughs Tower buoys for the next two years. The escort prompted local press to mock Trinity House, suggesting that when Joan and Penny were on Sealand, "It was hardly necessary to provide the Navy to protect a Trinity House vessel from two women." But the fact was that the family posed a threat no matter who was on board.**

---

* The full name is the "Corporation of Trinity House of Deptford Strond," or, formally, "The Master Wardens and Assistants of the Guild Fraternity or Brotherhood of the most glorious and undivided Trinity and of St. Clement in the Parish of Deptford Strond in the County of Kent."

** News articles and government documents are full of irritating condescension toward the Bates women, but one reporter for the *East Anglian Daily Times* was a bit less chauvinistic: "Passing ships soon see that the island is partly feminist. Guarding is often done by the wife and daughter of owner Bates, who has given his children a Spartan lifestyle. If any 'invasion troops' think they can take possession of the island by means of ropes and ladders, they are wrong because the ladies do not hesitate to immediately grab the large supply of petroleum bombs."

The *Vestal* incident was another "recrudescence of trouble involving the fort" that gave the Crown an in to go after the occupiers of Roughs Tower, which they of course still considered property of the British government. This time, Michael and Roy were officially charged with violating the Firearms Act of 1937 and were to be arrested as soon as they set foot on shore. Roy was charged with allowing Michael to use his .22 pistol in a way that would endanger life, while Michael was charged with possessing the pistol without a valid firearms certificate.

Sure enough, on July 16, Michael found himself in the back of a police car after being arrested, along with his father, outside of their home. Sirens blaring, he was whisked away to the Harwich Magistrate Court at top speed for questioning. Navy vessels sailed past Sealand at least five times to see if the fort had been left abandoned. But Joan simply stared down from the deck, mean-mugging them and making sure they knew she had weapons.*

Roy's barrister argued in court in Harwich that the Crown didn't have jurisdiction over the fort, and as such the Firearms Act couldn't be used to prosecute anything that happened on the tower. It was the same deceptively simple argument that had stymied officials for years, and court was adjourned for six weeks to figure out if this was true. The matter was bumped up to the higher Central Criminal Assizes Court in Chelmsford,** and the Bates boys were ordered to appear before Judge Justice Chapman in October.

According to Roy, this was all part of the plan.

---

\* Plans for a raid on the fort were in fact drawn up in case that opportunity presented itself. Option A was a boat raid in which a tall-enough boat would pull alongside the fort so marines could rush onto the platform, while option B was a helicopter raid with commandoes repelling down onto the fort from above. Rules of engagement included in the plans granted the marines permission to fire back at the occupants if they were directly fired on first. It would be preferable if the local police force did the actual arresting, the report noted, that way it wouldn't look like the military force was being mobilized for a civilian matter. The report also suggested bringing along female police officers, as the government imagined "it would take most of the sting out of subsequent allegations of excessive force or official brutality if it could be shown that Miss/Mrs. Bates was in fact apprehended by a Woman Police Constable."

\*\* The Assize courts heard cases passed along to them by local county courts called quarter sessions, which met four times per year. Minor offenses were heard by justices of the peace in petty sessions, also called magistrates' courts.

"We shot at a British ship—into the air, though—just to force the English to charge us with illegal possession of firearms before a British court, [a]nd to prove thereby that Britain possesses no jurisdiction here," he said.

On October 21, father and son appeared at the Shire Hall in Chelmsford, their wide eyes taking in the grand chamber whose wooden walls were shiny with polish. After some preliminary procedure, the hearing began. Mr. Boreham, arguing for the prosecution, dug deep into the annals of precedent to make the case that Roy and Michael were breaking the law, citing cases from as far back as 1536. Boreham argued that British courts have jurisdiction anywhere there is a British Admiral, which is to say on the seas and any fort thereon. If a British citizen commits a crime out at sea, as Michael and Roy did, British courts can punish the offender as if they had been committed on shore, he said.

Arguing for the defense from behind a Kafkan pile of documents, briefs, and scribbled notes, Mr. Eastham contended that, aside from cases of murder, bigamy, and treason committed by British citizens at sea or on British vessels, British courts only had jurisdiction over the soil of Great Britain and within the three miles of territorial waters, and Roughs Tower was of course outside this delimitation.

The debate about how far jurisdiction reached went on for over two and a half hours, with the barristers gesturing so vigorously as they argued that the sleeves of their robes bounced around like in a cartoon. When the court broke for lunch, Michael and Roy were escorted down to a holding cell and sat side by side on a cold bench. Lunch was refused, as they had too much to chew on mentally.

When court resumed, Justice Chapman deemed the whole affair a "swashbuckling incident perhaps more akin to the time of Sir Francis Drake" and agreed with defense barrister Eastham. "Parliament no doubt has the power to make it an offense for a British subject to have a firearm with intent to endanger life in Istanbul or Buenos Aires, or where have you, but I do not think it has done so," Chapman said. "I think the Admiral would be somewhat surprised to hear that if one British Subject picked the pocket of another on an artificial structure [that it would be] some concern of his."

In other words, Michael and Roy were not guilty of violating the Firearms Act of 1937 because British law didn't reach Roughs Tower.

The implications took a moment to sink in, but then Roy's jaw fell open and his bushy eyebrows rose in surprise as Sealand's supporters broke out in a cheer. *A judge, a judge whose authority was vested in him by the Crown, just said the British government didn't have legislative power over Sealand.* Even Roy expected in the back of his mind that he'd get punished. Instead, his reign as monarch of Sealand had apparently been confirmed. "The UK's trash was Bates' treasure," as one writer put it, and now Bates was free to do with it as he wished, up to and including declaring it his own country.

Scholars who have looked at this case note that the judgment reflected a precise reading of the law as it was at the time: Chapman didn't say the Crown *couldn't* extend jurisdiction to Sealand; he only said it *hadn't.* Conceivably the Crown could pass legislation clarifying the matter, and a meeting was called on November 5 to discuss possible appeals to Chapman's ruling. But the decision was never appealed. According to the minutes of a November 1968 meeting between governmental departments, there was no reason to use legal or physical force against Bates, since he wasn't doing anything seriously wrong. Plus, "there was some advantage in refraining from prosecutions which would enhance Mr. Bates's local reputation as a colorful adventurer prosecuted by authority."

But the victory absolutely did enhance Roy's reputation, and it was indeed "claimed by Bates as a further triumph over officialdom" as they feared. The 1968 Assize court decision is touted to the present day as one of the most defining events in the principality's history, and one of the two events most critical to affirming the principality's sovereignty.

"If we didn't have any rights in international law, they would have pulled us off years ago. We are a problem—but only to bureaucrats sitting in centrally heated offices in Whitehall," Roy said. "I think the government finally left me alone because I am a decent chap."

Fists pumped in victory, and their sovereignty confirmed by the very country who tried to deny it, the Sealanders were ready to introduce their country to the global stage. They would forge ahead with their empire, filled with a sense of duty bolstered by the remarkable decision by Justice Chapman and the logical case for Sealandic sovereignty. For Roy Bates, the future was always looking bright.

"If I was not serious about Sealand's future, do you think I would have given up everything for it? I had a very successful business, a large and comfortable house, and a Bentley," he said. "That is quite a sacrifice."

# CHAPTER 8

## BEHOLD THE TRAPPINGS OF STATEHOOD

*"I expected it to last six months, not fifty-something years."*
—Michael Bates

Roy and Joan's oldest child Penny was almost eighteen years old when her father declared Sealand sovereign in 1967. Even though the Chapman ruling opened up the platform to a world of new possibilities, it wasn't long before she decided she'd finally had enough of the adventure.

Penny was outgoing, pretty, and interested in leading a normal social life. Being isolated on a metal platform was not particularly conducive to doing so. Subsisting for days on flour biscuits made with painstakingly distilled seawater wasn't just an interesting anecdote in the Sealand story; it was a genuinely callous and shocking reality. She couldn't help but to take it personally that her father apparently didn't recognize the danger she and her brother had been in. "He'd shrug and say, 'You're all right now, aren't you?'" Penny recalled.

Penny's decision to divest herself of further responsibility to the fort created some serious waves in a family not known for its subtlety. The stress of the Sealand endeavor already caused explosive fights, which compounded the raucous arguments about politics and social issues. Dinnertime was often an event of significant volume, with Roy and Michael and Penny screaming at each other while Joan calmly dished out the meal, though she wouldn't hesitate to cut in with a harsh rejoinder of her own. On top of the umbrage he felt when things didn't go his way, Roy, the proud war hero and entrepreneur, was privately afraid that Sealand could fail. This fear was partly expressed in his disappointment that Penny would choose to forsake the project. Things were just getting started, and they needed all the help they could get! But just as Roy was a hardheaded individual, so is Penny, and she disappears from most press reports about Sealand in the early 1970s.

Penny's brother Michael, on the other hand, was fully invested in Sealand from its inception and continues as the country's Prince Regent today. Photos of Michael from the early years of the micronation's existence show him beaming alongside his parents out on the fort or standing guard in a knit hat and winter jacket, his fingerless gloves holding a shotgun and his mustache and sideburns framing a smirk. He willingly subjected himself to inhospitable conditions as the country was established and risked life and limb in doing so, always on guard against further invaders and frequently dangling from the ends of rusting protuberances to do repairs on obscure parts of the tower.

Despite his dedication, even Michael wasn't immune to the loneliness that came with being out on the fort. His longest consecutive stint was six months, and in total he estimates he spent the better part of twenty years stationed there—a huge chunk of his life that started when he left boarding school and ran until he got married in the mid-1980s. Oftentimes he would spend a month straight on Sealand, hitch a ride back as soon as he could, and then be instructed by his father that he'd have to turn right back around. It was hard to muster enthusiasm sometimes, and Michael has been known to take a step back and objectively question the wisdom of dedicating his life to the pursuit.

"The isolation must have had some effect on us, I suppose. I went back to the mainland every few months but I had few friends there," he said. "I expected it to last six months, not fifty-something years."

The loneliness of the fort abated somewhat as the micronation caught the attention of more people. The kind of people that wanted to pitch in were often the kind of people Michael got on quite well with. Two young Germans named Roland Teschner and Walter Mierisch became Sealanders in 1969 when they planned to hitchhike to Namibia but ultimately didn't have time to do the rounds of vaccinations required. They read about the principality in a German newspaper and ended up completing two long stints on Sealand, broken up by mandatory service in the German military. Other worthy additions to the crew were a tough-looking guy with a diving knife strapped to his leg named Barry Harcus, whose scowl and spiky blond hair made him look like he was from *West Side Story* or a punk band, and Gordon "Willy" Wilkinson, who managed the Bates family's Airfern business and became one of Michael's best friends.

A break in the isolation would also come from chatting on the radio with the captains of various area ships. A common sight from the deck of Sealand was a ferry that shuttled between Harwich and the Hook of Holland. Captain Wylde, the skipper, would throw over newspapers and messages weighted down with bolts, sometimes beers, and one Christmas he even attempted to launch a frozen turkey that unfortunately plummeted into the sea.

One of the biggest problems, Michael said, was that there were no women. Michael made the best of it, however, using Sealand's radio like a very early dating app. One young woman even hitched a ride with a local fisherman to come out to visit him. "We had a whale of a time," Michael said, though Roy was worried that the princely bacchanalia would become tabloid fodder and damage the principality's reputation.*

In order to break the monotony and raise money, Michael began looking into projects outside of Sealand, including harvesting cockles, a small, edible mollusk found in abundance on British coasts. The borough of Leigh-on-Sea in Southend, not far from where Michael grew up, was a particular hotbed for the industry and had been for hundreds of years.

The family already had a handful of boats for the white weed business that could be readily outfitted with the necessary equipment for cockling, though Roy warned that it was a precarious occupation with little chance of financial recompense. But the white weed market shrank in the 1970s due to depleted interest, and Michael realized

---

* Penny felt a similar longing but said that while there were tons of charming boys working for Radio Essex and the rugged handsomeness of the later crewmen was certainly appealing, she was too much of a "goody two-shoes" to pursue those kinds of relationships. "Initially it was quite interesting because it was full of young boys," she said. "That was quite interesting considering I went to an all-girls boarding school. [Sealand] wasn't as much fun because it wasn't a radio station. There were some fascinating young lads out there at the time but I didn't appreciate it."

how valuable a commodity cockles could be by exporting them to countries like Spain and Portugal that eat them more regularly than the UK. Michael bought a boat and outfitted it with the appropriate equipment, went off to Scotland for a few seasons to get the hang of the trade, and eventually returned to the Thames Estuary to begin cockling closer to home. (More about the Bates family's cockling ventures is discussed in chapter 19.)

Roy naturally insisted on maintaining the fort with unrivaled fervor. Offers to buy the fort were consistently rejected, even though they would have helped to alleviate the family's financial woes. At one point Roy turned down an offer of around three million dollars, supposedly offered by Aristotle Onassis. Things got so bad at times that the Bateses would have to sell furniture or records from Radio Essex in order to buy food or pay wages, and later on Michael had his home repossessed because he was pouring so much money into the fort that he couldn't pay his mortgage. "If he had no money, he wouldn't give it up. For no reason would he have given it up," Michael said.

In addition to the arbitrary hardships imposed on the family by Sealand, Penny, who looks a lot like Joan, said it was somewhat tragic that Sealand was so important to Roy because the isolation kept her outgoing and vivacious mother from pursuing the social life she found so engaging. Joan had gotten married at age eighteen and barely had a chance to develop a life of her own outside of her parents' home, but following the direction of her husband was just how things were at the time, Penny said. Even so, she was indispensable to the successful functioning of Radio Essex. She flourished under the pressure that came with managing the various family enterprises, and she certainly appeared to enjoy the celebrity that came with being Princess Joan. She was also quick to chastise reporters, take officials to task, and let authorities and invaders alike know she was packing. "Would you ask the same question of Princess Grace of Monaco?" she said sharply when asked if she was serious about her crown. Plus, the Sealand endeavor gave the Bateses an excuse to spend a lot of time together, which her mother relished tremendously, Penny said.

In any case, the isolation and privations were only going to be temporary, as Roy banked on Sealand becoming a much more productive industry. The intention was always to bring commercial enterprise to the principality, and the Sealanders got to work opening the micronation for business at the end of the 1960s.

"If you want to be a country, you have to act like a country, which is why you have to have visas to visit Sealand, and stamps and passports, coins and all the paraphernalia that go with it," Michael said.

## "CINDERELLA" STAMPS AND COINAGE

One day in September 1969, a helicopter flew across the North Sea and hovered over the principality. Michael and Roy ran to the landing pad on top of the fort to take down the mast so the chopper could land. Squinting to keep out the flying dirt and dust, Michael stared up awestruck at the thundering machine. It was so powerful and its engine so loud that it seemed to be summoning a power from the beyond. His dad grabbed him by the shoulder, snapping him out of his trance, and the two ran back down the steps to let the helicopter touch down.

Out of the chopper came a Belgian named Christian Hache, who was delivering a package containing the first edition of the Sealand stamps, which had been designed and printed in Belgium. In turn, as Sealand's postmaster, he was going to take the first mailbag from Sealand to Belgium, where the letters would enter the bloodstream of international postage and be dispatched around the world. The move was practical but also strategic: A functioning postal service would reinforce its status as a separate country. An official post office was developed in the sixth subfloor of one of the legs, replete with a teller window and a banner reading "Post Office."

"I'm sure our government will have no objection to handling this mail," Hache said. "Never before have I felt such enthusiasm for a new issue of stamps. I have become a Sealand enthusiast—the idea is wonderful."

A little while later, Roy handed Hache the letters to which were affixed some of the fresh stamps. The stamps were in denominations of 2 and 50 pence, and each stamp bore the visage of a famous explorer: Christopher Columbus, Vasco da Gama, Walter Raleigh, Francis Drake, Captain Cook, and Magellan. The most expensive of the bunch featured a somewhat obscure explorer named Sir Martin Frobisher who brought back tons of gold ore from the New World only to learn it was—*womp womp*—fool's gold.

Unfortunately, the postal services of the UK and Belgium didn't take to the plan. Both countries refused to recognize Sealand's stamps and returned to sender any letters to which they were affixed. A few hundred letters with Sealand stamps slipped through official cracks and were delivered over the years, but the Post Office admitted in court at one point that it had simply thrown out any letters addressed to the principality. The rejection wasn't necessarily a show of prejudice against Sealand specifically; it had more to do with the fact that the micronation was not part of the International Postal Union.*

Nevertheless, Sealand would issue many series of stamps over the years, including editions with famous ships, incredible sea creatures, and images of the prince and princess—all quite remarkable works of art. The Ipswich Post Office has an official Sealand address—Sealand Post Bag, IP11 9SZ, UK—the contents of which are picked up by the Sealanders when they come to shore.

Sealand stamps do have their enthusiasts, however, and not just among micronationalists. They are considered "Cinderella" stamps in the stamp-collecting community, a subcategory of philately that includes nonofficial postage stamps, stamp-like labels, and stamps from other nontraditional countries (such as Lundy Island, Sedang, Franz-Joseph Land, Occussi-Ambeno, Atlantis, and Montebello Island). Derek Watson, Secretary of the UK-based Cinderella Stamp Club, said that any competent printer can print quality sheets of stamps, but "finding a perforator is a bit more difficult."

---

* As part of the Universal Postal Union, countries have agreements where they reimburse each other for the cost of delivering mail. This is how postage rates are determined: When you buy a stamp, you aren't just paying the country you are sending it from to mail the letter; you are also paying the recipient country to deliver the letter for you. Basically, since no country had this kind of agreement worked out with Sealand, no country was going to pay for the labor of delivering letters sent from the principality.

That's why, as a fascinating episode of NPR's *Planet Money* pointed out, Chinese companies can send packages to US customers and not charge for shipping. The seemingly money-losing venture for China actually makes sense because the rates China has negotiated with the US (and vice versa) work out well enough for China that its postal system can charge super low rates to send stuff abroad.

If conditions are right, however, Sealand stamps could have some legitimate postal use. Joanne Berkowitz, of the International Society of Worldwide Stamp Collectors, said it's not uncommon during war or national disasters that private postal services will crop up to deliver mail. Sealand stamps could perhaps be used for this purpose. And this could even work in peacetime: A man in California creates postage stamps for his "Bat's Private Post," in which neighbors add one of his stamps to their letters in exchange for him taking the letter to the post office for them.

Today Sealand has stamps for sale on its website as curios alongside mugs and desk flags and T-shirts. The latest stamps, the 2010 edition, featuring a modern art version of the principality's silhouette, can be purchased in sheets of twenty in one of three colors for between $9.99 and $15.99, or all three colors for $29.99.

The first Sealand coins were issued in 1972. The denomination was Sealand dollars, written as SX$, and valued as 1:1 with the United States dollar. Roy and Joan flew to Houston a number of times to meet with a banker named George Garner to produce the first batch, which included 2,000 silver coins minted at SX$10 each. The front featured Princess Joan; the back was a ship. SX$20 silver coins and SX$100 gold coins followed over the next few years. "George proved to be honest," Michael said, and "there was a trickle of money coming out of our project." Most recently, coins were produced to commemorate Sealand's fiftieth anniversary in 2017, including an SX$25 coin featuring the faces of Roy, Joan, and Michael and an image of the flag-raising ceremony from 1967 on the back.

Collectors can even purchase coins boasting a strange minting error from the 1994 series. This run of coins came in SX$0.25 to SX$5 denominations, all of which bore the Sealandic crest on the front and an orca, a "Treasure of the Sea," on the back. The approximately seventy-five mistake coins came from the dies from Sealand coins being imprinted on the back of Navy Seal medallions on account of the shared nautical theme. However, the person who minted the 1994 coins seems to have ripped the Bates family off, as they have not seen a dime from the sale of these coins, which Michael said the seller is still actively selling. "That still infuriates me," Michael said, noting that none of the proceeds from the coins went to helping whales, which was part of the reason for minting them in the first place.

On top of the venture into the coin and stamp business, a "Las Vegas of the North" was discussed, replete with casinos and "houses of ill repute," and former Libyan dictator Muammar Gaddafi offered Roy a "pot of gold" to use the tower for undisclosed reasons. The rejection was partly a matter of logistics. Roy said he was offered gold bars for the platform but said the plane scheduled to transport the idea wasn't big enough to handle the weight of the gold. An offer by an American church to use the platform to beam religious broadcasts to Russia seemed promising as well, "until someone told me the church was a front for the CIA. I don't want Russians down my back, so I refused," Roy said.

The lack of development was disappointing, considering how much effort was going into keeping the principality afloat. "There's always a good lunch, some very decent wine, and then I tend not to hear from them again," Roy said with some amount of resignation.*

But Roy's fate would turn with the arrival of a mysterious group of Germans who would soon come along with impressively grandiose plans for the principality. The Germans pushed the argument for Sealandic sovereignty into overdrive and put into motion some of the most outrageous and defining events of Sealand's history. Roy was actively courting investment, but the partnership with the Germans would leave the Sealanders wondering what the hell they had gotten themselves and their country into.

---

* The Bateses weren't the only ones fielding proposals for the fort. In June 1972, a company called Safety Disposal, Ltd. wrote to the Ministry of Defence to ask about installing a toxic chemical waste incinerator on Roughs Tower. The remote location made the towers ideal, and the pollution it created at least wouldn't be right in anyone's face. The Crown would have no doubt loved to have plunked a toxic waste incinerator right in Roy Bates's living room, but the government never took Safety Disposal, Ltd. up on its offer. (Who knows what kind of headache would have arisen if a toxic waste platform declared itself sovereign?)

The Department of Energy did, however, commission a study on the concrete of the forts, as they wanted to see how well the concrete of the forts was doing since oil platforms were being built with concrete legs as part of the "Concrete in the Oceans" program. They were to take samples of the concrete and undertake studies such as "rebound hammer" and "ultrasonic pulse transmission" surveys of the concrete legs. No reports have surfaced that a Sealander fired on the DoE scientists, or if the scientists even approached Roughs Tower in the first place.

# CHAPTER 9

# ARRIVAL OF *DIE DEUTSCHEN*

---

*"It is inevitable that businessmen—solvent businessmen—will come to Sealand."*

—Walter Scheffel

The exact way in which the group of Germans and Dutchmen got in touch with the Bates family has been lost to time, but Michael said that sometime in 1973 his father was approached by the Germans, possibly in response to an ad placed in a newspaper, and was apparently taken enough by their enthusiasm for Sealand to go into business with them. The principality's square footage held a lot of commercial promise, but the Germans visualized a micronation with a much more commanding presence: a nation-state of apartments, casinos, oil refineries, and "perhaps even a coffeeshop." (Much more on that later.)

The Sealanders soon met the Germans in person, and, to put it mildly, they were a colorful lot.

Among the group was Walter Scheffel, a former tax adviser from Maintal with a thin red mustache who would become "Consul of Sealand." Scheffel was a crewmember on German bombers during the Second World War before becoming a secret agent for the Allies, while postwar he tended to his collection of ninety large cats of prey, of which "many a large zoo would be envious." He claimed he had been named Lord Multon-Harrington in 1977 by Queen Elizabeth II, but a British official said they could find no such record of the appointment.

Scheffel said he was in it for the adventure. "I believe in Sealand's development, and I always have great fun in completely new things which you can help to build up from the beginning," he said. "It is inevitable that businessmen—solvent businessmen—will come to Sealand; this will be an accompanying phenomenon experienced by all small countries today and decades ago."

Most infamous of these new investors would be Professor Alexander Gottfried Achenbach, a not unhandsome man in his midforties with an unsettling smile, said to be a former diamond dealer from the western German town of Aachen. His title of "professor" was not necessarily bestowed due to academic achievement; he had apparently been a guest lecturer at a few universities and/or had come upon the title through his involvement with a group of conmen who sold hundreds of fake titles and documents. Achenbach planned to spend his retirement years raising rabbits in Henri-Chapelle, Belgium, but he felt that the transformation of Sealand into a true maritime power would make for "the last great adventure of the twentieth century" and the venture drew him out of retirement. He told Roy and Joan he used to work for the CIA, smuggling people across the East German border, and he gave them a small carving that he said was from a representative of the UFO influence in the ancient Yucatan cultures. Though he would only visit the micronation once, Achenbach became the Minister of Foreign Affairs and later Prime Minister for Life. (Achenbach did not speak any English, so a man named Carl Wilhelm Tebroke acted as his translator and business agent.)

As the partnership got underway, a German named Detlef J. Kammerer, acting as "President of the Senate of the Principality of Sealand," and a few cohorts began sending inquiries to various governments about doing business on Sealand. The group bombarded embassies with a volley of letters so intense that one official called it a "diplomatic offensive." Achenbach later estimated that they sent inquiries to the governments of 150 countries.

The Germans then obtained a legal opinion about Sealand's sovereignty from a "Dr. Dr. Dr." Walter Leisner,* a professor at the University of Erlangen-Nuremberg. In short, Leisner says that while Sealand is not a naturally occurring piece of land, it does have a "national territory as it is based on a defined part of the surface of the

---

* The British government was unimpressed with the "Dr. Dr. Dr." title in front of Leisner's name, which Achenbach explained was a custom followed by European academics to reflect their expertise in numerous fields. Achenbach apparently didn't have much in the way of a response when a British official fact-checked this claim in front of him and proved that no such nomenclature existed.

earth" and is "immovably fixed to the surface of the earth," which is qualification enough for statehood. The Leisner opinion, professionally printed and bound in reflective silver cardstock, would be cited without fail in future advocacy for its legitimacy. Achenbach also helped draft Sealand's constitution, a twenty-three-article document based on British common law that the principality still uses today. Overall, however, the feedback to the diplomatic offensive was a bit underwhelming. Documents in the British National Archives show many a befuddled inquiry from state officials about the requests from Sealand, but the Crown government just sighed and told the countries to ignore them. Achenbach had also reached out to the UN, which wasn't interested. "The United Nations is an organization of governments, not gun platforms," a UN spokesperson said. "The secretary-general has a nut file for such applications."

The Crown government kept a wary eye on the "state on stilts," as it was unclear where all of this activity was going. It seemed like an extended role-play in statesmanship, but things got a little sketchier when members of Sealand's new government were arrested in Luxembourg on May 17, 1975.

The German Sealanders had previously set up a business in Luxembourg called "Sealand Information Gathering and Messaging Agency" (SIGMA) and had at one point managed to get entry stamps in their Sealandic passports. However, when Achenbach returned to Luxembourg and tried to sell Sealand coins and stamps, he and other SIGMA officials were arrested for "engaging in fraudulent business based in an imaginary country." They were jailed as officials looked into the legitimacy of the Sealander's claims. Meanwhile, Achenbach hired a Dutch lawyer known for his work in tricky international affairs to sort the issue out. The lawyer was Adrian L.C.M. Oomen, a rotund, middle-aged man "with thinning hair and an almost Hitler-like mustache," as Michael Bates described him. The group announced they were petitioning to have their case heard by the International Court of Justice in The Hague. As before, there was hope that the court's decision would force legal recognition. "I believe that the International Court of Justice could declare the Luxembourg action to be an illegal or unfriendly act, possibly even an aggression," Oomen said.

The Luxembourg authorities consulted the British government about the situation. Luxembourg was eager to help set things straight, as "they are very concerned that Luxembourg's financial name should not be sullied in any way." The men were facing up to two years in jail but were released three weeks later on bail and fined around $500 each for lesser charges. The judgment granting their release "made no reference to the legal status of Sealand" and thus the episode wasn't especially helpful.

Undaunted, Achenbach soon tried another experimental tactic. This time it was a bit more dramatic. On August 2, 1976, he petitioned the Administrative Court of Cologne to revoke his German citizenship so he could officially become a citizen of Sealand. The judicial officials listened with stunned amusement as he made his case. Achenbach argued he was one of 106 people who had been issued a "naturalization document" by what the court called the "Duchy of Sealand," obviating the need for German citizenship. Sealand was on the verge of being recognized by Ceylon, Paraguay, and Cyprus, Achenbach explained, and he was preparing to sponsor a Dutch athlete in the next Olympics to compete on behalf of Sealand. He explained the Leisner position and the requirements of the Montevideo Convention and rested his case. After considering Achenbach's arguments, the court found that the "action was admissible, but unfounded."

The court's subsequent decision, *In re Duchy of Sealand* 80 I.L.R 683, became a classic document of the Sealand story, cited with as much fervor as those who cite the 1968 Chelmsford Assizes decision in favor of Sealand's sovereignty. The court acknowledged that Achenbach had not lived in his home country since late 1975, but just because he lived elsewhere did not mean that he had acquired the citizenship of another territory. Moreover, they said, an abandoned fort did not constitute territory in the sense necessary for statehood.

First, the court said, the root word of "territory" is "terra," which is synonymous with "earth," meaning that any would-be country must be on naturally formed land. And while the size of a country is not a deciding factor of its legitimacy as a state, the citizens of any would-be nation must form a "cohesive vibrant community" ruled by a government who respects and carries out the aims of this community. Sealand does not do this, the court argued, as it is "neither state territory nor a people nor a State government."*

Their decision was final, and Achenbach was forced to keep his German citizenship.

Unbeknownst to the Bates family, Achenbach was facing unrelated legal troubles around the same time and had to appear in court soon after for his alleged role in a false document scheme. These were the days before the internet, Michael said, and had the family been aware of the extent of his chicanery, they might have anticipated the shadow soon to be cast over his involvement with Sealand.

In essence, Achenbach was accused of being a broker for a crew of conmen who sold hundreds of fake titles and documents under the guise of a humanitarian organization called the "Anglican Free Church." Six men and one woman behind the scam had ultimately been arrested, and Achenbach told the court that the church's founder had ripped him off.** "We had agreed on a commission of 20 percent, and the 370–400 addresses I had given to the Anglican Free Church represented a business value of three million. That would have been DM$600,000 for me," Achenbach said.

---

\* According to the opinion, the State *has the duty to promote community life. This duty does not merely consist of the promotion of a loose association aimed at the furtherance of common hobbies and interests. Rather, it must be aimed at the essentially permanent form of communal life in the sense of sharing in a common destiny…[A] State community must play a more decisive role in serving the other vital human needs of people from their birth to their death. These needs include education and professional training, assistance in all the eventualities of life and the provision of subsistence allowances where needed.*

Moreover, the idea that territory has to be natural land is outdated and probably never true in the first place. As Vince Beiser writes in his incredible book on sand, *The World in a Grain*, humans have been dredging sand or damming water to expand shorelines for hundreds of years. Beiser notes that humans have added 5,237 square miles of artificial land to the world's coasts since 1985, such as the ninety-two-acre Battery Park City in New York City, and notes that Dubai's Palm Jumeirah, the luxury neighborhoods built on a palm-tree-shaped manmade sandbar, is so large it can be seen from space.

\*\* Dozens of professionals duped by the fraud were scheduled to testify at the trial, but almost all of the witnesses claimed they were ill, busy, or out of town. The judge threatened to require medical examinations to validate their excuses, and suddenly many people were able to come to the trial.

The judge eventually handed down nine-year prison sentences to the perpetrators, though Achenbach was able to evade jail time since he wasn't one of the movers and shakers. He went back to his duties as Sealand's Minister of Foreign Affairs, somewhat chastened by the close call but feeling emboldened by the various legal judgments against him. They wouldn't be hounding him so hard if he wasn't onto something, he figured, and so, undaunted by the *In re Duchy of Sealand* judgment and the ignominy of the Free Church affair, the Germans hid their questionable sides and ushered the plans to expand Sealand forward. Roy Bates may have had big plans for Sealand, but the Germans seemed to help him think even bigger.

## THE GERMAN SCHEME

It began with a brochure.

The Germans put together a pamphlet touting their plans, illustrated with clean, pleasant diagrams that wouldn't be out of place as IKEA instructions. Just as the Maunsell Forts had originally been floated out to sea on concrete pontoons and then sunk, the pamphlet described a network of platforms that could be pieced together in a honeycomb-like design and expand the nation indefinitely.

The plans were modest: money exchanges, post offices, duty-free shops, drugstores, an administrative complex, heliports, hotels, apartments, casinos, staff accommodations, and a lounge. There was also to be a radio station, a cafeteria, and a separate island to provide a greenspace for guests. Various weapons would be integrated into the design for security purposes. They were courting investors for this project and assured interested parties their investments would be backed with shares in a Zurich steel fund.

The most ambitious part of the plan was an oil refinery on Sealand, which would take advantage of the North Sea oil reserves in Sealand's territorial waters. The refinery would be connected to the British mainland by a pipeline while Sealand itself would eventually be joined by a bridge to the coast. All told, the expansion of "old Sealand" was estimated to take around two and a half years and would cost $36–55 million. "It simply takes longer to expand a State in the sea than to build a factory on green fields," Achenbach explained poetically.

Interested parties could write to an address in Berlin to get a copy of the pamphlet, and Roy and the Germans began spotlighting the project in newspapers and on a forty-five-minute special on German TV. One British official noted that the film was shown during a children's cartoon hour and might not have reached many people, but the advertising did generate some interest. Scheffel took calls from a gardener who wanted to plant flowers on the fort and from a circus looking to reinvent itself as "Circus Sealand."

The Germans' plans were bolstered by another legal opinion in favor of Sealand's sovereignty, this time from a professor of international law at the University of Nijmegen in the Netherlands named Bela Vitanyi. Sealand had governance over its own affairs while at the same time participating in the international system—classic hallmarks of any state, he said. If this isn't enough, Vitanyi also invoked squatter's rights as further justification for the Bates family's "intellectual" and "physical" occupation of the fort.

According to Roy Bates, more than 90 percent of the funds necessary to expand Sealand had been collected by early 1978, and it was only a matter of time before Sealand became Seacontinent. But not everyone thought as highly of the Germans.

Guy Hawtin, an acquaintance of Roy's and a reporter at the *Financial Times*, surmised that Roy was being taken advantage of, that he was a "reasonably honest fool" whose essentially innocent aspirations were being exploited by the Germans for as-of-yet unknown ends. As close as Hawtin could figure it, it appeared they were trying to con Roy, installing themselves on the fort and vying for diplomatic recognition in an effort to transform Sealand into a financial institution that could obfuscate the movements of large sums of cash.

Hawtin was so wary of what apparently lay ahead that he met with Achenbach and played dumb about the German's plans so that Achenbach would give him copies of documents outlining their financial dealings. Hawtin noted that it seemed like the "Carlo Ponzi" approach was being employed in funding the project, prompting him to secretly reach out to the police about the possibly questionable dealings going on out at Sealand. The Crown speculated that plans for Sealand's expansion were orchestrated to drum up publicity (and funds) for the actually feasible tax haven project.

Eventually, the Germans weren't even shy about their intentions to develop a tax haven on the principality. The Sealanders began looking for banks to handle the principality's transactions. Denials from bank officials were common—"I hope you will understand that the Federal Ministry of Finance has a heavy burden of work and that it will not be possible to comment on this matter further," wrote one official—but the questions led to the governments of Germany and England double-checking that there were no loopholes that would allow citizens from either country to avoid paying taxes while on the fort. But this didn't mean it wasn't worth pursuing, as the situation wouldn't be so easy to resolve given that the fort was still in international waters.

"The British government has been lucky in that over time Bates has only courted a succession of dreamers and oddballs, with the fort never having been put to any genuinely nefarious purpose," writes British FCO researcher Grant Hibberd. But money has a way of corrupting things, and in August 1978, Sealand would come as close as it ever had to being used for a genuinely nefarious purpose. The German-born Sealanders would stop at nothing in pursuit of their microempire.

"[Sealand] was meant to be a way of making money, but it turned into more of an adventure," Michael Bates said in what might be the understatement of the century.

# CHAPTER 10

# THE COUP: WORLD WAR SEALAND

*"It is the differences in preference, the differences in will, that make groups depart from one another. It is also the differences in will that further solidify the social bond between the members of any one group. As the groups began to grow, the collective will within the groups would grow more diverse, and split again."*

—Andrew HE Lyon,
"The Principality of Sealand and its Case for Sovereign Recognition"

A Mercedes 350 SE made its way down the streets of Amsterdam, a smart leather briefcase containing legal arguments and a Sealandic Diplomatic passport. The car was driven by Gernot Ernst Pütz, a young German lawyer with studious glasses and a full head of dark, curly hair. Pütz had helped Alexander Achenbach in his bid to legally renounce his German citizenship and had been awarded Sealandic citizenship for his efforts. This time, however, Pütz's task fell a little outside the normal parameters of legal work: He was given license by Achenbach to secure ownership of the fort by whatever means he could. It was August 10, 1978, and Pütz was on his way to a helipad to await a signal from his boss.

At the same time, Roy and Joan Bates were in Salzburg, Austria, to meet with Achenbach, who had broached the idea of buying the platform outright from the Bates family. Achenbach had proposed DM$1 million and Roy countered with DM$10 million; negotiations were to happen forthwith. Unbeknownst to Roy and Joan, Achenbach had no intention of engaging in serious negotiations. He knew that Michael would likely be alone on Sealand when Roy and Joan came to talk business, and this was the real reason he had invited them to Austria.

## AN "APPEAL TO THEIR CONSTITUTIONAL RIGHTS"

Back on the fort, Michael lifted his face to the breeze and inhaled deeply. A big breath of fresh air always invigorates the spirit, and

Michael partook in this refreshing ritual as he went about the seemingly endless number of daily chores. But his reverie was interrupted by a telltale thrum. Michael, who had just turned twenty-six, squinted and saw a helicopter making its way toward the fort.

His Spidey sense started tingling. It was too early for his parents to be coming back, they didn't like to travel by helicopter, and no other visits had been arranged. Soon the chopper was overhead, blowing rust and loose bits of material. Inside were a handful of men staring expressionlessly down at him, one of them filming, waiting for the mast to be taken off the helipad so the chopper could land.

A rope was tossed out of the helicopter and a portly man named Winifred Brings shimmied down onto the deck. He shook Michael's hand for an uncomfortably long time as more men slid down and took up a position behind Michael. Michael recognized the men as Evert Boss, Helmut Eck, and Oldenburg—men with whom his parents had been in business over the past few years—but the unannounced visit did not in any way auger anything good.

Brings had a telex saying Roy had signed a contract to sell the fort and that his son should hand over control to the Germans. But he wouldn't let Michael examine the telex himself, and so Michael tried to get them to leave and come back later when his father—or anyone else at all—was there with him. Eventually the "oily bastard" Brings agreed to leave, but not liking to fly, he begged for a drink to calm his nerves. Michael agreed to get him a drink if only to expedite his leaving, and he went to the storeroom to grab some scotch.

Suddenly, Brings rushed up behind Michael, pushed him into the storeroom, and slammed the door closed. He then braced the door shut with a nearby camera tripod.

It took Michael a moment to realize what had happened. He'd been in the storeroom countless times, but he noticed for the first time how inescapable it actually was. The room was only about three feet wide and seven feet long—a chamber uncomfortably like a tomb. There was a two-inch-thick steel door and two small portholes, neither of which was even close to big enough for a grown man to slip through.

Michael soon heard the helicopter take off from up above. He remained motionless, trying to determine if he could hear anything in the thunderous silence that followed. Trying to control his mounting panic, he began pulling at the ceiling and wall to see if there was a way to get himself out. He reached a hand through a gap and was immediately whacked on the knuckles by someone on the other side. Well, at least they're still there, he thought.

Michael was left in the room overnight and well into the next day, keeping himself warm by wrapping himself in a Sealand flag and using a cookie tin to relieve himself. Eventually, his captors told him to stick his hand through the porthole window (which they had smashed out) so they could handcuff him. Michael was walked out onto the deck while Eck and Boss consulted about what to do.

When they got close enough, Michael kicked one of the men square in the nuts and grabbed the other by the lapels of his coat and head-butted him in the face. But the two men knocked him down and began kicking him, subduing him enough to bind him up. They tied Michael at his hands, elbows, and knees, tying his hands to his knees.

"Let's chuck this bastard over the side," one of them said.

Instead, Michael was taken from one room to the next before eventually being tossed and locked in the radio room. His hands screamed with the pressure of the binding, looking like purple sausage balloons about to burst. He kept himself busy getting the ropes loose before lack of circulation made his hands fall off. "Thank God for my years spent around fishing boats and experience of working loose, seemingly impossible knots," he said.

The next morning, a trawler pulled up under the fort, and five more men ascended onto the platform. Michael was led out into the sunshine. He inhaled deeply, happy to take in the sun and some fresh air. Lawyer Gernot Pütz had arrived by helicopter from Amsterdam and was calling the shots.

According to Pütz, Michael was to be dumped onto the trawler below, sail through the night, and be kicked out in Holland. Sure enough, he was put on the boat and spirited back off under the cover of darkness, and Adrian Oomen, the Dutch lawyer who had helped Achenbach when he was arrested in Luxembourg, paid the skipper for his troubles. The skipper in turn let Michael stay at his house and helped him book a flight back to Southend.

It appeared that the invading Germans were now in control of the principality.

"In this modern day we call them terrorists, in those days I don't know what we called them," Michael said.

The invaders decried such a characterization and described the takeover as a desperate move to save Sealand from Roy himself. In an article called "Putting things in the right light" published in the second edition of the government's Dutch-language magazine *Neue Sealand Journal*, the authors explained that Roy had contravened the Sealandic constitution with his "intention to sell states' rights to a consortium" and take control away from the business partners. Under these desperate circumstances, Achenbach had amended the constitution to transfer Roy's powers over to Oomen, who acted as functional head of state while the coup was underway. It was an "appeal to their constitutional rights" and a duty necessary to keep the micronation afloat. Roy would have had the right to appeal the decision to a Sealandic court, but he abdicated that right by working so brazenly in his own self-interest.

Meanwhile, Roy and Joan arrived in Austria and were met by a handful of suspicious-looking men who said the meeting would take place later that day. When the men never showed for the meeting, Roy and Joan started to get worried and tried to get in touch with someone back in England. "We phoned different people who worked in the area—fishermen and the Coast Guard. One of them said, 'I saw a big helicopter hovering over Sealand.' It didn't feel right," Joan said.

They rushed back to England and linked back up with their son, who was recuperating at his grandma Lilyan's house. When he told them what had happened, the reception wasn't particularly warm.

"How can you throw away our life's work?" his mother asked him in tears.

"What have you done since you've gotten back to resolve the situation?" Roy thundered.

As Michael recalled in his memoirs, he felt like shit.

But no amount of grousing would change what had already transpired. Once tempers had calmed, the family realized the only possible solution was to retake the fort, just like they had when Radio Caroline's men turfed them off Knock John back in '66. They needed to smite the opposition to such a degree that they would never try anything so foolhardy again. Fortunately, they knew a few guys, and one of them had a helicopter.

## AN "ACT OF PIRACY THAT VIOLATED ALL EXISTING LAWS"

The temporarily deposed Sealanders gathered at a regional airfield a few days later, joined by some friends who felt "sheer disgust at what had happened" to the Bateses. Michael's best friend Gordon "Willy" Wilkinson was so eager to avenge the dishonor that he left his hospital bed and the tests he was undergoing to join the fight.

It was 3:00 a.m., and the assemblage was fearsome. They had a few pistols that Joan had retrieved from her mother-in-law's cottage, while Michael had tucked inside his coat a sawed-off shotgun that dangled from his neck by a piece of cord. They'd gotten word that Belgian mercenaries with machine guns were on their way to the fort as reinforcements, and time was of the essence.

"If we're going to do something, we have to do it now," Michael said.

The plan was simple: A man named John Crewdson, who had flown helicopters as a stunt pilot in the 1969 James Bond film *On Her Majesty's Secret Service*, was going to transport the group out to Sealand. There they would slide down ropes they'd dangle from either side of the chopper and do whatever they needed to do to depose the Germans. It was the pilot's first time conducting an actual armed raid, and there was real ammo. Crewdson was elated.*

And if that didn't work, there was another option.

"No crook will rule Sealand. I will blow it up first!" Roy declared.

The night before the raid, the group practiced repelling out of the helicopter by descending from a metal bracket attached to the front of the Bates family's factory. The helicopter doors were taken from the hinges and piled in the hangar, while ropes were tied to the doorframe and coiled on the chopper's floor. When it was go time, Michael, Roy,

---

* Tragically, Crewdson would die along with three other people in a helicopter accident on June 26, 1983, at age fifty-seven. His son is now a commercial airline pilot.

Barry Harcus, and Willy piled into the chopper alongside the pilot, leaving one man behind who literally cried tears of frustration that there wasn't enough room for him to come along.

The helicopter took off and rushed out to sea, the sun rising and the waves crashing below in spectacular cinematic fashion. One of the Germans had fallen asleep on the deck on his watch and awoke to see a helicopter triumphantly ascend from below the level of the deck. The chopper whooshed into the air and hovered a hundred feet above him, with fierce and determined (and armed) men standing on the skids. The ropes uncoiled down toward the deck, and the men, with rags wrapped around their hands to prevent rope burn, dropped smoothly out of the sky like avenging angels.

Michael literally hit the deck running as Pütz and another man ran out of the doorway with a pistol to see what was going on. A look of sheer surprise came over his face when he saw Roy, who he'd only ever seen wearing a suit, looking much tougher than before right in front of him. Michael jumped from the helipad down to the surface of the fort, tucking and rolling as he landed, in the process firing a shot from the sawed-off shotgun around his neck. Pütz, Eck, and Boss immediately surrendered at the thunderous report. A few minutes and a black eye or two later, the invaders were sitting on their hands on the deck, scared and sheepish at their predicament.

"You don't serve seven years in the army without learning something," Roy said.

The prisoners were shuffled onto Sealand's deck to be photographed by the boats full of reporters, who had begun arriving within ten minutes of the countercoup. Armed Sealanders, looking like henchmen from a 1970s movie, stood guard over the prisoners, who looked away from the cameras in disgrace. A trickle of blood dripped down Pütz's lips.

"They must have fallen over," Michael said with a wink.

Reporters shouted questions up at the fort.

"Do you speak English?" one asked. "We thought there'd been a coup d'état."

"Yes, and at dawn this morning we coup-de-état'd the coup d'état," Michael yelled back.

"Marvelous! Absolutely bloody marvelous!"

"[W]e have to police ourselves, look after ourselves, defend ourselves," Michael said. "We have come under attack before, and therefore we're not going to sit there like pussycats, are we?"

The Sealanders told reporters that the invaders had done $25,000 worth of damage, smashing furniture, ripping out wiring, and putting the generators out of commission. "You wouldn't believe it when you saw it. We had to have them cleaning up the mess they made—they were living like animals," Michael said. "I think they were hysterical."

The crisis on the micronation quickly caught the attention of the prisoners' respective embassies. On August 29, a Minister at the Dutch Embassy named Schaapveld wrote to the British government and said he'd received a telex from Adrian Oomen that Pütz and the other men had been "manhandled" and were being kept under armed guard. A Dutchman, Hans Lavoo, who had sailed over to the fort to negotiate the prisoners' release, had been taken prisoner himself before he could encourage Pütz to throw himself overboard. Perhaps the British government could ram a boat into the fort and knock it over, Schaapveld suggested. For their part, the Federal German Republic encouraged the British government to classify the Bateses' effrontery as piracy—a serious criminal offense that could be dealt with on the high seas by any country.

Conveniently, the British government absolved itself of any responsibility in the matter. "If Pütz is falsely imprisoned, he is not falsely imprisoned on British territory," said one official.

There the matter stood, at least until Pütz was sentenced in Sealandic court.

## THE SENTENCING

On August 30, 1978, just short of three weeks after the countercoup, the Sealanders decided their prisoners needed to be tried for their crimes. Eck and Boss were granted parole, as was Hans Lavoo, thanks to a treaty brokered through a Dutch journalist. But a special tribunal was convened to try Gernot Pütz, who had earlier been granted Sealandic citizenship and was thus considered a traitor on top of an invader.

Pütz was retrieved from his cell in the sixth subfloor of the tower and perp-walked to the fort's living room.

Present at his trial were a few Sealanders, the son of Roy's attorney Lionel Conway, and members of the press. The assemblage towered over Pütz, who sat shackled on a couch. Michael prosecuted, phoning in the performance because it was a fairly open and shut case.

Roy Bates's hair was thoroughly white, giving him the sagacity of an experienced judge.

"Gernot Pütz," he intoned. "You are charged that on August 13, 1978, you committed an act of treason in that you were a member of an armed party who attempted by force to overcome or hold by force against your Sovereign Roy of Sealand and the island of Sealand."

Pütz hung his head.

"This Court accepts your plea of guilty to the charge of Treason. You are summarily fined the sum of DM$75,000 [around $18,000 at the time], and you will remain at Sealand until sometime in October if this sum is paid forthwith, or until this fine is paid," he said.

No gavel was present, but Roy's words rang heavily enough.

Pütz was ordered to hand over the documentation attesting to his Sealandic citizenship, and the vaunted, rare nationality was stripped away. Pütz was to be put to work around the fort, cleaning toilets and making coffee. All things considered, he was lucky he got off so easy.

"In Britain, people can still be shot for treason," Joan said, "My husband seems and is often a very friendly man, but under his clothes he can often be a barbarian."

Roy felt capital punishment wasn't necessary. "I've killed a lot of Germans in my time," he said, recalling his service in World War II. "Another one wouldn't have made much difference, I suppose, but I didn't want to kill anything else, really."

Still, being stranded on the fort could be punishment enough for the uninitiated. A reporter from London's *Evening News* named Barry Gardner was permitted to conduct an interview with Pütz and filed a report from Sealand a little over a week after the sentence was handed down. Gardner gave the contrite Pütz space to talk about the reality of the situation and plead for some kind of international relief. The beleaguered declamation is worth printing in its entirety:

"I regret ever getting involved with this thing," Pütz told him.

*At the time I did not realize these men wanted to take over Sealand. They told me they had a contract for the island and as I hold a Sealand passport they needed me to go out there. About a dozen of us arrived in a helicopter and boat. Believe me I did not know they had weapons on board. Later, I realized what was going on and wanted nothing more to do with it. If these men do come back I will not help them again.*

*I am being treated very well. I can eat and drink with others out here, but I miss home. I obviously miss my wife, Hannelore, and I must get home soon or my business will suffer. While I am here I spend the day cooking and washing-up for the others. Otherwise I read or sunbathe perhaps. At night I just lock myself in my tiny bunkroom because I am frightened. What of?...well maybe what is here. I am getting a little depressed being here. It's not an easy situation. Roy and the others have made their point.*

*I have been fined DM$75,000, but that's a ridiculous amount—it's the highest fine you can get in Germany. I don't know how I will raise that kind of money. I have written to my wife in Dusseldorf and told her what has happened. I think she will try to contact the men who came out here to ask them to pay the fine.*

"If they don't, I don't know what will happen," Pütz said, forlorn. "Have you heard if the German embassy has managed to do anything for me? I must get away from here as soon as possible."

## WIRETAPPING AND PIRATE RADIO IN 1978

At the same time, back in Southend-on-Sea, officers from the Post Office began looking into an illegal radio station the Bates family was said to be running from their home (thanks to a tip from Dutch lawyer Adrian Oomen). The Bateses weren't broadcasting pop music but simply communicating between the principality and the English homestead, but according to prosecutors they were using international distress frequencies to do so. This was still illegal under the Wireless

Telegraphy Act, and so the Post Office's technical officers set up a sting operation to listen in to the communications.

Handwritten logs of intercepted communications document the banal side of life on Sealand. The Bateses discussed the weather and had the "usual chat[s] about getting things from land," such as batteries, light bulbs, Marmite, and curry powder. "Is your mother well?" Roy was quoted as saying. "I couldn't find that bloody magazine but everything else is alright." In an impressive piece of detective work, an officer named Raymond Cassell noted he found a sack of potatoes in the trunk of the family car that was intended for Sealand because he'd heard about it over the radio.

Having documented enough illegal radio usage, the Post Office obtained a search warrant for the apartment on Avenue Road, while local police and Customs drew up their own warrants based on the tip that Roy and Joan were in possession of illegal firearms. On October 3, four Post Office officers showed up at the Bates apartment. Officers began forcing open the door but stumbled into the foyer when a pajama-clad Roy opened the door.

Cassell and an officer named Michael Hawkins guided Roy into the kitchen. Cassell took notes of the encounter.

"What is your full name?" Hawkins asked.

"You know who I am," Roy said.

"I do not know your full name."

"You'd better guess it then."

"Unfortunately Bates was both aggressive and truculent in his manner, and his stock answer to questions was to say, 'Do the job you came to and bugger off,'" Cassell wrote.

Roy was called upstairs to a bedroom where the officers had found a bookshelf that held homemade transmitting equipment. Asked about this assemblage, Roy stayed mum.

"I told you I have no comment to make, I am telling you to get out, I am getting annoyed and if you stand there much longer I will knock you down," he said.

The equipment was confiscated, and the officers moved on to the offices of Airfern, Ltd., the Bates family's white weed-processing facility on Wickford Road. A simultaneous raid had uncovered a DIY receiver-transmitter in a cabinet. The equipment and the cabinet were both confiscated. Roy was given a receipt itemizing the things they'd taken, with the most expensive piece valued at £4. "They were looking for arms but I haven't got any," Roy told a reporter minutes after the raid. "They made a thorough search, but I don't think they were going to find guns in pairs of knickers."

Not long after, transmissions from Airfern apparently began again and officers were dispatched to the warehouse. A nearby officer was monitoring transmissions on Wickford Road and noted they stopped as soon as Hawkins knocked on Airfern's door. Once inside, Hawkins saw more transmitting equipment and a car battery to power it. The back-and-forth began again.

Bates told the officers he could tell they'd been drinking.

"You can smell it, can't you?" he asked Joan.

"Yes, I can, as soon as they came into the room," she said.

Another officer smelled Hawkins's breath, noted that he was sober, and they once again confiscated the equipment.

Roy's friend and solicitor Lionel Conway wrote to the British Home Office and explained Sealand's need to communicate with the outside world. The people on the fort "had been instrumental in effecting something like thirteen rescues" out at sea, and because there was no doctor on Sealand, radio equipment was necessary for emergencies. The Sealanders were under constant threat of "villains" who wanted to take over and use the fort for drug smuggling and gunrunning, Conway said, and he reminded officials that the Seal-anders had once helped police locate a plane that landed nearby for such purposes.

The appeal fell on deaf ears, and Roy was once again due to appear before the Southend Magistrates on three charges of broadcasting without a license.

## THE CRISIS CONTINUES

Meanwhile, the Federal Republic of Germany did not appreciate Britain's nonresponse to the prisoner crisis on Sealand. It wasn't only the embassy that wrote in "despairing" tones—Gernot Pütz's wife Hannelore had been petitioning the FRG government to check on the well-being of her husband.* "[They] may feel that they have lost face as a result of this affair, whose funny side they may not appreciate," wrote one official.

With neither the FRG nor Hannelore Pütz getting a satisfactory response from the Sealanders, the German government did what any government would do: send a diplomatic official to investigate to negotiate the prisoner's release. Dr. Christoph Neimoller, a "sallow complexioned and cadaverous-looking diplomat," as Michael Bates recalls, and head of local and consular affairs at the German embassy in London, was to go to the Principality of Sealand on what was undoubtedly one of the strangest assignments of his career. "I hope for an early solution to the problem," he told a reporter.**

Joan Bates met Neimoller at the Southend airport. She smiled as she explained that anyone visiting the platform had to be searched for weapons. Neimoller bristled at the demand. He took out his diplomatic passport and yelled he wouldn't be subject to such a dishonor.

"OK, then you can't visit and I will go," said Joan.

Neimoller glared at her but conceded to the search. Joan called over a nearby police officer.

"Young man, would you be good enough to search him for me?"

The officer took to the task with zeal and frisked Neimoller extensively.

Despite the indignity of the search, Neimoller was in awe at seeing Sealand and the North Sea from far up in the chopper. He was searched again once on the principality, and his passport was taken and stamped with a Sealandic emigration stamp. "Lucky guy, an exclusive club," Michael said.

Roy ordered Pütz to make coffee before Pütz and Neimoller were allowed to meet in private for half an hour. Not long after, the diplomat returned "empty-handed and rather baffled" to the mainland, having

---

* Michael maintains Hannelore "certainly didn't seem too interested in sorting out his release and had only very grudgingly sent a box of letters he had requested several times to our lawyers."

** A handwritten addendum to a note from the Western European Department expressed concern that Neimoller would be mistaken for an agent of Achenbach's and imprisoned as well.

failed to secure Pütz's release. But keeping Pütz there was more trouble than it was worth, and the Sealanders suddenly decided to free him a few days later. Pütz, who was given a little cash and one of Michael's jackets, was to be dropped off in Harwich, UK. "He drove us bloody mad," Michael said.

A small crowd of TV and newspaper reporters rushed down to the dock to meet the boat as it pulled up to the public harbor on September 28. Roy Bates clapped Pütz on the back and told the reporters that the crisis had been one big misunderstanding.

"Originally I thought [Pütz] was involved in this rather violent takeover, but I found out over a period of time—we had a lot of people checking the matter—that he was fed false information and was deliberately used," Roy said. "It has taken all this time for us to complete our investigation. Now he is being reinstated as a Sealander, and he is going back to Germany as a Sealand representative."

"We are all friends now," he added.

Harwich police and a Customs officer standing nearby rolled their eyes.

To this day, it is hard to know how to take the coup and the imprisonment that followed. Pütz "seemed happy and even posed for pictures," according to an account in the *Colchester Evening Gazette*, and many wondered if the whole thing was a well-done publicity stunt. Neimoller even noted in his report that Pütz seemed to be enjoying himself more than one would expect from a prisoner.

However, the situation did require the intercession of a representative of the international community, which was obviously a fairly serious response, and Michael maintains that he suffered nerve damage to his hands and to this day can't sit with his back to a crowd. It's possible that a tense civil war just happened to come to a fairly peaceful conclusion instead of ending with casualties. Perhaps the easiest solution for all involved was just to play nice, so nobody would have to face the authorities back in Europe.

The Germans retreated back home after the failed coup, licking their wounds and stewing in their dismay. The countercoup by Roy Bates was "an act of piracy which violated all existing laws," they said, but fate was on the prince's side. The Germans' plans for the fort, whatever they were, were not meant to be. Not unlike the legend of Atlantis, a thriving seaborne utopia was imploded by the inhabitants' wild greed.

Achenbach and Co. would go on to establish a Sealandic government-in-exile, a strange entity with even more eyebrow-raising ambitions than before. The exile government maintains it is the legitimate ruling body of Sealand to the present day, and its activities have added colorful—if not completely headache-inducing—elements to the true Sealand's history. (The many capers of the exile government will be discussed in chapters 12 and 17.)

Following the coup, Roy Bates continued to tout his plans to expand the principality, and he seemed to do so in the press with newfound vigor. The country was his and he was in charge. Sealand's sovereignty "is an internationally-established fact—all the lawyers will tell you that!" he said.

But the most important outcome of the whole affair was the remarkable gift Sealand had been given in the effort to get Pütz released: *an embassy official to Sealand to negotiate the release of one of its citizens.* The Federal Republic of Germany had interacted with Sealand as it would a peer nation, carrying out a diplomatic protocol practiced the world over. Ten years earlier a British judge had ruled that British laws could not be enforced on Sealand, and now that same territory was engaging in international diplomacy with a major country recognized by every nation on the planet. It was an interaction that profoundly reinforced the principality's ideological underpinnings and speaks for its sovereignty in the present day.*

## CODA TO THE COUP

There was one more thing the Sealanders had to do to bring the coup saga to a close. On January 22, 1979, Joan and Michael were to fly to The Hague to file a complaint with the Netherlands Bar Association against Adrian Oomen, who had reportedly been calling the Bates

---

* Some scholars argue that even if a diplomat visited Sealand, such an official wouldn't have the authority to change Sealand's status or express the official position of his government, not to mention that diplomatic officials intervene in affairs all the time without affecting the territorial status of the place they are visiting.

home and threatening them following the Germans' defeat. Joan had documents detailing the threats and was going to present them to the higher authorities. "The law society will consider whether this lawyer was guilty of conspiracy against my husband, for whom he was working at the time, and for an act of piracy on the high seas," she said.

The family was also considering filing a suit against KLM, the Dutch television company who had supplied the helicopter used in the takeover of the fort. A camera crew had flown along with the coupsters out to Sealand, and it is unclear if they knew what was going to happen. Either way, Achenbach sent the DM$17,000 bill for the helicopter's rental to the station's headquarters.

In response, Oomen told the Bateses that he would have them arrested as soon as they set foot in Holland. Michael and Joan weren't sure how seriously to take this but said they would be going straight to the public prosecutor to file the complaints nonetheless. Storms canceled their flight, so they ended up taking a ferry. Dutch customs officials came aboard the ferry to escort the Sealanders, who flashed their diplomatic passports. "Any arrest plan was outfoxed," Joan said.

At The Hague, Michael stood in awe at the tradition of diplomacy and justice around him. "[It was a] strange place to be, where despots and tyrants had stood trial for mass murder, genocide, and war crimes," he said. He and Joan pleaded their case for almost three hours and were represented in the proceedings by none other than Gernot Pütz. Proceedings were adjourned to take more witness statements the second day. "Things are looking pretty black for the lawyer," Joan said.

The next day, Oomen admitted he had taken part in the coup and that he had introduced himself as the spokesperson for the nefarious Germans in the threatening telephone conversations. He also admitted he had threatened the Bateses with physical violence, though he explained this necessary to get two hostages off the platform and that he didn't necessarily intend to follow through with any act of force. The principality stayed on high alert after their appearance at The Hague, as an anonymous caller would periodically warn that a raid by mercenaries with automatic weapons was imminent, though no further attacks ever occurred.*

In the end Oomen was temporarily suspended from practicing law for a month. He appealed the decision the next day, and the ultimate decision of the Bar Association's disciplinary committee was not released to the public. "What is being said is wrong and I am in no way willing to give my own version to anyone," Oomen said.

Back in England, Roy Bates pleaded guilty to all five charges of unlicensed broadcasting brought against him in 1978 and was fined and made to forfeit his broadcasting equipment for good. "Many of the transmissions were personal in nature and orders were even made to supply Sealand and I do not understand that anyone can be so stupid as to use official PTT frequencies for such purposes," the judge said. "I hereby conclude that Mr. Bates is ordered to pay a fine of £200, he must pay the costs of the trial, £100, and that the confiscated equipment, valued at £2,000, will be forfeited."

Defiantly, Roy gave his address in court as "Sealand in the North Sea." He paid the charge as if it were nothing and strode out of the courtroom proudly.

The 1970s closed on a note of love, however—a show of romance second only in grandiosity to giving someone her own private island. Gordon "Willy" Wilkinson, manager of Airfern, Ltd., longtime Sealander, and one of the men who had helped recapture the fort, planned to marry his sweetheart Karen Huxtable, a mannequin's wigmaker, on the Principality of Sealand on May 5, 1979. Approximately fifty-five

---

* However, this didn't mean that another raid wasn't being planned. Achenbach met with a professional mercenary named Paul "Pistols" Wilking at least twice about forming a private army and re-retaking the fort. Wilking said he was offered "millions" by Achenbach's men and that he even flew a surveillance mission over the fort to see what he was up against. The Sealanders shot at him immediately, and when he arrived back at the airport, Achenbach told him to call it off. Apparently Oomen was getting stressed about all the negative publicity he was receiving in the Dutch press and refused any further attempts to take the fort.

Roy Bates said Wilking had in fact approached him about taking the fort back from the Germans but that he'd turned him down. "First of all, I have plenty of people myself and second, when I talked to him, it was as if I was a super professional tennis player playing against the smallest amateur in the world," Roy said. Wilking laughed at this characterization and said he never met Bates, but either way, his involvement with the matter ended there.

guests were to travel out to the fort, which was given a new coat of paint for the occasion.

"It will be a traditional wedding with the bride in white, and a wedding cake. The only difference is that it will be the first wedding in this country," Joan Bates said. "I think it will be the wedding of the year."

One snag was getting a priest to officiate, as Sealand was not in the jurisdiction of any diocese. Roy couldn't perform the wedding because he was not a captain and Sealand was not a ship. While these formalities wouldn't have mattered on Sealand itself, the couple needed the marriage to be recognized in the UK.

The Bishop of Colchester told a reporter he hadn't yet met the couple and wanted to make sure the wedding wasn't just a gimmick. Once he was assured of their devotion, he put out his feelers for a clergyman willing to perform the ceremony. Eventually, the Reverend James Chelton, Vicar of St. Nicholas in Harwich, was given permission to conduct it. According to Chelton, the wedding would be a relatively easy affair since it wasn't on UK soil and thus didn't entail some of the bureaucratic processes of English weddings. "This will certainly be the most unusual wedding I've ever conducted, but I'm looking forward to it," Chelton said.

On the hallowed day, a small sound system played the wedding march and other traditional tunes as the guests mingled and took in the view. Chelton had supplied the music, which soon was drowned out by the noise of an approaching helicopter, which soon alit on the upper deck. Sitting in the bubble dome of the chopper, Karen looked radiant in her wedding dress, veil in place and holding her bouquet. An additional bouquet adorned the helicopter's controls. Roy looked serious but happy as the helicopter touched down. John Crewdson, the pilot who flew the countercoup mission, got out and opened the door. Karen's dad walked happily up the stairs to the helipad, took her hand, and lowered her from her seat.

Chelton addressed the couple and the crowd with words of wisdom and the joys of matrimony, uniting them as one sixty feet above the sea. A ferry bound for Harwich pulled close to Sealand and the passengers cheered and waved at the happy couple. Being hailed by the ferry was one of the highlights of the wedding and the time on

Sealand, Roy said, a show of widespread support for the micronation on the jubilant occasion of bringing Willy and Karen together.

The couple went back to the mainland in one of the micronation's rigid inflatable boats, and the guests threw rice on the couple as the boat was lowered down to the sea on the winch. All of the invitees had come with one exception: Prime Minister Margaret Thatcher. "Remember that she leads a busy life and therefore she could not attend the ceremony," Roy said.

Buoyed by the energy of the newlyweds and emboldened by the diplomatic recognition, the Sealanders would plunge headlong into the next decade of their existence. Importantly, the 1980s would introduce the third generation of the Bates lineage: three children who would be raised as the heirs apparent to the glorious offshore kingdom.

# CHAPTER 11

# THE DYNASTY EXPANDS

*"I mean, honestly, who would let their fourteen-year-old boy make Molotov cocktails? Or hold a sawn-off shotgun and automatic pistols?"*

—Michael Bates

The 1980s were a time of significant ideological change in the UK and a lot of the Western world, with leaders such as US President Ronald Reagan and British Prime Minister Margaret Thatcher moving their respective nations significantly to the right. While the Sealand issue didn't register high on the list of UK concerns, there was still significant discussion in the British government about the principality following the diplomatic quasi-crisis sparked by the attempted coup in 1978. The issue was still quite vexing, with officials passing responsibility for the fort to other departments like a game of diplomatic hot potato. "There must be someone in your vast organization who admits responsibility for Sealand," wrote one British official pleadingly. As usual, there were numerous events that took place that made the issue even more complicated for the British government. But the Sealanders were just as readily learning about some of the difficulties that come with being a sovereign state.

On November 21, 1980, an official in the British Navy got a surprising midnight call from a Sheriff Moffat in Kansas. Moffat had in his custody a prisoner who was claiming to be a citizen of Sealand, and Moffat wasn't sure how to go about deporting the prisoner back to the North Sea. He had already called the British Foreign Office and the British Embassy in Washington, DC, who gave the sheriff the puzzling reply that they'd never heard of such a state. Shaking his head in annoyance, the naval officer told the sheriff that there was a platform in the Thames Estuary that had supposedly declared itself its own state but that so far the platform's sovereignty had not been accepted by his Crown superiors. The sheriff thus had to find another way to deal with his wily prisoner while British officials got in touch with Sealand's Prince Roy Bates to see what he knew about the situation in Kansas.

"I think the sheriff has become the victim of some kind of joke or that the prisoner concerned has been watching television too much. Recently there was an extensive report about my empire on American television," Roy said. "A total of perhaps two hundred passports have been issued by me and I have always been very well informed about the people who applied for a passport. I can't imagine a fellow countryman going wrong and now being imprisoned in America."

But the more he thought about it, the more annoyed he got.

"If the man will indeed be deported and delivered to the platform and he turns out to be a criminal, there is only one possibility: throw him directly into the sea."

Needless to say, the criminal was not repatriated by the Bates family, regardless of the citizenship he claimed. Forged Sealand passports would in fact become a major international issue later on (see chapter 12), and Roy vowed once again that he would never do anything to threaten the law and order of any established country. In fact, not long after the Kansas prisoner incident, Roy had the chance to demonstrate the loyalty he still felt to his original homeland.

On April 2, 1982, Argentinian troops began occupying the Falkland Islands, an archipelago off the Argentinian coast that had been colonized by the British since the early 1800s. The sovereignty of the hundreds of islands was a long-standing bone of contention, with both countries claiming control over them, and a small-scale but furious war broke out, with serious battles on land and sea. The British government set up an air base on Ascension Island in the middle of the Atlantic Ocean as a refueling location for its fighters on the way to South America, and the Argentinians began looking for a similarly strategic location closer to England. "It was during the Falklands conflict and I was approached by some Argentinians with the idea of selling them Sealand," Roy Bates said. "They wanted their own 'Malvinas'* right on Britain's doorstep."

---

* Argentina refers to the Falkland Islands as "Islas Malvinas."

The proposal was a little surprising but not totally unexpected, as Roy had been approached in the late 1970s by representatives of the Spanish government who hoped to get Gibraltar back for Spain. Roy rejected the Malvinas overture in the strongest possible terms and reiterated his support for the UK in the miniature war. "Of course I sent them away. I'd never do anything that would pose a threat to the UK," he said.

Ultimately around a thousand people died in the Falklands conflict, which concluded with an Argentine surrender ten weeks after it started. There has been no clear resolution to the question of ownership, even in the present day. The Falkland Islanders voted by a margin of 99.8 percent to remain British in a 2013 poll, but Argentina doesn't consider the poll valid.* "Looking out over the bleak landscape, after weeks of gray skies and horizontal snow…'you'd have to be English to want this,'" writes Rodolfo Fogwill in *Malvinas Requiem*, the Falkland War's version of *Catch-22*.

## SEALAND ROYALTY V. 3.0

The year 1985 was a happy occasion for Michael, as he married Southend florist Lorraine "Lozzie" Wheeler and was able to take some much-needed time off from the fort to try his hand at family life. The pair met when twenty-one-year-old Lorraine was interviewing with Michael to do some arrangements for the family's white weed business. The two were smitten with one another from the start, and when she got home Lorraine told her sister, "I'm going to marry that man." Sure enough, within five days the pair was engaged. "You can say it was a whirlwind romance," she laughed.

Lorraine recalled seeing a feature on television about the 1979 wedding on Sealand, but she didn't realize at first that she was marrying into a royal family. Lorraine came from a "fairly normal background" and so the culture shock was significant. "It was all quite overwhelming to begin with," she said, "but very, very exciting." She

---

* In 2016, a United Nations commission unanimously ruled that the Falkland Islands are in Argentinian territorial waters. The commission extended Argentine waters to 350 miles, adding 1.7 square kilometers of area to the country's waters. The UK "downplayed" this judgment and the dispute continues to simmer.

was immediately taken with Roy and Joan, who welcomed her into their family and treated her like a princess. "I was in awe of my mother-in-law—she was the most beautiful woman I'd ever seen," she said. "Roy was an extreme gentleman—the typical English gent. He was a remarkable man, and I absolutely adored him." Having met the prince and princess, it was soon time for Lorraine to see the Bates empire for herself.

Her Sealand excursion did not proceed as seamlessly as hoped. First, the winch broke as she was being raised up to the platform, sending her plummeting down like a ride at an amusement park she didn't ask for. Fortunately the sudden drop wasn't far, and she didn't slip out of the cage raising her up, but it wasn't a great start to the tour. Then, after she had reached the solid ground of the platform deck, one of the diesel generators broke and started spewing flames and oily black smoke. She stood in shock, unsure of where to run if the thing was about to blow and deaf to her husband's desperate pleas to climb the ladder back out of the room and wait in the fresh air of the deck. Her interest in tending to the fort's operations or taking a more active role as micronational royalty quickly ended when she got a lungful of toxic fumes. Plus, it was freezing cold, with only a small paraffin heater to huddle around, and to make matters worse, Lorraine was six months pregnant at the time with a little boy they would call James.*

Fortunately the incident was scarier than it was harmful, and James was born healthy and kicking in July 1986. "We were both very proud of him and would show him off at every opportunity," Michael said. "You would think we had invented having babies."

As James grew, Michael reflected on his own upbringing and couldn't believe the responsibility his dad gave him at a fairly young age. Imbued with a sense of protectiveness and duty that comes with being a father and husband, he saw with fresh eyes just how intense a childhood he and his sister actually had. He survived, no worse for the wear—and certainly tougher for it—but he intended to be a little more circumspect when it came to the upbringing of his own kids. "I mean, honestly, who would let their fourteen-year-old boy make Molotov

---

* Most of Lorraine's subsequent trips to Sealand were taken via helicopter, given the scare of her first journey.

cocktails? Or hold a sawn-off shotgun and automatic pistols?" he said. "I do remember asking my dad, 'If someone gets on when I'm aboard, do you want me to shoot them?'" Michael was told it was up to him to make that decision when the time came.

But this didn't mean the boys wouldn't grow up to be hardy Sealanders. James was joined by Liam in November 1988, and the brothers were acquainted with the fort at an early age. The boys would stay out there for a week at a time, learning how to fish and shoot. Michael had them do laps around the micronation to wear themselves out, even though the guard rails weren't especially high. "Well, you were only this tall," Michael said, rationalizing like Roy.

James said one of the earliest memories of the fort was when he was winched up to the platform alongside his brother Liam in an old oil drum. His dad would yell, "'Don't lean over the sides!' as it's being lifted up by these four little strings," he said. "Me and Liam at the same time—all your eggs in one basket."

The family would be rounded out by a third Bates child—a girl named Charlotte—in 1991. Charlotte wasn't especially interested in the fort out at sea, preferring instead land-based entities such as horses and dogs, but as any young sibling does, she looked at the trips her brothers and dad took with envy. However, she used to go out there with such frequency that her mother recalls her lamenting about having to take yet another helicopter ride.

Sometimes the Bates kids would brag to schoolyard chums that their family owned their own country, but it was a boast indistinguishable from the tall tales told by their peers. "I'd take newspaper clippings into school and nobody would ever believe me," Charlotte said. "People would always think us nuts, to be honest, there's no other way to put it." James one-upped the evidence of Sealand's veracity and took some friends out there for a very unique kind of slumber party when he was eleven years old. "It was a real adventure for my children growing up," Lorraine recalled happily. "My boys are really proud of their grandfather's achievements and their father's. I'm very proud of all them."

Michael and Lorraine would divorce about ten years later but have remained great friends to the present day. They make a point to spend the holidays together with their children and still meet regularly for family dinners.

## THE "INCORRIGIBLE WEINER"

Pirate radio was experiencing a bit of a resurgence in England in the 1970s and 1980s, with a new squadron of broadcasting ships playing music from fifteen miles out to sea and clandestine stations located in apartment buildings. The pirate stations were once again filling an important gap on the airwaves, playing music that wasn't getting a lot of attention on mainstream radio—especially music of interest to the black community. Like the 1960s, the stations played a game of cat and mouse with the authorities bent on shutting them down.

The Radio Investigation Service of the Department of Trade and Industry* went after many illegal broadcasters throughout the 1980s, and the Marine Broadcasting (Offences) Act of 1967 was still the go-to law for squashing illegal radio operations. Fines were meted out and stations were raided, and a sweeping 1985 operation against pirate broadcasters was popularly known as "Eurosiege."

Just like in the 1960s, competition between pirate stations could be fierce.

"We used to have a team of security up on the roof waiting for other pirates. If it was the DTI, you'd tell them to take the transmitter and they'd look the other way, but if it was other pirates there would be a fight," said Gordon Mac, who founded the underground station KISS. "It became a really heavy scene towards the end of it, which is why I was so pleased when we could go for the legal license because you can only do that for so long."

Sealand had a part in the resurgence of pirate radio as well, though in a less-antagonistic capacity than before. A group of HAM radio operators transmitted from the platform on the fifteenth anniversary of the micronation's existence in 1982, and widely publicized plans to open three radio stations on Sealand were announced in 1986. Free of

---

* The Department of Trade and Industry no longer exists. It transitioned into the Department for Innovation, Universities, and Skills and then the Department for Business, Innovation, and Skills before finally becoming the Department for Business, Energy, and Industrial Strategy, which it remains today.

UK needletime restrictions, the new transmitters were said to have the capacity to reach up to 200 million listeners. "There will, of course, be those who will not hesitate at laughing the whole thing off as a joke, but it is not. No many [*sic*] spends twenty years, and millions of pounds working for something that is merely a joke," as one newsletter stated. But plans for a new radio-based operation fizzled out before they went anywhere, at least until the Sealanders got involved with an equally rapacious radio pirate from the United States named Allan Weiner.

On July 28, 1987, Weiner, a reedy thirty-five-year-old, sat handcuffed on the deck of a rickety ex-fishing trawler called the *Sarah* about four miles off the coast of Long Island, New York. Next to him was fellow DJ Ivan Rothstein and a journalist from the *Village Voice* named RJ Smith, all in shackles and roasting in the summer sun. The FCC officers had sped out in one of their cutters with men stationed at the machine guns on deck and boarded the ship at 5:35 a.m. A Coast Guard captain was keeping watch over the prisoners as FCC officials went to work below decks. This was all after Weiner's radio station, Radio Newyork International, had broadcast for a week across several frequencies and could be heard up and down the US.

Weiner wept "tears of rage" as he listened to what was going on underneath him. The agents were cutting apart Weiner's equipment like mafia goons punishing those who didn't pay protection money. The resulting mess "look[ed] like an explosion in a radio tube factory," Smith wrote. The *Sarah* would be impounded, along with the equipment that wasn't dismantled, and the DJs faced the possibility of quarter-million-dollar fines and five years in jail. But Weiner, who had already been arrested a few times for illegal broadcasting, vowed he wouldn't be defeated.

Weiner had a longstanding fascination with radio and a passion for democratic broadcasting that put him in intellectual kinship with radio pirates around the world. A teenager in the 1960s, "I was one of the technical nerds, running around with pocket protectors and all that," he said. "As a kid in high school, I said, 'What can I do to help?' I'm into electronics, I'm into radio, why don't I get into this radio thing?"

Weiner was arrested at age nineteen for broadcasting from his basement and was dinged for unauthorized use of frequencies numerous times in the early 1980s. He eventually linked up with Radio Caroline, the first pirate station in the UK, and planned to start a similar venture in the United States. But he needed a ship to do so.

In July 1984, a Japanese trawler registered in Panama called *Lichfield I* broke down off the coast of New York, supposedly with substantial amounts of marijuana on board, and was towed into Boston to be auctioned off by the United States Customs Service. A man paid $100 for the vessel and won, which had somehow been renamed "S/S *Litchfield*" (note the addition of a *T*) while in custody. The sale itself was suspect—it was done on a holiday with little attention to protocol—and the ship was eventually sold to Weiner. He in turn christened the ship *Sarah*, after an ex-wife of his.

In the summer of 1986, the *Sarah* was outfitted with radio broadcasting equipment and a five-ton anchor to keep the engineless ship stationary 3.5 miles off the coast of Long Island. The station was called RNI, or "Radio Newyork International," a convenient abbreviation that allowed Weiner and his DJs to reuse old jingles from an old Dutch pirate station called "Radio Northsea International." The following summer, the *Sarah* was towed to the predetermined location and the enormous anchor dropped. Transmissions began on July 23 on 1620 kHz AM, with the station billing itself a music-lover's radio station that played deep album tracks and promoted a philosophy of "peace, love, and understanding."

RNI's operations, like most radio pirate projects, were seat-of-the-pants. The leaky ship, previously a fishing vessel, was kitted out with insulation to help keep the fish frozen, but in the absence of the freezers, the insulation worked to keep the heat in. The crew at times subsisted on crackers, cornflakes, and beer, but like their forebears in the UK, the trade-off was worth the chance to bask under a beautiful night sky in which shooting stars were legion.

The ship's broadcasts were heard as far as Florida, and the FCC was alerted to the operation when it picked up one of the broadcasts in Michigan. A Coast Guard ship told them to stop broadcasting, but the spirit of pirate radio was strong. "The FCC is trying to say they have jurisdiction beyond the borders of this nation," Weiner said. "We aren't pirates because we are not breaking the law." Federal authorities disagreed, and that's when the Coast Guard vessel zoomed out to the *Sarah* and clambered aboard. The Coast Guard officers complimented the DJs on the music they were playing the night before as they hand-cuffed the staff and dismantled the equipment.

The charges against Weiner and RNI were ultimately dropped, with Weiner promising not to broadcast again. Undaunted, he looked for a workaround to the prohibition. Weiner knew about the Princi-pality of Sealand from Radio Caroline and was aware that the Sealanders were always on the lookout for new commercial possibili-ties, so he got in touch.

"I always respected the Bates family and what they were trying to do," Weiner said. "I believe a group of individuals can get together and become sovereign, become independent. I believe in their mission, and that's why I contacted them."

Weiner proposed a partnership with the micronation and found that Roy was very pleasant and easy to deal with. The plan that resulted was ambitious in scope. Weiner and Michael Bates developed a series of corporations to buy, sell, and register the *Sarah* in Sealand through a series of shell companies in the UK run by Michael. The new regis-tration in Sealand would allow Weiner to circumvent not only his own prohibitions against broadcasting, but US and UK broadcasting laws in their entirety. After all, Sealand makes its own laws, and the ability to register ships would underscore Sealand's status as a sovereign nation. The *Sarah* soon headed back to sea to put these new credentials to the test.

## THE TERRITORIAL SEA ACT OF 1987

Roy Bates had all the while been advocating for Sealand's sover-eignty, pointing out to the Crown government the series of smaller-scale affirmations that added up to a significant argument for its independence. He noted that recognition was granted (albeit temporarily) by Abu Dhabi and a diplomatic relationship was successfully established between Sealand and the Princi-pality of Hutt River, a micronation in Australia founded by Leonard George Casley in 1970 in response to the government imposing wheat quotas on his farm.* Roy also submitted once again the legal opinions from Dr. Dr. Dr. Leisner and Bela Vitanyi to the Crown, though they were dismissed as being too old and by authors not eminent enough in their field.

"Their arguments make the so-called 'Principality' even more Alice-in-Wonderland-like!" wrote one official, but the Crown was still unsure about the most efficacious way to shut down Roy's claims. It was a surprisingly difficult position to be in, as the language of the Continental Shelf Act of 1954 and the Oil and newly-passed Gas Enterprise Act of 1982 was not specific enough to apply to an abandoned military platform with no resources-exploiting capabilities.

To this end, the Crown finally began the long-awaited process of expanding Britain's territorial waters. The Territorial Sea Act was drafted in May 1987 and officially demarcated Britain's waters to reach twelve nautical miles from the shore. The move wasn't done specifically to go after Sealand but rather to bring the UK up to date with what other countries were doing. The expansion would not only encompass Sealand but the waters far beyond it, and was planned to go into effect on October 1, 1987. "Were nothing to be done, the argument about acquiescence and squatter's rights may become progressively more difficult to counter," said one official about the act's effect on Sealand.

However, Bates still had some latitude to parry this maneuver. There was no retroactivity clause in the Territorial Sea Act, meaning that it couldn't preempt Sealand's declaration of independence. In any case, Roy bought some time the day before the UK's expansion went into effect, declaring Sealand's waters to be

---

* The Australian Governor General once sent Casley a letter addressed to the "Administrator of the Hutt River Province," which Casley took as de facto confirmation of his independence. Recently, Prince Leonard received an interesting letter from the Queen of England that gave more weight to Hutt River's claims of independence. The letter was a response to Prince Leonard's letter to the Queen, in which he bid her a happy ninetieth birthday. The Queen conveyed her good wishes to Prince Leonard, who was also ninety, and wished the country well on the forty-sixth anniversary of its secession from Australia. A birthday celebration was planned on the principality, with "pies, pasties, sausage rolls, hot and cold drinks" available in the principality tearoom. Prince Leonard passed away at age ninety-three in February 2019.

eighteen miles from the fort in all directions in accordance with international custom. Radiating outward from Sealand, the territorial waters encompassed a sizeable amount of the UK, including Harwich and Felixstowe.

If Roy could get any sort of respectable acknowledgment of Sealand's independent status, it would go a long way in counteracting the expansion mandated by the Territorial Sea Act. The more official clout he could get, the better off he and the other Sealanders would be, which is why the idea of registering a ship on Sealand took such hold at this time.

By August 1988, the *Sarah* was repaired, registered to the Principality of Sealand, and towed back to the waters off Long Island to resume broadcasting in October. Weiner stayed off the ship during this time, but the Coast Guard promptly shut it down regardless. All told, RNI had broadcast for a total of ten days, from July 23–28, 1987, and October 15–18, 1988.*

Weiner appeared in US District Court in October, represented by a lawyer from the American Civil Liberties Union named Gutman. A judge reminded Weiner of his agreement not to broadcast again. "I guess I didn't read that letter too carefully," Weiner said.

Weiner's secret weapon was the Sealandic registration and the freedom inherent in the principality's laws. Initially, the US government didn't know what to make of it. The ship's registration was already thorny before Sealand—it had been named and renamed with a fake paper trail—and the US government requested a representative from the UK provide an opinion about the ability of Sealand to register ships. James Murphy, a Department of Trade and Industry inspector, did some research and submitted a statement delineating reasons why Sealand isn't a country and can't register ships. The government essentially laughed off Sealand's claims, and the "incorrigible Weiner," simply issued an injunction to stop further broadcasting, once again evaded prosecution. The judge went further to say that Weiner could

---

* Based on the cost of putting the ship and station together, each day of broadcasting was around $50,000.

apply for a license when more of the AM spectrum was opened to commercial interests in 1990.

While Weiner was tied up in court, another group of radio operators began negotiations to buy the *Sarah* and everything aboard—and consequently became some of Sealand's most vitriolic enemies to date. The group represented a US station called MPLX and a UK station called Wonderful Radio London, or WRLI. The idea was to use the ship to broadcast "an alternative to the BBC World Service"—not a pirate station, but rather a legitimate enterprise anchored off the coast of England.

According to WRLI producer Paul John Lilburne-Byford, Weiner assured the WRLI/MPLX staff that he owned the *Sarah* and had the clear papers to prove its ownership and registration. MPLX presenter and staff member Genie Baskir flew to meet Weiner and purchased the boat for several thousand dollars. They weren't aware the ship had been registered in at least three locations, and when the paperwork attesting to the valid registration of the ship was never turned over, the new owners couldn't legally move it.

While this was going on, Weiner allegedly moved all the broadcasting equipment onto a new vessel called the *Fury* and sold the *Sarah* to an MGM studio. The *Sarah* appeared in the 1994 Jeff Bridges and Tommy Lee Jones movie *Blown Away*, in which it was, in fact, blown away in a spectacular explosion (with the injured protagonists narrowly escaping the fireball by jumping off a dock in slo-mo).

Infuriated at being ripped off, Baskir worked with US authorities to get the *Fury* and what was supposed to be her equipment impounded. Though Inspector Murphy determined that the Sealandic registration was invalid, the US government declined to prosecute Weiner and instead took possession of the equipment previously on the *Sarah* and destroyed it, leaving MPLX without a ship or the radio equipment that they thought they paid for legally and in good faith. "We were finally blown off from ever obtaining a resolution and restitution of our own part in this complicated saga of misfeasance, malfeasance, and nonfeasance by government officials, who in the end were sick and tired of anything to do with the *Lichfield I*," write WRLI associates Eric Gilder and Mervyn Haggard.

WRLI explored its legal options for going after Weiner, but the courts in Essex (and elsewhere) refused jurisdiction. One judge told Lilburne-Byford that he had to prove Sealand is a part of the UK and even suggested they take up the matter in Sealandic court. The WRLI staff was shocked at the apparent indifference to their plight and regarded the opinion especially egregious in light of Sealand's history of armed struggle, which they felt should've prompted swift action from the government years before.*

Lilburne-Byford was personally hit hard by the whole affair and was filled with rage and a sense of serious injustice. A Chelmsford court declared him "bankrupt for life" following a failed lawsuit and put the government in charge of his financial affairs. (According to Lilburne-Byford, the action was carried out "by corrupt toady individuals who would have no shame in nodding with approval at Saddam Hussein, if he happened to be their boss.") And then, when taking an odd job to make ends meet, he was struck by a car traveling more than seventy miles per hour, leaving him with a physical handicap and in constant pain. Lilburne-Byford eventually hopes to "sue every sniveling miserable bastard...who has helped to make my life a miserable hell."

Allan Weiner emerged from the situation relatively unscathed and laid low before applying for another broadcast license in 1992. An FCC review board denied the license on account of Weiner's "brilliant pattern of contumacy" despite "Weiner's recent candor and epiphany" that what he'd done was wrong. Weiner was finally able to open a legitimate shortwave radio station in Maine in 1998 called WBCQ, which he runs—legally—with his wife to this day. "It's kind of like the Bates family—it's a family affair," he said.

Weiner's mission remains the defense of free speech. To that end, the station has aired programs such as the Hal Turner Show, a revoltingly racist talk show that is about as extreme speech-wise as can be imagined. "Everybody must be able to speak or nobody will be able to speak," Weiner said. "That's been our mission, that was our mission back when we contacted Roy, and that's still our mission with WBCQ.

---

* Gilder and Haggard also contend that Michael's registration of the ship was in fact met with Roy's staunch disapproval, to the degree that the father even considered his son's actions traitorous.

It will be our mission until we're not here and other people carry the flame."

The prospects of Sealand radio in the 1980s fizzled out with the *Sarah* experiment sinking into a quagmire of legal drama. However, Roy was simultaneously developing an even bigger challenge to those who believed they owned the airwaves: He was planning to move forward with Sealand TV.

## "SEALAND TV 'LIVE IN 12 WEEKS' TIME"

In June 1987, a flurry of newspaper articles breathlessly announced "Sealand Television," a TV station to be developed on the principality whose signals were estimated to reach at least twelve million homes. The projected date of the first broadcast made perfect sense: It was to be on September 2, 1987—twenty years to the day after Sealand was founded.

The TV station reflected the earlier struggle that launched the micronation. At the time, there were only four television channels available to UK viewers: two BBC channels and two commercially funded channels, ITV and Channel 4. TVs were sold with dials tuned to these stations, with additional slots for future stations; Sealand TV was to be the fifth channel available to UK audiences. A brochure made the rounds, complete with market research about age demographics in the viewership area. Because Sealand's sovereignty had been "acquiesced to" by Britain, UK prohibitions on broadcasting didn't apply to broadcasts emanating from the fort, the Sealanders argued. The channel would feature "No news, no politics—just fun, fun, fun." All viewers would have to do was tune in to Channel 5.

"That's right folks, no new taxes, no cable fees, no satellite dishes costing thousands of pounds. Our service is *free* to the viewers, and what's more important, it's *for the viewers*," the brochure stated. "Sealand TV is leading the Revolution that will drag the United Kingdom into the eighties, prying control of the air waves out of the hands of the Home Office."

The plan was to construct a 1,000-foot-tall broadcasting antenna from the fort at a cost of $600,000, with programming transmitted to Sealand from studios in Tulira Castle, Ireland, and then via a series of relays from Sealand to satellites, which would beam it to the UK and on the European continent. Sealand TV would broadcast daily from 5:00 p.m. to 2:00 a.m., with "twenty new films each month, plus sports events, music videos, and variety shows."

"Let's face it—television in this country is diabolical at the moment," Joan said. "Sealand Television will be sheer entertainment for people who want to relax at home."

According to the *Colchester Evening Gazette*, "If Sealand television does get off the ground...the name of Roy Bates will surely become a household one yet again."

In order to launch this ambitious endeavor, Roy Bates teamed up with a fifty-five-year-old Texas businessman named Wallace Clegg Kemper who was living in London and managed an investment company registered in the Bahamas. (He also owned an oil company in Texas called "Ewing Oil," a deliberate nod to the TV show *Dallas*.) Some of the start-up costs for Sealand TV came from a trust owned by Kemper's children, with advertising rates to sustain the station once it got up and running. According to the brochure, it would cost £3,500 for a ten-second spot and £10,000 for thirty seconds. Roy was to receive around 25 percent of the station's profits.

Ken Hanlon, Sealand TV's managing director and formerly a nightclub owner, said that while the station wouldn't engage in "petty censorship," the aim wasn't to be a free-for-all. "Definitely no porn," Hanlon said. "I'm a family man and I don't think people need that sort of thing. I used to run wet T-shirt competitions in my nightclub, but there was never any nudity."

Suzanne Mizzi, a model whose body was once insured by a lingerie company and who later found renown as an interior designer and abstract artist, was to be Sealand TV's presenter. Her natural good looks made her the ideal choice to link programs with their sponsors, the brochure said. "She's the image of enthusiastic youth we want," Kemper said. "I'm talking to Roy Bates about making her Sealand's first countess."

The British government prepared statements to give to the press in anticipation of the interest surrounding the project, and they also noted that anyone who broadcasts from Roughs Tower will be prosecuted under Roy's old foil, the Wireless Telegraphy Act of 1949. But overall, they took the announcement about Sealand TV surprisingly well. According to an article in *Campaign* magazine, "Officials from the Department of Trade and Industry, the Foreign Office, and the Home Office broke into peals of laughter" when asked about the plan. "Let's just say I'm not losing sleep at night," said the sales director of another station.

Nevertheless, the Crown's guard was up. A representative of a UK communications equipment manufacturer named Mr. Bones alerted the Home Office that representatives from Sealand TV were inquiring about getting equipment manufactured for the unlicensed station. Included in UK government files on Sealand is a list of equipment manufacturers in every country in Europe with checkmarks next to the names indicating they had been asked to avoid working with the principality.

But the Crown also knew Sealand TV involved at least one person with a checkered past and expected the endeavor would implode accordingly. Wallace Kemper was alleged to be one of the two masterminds behind a scheme to make big returns from an international arbitrage transaction that ripped off rich and poor alike,* and the Texan was indicted in Los Angeles in March 1987, along with six other associates, on twenty-nine counts of fraud. Roy and Joan Bates told one newspaper they knew of the impending fraud charges in the US but that they still had faith in Kemper's involvement with Sealand TV. "Wallace dismissively reassured us that it was nothing but a misunderstanding, and would 'blow over,'" Michael said.

Not long after, Kemper went MIA, and it turned out he was in jail. In addition to the charges he was facing in the US, he had also been

---

* Quoting federal prosecutors, a contemporaneous article in the *LA Times* explained that "[t]he defendants allegedly told borrowers that they could obtain promissory notes from leading American banks and AAA-rated bonds that would be used as collateral for the transactions. To enhance their credibility, they used a Panamanian corporation that purportedly had billions of dollars to lend at low interest rates and a Caribbean bank doing business in London that supposedly accepted deposits of borrowers' fees...Advance fees obtained through the solicitations were laundered through various corporate accounts in the United States and London and eventually turned over to the principals in the scheme."

charged with conspiracy to defraud in the UK in 1986 in an unrelated incident involving a $3 million bank draft. His extradition back to the US was delayed on account of the UK charges, and once he was freed, Kemper told the Bateses he was through.

"The British courts imprisoned me for something I didn't do," he said. "I'm not staying one more day in this goddamn banana republic."

As Michael put it, "With that came the unceremonious end of Sealand TV." The employees who moved for the job relocated back home, and the equipment was gotten rid of. A legitimate Channel 5 station would begin broadcasting in 1997, licensed not to Sealand TV but to Channel 5 Broadcasting Ltd., a fully licensed entity comprised of media groups and equity firms and entirely approved by the UK government.

## TROUBLE ON THE HORIZON

Sealand and the UK were two rivals eyeing each other from afar, but a third party would soon rejoin the dispute. Sealand's exile government, headed by 1978 coupster Alexander Achenbach, was going through some changes in the 1980s as well.

Achenbach reappeared in the press in the late 1970s and early 1980s in connection with a man named Pim Lier, who joined the Dutch royal family when it was determined that Lier was the illegitimate son of the current queen's brother. As Achenbach related to a Dutch magazine, he had met Lier, also known as Prince Albrecht zu Mecklenburg, at a society party and promptly installed him as a prince of Sealand.

However, Achenbach was intermittently doing stints in prison for fraud unrelated to the principality during the same period. Over the years he had been arrested and convicted of fraud in Greece and he subsequently went bankrupt. He was also said to have done shady construction deals in Mallorca and Germany. But Achenbach also boasted that he was once again wealthy thanks to the returns from a (literal) gold mine he owned and the profits he'd gotten reselling eighty million dollars' worth of coal he bought from a Frenchman. He and the ex-Sealanders were even looking into setting up a new extraterritorial state. "On one of my many journeys I discovered an island,

Bréchou, in the Channel between England and France, for sale for thirteen million guilders," he said. "I will soon buy it."

But he still had Sealand to look after, and the best thing was to transfer his power given his intermittent stays in prison. An amendment to the Sealandic constitution appointed Dutch lawyer Adrian L.C.M. Oomen as *syndic* (i.e., a transitional official endowed with leadership powers), who eventually appointed a man named Johannes W.F. Seiger as Prime Minister in 1989. A new constitution was developed the same year, establishing German as one of Sealand's national languages and augmenting the structure of the government so that the power of Prince Roy and Princess Joan was held in check by the "Privy Council," which was headed by Seiger.

"I'm more optimistic about the future than ever before," Roy said, unaware of the trouble for the fort that was brewing all over the world. Some far-less scrupulous people felt just as good about their aims for Sealand, and the 1990s would show just how unscrupulous they could get.

# CHAPTER 12

## SHOTS FIRED, FORGED PASSPORTS, AND OUTRAGEOUS CRIMINALITY

*"Life should be made difficult for Bates."*
—anonymous Crown official

It had been a while since the Sealanders fired upon an approaching vessel in self-defense, and it was high time they do it again. On February 23, 1990, the Thames Coast Guard received a distress signal from a Royal Marine Auxiliary Vessel called *Golden Eye*. The *Golden Eye* reported it was under attack—someone standing on a platform in the North Sea was shooting at it. Unbeknownst to the vessel, it had entered Sealand's territorial waters. The ship retreated and was able to make it back to shore with its crew intact.

"I almost choked on my cornflakes," said one Crown official when he heard about the incident.

The British government promptly investigated.

Prince Roy, who was sixty-eight at the time, conceded that shots had been fired at the *Golden Eye*, but not in aggression. The *Golden Eye* appeared to be sailing too close to the legs of the platform, and Roy wanted to make sure the ship knew of the geographic danger.

"The rifle shots were a warning, used like a flare from a lighthouse. The vessel had not responded to repeated radio calls and there was some concern," he explained.

"Life should be made difficult for Bates" following the *Golden Eye* shooting, wrote the man who choked on his cornflakes, but the police's response, if there was any, has apparently been lost to history. There was no counterattack by the British government, and Joan said that repairmen have called to ask permission before coming to service the buoys since then.

But no matter how much the principality's territorial waters were respected, money was still required to keep Sealand solvent. Plans being discussed in the 1990s included setting up a "giant hypermarket" on the principality that sold duty-free cigarettes and alcohol to passing ships and continuing to allow companies and ships to register on Sealand, as it had done for the pirate radio ship *Sarah*.

Roy's bullshit detector was always on high, though, following the attempted takeover by the Germans, the approach by the warring Argentinians, and the Sealand TV investor going to jail for fraud. It wouldn't be until the very end of the 1990s that a serious venture finally got up and running on Sealand. And when it did, it would prove to be exactly the kind of principled, envelope-pushing project the micronation was made for.

As it happened, however, most of the business involving the principality in the 1990s took place without the royal family's knowledge or consent. The first inklings that something was seriously amiss came when the Bates family found themselves mixed up in a horribly grim crime.

## THE VERSACE AFFAIR

Michael Bates was caught off-guard by a newspaper item he read in late July 1997, claiming that he and his parents were connected to the murder of Italian fashion icon Gianni Versace. According to the article, a passport issued by the Principality of Sealand was found on the houseboat where Versace's murderer had committed suicide.

Michael squinted at the paper and continued to read.

On July 15, 1997, Gianni Versace was leaving his opulent mansion in Miami Beach when he was gunned down on his front steps by a twenty-seven-year-old psychopath named Andrew Cunanan. Allegedly distraught that a rich benefactor had cut him off, Cunanan had embarked on a kill rampage across four states earlier that summer, murdering two former lovers and two strangers before coming back to Miami and killing Versace for seemingly no reason. When police finally tracked him down, Cunanan led them on a chase, broke into a houseboat, and shot himself.

The owner of the houseboat was a strange German character named Torsten Reineck. Reineck, age forty-nine, is described by some acquaintances as well-spoken and polite but by others as "obnoxious, unpleasant, disgusting." He had a number of real estate investments in Miami and owned a Las Vegas health spa where orgies allegedly took place, running it under the pseudonym "Mattias Ruehl"—the same name as was listed on a passport issued by the Principality of Sealand found in the houseboat following Cunanan's suicide. Reineck also had Sealand "Corps Diplomatique" vanity plates and was known to flash the Sealand passport around and pass himself off as someone important. Authorities quickly began looking into the principality to determine its connection to the German fraudster and Versace's murder.

It was true that Roy had produced Sealand passports starting in the 1970s and had given around three hundred out to trusted friends, family, supporters, and businesspeople. It was also true that the passports had occasionally ended up in the wrong hands, but the fact that a Sealand passport was being associated with the killing of Versace left Roy baffled, enraged, and embarrassed. He was emphatic that the principality had nothing to do with this sordid business, and that Sealand, while prone to defend itself, would never involve itself in something as dishonorable as cold-blooded murder. An agent from Interpol's fraud squad came to speak with the family directly, and investigators ultimately confirmed there was no connection between Sealand and the Versace murder. "Nobody is more honest than my husband. He's so honest he creaks," Joan said.

Reineck's role in all of this was hard to figure out. He used the alias Mattias Ruehl in some of his dealings (including opening a number of shell companies registered at the address of his boat), but then the real Mattias Ruehl showed up at the houseboat when police were investigating. He and Reineck seemed to be connected to a bunch of wealthy German flimflam men that lived in Miami, but both disappeared before police could interview them. Reineck ultimately turned himself in to authorities in Frankfurt a few weeks later and was sentenced to three years in prison for 152 cases of fraud and intentionally delaying bankruptcy proceedings.

Although former Miami Beach Police Department Chief Richard Barreto, who was chief at the time of the Versace killing, said Cunanan possibly knew Reineck from the gay porn scene and had probably been on the houseboat before, police ultimately determined that Cunanan probably had no connection to Reineck and that he had likely broken into the houseboat at random.* In any case, the Bateses were cleared of any connection to the deadly rampage, but it turned out that the problems involving bootleg Sealand passports were only just beginning.

## THE SPANISH CAPER

On April 4, 2000, a trim, handsome forty-six-year-old man named Francisco Trujillo Ruiz made a few adjustments to the odds and ends in his office at 210 Paseo de la Castellana, a street in a fashionable part of Madrid, before sitting down to speak with a newspaper reporter. Trujillo Ruiz, a flamenco club owner and former police officer who'd been kicked off the force for burglarizing a home, was going to speak about his duties as a high-level government official.

The reporter had just turned on her recorder and had pen poised above her notepad when a klatch of green-uniformed members of Spain's Guardia Civil came through the office's door. Trujillo Ruiz jumped up in surprise, and the officers promptly boxed him in and got to the point: He was under arrest for his membership in a gang that had allegedly sold more than two million gallons of diluted gasoline.

Trujillo Ruiz was momentarily nonplussed, but then he pulled out a diplomatic passport and claimed immunity. The police had no right to be there, he said, as they were actually outside their jurisdiction—his office was the Sealandic consulate in Spain.

The reporter, still sitting, looked back and forth between her subject and the police. The passport was apparently a very formidable fake, with a rubber coating and foil-stamped seals, and it gave officers some pause when considering how to handle the arrest. But it was soon confirmed that Sealand was not a member of the Schengen Agreement (which covers passport and visa issues between twenty-six European

---

* Of course, conspiracies abound: Some have postulated that Cunanan broke into the houseboat looking for Reineck, as Cunanan may have been worried that he was HIV positive and was looking to take revenge on Reineck for operating a gay bathhouse where casual sex was supposedly commonplace. Post-mortem testing confirmed that Cunanan was HIV negative. Even wilder (and completely baseless) theories claim that Cunanan was going to sail the houseboat to Sealand. Either way, the houseboat sank under mysterious circumstances five months later.

countries) and that arresting Trujillo Ruiz would not violate any international laws. In fact, far from being a diplomat, authorities soon learned that in addition to selling bunk gas, Trujillo Ruiz was one of the prime movers and shakers of a gang of scam artists operating throughout the world, a "very cold and calculating person, with an enormous capacity to invent things and trick anyone," as one officer put it. He was officially placed under arrest and taken into custody for fraud, falsification of documents, and "usurpation of functions."

Investigators subsequently found that one of the gang's primary sources of income was the sale of passports, nationality cards, and university degrees over the internet, all from businesses and universities supposedly based on the Principality of Sealand. Customers shelled out between $9,000 and $55,000, depending on which document was needed, and they were free to use them for whatever purposes they wanted.

Not long after Trujillo Ruiz's arrest, officers crashed two more Sealandic "embassies" in Madrid, one of them located in an office that managed bingo halls. At least twenty fake diplomatic passports, hundreds more blank passports, and 2,000 official documents were seized in the raids, as were two vehicles with Sealand diplomatic license plates that had been escorted through Madrid by Spanish police on more than one occasion.

Michael Bates was tipped off to these strange goings-on around the same time, when a friend asked him about the documents for sale through the Sealand website.

"Excuse me?" Michael asked.

"On your website. The diplomas and passports."

Michael scratched his chin. Sealand did have a website, but it was in its infancy. And it certainly wasn't selling official paperwork.

He turned on his computer, clicked on the browser icon, and listened to the dial-up connection's rasp. He typed in Sealand's then-URL: *www.fruitsofthesea.demon.co.uk/Sealand*. The site was how he had left it. He then searched around and turned up a Sealand site with a much more manageable domain name: *www.principality-sealand.net*. Lo and behold, it was a website purporting to be the official mouthpiece of Sealand, and you could indeed buy a number of Sealandic documents.

Michael wrote to the address listed on the website and heard back from someone claiming to have close ties with Spain's King Juan Carlos. The group was working "in the best interest of the family," the man said.

"I'm thinking, what the hell is this all about?" Michael said. He considered going to Spain to confront them himself. "I'd be only too happy to. They are doing us a dreadful disservice." (All of this was going on, incidentally, while Paddy Roy and Joan were on vacation in Spain [and had traveled there on British passports].)

The breadth of the gang's plans was impressive: Diplomatic credentials were sold to Moroccan hash smugglers, one "itinerant ambassador" attempted to acquire 1,800 cars from a car factory using forged documents, and a churro proprietor in Madrid tried to use Sealandic documents to secure a twenty-million-dollar loan for two private planes. Uniforms were designed for the Sealand Army, labels were printed for Sealand whisky, and the group was selling shares of a Sealand expansion project for the small fee of £6,000, with a £350 "goodwill deposit" required to even get the conversation started.

Incredibly, Sealand's "Secretary of State" Miguel Palacios Massó and "Minister of Transport and Trade" Simon Montolio Solsona had even begun negotiating with members of the Spanish Russian Mafia to buy tanks, helicopters, bombs, missiles, and ammunition through a shell company to sell to Sudan, which was under embargo by many governments of the world for being a terrorist state. Money was supposedly laundered for "mysterious Russian and Iraqi clients" as well, but the accusations were disputed.

"Neither I nor anyone has committed any criminal action or obtained economic benefit," Massó said in a note slipped to a newspaper.[*]

---

[*] Most of the gang's members had previous arrests for financial misdeeds. Palacios Massó was convicted of a host of "economic crimes," Secretary of State Carlos Gallego Poveda was a financier with a history of forgery and fraud, and Igor Popof, Sealand's Foreign Minister, skipped out on a $3,000 hotel bill in Madrid. Additionally, the country's political advisor had ties to an Italian Fascist Party and Berlin's underground Nazi Party, and the son of the former personal secretary of Benito Mussolini claimed Sealandic citizenship as well.

The gang went as far as to set up some seemingly legitimate cultural organizations as fronts for the scams, including the "Goya Foundation," and even managed to get members of Spain's actual royal family to sit on its board. (The Royals later resigned in embarrassment.) It also came to light during this period that the group had sold four thousand bootleg Sealand passports in Hong Kong for $1,000 apiece when the territory was transferred from British to Chinese control in 1997.

"They're stealing our name, and they're stealing from other people. How disgusting can you get?" said Princess Joan.

Trujillo Ruiz reportedly first learned about Sealand while working in a German town called Erwitte for a company owned by Friedbert Ley, who had launched his own Sealand fan website in 1998 and had asked Trujillo Ruiz to go back to Spain to set up a Spanish branch office of the Sealandic government. When confronted by investigators with the fake passports, Trujillo Ruiz conceded they were made in Germany but insisted that he'd been appointed as acting head of state by the Bateses and was authorized to issue Sealand passports. "Roy Bates is a vegetable, his son Michael chose me, and I accepted the position," Trujillo Ruiz later told reporters.[*] Meanwhile, Trujillo Ruiz's father, who shares the same name, told a reporter it was bad fortune that he had passed his name to such a numskull. "[He] never amounted to anything because he's always been undisciplined," the father said.

The passport scam was merely the latest in an apparently lifelong series of screwups. The father explained that he had called in some favors to get his son a position with the police. When that fell through, he helped his son set up a clothing store, a grocery store, and a video rental store—all opportunities the younger Trujillo Ruiz botched.

"I knew this Sealand affair was not going to turn out well. I'm convinced they used him because he doesn't have the ability to pull off something like that," the elder Trujillo Ruiz said. "He doesn't even have his high school diploma."

The investigation into his son's criminal activities resulted in the elder Trujillo Ruiz's bank account being frozen, and the younger Trujillo Ruiz's overall good-for-nothingness had contributed to his parents

---

[*] Roy was very much active and well at the time.

getting divorced. Moreover, the son was married with three kids but didn't send a peseta home to help his family with the rent when he was living in Germany. The Germans were a bad influence, the elder Trujillo Ruiz added.

The investigation also revealed that Ley and a man named KH Schrimpf had gotten their passports from the same group of people as Torsten Reineck. As it turned out, behind the Germans and their dubious passports was allegedly none other than the masterminds of the 1978 coup, and longtime thorns in the legitimate first family's side: Alexander Gottfried Achenbach, and his cronies, including Johannes W.F. Seiger, who became "Prime Minister of Sealand" via constitutional amendment in 1989.

For their part, the exile government refuted Ley's assertions in a missive published not long after Trujillo Ruiz was arrested. According to Minister for Special Affairs Hans-Jürgen Sauerbrey, the exile government had allegedly been approached by Ley and Schrimpf, who offered money for diplomatic posts and bootleg passports in exchange for official recognition by the Spanish government. The exile government claimed they knew they were dealing with criminals and didn't play ball. They also said that the passport pictured on the website as an example of the documents for sale was stolen from Prime Minister Seiger.

In fact, Sauerbrey claimed, instead of investigating the real criminal, the various diplomatic and trade missions of the exile government had been searched by German authorities "in violation of its diplomatic immunity and in contravention to the Vienna Treaty." The exile government claimed the German government was actually looking for Nazi documents and information about flying saucers, caches of silver and gold, and a "multitude of cultural goods of immeasurable value… as well as highly sensitive documents from the Stasi files" that had been entrusted to the exile government. The misdirected focus allowed the criminal activity in Spain to continue, Sauerbrey said.

Despite Sauerbrey's disquisition, investigators noted that the circumstantial evidence linking the Germans to the scam was pretty strong and that the Bates family once again had nothing to do with an international crime. And besides, police in another part of Europe had been investigating Achenbach for the past few years for questionable banking activities in Slovenia, as the mastermind behind a scam that likewise trafficked on the name of Sealand.

## THE RETURN OF A GERMAN SCHEMER

In the mid-1990s, Achenbach had set up a company called "The Sealand Trade Development Authority Limited" (STDAL) through an infamous Panamanian law firm called Mossack Fonseca, which had offices in thirty-five other countries and was said to be one of the world's top creators of shell companies. According to information revealed in the Panama Papers leak of May 2016*, STDAL was set up in the Bahamas using Sealand passport number C000002 and envelopes using Sealand stamps.

Using Sealandic documents and STDAL credentials, Achenbach and an Austrian couple named Josef and Eva Baier opened a bank account at Banka Koper in Slovenia in 1996. (Josef Baier was a long-time associate of the exile government and had designed some of the coins the exile government minted in the late 1970s.) The account caught the eyes of Slovenian authorities in March 1997, when €6 million suddenly appeared in the account from Luxembourg, Germany, and the UK. Officials expected the money was being laundered or had come from a pyramid scheme. The account might have aroused notice sooner, but "there are so many new states and young countries now that the bank official accepted the passport as identification to open the account," said one investigator.

---

* According to the International Consortium of Investigative Journalists, "The Panama Papers is an unprecedented investigation that reveals the offshore links of some of the globe's most prominent figures. The International Consortium of Investigative Journalists, together with the German newspaper *Suddeutsche Zeitung* and more than 100 other media partners, spent a year sifting through 11.5 million leaked files to expose the offshore holdings of world political leaders, links to global scandals, and details of the hidden financial dealings of fraudsters, drug traffickers, billionaires, celebrities, sports stars and more...ICIJ's analysis of the leaked records revealed information on more than 214,000 offshore companies connected to people in more than 200 countries and territories."

Lamentably, while the findings are remarkable in their scope, international outrage seems to be lacking. To paraphrase an internet meme, "remember that time all those documents came out proving the world's rich were actively hiding their assets and defrauding the entire world and nothing happened at all?"

Not long after, the Baiers came to the bank and withdrew €200,000 from the account, again using Sealandic documents. When the couple attempted to withdraw €4 million more a little while later, the bank gave them a smaller amount and sent them on their way, with the authorities arresting them as they tried to cross into Italy. The couple was granted bail and fled to Austria, where they remained.

Slovenia had long since put a hold on the account, but the hold touched off an eight-year legal battle between Achenbach and the Slovenian state, who struggled to prove that the money had come from an illegal source. In 2005, the court ruled that the bank had to release the €6 million to Achenbach because they couldn't prove it was related to any criminal enterprise. The money had in fact come from a gambling enterprise in Poland, but it was an aboveboard operation. A higher court later affirmed the ruling in Achenbach's favor.

Achenbach had the money transferred to an account in the name of his lawyer Daniel Starman. (He couldn't use his own bank account because it too had been opened with fake documents.) The money was released to Starman, and Achenbach sued Slovenia in 2010 for €1.3 million for preventing access to his money. The government denied the appeal, arguing that Slovenian law stipulated that any seized assets that were returned would be done so without interest.

Achenbach was charged almost €9,000 in court fees for his lawsuit, which he of course appealed, but he soon found himself back in court because the paperwork he'd used to sign the funds over to his lawyer were STDAL documents, which were obviously illegitimate. He was also sued by a former colleague who alleged that the money was his and that Achenbach had conned him out of it.

The banking saga "presented us with a strange philosophical question," said one Slovenian investigator later on, especially in that part of the world. "It was about territoriality and recognition. Did we recognize these passports or not? Who is to say what is or isn't a country? For a time in 1991, after Slovenia was briefly caught up in the Bosnian war, many countries refused to recognize our nation."

The strange legal and financial quagmire was a fitting final chapter in the life of someone who had spent a lifetime involved in dubious ways to get money. Achenbach was seventy-nine when he filed the lawsuit in 2010, and he succumbed to old age in the middle of the litigation at age eighty. Starman, his lawyer, had also died, and so the case simply faded into oblivion and the money was absorbed by the state.

Roy Bates felt that the attention the dubious passports received was disproportionate and not a reflection of any problem with the true Sealandic government. Instead it was an unintentional association that sullied everything he had been working toward. "Every country in the world has problems like this," he said grouchily. "The world is awash with fake passports. I'm just angry they're faking mine and using them for illegal purposes."

Given the Trujillo Ruiz affair, the Slovenian bank scam, and the thousands and thousands of fake Sealand passports circulating around the world, the family put a moratorium on issuing passports and effectively ended the practice for good following 9/11.

## THE CAZIQUE OF POYAIS

Sealand was not the first and certainly won't be the last territory to be exploited by scammers. Fraudsters have been very adept at channeling the promise of a fake country, and many people have found themselves duped, broke, or even dead as a result. Gregor MacGregor's Territory of Poyais is one particularly tragic example of how the claims of nationhood can be used for despicable ends.

Gregor MacGregor, the man who would style himself "the Cazique of Poyais," was born in 1786 in Scotland. He joined the British Army at age sixteen and ascended through the ranks, sometimes advancing thanks to genuine soldierly skill and sometimes by paying for rank, which wasn't an uncommon practice at the time.

MacGregor set sail for Venezuela in 1812 with the intention of joining the country's war of independence against Spain. He fought in several battles and was cited for some legitimate acts of heroism, but in April 1809, he abandoned his troops during a battle, fleeing the scene to save his own skin. He eventually reemerged in Honduras and was given a large swath of land as a gift. This gave MacGregor the impression he was king of his own territory, and he was warmly received in London society as "Cazique" of this territory, a title he said was bestowed upon him by an area chieftain.

The "Territory of Poyais," as he called it, supposedly encompassed around eight million acres in the east of Honduras and north of Nicaragua. Rebellions and leaders came and went in Central America, so it wasn't too out of the ordinary that a new nation could pop up relatively unannounced. Investors knew of the limitless opportunities for development in that part of the world, and so MacGregor pitched the chance to develop Poyais. He promptly established a business office in London, drew up official-looking paperwork, and put together promotional literature touting Poyais's abundant resources, friendly natives, and convenient location, and promised a significant return on any investment. MacGregor would ultimately walk away with the equivalent of about four billion investor dollars as a result of the Poyais scam.

But things got especially tragic when 250 settlers took MacGregor's enticements at face value and set out for Poyais on two ships. They reached the supposed location a few months later and found that it was basically uninhabitable. Conflict swept through the settlers' camp, and people began to die from disease, starvation, and suicide. Ultimately, more than 80 percent of the settlers perished on "Poyais," even though a passing ship was able to get people off the putative paradise and into neighboring countries. MacGregor had effectively sentenced two hundred people to death through his scheme.

As news about the failed excursion reached England, MacGregor claimed that he himself had been duped by fraudulent business partners. Many people—including survivors of the ill-fated journey—defended him. But Poyaisian development stock plummeted and the scheme fell apart. Eventually MacGregor was arrested with a few of his cronies, but he was able to wriggle his way out of jail and return to Venezuela, where he was given the reception of a war hero and buried with full military honors in 1845.

Sealand passports, legitimate and fake alike, are now on a list of documents European Union Customs officials are supposed to watch out for—an honor Sealand shares with documents from other banned locations such as the Byzantine Empire, the Confederate States of America, the Republic of Koneuwe, Waveland, and Atoomvrijstaat, the "Nuclear-free State."

Despite his passing, Achenbach's legacy certainly lives on in the present day. Sealand's government-in-exile is as active as ever under the leadership of Prime Minister Johannes W.F. Seiger, who was appointed by Achenbach in 1989 and has taken the dark mirror Sealand in some peculiar directions (see chapter 17).

ROY WAS ALMOST eighty, and Joan in her midseventies, as the 1990s drew to a close, and the heavy duties of running the micronation were beginning to take a toll. Michael Bates was named "Prince Regent" and given much more authority when it came to all matters Sealand, but it was by family agreement that the Sealanders embarked on the next wild, boundary-pushing endeavor. This project was undertaken with the true royal family's utmost blessing, and internet geeks, legal scholars, and Matrixian libertarians the world over would suddenly start paying attention to the rogue principality far out at sea. If all went according to plan, the techno-scheme on Sealand would make everyone involved fantastically rich.

PART III

# SURVIVING THE CYBER AGE

(2000–present)

# CHAPTER 13

# CYPHERPUNKS AND OFFSHORE DATA STORAGE

*"A tiny bastion of freedom in the middle of a cold sea, surrounded by large socialist nations in every direction. I wanted to ask for political asylum and move in that very day."*

—Sean Hastings

On a grim day in March 2000, storm clouds threatened on the horizon as a bespectacled man with curly hair named Simson Garfinkel was being hoisted up on the famous Sealandic winch. The North Sea was characteristically turbulent, and part of the trick to getting up to the platform was timing the swell of a wave with a hop into the swinging chair attached to the winch. Garfinkel was on assignment for the pop-tech magazine *Wired*, and the journey across the waves was not something he ordinarily undertook as a geek reporter.

Garfinkel was there to explore a dotcom-era version of Sealand. Specifically, he was paying a visit to a group of young and principled cypherpunks who were getting the rooms in the fort's concrete silos ready for racks of servers, computers, and satellite equipment. Sealand was in the process of being transformed into a sort of digital fortress—an oceanic castle whose sovereignty and inaccessibility made it the perfect "data haven."

Similar to a tax haven, data havens offered a no-questions-asked data storage, web hosting, and encrypted communication as a response to increasingly intrusive government regulation of the internet. Sealand's extraterritoriality made it the perfect home base for internet services theoretically free of any other nation's regulations.

The company Garfinkel was going to visit was called "HavenCo," whose founders had worked out a deal with the Bates family to base their operations on Sealand the previous fall. With Garfinkel on the boat was a stoic twenty-one-year-old named Ryan Lackey, whose pallid complexion, shaved head, and all-black clothing spoke for his stature as a serious cyberwarrior. Indeed, it was Lackey who cofounded HavenCo and helped drum up the funding to get the project started. His journey out with Garfinkel was his first taste of the physical reality of Sealand/ HavenCo, and he sat on the boat with a look of intense concentration as the strange silhouette on the horizon got steadily larger.

Lackey followed Garfinkel up the winch onto the deck, where he stood quietly and looked around, taking in the views from the concrete island. Sealand was much smaller than he expected, but the success of his mission was more important than the comfort of his physical location. Besides, he thought, were he back home in the Bay Area, he'd be sitting in his apartment in front of his computer with the shades drawn anyway. Lackey walked off to stake out his living quarters while Garfinkel chatted with the security guards.

Garfinkel was shown the living areas and kitchen and passport control and then taken to the South tower. The grate to the ladder in the floor was pulled back, and Garfinkel descended the steep stairs down into the first level. He was skeptical but intrigued. At this point, the room (and those below it) was almost comically bare: no storage space, no furniture, a single lightbulb hanging from the ceiling. Notably, there weren't even any electrical outlets. However, the room had been given a fresh coat of paint, which made it seem a little more professional. Besides, it was still early on in the experiment, and there were many more boatloads of stuff to be brought to Sealand to put the HavenCo infrastructure together.

After Garfinkel completed the tour and spent some time speaking with those aboard the fort, he was lowered down onto a waiting boat and departed for land to write his story for *Wired*. Lackey stayed on Sealand, and he would remain there for the foreseeable future to get HavenCo up and running. Speaking a few years later at a tech conference, Lackey held aloft the Sealand passport he'd been officially issued by the royal family. "This cost me $220,000 and three years of my life," he said.

## HOW TO START YOUR OWN COUNTRY

In the late 1990s, the tiny Caribbean nation of Anguilla was home to an interesting cluster of expatriates. With its nonexistent taxes and incredible beaches, it was the perfect place for self-employed computer geeks to develop projects during the dotcom boom. Lackey moved there after dropping out of MIT. He had been a hacker since the early 1990s—before he was even a teenager—and the democratic possibility of computers meshed with his political outlook. "I was interested in how individuals could stand up to large groups, even nation states, using mathematics," he said. "Learning about computer security meant I was able to subvert security systems, and this gave me access to things I wasn't supposed to see."

Lackey cofounded an early electronic payment mechanism on Anguilla, but the project was eventually abandoned and he was on the lookout for his next venture. As it happened, the Second International Conference on Financial Cryptography was hosted on the island in February 1998, and it was at that conference that friends of his (who happened to run Anguilla's ".ai" domain name) introduced him to a Michigan native named Sean Hastings.

A few years older at twenty-nine, Hastings had left the University of Michigan on account of the excessive humanities requirements and had since made a living playing professional poker and programming. Hastings and his wife Jo found their niche in online betting services, as Sean wrote software for sports betting operations while Jo undertook market research for casinos across the US. The Hastingses found themselves on Anguilla after an online betting startup in Costa Rica didn't come together as planned.

Both Lackey and the Hastingses were ardent Libertarians of the computer age. As they saw it, increasing governmental snooping and corporate influence were eroding personal freedom. They were part of the "cypherpunk" movement—a term encompassing hackers and rebellious techies who developed technology with the intention of subverting this Orwellian encroachment.* Hastings met a man named Vince Cate who had tried his own data haven project on Anguilla, and they began working together on a similar venture. Among other uses, data havens could be useful to political dissidents, gambling

---

* Some notable cypherpunk projects include currencies like Bitcoin and unbreakable encryption.

websites, pornographers, and those simply interested in keeping their business their own.

Hastings discussed the idea of a data haven at the Financial Cryptography '97 conference with fellow cypherpunks and proffered some ideas about how they could keep hands off their data. One he dubbed the "toxic barge project": one would buy a ship, outfit it with servers on top and toxic waste on the bottom, sail it out to international waters, and open the servers up to anyone who needed to rent space on unassailable servers. Nobody would want to board a ship filled with toxic waste, and the militaries of nearby countries would likely ensure that nobody messed with the ship in order to keep an ecological disaster at bay.

"The beauty of the idea is that your defense system actually earns you cash. The people producing this nasty toxic waste will pay you to take it off their hands and store it at your facility. The drawback," he said, "is that toxic waste isn't very popular, and it is hard to market something called 'Toxic Barge' to the general population." The proposal was tongue-in-cheek, but the concept was resonant and sparked enthusiasm for a real data haven.

Meeting Lackey at the conference was fortuitous. Anguilla proved not to be as much of a hands-off haven as Hastings and Lackey thought. Pornography and gambling were explicitly illegal according to the country's constitution, meaning that Anguillan servers hosting even mild versions of this content were subject to prosecution. The country's tax policy was beneficial for foreign businesses and individuals who wanted to obfuscate their funds, but the country often required participation in a graft system to do business. Hastings and Lackey decided to partner up on the data haven idea, and they began looking for somewhere that could legally assure the no-questions-asked privacy the concept demanded. That's when Cate handed Hastings and Lackey a book by Erwin Strauss called, appropriately, *How to Start Your Own Country*.

It's hard to overestimate the amount of influence Erwin Strauss's book *How to Start Your Own Country* has had on the story of the Principality of Sealand and similar ventures that have popped up over the years. Strauss said he is aware of the book's popularity and influence, as he is the go-to guy for reporters whenever a new country-type situation pops up. The book has sold a few thousand copies and was adapted into a British TV show of the same name, in which the host declares his own country in his bedroom.

The book came from an experiment in the 1970s in which Strauss and a few cohorts attempted to set up a gambling operation in international waters in which they would take bets by CB radio. Strauss and a small group of backers got together money for a ship and the necessary equipment. "We got involved with some of the narco people and their bankers and agents because they were willing to buck the system to do it. The thing that broke that camel's back was that we got word that General Noriega in Panama wanted to have a cut of the business," he said. "It was really getting heavy."

The offshore betting ship never got off the ground, but Strauss realized he had amassed a significant amount of material about new countries and information about how to take advantage of being in international waters. Loompanics publisher Michael Hoy suggested Strauss compile the information into a book, which he would publish. The book would fit right in with other titles that appealed to armchair adventurers who wished they were soldiers of fortune, such as *50 Ways to Kill Your Neighbor*. Strauss fleshed out the manuscript with documents from an early chronicler of micronations who had a Sam Spade-ian office in St. Louis full of filing cabinets and trunks full of related information. Thus, *How to Start Your Own Country* was born.

Strauss's book was first published in 1979 by Loompanics Press, an underground publishing outlet that distributed an incredible amount of titles spanning the extremes of politics, religion, and conspiracy theories, as well as practical manuals about how to shoplift, make a composting toilet, and cook meth. "I liked presenting a variety of outrageous and controversial viewpoints," publisher Michael Hoy said.

Among a host of other considerations, Strauss lays out in *How to Start Your Own Country* the legal technicalities and defense considerations of starting a new nation. The book also catalogs an impressive list of attempted nations throughout the world, including New Atlantis, the United Moorish Republic, and some horrible venture called "Aryana" that was supposed to be a white nationalist enclave on an island near Antarctica. According to the book, the only self-made country that came even close to actual success was the one that graced the book's cover: the Principality of Sealand.*

Lackey and Hastings were impressed with Sealand's longevity and bellicose history and found in the Bates family a similarly antagonistic, pro-individual idealism. If there was some legitimacy to its sovereignty, Hastings reasoned, then the country could enact laws that would put an emphasis on protecting data, providing a legal basis for hosting material others might find objectionable. Hastings compiled as much information on the principality as he could and engaged a lawyer college buddy to assess the micronation's international standing. The situation was "unresolved," the lawyer said—a sufficiently vague determination that made Sealand ideal for a data haven.

Hastings reached out to the Bates family in July 1999, with a letter describing HavenCo as "pirate internet," a characterization that immediately resonated with the former radio pirates. The plan he proposed was simple: Sealand would become the host to a set of computer servers that would in turn host websites, process payments, and store

---

* The book found a receptive audience when it was published, as it came out at the tail end of the popularity of the hippie movement, communes, and people interested in developing a new way of life. Strauss could appreciate the interest, as he has always been somewhat of a loner and could sympathize with the idea of just wanting to be left alone. But when the 1980s rolled around, with the advent of leadership like Margaret Thatcher and Ronald Reagan, there was less tolerance for perceived threats to the established order and the number of attempted new countries fell drastically. The "world got much more serious, with not much room for fun and games," Strauss said.

Strauss said his book often gets lumped in with the survivalist/doomsday prepper circles and has occasionally made an appearance in some less than savory places. The book was found in the library of the Heaven's Gate cultists following the mass suicide at the arrival of the Hale-Bopp comet in 1997, and the book has also been cited as ideological guidance for right-wing separatist movements such as the Sagebrush Rebellion and the Montana Freemen "Christian Patriot" militia. Strauss was not involved with any of these groups and disavows much of their thinking, but he was aware that the associations might raise some eyebrows. "I thought the FBI would come knocking after one of these incidents," he said. "But the knock never came."

Following the publication of *How to Start Your Own Country*, Strauss took his degree in physics and began working in the computer business and evaluated proposals for a government contractor. He retired at fifty-five and now makes the rounds at science fiction conventions, where he is a well-known "filk" musician, or folk music based on science fiction. Strauss helped produce a full-scale filk musical for the 77th World Science Fiction Convention, which was hosted in Dublin, Ireland, in August 2019.

information with almost no restriction on content—save for child pornography, hacking, and spam. HavenCo's internet would come from fiber optic cable, microwave link, and satellite feeds.

"We've had dozens and dozens of proposals and we've turned them all down," Roy said. "This is the first one that seemed to be really suited to what we are."

The project was pitched at a good time. Roy wasn't as spry as he used to be. On the fort he had a flare-up of malaria he'd contracted in the war and spent a few days wrapped in a blanket and holding a shotgun in a delirious attempt to ward off hallucinated invaders. Establishing a viable new project, at the height of the dotcom boom, on Sealand not only meant a healthy influx of money; it was also an excuse to get Roy off the platform and back in the UK for good.

It's impossible to know just how much money had gone into Sealand—the standard estimate is "millions of pounds"; one writer described the venture as a "quixotic financial sinkhole"—but the upkeep of the fort had taken a toll on the Bates family's finances after more than three decades of hard-scrabble living and diplomacy. Roy stayed out there so long because there wasn't money available to pay staff. Even in his old age, he was too proud to loosen his grip on the project that he'd spent a huge percentage of his life building. "My father would never, ever back down from anything. If he decided to do something, he was going to do it. He would've stayed there until he died if I didn't do anything," Michael said. With this in mind, the Sealanders invited HavenCo out for a visit in the fall of 1999.

Sean Hastings chartered a helicopter to Sealand in November so he and Jo could meet the Bates family and take a tour of the facility. He saw that the server room had been meticulously cleaned and repainted a soft pink, created by dropping food dye into white paint. Hastings took as a good omen that Sealand had a functional TV on hand—not because he wanted to watch TV but because the Sealanders were using it without paying the appropriate usage fees to the BBC. "Reading about something—even seeing photographs—it's just not the same as laying eyes on it. A tiny bastion of freedom in the middle of a cold sea, surrounded by large socialist nations in every direction.

I wanted to ask for political asylum and move in that very day," Hastings wrote.

The group hammered out a plan. The Sealanders would continue to provide security and logistics for the platform while HavenCo would handle the tech side of things. Hands were shaken, congratulations were in order, and the Sealanders began getting the platform ready to host a high-tech informational fortress. HavenCo, Ltd. was incorporated in Anguilla and then Cyprus, a country similarly known for facilitating anonymity in business.

Back in the US, Lackey and Hastings began raising money for HavenCo. Much of the first $1 million came from heavy hitters of the early internet age. Avi Freedman, a developer who always seemed to be wearing shorts, sandals, and a Hawaiian shirt regardless of the weather, put in $500,000, while Joichi Ito, a thirty-four-year-old tech entrepreneur, invested $200,000. Sameer Parekh, a techie and libertarian newspaper publisher the group met at the Anguillan cryptography conference, became chairman of the board. (Parekh thought Hastings's "toxic barge" idea was so funny that he registered the domain name "toxicbarge.com.") A further $400,000 came from a group of anonymous donors. All were advocates of the same techno-libertarian principles. Of this, the Bates family was rumored to have received an initial very helpful sum of a quarter-million dollars to let HavenCo use the fort. "Until HavenCo came along, there wasn't much money about and that was a big thing for me," Michael said. "HavenCo provided some money, and I gave it all to my dad."

The investors were cautious about truly believing in Sealand's sovereignty, but there was argument enough to be made for its independence, and a precedent-setting internet business might be key to establishing this status for good.

"Personally I was as interested in testing what governments would do as we started ramping up," Ito said. "I don't think anyone believed that it was absolutely a sovereign territory, but they definitely had some good claims."

Hastings said he knew that HavenCo was going to be treading on some touchy ground but was prepared to face the consequences that might result, including being exiled from the United States. "If this was just about secure colocation, I wouldn't be investing," he said. "There is idealism involved. This is not strictly economic."

Hastings and Lackey began making plans to move to Sealand full time.

## THE HAVENCO EXPERIMENT

On that forbidding day in March when Garfinkel visited Sealand and Ryan Lackey set foot on the principality for the first time*, the boat was also ferrying tools, equipment, and a larger cache of food than usual on account of the beefed-up security and the influx of people who would be setting up HavenCo's operations.

The principality's south leg was to be the HavenCo HQ. One of the leg's rooms would hold the servers, processors, and memory banks, while another room would function as the Network Operations Center, or NOC, where Lackey would oversee the workings of HavenCo from behind a desk with at least four monitors.

Customer costs for hosting on Sealand weren't cheap, but they weren't outrageous either. Customers would pay around $1,500 for a dedicated server, $750 in startup costs, and between $300 and $750 per month for colocation services and 128 kbps of bandwidth, which at the time was equivalent to a decent home internet connection. The satellite connection would be established in May 2000, with the microwave connection and cable slated to be put into place by September.

HavenCo's only responsibility was hosting material; policing the information that may get people in trouble in their home country wasn't their concern. Lackey anticipated that the majority of the customers would be hosting porn, which would be good for both HavenCo and its other clients because more traffic would help obscure the traffic overall. "Our customers don't want to break the law, they want a different set of laws they can comply with," he said.

Client data would also be protected by HavenCo's rigorous physical security. The four guards would carry machine guns and the rooms holding the servers would be filled with nitrogen gas and accessible

---

* While this was Lackey's first visit to the platform, he had previously met Michael on his way to a rave in Hungary.

only with breathing equipment. In the event that an unstoppable raid was imminent, the servers would be unplugged, smashed, and thrown into the sea. Customers would be provided with stock servers installed by HavenCo that would be assembled on site and scanned for spyware, but customers would never be allowed to access the physical equipment themselves or even set foot on the principality. In the event that the UK shut off Sealand's internet, HavenCo had numerous backup plans.

"With three satellite connections, many transit providers, and lots of peering, it's going to be very hard to shut HavenCo down," Freedman said.

Even if a country was so pissed off at HavenCo that it did decide to attack it, such an attack likely wouldn't be possible. Any attack mounted on Sealand would be done so in close proximity to a number of other nations who would not stand for warships passing through their waters or launching attacks from somewhere on their shores. Attackers would have to contend with the complete PR catastrophe that would befall a major country which invaded the world's smallest country over a free-speech issue, Lackey said, and he couldn't imagine any elected government taking that risk. Hostile interactions with neighboring countries would presumably be resolved in court, the proceedings of which "would constitute further evidence of recognition as a nation, and strengthen our case in the world court," according to HavenCo's business plan.

At the very least, even if Sealand was attacked and destroyed by terrorists or another nation, such an event wouldn't violate HavenCo's commitment to security, as the data they want to protect would presumably be destroyed along with the platform, thereby keeping the authorities from seeing it. "Basically our security model is that we can be destroyed. It wouldn't be that hard to physically destroy all of Sealand…if I weren't involved with HavenCo I could probably (destroy) it," Lackey said.

Everyone at HavenCo was optimistic about the popularity of the service. An estimated nineteen employees were going to be needed within a year. Revenue would be $65 million in three years. Equity was split between the royal family, the HavenCo founders, and various advisers. An IPO was expected on the distant horizon. The group envisioned more facilities opening in permissive locations as HavenCo's reputation grew.

"Initially, we were motivated primarily by libertarian principle, but that *includes* a desire to make money," Lackey said. "The business would not be possible, nor would we pursue it, if it did not hold the promise of being wildly profitable if successful."

The first HavenCo data haven opened for business on Sealand in June 2000.

## LILBURNE-BYFORD'S REVENGE

Ryan Lackey fell into a routine on the principality as he attended to the needs of HavenCo's clients, which included gambling websites, groups hosting sensitive stock market investment information, websites for the makers of unauthorized computer add-ons, and the website of the government of Tibet.

Every day Lackey would wake up in his bedroom in the North tower, ascend the ladder to Sealand's small kitchen, pour himself a bowl of cereal, and go to work in the other tower. Lackey sometimes slept at his workstation—a less-hazardous choice than trying to climb into and out of concrete rooms on narrow ladders.* There was a weight bench and a library of DVDs and cheap paperbacks for breaks between work, but Lackey's routine didn't leave a whole lot of time for activities outside the confines of the tower.

Garfinkel's article about HavenCo and Sealand adorned the cover of the July 2000 issue of *Wired*. The story, "one of the greatest pieces of tech journalism of all time," was a sensation, and HavenCo suddenly found itself inundated with thousands of requests for interviews and TV appearances. The interest was encouraging but incredibly distracting. At one point Lackey was doing all of HavenCo's accounting, billing, and sales work alongside taking care of all of the "technical stuff" necessary to make the project work. "We had so much press inquiry that nobody did any other work. Every day people would fly

---

* Being aware of what you were doing on Sealand is always paramount. As one reporter noted, a wind generator sat above a stairway that sometimes decapitated birds with its blades.

out on a helicopter and talk to the press and go back and go to sleep, and that's it. I was the only person doing anything other than talking to the press," he said.

The publicity also drew official statements from the UK and US governments about the data haven. A Home Office spokesperson said that the UK doesn't recognize Sealand as an independent state, and that if they set up an internet host in UK waters they might be required to let authorities view this data. The US government was a little more lax about the concept but still paying attention. "Right now, we aren't even concerned with something like Sealand because they are not representing any kind of a threat," State Department official Susan Elbow said at the time. "It would not be an issue for us unless, for example, they are hooking up with Osama bin Laden."

HavenCo had to contend with regular tech problems on top of all of this. Denial-of-Service attacks by mischievous netizens meant that clients lost connectivity for many days at a time, and then the company scheduled to provide their fiber optic infrastructure went out of business in the dotcom crash and cut out connectivity for two months straight. The company had a few thousand customers waiting to sign up when the company opened, but this potentiality was greatly reduced by the lack of internet.

Not only was Lackey working hard to get HavenCo up and running but he was doing so on a fairly inhospitable environment. Ferrying out food, equipment, and diesel was expensive (chartering a helicopter cost around $5,000 a trip), and they had to upgrade the winches on the platform to pull up heavier loads. Eating some variant of corned beef hash or rice pudding gets kind of old after a few days, he admitted. "We have hundreds of people send in resumes," Lackey said. "But it's hard to get people to stay once they show up, because then they realize they're stuck here for a couple of weeks at a time." One employee lasted only a single day. ("I have the internet, so I don't care," Lackey said.)

The Hastingses were afflicted with a similar sort of cabin fever. Despite the success of bringing their beloved dog to the fort for company, the pair decided they'd had enough and left the company in mid-2000.* "People that were willing to come work out there were crazy people. There's a reason people do this, and that's because they don't fit into society," Sean Hastings said.

But things were looking up. Many clients were supportive for ideological reasons and were perhaps a little more forgiving of the start-up's missteps. The two-month internet outage only cost them around a quarter of their accounts. Plus, they got a 25-gallon-per-hour water maker, which allowed the HavenCo staff to take showers.

The business worked out well for Sealand's sovereigns as well. In addition to Roy's bout on the fort with delirium-inducing malaria, life on the fort proved unsuited for Joan's worsening arthritis, and she had long decamped from the concrete and steel enclave to their home in Essex. Thanks to the cash influx for leasing Sealand, they were able retire to the perpetually sunny beaches of Spain. It was a welcome change, and one they could accept with pride. It seemed that Roy and Joan were poised to pass the Sealandic torch to a new generation of iconoclasts.

By 2001, HavenCo was a "reasonably successful company," Lackey said. "It looked like in a year or two it would go quite well." Around this time, however, a surprisingly vitriolic anti-Sealand publication came into being. Called *Rough Sands Gazette*, the e-newspaper was almost comical in its hyperbolic opposition to the "long-running Bates Family farce and con-game." Articles such as "Why Roy and Michael Bates are irresponsible thugs" were commonplace, and the newspaper attempted to sound the alarm that the UK had terrorists squatting on a "military base" right on Britain's shores. At one point the *Gazette* even published Michael's home address in England.

Sealand has certainly had its detractors over the years—check the comments on online articles discussing Sealand's sovereignty; people get disproportionately angry about even a lighthearted look at the whole situation—but it was perplexing as to where an entire newspaper dedicated to trashing Sealand's name had come from. At least until one spotted the bylines of Genie Baskir and Paul John

---

* Michael Bates recounts the dog transporting operation in his memoir *Holding the Fort*, along with many other adventures and misadventures from the HavenCo years, including some endearing impressions of life in America.

Lilburne-Byford, the radio producers from MPLX who had been embroiled in a legal battle over the radio ship registered in Sealand they had purchased from American DJ Allan Weiner.

Following the investigation into the *Sarah*'s true background, the MPLX personnel tried to obtain compensation for the ship from Weiner. The suit developed into a ten-year legal battle that only hardened Baskir and Lilburne-Byford's cynical appraisal of the British government. The *Rough Sands Gazette* authors were stunned by the HavenCo scheme on Sealand and were appalled that the UK seemed to be encouraging it by not shutting it down. They hoped that by advocating to the public about the problems they'd had with Weiner and Sealand, the public would turn on the principality and that "Roy and Michael Bates may at long last be facing the beginning of the end in their saga of lies and violence."

In Lilburne-Byford's suit to gain compensation for the boat registered in Sealand, he had to prove in court that Sealand was part of the UK. He put together a document outlining twelve offenses that the Sealanders had committed that violated the Firearms Acts of 1968–1997 (evidence of which was recorded for a TV documentary) and cited the statement given under oath in US court by Department of Trade and Industry inspector James Murphy in which he delineates reasons why Sealand isn't a country.* The "Demand for Essex Police to Enforce the Laws of the United Kingdom—Arrest Roy Bates" was presented to the Chelmsford Magistrates' Court on October 5, 2000, resulting in an opinion that was not favorable to the principality.

"The court ruled that Sealand, Roughs Tower, is part of the UK and come specifically under the jurisdiction of the Southend Magistrates' Court," Lilburne-Byford said. "We will now be taking our case further and bringing more information to the court."

According to a newspaper account at the time, the Sealanders were "shocked to hear a court's decision that their 'country' is not a principality."

"We accept British territorial waters go round our territorial waters, but that does not make us part of the UK. If Britain imposed itself on

---

* However, they would later write, this inspector was apparently very untrustworthy. He "was a living pun," they wrote, nothing he "ever attempted was true and correct, he bungled everything—including his Sworn Statement of 1989 for the Official Solicitor."

us in that way it would infringe basic human rights," Michael Bates said. "How many other countries around the world could just take over other smaller lands simply by extending their waters from three to twelve miles? You cannot arbitrarily take action like that—it is a ridiculous suggestion."

The court threw out one of the charges against Sealand relating to its use as a data haven because Lilburne-Byford presented incorrect information to the court, and the British government didn't make any moves to get the Sealanders off the fort. But in the general interest of making things difficult for the Bates family, the petition was a success. Ryan Lackey became aware of the Allan Weiner/Sealandic issue and resulting lawsuit through the *Gazette* website, as the proceedings hadn't been well publicized until then. The issue stoked Lackey's growing distrust of the Bates family, and the *Gazette* authors watched gleefully as optimism about HavenCo started to wane.

## A DATA HAVEN'S DEMISE

Michael and Lackey had long been butting heads, with the demeanor of a no-nonsense sea salt clashing with the dubious social skills stereotypically associated with computer geeks. Lackey considered Michael boorish while Michael felt Lackey was condescending and didn't have a practical appreciation for what the project actually entailed. When a dispute arose, the interactions could be downright excruciating. "It came to the point that I would make him come back when he [sulked away] and stand in front of me like a child until he answered my questions clearly and concisely," Michael recalled.

In fall 2001, the Bates family brought in their own technical adviser to help them with the project. The adviser nixed a cryptocurrency idea because it seemed like it could be easily used to launder money. Lackey felt that the adviser had no idea what he was talking about and balked at the idea that some of HavenCo's sensitive information, such as payroll records and personnel files, would be stored on a regular desktop computer in England. In the end, the Bateses took the advice of the adviser against Lackey. They were also upset by Lackey's secrecy, as he set up various services for other clients that the Bateses didn't know about or approve.

Tensions continued until May 2002, when the proverbial shit really hit the fan. An early progenitor of streaming video named Alex Tan contacted HavenCo about restarting a "blatant pirate" movie-streaming site previously hosted in Iran. The idea was to take legally purchased DVDs and rent streaming rights to viewers while ensuring that no movie could be rented by more than one person at a time.

According to Lackey, the idea "might have been legal under Sealand law because we could have written it," and the proceeds from such a scheme would have paid off the company's debt and paid their expenses "4-5 times over." But Roy Bates said Sealand had a duty to the world community, and he certainly didn't want to get embroiled in an expensive scandal like the Napster debacle in the US.

To Michael, it was simply a matter of common sense and legal practicality that there be some limits on what HavenCo hosted. At one point someone wanted to host a website to auction off human organs. "You think, maybe there's a place for that, but then you think a little further and you hear about the execution rates going up in China where they sell the body parts," he said. "[Y]ou have to have certain levels of where you say no."

In fact, both the UK and the European Union passed legislation around this time that seemed specifically tailored to address loophole-exploiting internet endeavors like HavenCo. The UK's Regulation of Investigatory Powers Act of 2000, similar in scope to the USA PATRIOT Act, gave the British government the power to monitor electronic communication, while the European Union passed European Copyright Directive in 2001, which shored up copyright law. Data hosted in Sealand but accessed in other countries meant the data was subject to those countries' laws, obviating the need for offshore hosting.

But to Lackey, the disinterest in pushing the boundaries of these kinds of laws was something close to philosophical cowardice. If they didn't believe they could host this thing, he wondered, did they really believe in Sealand's sovereignty? "They were very good at trying to simulate a real country there because they acted like politicians," he said.

From the UK National Archives, as catalogued in Turner, The Maunsell Sea Forts

Roughs Tower, the fort that would become the Principality of Sealand, was built on the wharfs at Gravesend as a midocean fort to shoot down incoming Nazi bombers. The fort's unconventional design was the brainchild of Guy Anson Maunsell, who was known for his unusual, though utilitarian, concrete structure. Here, the ready-made lining of one of the seven rooms in each leg of the tower is lowered into place.

From the UK National Archives, as catalogued in Turner, The Maunsell Sea Forts

Roughs Tower was towed to its present location in 1942. The tower was built in its entirety on land on top of pontoons, which were then filled with water to sink the bottom and anchor the fort. Men were aboard the fort as it sank.

Penelope "Penny" Bates was seventeen when Sealand was declared independent in 1967. She spent a lot of time during her teen years helping her parents' pirate radio station that preceded Sealand. No stranger to the perils of life on the fort, she and her brother Michael sometimes had to eat biscuits they made from flour and distilled seawater.

Michael Bates, shown here as a teenager, dropped out of school at age fourteen to help his parents with life on the fort. He was often left alone as the only guard in the middle of the sea and was tasked with shooting or throwing bombs at any invaders that attempted to take over his family's hard-fought possession.

Penny Bates posed for a photographer on Sealand for a newspaper story in 1966. Roy Bates said he didn't mind Penny showing off the pistols, but she should have known better than to keep her finger on the trigger when handling the guns. (Note the Molotov cocktails in the background.)

Penny hugs her mother Joan Bates, Roy's partner in crime—literally—for sixty years. Joan was no stranger to the intrigue that came with holding the fort, managing the radio station and wily DJs that preceded Sealand, and sleeping with a .38 under her pillow once the micronation got up and running as its own national territory.

Michael, Joan, and Penny Bates share a cup of tea on Sealand in the late 1960s. Joan said that while life as a maritime monarch could be challenging, she really enjoyed and appreciated the time it allowed her to spend with her family.

Roy and Joan met at the Kursaal Dance Hall in 1948 and were married six weeks later. The two embarked on many adventures, including importing rationed poultry, running a rubber swim fin factory, and harvesting white weed from the ocean for flower displays. The only time Joan vetoed the plans was when Roy suggesting moving to Kenya during the Mau-Mau uprising.

Roy and Joan would often do interviews about Sealand together, explaining the rationale for their unique quest and rebuffing doubts about the legitimacy of their crowns. The couple retired to Spain in the late 1990s and then returned to England to be with their families as they entered the twilight of their lives.

Roy and Michael, looking indescribably cool in the 1970s, were always looking for ways to build up Sealand and increase its financial and cultural cachet. The battles for the fort of the 1960s prepared them for the rogues and shadowy characters who would later associate themselves with the principality.

The Bates family raises the Sealandic herald aboard the principality in the early 1970s. Sealand became their adopted homeland and a point of family pride as its renown grew after the declaration of independence. Michael estimates he's spent roughly twenty cumulative years of his life aboard the fort.

Many people were eager to become Sealanders, including Roland Teschner and Walter Mierisch, two Germans who traveled to Essex to seek out Roy Bates after their plans to hitchhike to Namibia fell through. The two would spend years building up the fort and repairing machinery, their long stints aboard the fort broken up only by mandatory military service in their homeland.

Visitors are only able to access Sealand by helicopter or boat—if the Sealanders permit it. A mechanized winch pulls visitors up from the deck of a boat while a large mast has to be taken down for helicopters to land. In 1979, a helicopter delivered the bride to the fort for Sealand's first wedding.

## LOG EXTRACT

Mon. Stn. QTH ........ Date 3-9-197 ..... For attention of: R.T.D. I.I.2.

| TIME G.M.T. | FREQ. MHz | MODE OF EMSSN. | STATION CALL SIGNS | | BEARING | | OTHER INFORMATION (TEXT, DIALLET, NAME, LOCATION, CONDITIONS ETC.) |
|---|---|---|---|---|---|---|---|
| | | | TO | FROM | QTE | CLASS | |
| 1010 | 2420 | A3 3/3 | SEALAND | | | | VOICE OF H.H. PRINCE ROY (ROY BATES) - YES FINE DARLING - HE DOESN'T START U SAY? - YES. BATTERIES - JUST CLICKING WAS IT - ALRIGHT, THE BATTERIES ARE FLAT - NOT CHARGING - YOU'VE GOT JUMP LEADS - YOU'VE GOT IT STARTED, BUT NO CHARGE - I DON'T KNOW WHETHER IT'LL GO IN THE CAR - THE BOOT DOESN'T OPEN RIGHT UP WELL, LET THEM COME AHEAD - I'M GETTING FED UP WITH THEM - LET HIM COME - I SHALL KEEP HIM AS A GUEST AS WELL. IF THATS HIS BLOODY ATTITUDE, DEAR OH DEAR - HE'S TALKING ABSOLUTE TRIPE - LET HIM MEET ME OUT HERE - HE'LL GET A HOLIDAY AS WELL - THEY MUST PAY THE FINES FOR THE DAMAGE - YES DARLING I HEAR OK - I WILL DO - HE'S GOT TO PAY HIS FINES - HE'S DONE A LOT OF DAMAGE - THEY'VE GOT TO PAY THOSE FINES - SOMEBODY'S GOT TO PAY IT - OR WE GET GUARANTEE OF IT - AND THEY'VE GOT TO GIVE ME SEVERAL OTHER GUARANTEES TO - |
| 1021 | " | " | " | | | | |

Signature

The Bates family continued to use unauthorized radio equipment in the 1970s as a way to communicate between the UK and Sealand, so British authorities set up a sting to catch them using emergency frequencies for their own communications. Government agents' daily call logs often recorded mundane details such as grocery lists and the small talk between family members.

The first set of Sealand stamps were issued in 1969 and feature famous explorers. The idea was to fly letters with the stamps to Belgium, where they could be slipped into the postal bloodstream. Sealand has since issued stamps and coins with beautiful designs that can be purchased by collectors through Sealand's website.

Alexander Gottfried Achenbach was the mover and shaker of a shady group of Germans and Dutchmen who attempted to take over the Principality of Sealand in 1978. A professional confidence man and raconteur, Achenbach would be in and out of legal trouble for years and launched Sealand's government-in-exile, which continues to create strange problems for the principality to the present day.

The Bates family welcomed the third generation of Sealanders starting in 1986. Roy and Joan were the smitten grandparents of James, the first of Lorraine and Michael Bates's three children. The kids spent a lot of time on Sealand growing up, though Michael was a bit more circumspect than Roy about letting them handle weapons.

Though conditions on the fort can be miserable, the Bates family and associates steadily transformed Roughs Tower into a homey castle-state. In addition to the sleeping quarters, storerooms, gym, and chapel, the living quarters boast all the amenities of home, including a full kitchen, a small library, and an office.

Athletes from many sports have competed on behalf of Sealand, in many cases competing on the global stage and setting world records. Slader Oviatt, hailing from Canada, carried the Sealand flag to the summit of Muztagh Ata, a 25,000-foot mountain in China, in 2004.

All of these issues suddenly came to light in August 2003 at Defcon 11, one of the most prominent hacker conventions, when Lackey gave a talk entitled "HavenCo: what went wrong." Standing in front of a crowd and wrestling with a troublesome projector, Lackey spoke at length about his data haven experience and laughed nervously as he revealed the startling truth: the technology, the machine guns, the room filled with nitrogen, the multitudinous customers—all of it was extremely exaggerated, if not completely made up. Observers were caught unawares by these revelations, as up to this point it seemed like HavenCo was resolutely fulfilling its libertarian quest.

Lackey said that journalists who visited the fort were shown a "demo room" of equipment purportedly representative of the huge network stored below, but the reality was that racks of servers put up for display were in fact HavenCo's actual servers, and the only ones they had at that. The number of customers was exaggerated to keep up appearances, with the company having no more than a dozen clients, most of which were online gambling groups. HavenCo appeared to be profitable in 2001 because they weren't counting the substantial bills that would come due in the future, he said.

Lackey attributed most of the hype to credulous tech journalists and the lack of any deep examination into what was actually going on. Why this scrutiny wasn't applied, he wasn't sure. The single cable running along the floor into what was supposedly the server room, powering the servers and the cooling and heating operations of the power-hungry machines, should have been a clue that things weren't what they seemed.

Lackey and the Bates family ultimately agreed that he would decamp from Sealand and HavenCo a few months before but continue assisting in an advisory capacity. However, Lackey soon found that the Sealanders had cut all ties with him and locked him out of his former company, supposedly refusing to even give back his laptop and the money he was owed. Hence, the scene with Lackey holding up the Sealand passport and saying it cost him more than $200,000 and three years of his life.

The Defcon audience laughed when someone asked Lackey if he'd thought about mounting an armed insurrection on Sealand.

Lackey said he'd considered it for a few minutes but then realized he'd be stuck out on the fort if he succeeded.*

HavenCo was still up and running at the time Lackey was giving his presentation, but ownership had changed hands and the venture was being overseen by the Bates family and their adviser. It offered hosting services but with a more delineated acceptable use policy, rules that made its services no more or less restrictive than the average Western country. Now owned by people who didn't have the technical knowhow to keep it afloat, HavenCo floundered and finally went offline in 2008.

Nevertheless, everyone involved seems to have been able to appreciate the wild adventure for what it was—an experiment at the forefront of cyberethics in the digital age, even if it did cost them their investment.

"The venture was a really interesting idea, but it was early, the team was not experienced enough, and it was a really hard problem. Unfortunately, the project ended before we were able to test some of the more interesting questions in court or on the battlefield," investor Joichi Ito reflected. "While it was ultimately unsuccessful, the project was possibly the closest any group has ever gotten to creating a jurisdictionally independent data haven."

HavenCo briefly resurfaced throughout the 2010s and promised to once again become a player in cybersecurity. This iteration would not offer the services of a data haven but rather the tools needed to

---

* Lackey was set for more adventures in inhospitable places, as he eventually set up shop in war-torn Iraq putting together internet services for the US military and government contractors under the moniker Blue Iraq. Going about his business required wearing body armor and a Kevlar helmet, and he was frequently flown via helicopter to set up internet at obscure forward-operating bases subject to insurgent attack. But this only meant his services were in high demand.

"There's sort of a dark calculus when people are afraid," Lackey said. "Prices for everything go up. And if you understand the risk better than they do, you can price that into everything."

The lack of banks meant that he was paid in cash, and he'd have to catch a ride to a bank in Dubai to deposit his suitcases full of money. "After enough close calls with explosions and helicopters, and missing the Bay Area, I moved back to work on a more "conventional" tech startup," he said. He has since been involved in numerous cyber projects that align with his ideology and continues to do so today, still clad in all black.

better protect one's privacy online. The revamped HavenCo would help users set up a VPN, store encrypted information in the cloud, and store data in back-up servers on Sealand, which they maintained would be completely inaccessible through any means but physical invasion.

According to an announcement on Sealand's website, "You don't expect every letter you send in the post to be opened prior to arrival, so why is it acceptable to expect less privacy from actions you take online?" Avi Freedman was once again involved with the project, but HavenCo 3.0 struggled to get off the ground. Each member of the team found themselves spread a little too thin, and so despite the enthusiasm and meetings that pushed the idea forward, HavenCo disappeared for good around 2013.

The micronation is still full of mementos from the HavenCo days, including fliers taped to walls or tacked to corkboard announcing upcoming meetings in 2003 and an extensive intra-Sealand phone system that facilitated communication between every room of the fort. The Bates family is still in regular contact with Freedman and meet up with him for dinner whenever they're in the same area.

As for the Bates family, they take the rise and fall of HavenCo in stride as well. It was sometimes difficult to appreciate how young the HavenCo crew was when they started the business, Michael said. But Sealand came out no worse for the wear, and the reinvigorated interest in the micronation would lead to a newfound prominence and more exciting adventures overall.

"HavenCo ended up owing millions of dollars to my family. But hey, it was a fascinating project where I met some very interesting people and I have no regrets," Michael said.

# CHAPTER 14

## SEALAND IN THE NEW MILLENNIUM

*"The important thing in life is not the triumph but the struggle. The essential thing is not to have conquered but to have fought well."*

—Pierre de Coubertin

The ladders going between the floors of the former Roughs Tower still have the same wooden stairs they've had since the fort was built, worn and polished by countless boots over decades of use. But that the ladders are the only way of transport between floors (aside from the long out-of-commission lift shaft that is now a treacherous hole) underscores how claustrophobic it must have been for the more than one hundred marines who lived and worked on the fort at a time. As the ladders are tilted at seventy-five-degree angles and are little more than two feet wide, it's stressful imagining what it would have been like in an emergency situation where dozens of men were pushing and jostling to ascend them at the same time.

Sleeping on the fort must have been filled with perpetual unease as well. The bedrooms were sandwiched between the generators on the top level and the fuel and ammunition stored below, so if anything happened either above or below the sleeping quarters, the marines were, in essence, sealed in an underwater concrete mausoleum.*

Fortunately, no super-serious injuries have happened on Sealand over the many years of its existence, but in June 2006, a caretaker on the fort got a sense of the aching helplessness the men must have felt when they found the fort under attack.

---

* Air flow is always a preeminent concern even in nonemergency situations. Today, ribbed white tubing like that used for clothes dryer vents snakes down the disused lift shaft and provides ventilation to each floor.

## SEALAND, SEALAND, BURNING BRIGHT

At around 11:30 a.m. on Friday, June 23, 2006, pedestrians and fishermen on the shores of Felixstowe and Harwich saw a great plume of black smoke appear on the horizon. People stopped what they were doing and shielded their eyes with their hands. The immediate assumption was that something had gone awry on one of the many fishing vessels or sailboats. A few people even pulled out binoculars and telescopes to get a better sense of what was going on.

It turned out the source of the smoke was the infamous sea fort. Sealand was burning, and when its plight became known, firefighting boats from at least six jurisdictions sped out to sea to take on the blaze.

Up on Sealand, a watchman collegially known as "Pecker" had been attending to his duties as a caretaker when one of the generators suddenly came apart and exploded. Pecker grabbed a fire extinguisher and ran toward the south end of the micronation to see what was going on, but batteries and gas cans began exploding as the fire spread, driving him back. A few more explosions rocked the fort and the huge plume of smoke escaped to the heavens. The fire spread from the generator to the country's living room and threatened to engulf the entire nation in flames.

Pecker frantically looked over the side as the prospect of being stuck on the burning micronation became more serious. He knew that a plunge into the sea carried a tremendous risk of breaking bones and then drowning, and it was beyond the abilities of most mortals to swim seven miles to shore. He looked back and forth between the smoke and the water, aimed the fire extinguisher, and tried the piddling foam to no effect.

A helicopter carrying rescuers from the National Maritime Incident Response Group soon thrummed in the sky. The chopper made a few circles above the principality but determined that the fire was too serious to make a safe landing. Part of the tarmac had even melted from the heat. The pilot gulped as he saw Pecker frantically waving his arms to let them know he was there. Pecker was pulled up into the helicopter, hacking and wheezing. His face was red and black from the fire and smoke, and he was rushed off to Ipswich Hospital. The rescue chopper then returned to the fort, hovering nearby in case it was needed.

The firefighters decided that since there was no further risk to life, it wasn't worth endangering their safety by lowering themselves onto the fort. Instead, a Felixstowe port fire tug began pumping ocean water up onto the principality to combat the blaze, in the process punching out the windows in the living room and inundating Sealand with so much water that it began filling the tower's legs. The blaze was brought to a manageable level a little after 3:00 p.m., and Pecker was released from the hospital the following day, a little shaken up but no worse for the wear.

Michael was in Spain visiting his parents when he got the news from the Coast Guard that his entire country had almost exploded. He caught a flight back as soon as he could and boated out to the platform with his sons Liam and James. As there was nobody there to hoist them up, they had to ascend it the old-fashioned way, using a ladder hung precariously on the edge of a beam. Just as Roy looked on in worry as Michael climbed onto Fort Knock John Forty-one years earlier, so too did Michael watch his son legitimately risk his life clambering up to the deck. A cheer went up from the boat when James pulled his legs safely over the side, and Michael let out a huge fatherly sigh of relief. The remaining Bateses were spared the climb themselves when James lowered down the winch.

The Sealanders weren't prepared for what awaited: The generator was destroyed, smoke had damaged everything, and the living quarters were utterly soaked. There was broken glass everywhere. Charred debris smoldered and released a toxic chemical stench. "There is an awful lot of damage. It is worse than we expected," Michael said. It was truly heartbreaking.

The prospect of getting the country back on its feet was beyond daunting. Michael estimated the damage to be around half a million pounds, and as the principality was not insured, they'd have to foot the bill themselves. Moreover, there was a strong possibility that the family would be responsible for the cost of sending out firefighters, adding thousands of more pounds to the bill. The father and his sons kicked at bits and pieces of the wreckage and Michael sat on a gunwale to collect his thoughts.

"After the fire it was the only time we sort of said, 'It might be time,'" James said.

But the pessimistic appraisal turned a little more positive on a subsequent trip to survey the damage. Instead of being overwhelmed at the damage, caretaker Mike Barrington was apparently eager to get to work.

"We were out there looking around and Mike said, 'Oh shit, my emergency mattress is wet!' and he started wringing it out. We thought, 'Well, he must be staying!'" James recalled.

Fortunately, the generator had blown up at a good time. "It was summer, thank god—all of the windows were blown out but the weather was nice," Barrington said. From then on, the drive to rebuild was resolute.

The Sealanders began the slow process shuttling back and forth between England and Sealand to clean up the mess. A fundraiser was launched to help pay for some of the repairs. "Save Sealand" T-shirts were produced, and supporters could even buy damaged bolts from the principality for £3.99. A one-mile exclusion zone was declared so as to prevent interference with the cleanup efforts.

In November the Sealanders caught another break when the various agencies involved in fighting the blaze decided not to charge the Bates family for their services. A spokesperson from the Ministry of Defence said that the British government accepts responsibility for search and rescue operations irrespective of the nationality or status of the people they are helping. "It is not general practice for the [Maritime and Coastguard Agency] to attempt recovery of costs following a search and rescue (saving of life) incident," he said.

To Michael, this was a show of comity between the nations. "I think it is a nice example of *entente cordiale*, one country helping another. We have helped the Coast Guard many times in the past through our lookouts," he said.

Within a year of the fire, after much backbreaking labor and hefting charred bits of metal and destroyed mementos away from the fort, the principality was back to normal. Taking care of the fort was a lot for one family to handle, and perhaps this is why the principality soon went up for sale through a Spanish real estate agency.

The asking price: one billion dollars.

## SEALAND FOR SALE

Michael had been informally chatting with an agent in Granada, Spain, not long after the fire damage had been repaired, to see what he could learn about selling the principality. But the discussion suddenly took on a life of its own when the real estate agency, InmoNaranja, announced it had a country for sale on its website.

Michael returned home from running some errands after the news broke and found reporters camped out on his front lawn. The news that the principality was up for sale (for hundreds of thousands of dollars per square foot) brought more reporters than any event in the nation's history, including teams who flew in from opposite sides of the world to cover the story. The disruption was annoying, but the possibility that someone might actually be interested in paying €750 million for the fort was enticing, and Michael figured he might as well go along with the listing. "My father is eighty-five and my mother in her late seventies and I'm fifty-four," he said at the time. "I believe the project needs a bit of rejuvenation."

Gabriel Medina Vilchez, the head honcho at InmoNaranja, was experienced with this kind of thing. He had begun selling islands the year before, including some in his portfolio off Nicaragua, Fiji, and Ghana. He had approached the principality about the sale due to client requests. "All those who asked about the islands commented, half-jokingly, if it would be possible to become kings of them and create their own nation," he said. "So we thought of places to fulfill this desire and found the closest thing to a country."

Sealand's sovereignty was its selling point, of course—an ineluctable quality that evades financial quantification. As the Sealanders did not have an official deed to the place, the arrangement was to transfer the sovereignty of the platform—not the platform itself—with the new tenants contractually obligated to abide by the Sealandic constitution. "Technically, it's not a sale, it's a transfer, the government, the history, the concept of Sealand is transferred," Medina said. "It is a difficult transaction, the economic issue on the one hand, but there is also an inescapable condition of not attacking British interests."

Michael said that potential buyers would have to be vetted, noting that he wouldn't want to sell it to a "Blofeld-type person out of a Bond film, with a dodgy suit on stroking a white cat…but possibly somebody that doesn't want somebody looking over his shoulder the whole time with his financial dealings, or maybe some wealthy Russian who doesn't want a radioactive isotope dropped in his cornflakes when he's not looking."

An announcement about the sale went up on the principality's website, and Michael took to pitching the place himself. "Most places in the Western world with a sea view do get a really good price, don't they?" Michael said in an interview with Canadian VJ George Stroumboulopoulos. "The biggest swimming pool in the world [is] right outside your door."

As the Bates family waited patiently to field offers, they also began receiving a few intriguing inquiries about using the fort for other reasons, including a few individuals hoping to be granted political asylum there.

## HACKER HAVEN REDUX?

Numerous branches of the US military were put on high alert in February 2001, and then again in March 2002. Operating system files from nine computers had been illegally accessed and deleted, taking down army computer networks and computers at a naval station used to monitor the location and battle-readiness of naval ships. A vague threat also appeared on a military website. "Your security is crap," it said. The events would come to be called the United States' largest military computer breach, and it was pulled off by a thirty-five-year-old Scottish systems administrator named Gary McKinnon from his bedroom at his girlfriend's aunt's house in London.

The ensuing investigation revealed that McKinnon's hack accessed fifty-three army computers, twenty-six navy computers, sixteen NASA computers, and one computer each at the Department of Defense and the Air Force. McKinnon also copied data onto his own computer, including operating system files with encrypted passwords. The military estimated it was going to cost $700,000 to clean up the mess he made.

McKinnon's hack wasn't malicious but rather a fact-finding mission. "I knew that governments suppressed antigravity, UFO-related technologies, free energy or what they call zero-point energy," he told *Wired* in 2006. "This should not be kept hidden from the public when pensioners can't pay their fuel bills."

McKinnon was arrested in March 2002 for the breach, but it was determined he wouldn't face any charges in the UK, since no British computers were involved in the crime. He was, however, indicted in a Virginia court, and the United States requested his extradition in October 2004. He was facing seventy years in prison and around $2 million in fines.

McKinnon and his legal team attempted to resist the extradition, but matters became even more complicated when a treaty went into effect allowing Britain to extradite US citizens with little evidence they'd committed a crime. McKinnon purchased potassium chloride with the intention of committing suicide if the extradition was put into motion. He had seemingly nowhere to turn, which is why he turned to the Principality of Sealand for help in early 2007. The news was surprising to Michael, and it was already the second such controversial request that had popped up so far that year.

Earlier in 2007, infamous Swedish torrent-sharing site The Pirate Bay began talks with the royal family about hosting their servers on Sealand. The Swedish government raided The Pirate Bay and confiscated their equipment the previous spring under pressure from the Motion Picture Association of America and the US government (who threatened sanctions against Sweden unless action was taken), bringing the site down for three days. Though InmoNaranja was listing the country for one billion dollars, the Bates family said they would accept $65 million from the Swedes.

A crowdfunding campaign was launched to buy the principality on behalf of Pirate Bay. Citizenship was promised to any backers. "It is not clear if Sealand is an independent territory, but we are pirates and we are not going to wait for a decision of the British government," said Tobias Andersson, one of Pirate Bay's founders. "If they want to denounce us, perfect, although I'm sure they do not want a fight with us, because we have the support of thousands of hackers around the world."

But the crowdfunding campaign only brought in $13,000, and the Sealanders ultimately erred on the side of maintaining cordial international relations. "It's theft of proprietary rights, it doesn't suit us at all," Michael said at the time. "In fact, I've written a book and Hollywood is making a movie out of it, so it would go right against the grain to go into the file-sharing thing." According to a sarcastic internet posting, the money raised by Pirate Bay was reportedly used instead to buy trees, "allegedly in Cambodia to conceal King Kong's whereabouts."

In the meantime, back in the UK, hacker Gary McKinnon had spoken of what he'd found during his snooping expeditions: edited and unedited photos purportedly showing UFOs and mysterious Excel spreadsheets. One spreadsheet entitled "Non-Terrestrial Officers" contained names and ranks of US Air Force personnel who are not registered anywhere else, as well as information about ship-to-ship transfers on vessels whose names didn't appear anywhere else, McKinnon said. Unfortunately, someone in the system noticed the breach and closed McKinnon out of the system before he was able to download the hi-res UFO images over his slow broadband connection.

The Sealanders finally decided they were not interested in hosting McKinnon on the fort, however. With its constitution influenced by the honor of a stiff-upper-lip war hero, Sealand wasn't in the practice of accepting asylum-seekers attempting to evade the legal processes of other states. In fact, to distance themselves, a Sealand spokesperson said the notion that McKinnon would be granted asylum was a rumor "wholly without substance, appear to have originated from sources of fantasy, and should be disregarded." Furthermore, "our application list for general visas has been suspended for some years and remains suspended; this is to protect our citizens and residents here and is strictly enforced."

Fortunately for McKinnon, the extradition to the US didn't happen. Then-Home Secretary Theresa May said that McKinnon's extradition would give rise to a risk of suicide that would be incompatible with his human rights. McKinnon was glad he had taken the stand he did. "Slavery and forced labor will always be wrongs; freedom of thought, belief and religion will always be rights," he said.

All was quiet on the Sealandic asylum front until October 2012, when rumors abounded that Sealand was preparing to host the WikiLeaks servers and/or offer asylum to WikiLeaks founder Julian Assange, who by that point had been holed up in the Ecuadorian Embassy in London for a few months in order to evade arrest by British authorities. "There has been contact but we cannot really talk about it," Michael told the *Ipswich Star* at the time. "Any such dealings would be a private business arrangement and all our dealings with our clients are confidential."

In the end, hosting WikiLeaks and Assange on Sealand never came to fruition. There were many practical concerns that went into the decision. The secrets revealed by WikiLeaks could potentially endanger the safety of government officials and troops abroad, the Sealanders said, and the micronation's sovereignty could actually work against WikiLeaks. If they pissed off the right country, there would be nobody to protect Sealand except themselves. Fighting off invading fishing boats was one thing; the full force of a nation's military was another.

Sealand was still for sale during this time, though InmoNaranja was no longer fielding any offers, as the company closed its doors in 2008 on account of the economic crisis in Spain. There wasn't much of a market for private islands at the time, but the experience was "intense and very fruitful," Medina said. He soon opened a new business promoting tourism closer to home, hyping Granada "as if it were really a private island, an independent country." Sealand isn't officially for sale today, but the Bates family would no doubt entertain the right offer, provided the buyer abides by the Sealandic constitution.

## SEALAND ON THE BIG—AND SMALL—SCREEN

The history of the principality is obviously cinematic in scope, and Roy Bates had been speaking to the press about the possibility of a Sealand movie since at least the 1970s. But it wasn't until 2003 that Sealand got its first real brush with Hollywood fame when a young writer named Sean Sorensen sold a movie script of the story of the principality to Warner Bros. Sorensen befriended the Bates family a few years earlier and became the first American citizen of Sealand, and he used the $20,000 he won on a short-lived Fox game show called *Greed* to sustain himself as he worked on the script. Based on Sorensen's treatment, the story was billed as a "modern-day *Braveheart*."

Michael first met Sorensen at a party hosted by a mutual friend, and he was intrigued by the fact that Sorensen was sitting quietly by himself reading the script of *Gone with the Wind* in the middle of a social event. They got to talking, became friends, and Michael worked with Sorensen to bring the script to life. Roy Bates is probably the most interesting man in history, Sorensen said.

"I first heard about this project when I was nine, and when I became reacquainted with the story last year, I tell that it was such an empowering story I had to make a movie about it," he said. "It's an audacious and inspirational story about people that achieve seemingly impossible dreams."

Since then, Michael has sold the film rights to the family's story no less than three times, which has paid handsomely and has gone on to benefit the operations of the micronation. Director Mike Newell (of *Donnie Brasco* and *Harry Potter and the Goblet of Fire*) was set to direct the piece, with A-listers such as Russell Crowe, Mel Gibson, and Emma Watson rumored to star throughout the years. Most recently, Michael Bates met with the director of a major film franchise who was interested in the project, though disputes with one of the scriptwriters and the directors left the project hanging once again. Part of the problem was the difficulty in trying to determine whether the adaptation would work best as a love story, comedy, or action film, Michael said. He prefers the latter—"It's more like Mel Gibson and *Lethal Weapon*"—but he said if a love story will sell the film, then so be it.

Though not a movie, Michael and his sons did partake in a pilot for a reality show about Sealand in which a film crew would follow them around on their daily business running the fort. Eric Roberts, Julia Roberts's brother, was involved and especially excited about the project. Cameras did in fact follow them around, and one scene from the pilot included a drone Michael bought breaking and falling out of the sky and almost hitting an elderly lady. Another segment included the father and sons fielding pitches from people interested in building up the fort. The Sealand reality TV program never made it past the pilot stage, but it was of course a fun experience and something the family might never have gotten to do otherwise.

Sealand has received representation in other forms of media independent of the family's involvement. It features prominently in *Hetalia: Axis Powers*, a Japanese manga comic and anime that features anthropomorphized countries reenacting historical events and ironing out geopolitical issues. Along with characters representing most macronations, a number of micronations are represented in the series, including Molossia, Wy, Seborga, and the Principality of Hutt River. Sealand is portrayed in *Hetalia* as an enthusiastic little brother to England, always insisting that he'll be taken seriously someday. None of the Bateses had heard of Sealand's inclusion in the anime until one of the boys' young cousins, a fan of the show, showed them an episode.*

The print editions of the *Hetalia* manga comics topped the *New York Times* bestseller lists, and *Hetalia* fans around the world custommake the *Hetalia* Sealand costume of a white sailor shirt, blue capris, and white knee socks for cosplay and convention purposes. Liam Bates said it is easy to know that some people came to follow Sealand's social media accounts thanks to the show, as the followers' avatars are often anime characters. That Sealand would become a cutesy character in a cutesy Japanese cartoon was another outgrowth of the micronational experiment that Roy and Joan scarcely could have imagined.

"It's great and it's unbelievable the huge following the cartoon has," Michael said. "It would be great to honor the writer/author."

Sealand is also a character in the meme comic series "Polandball," a satirical take on current events and world history as told through the adventures of nations represented as balls colored as the nation's flag.

---

* According to an overview of the character on a *Hetalia* Wiki, "[Sealand] attempts to attend a world meeting with the other nations, though his presence winds up going ignored. Sealand managed to get Japan to notice and nod his head toward him (Japan then turned around and continued walking in the direction he was heading), but it was seen that Japan looked rather uncomfortable and England stared at Japan with a harsh look. Sealand manages to get Lithuania to notice him and is given advice on how to become an actual nation."

The series does not have a definitive author but is rather an ongoing crowdsourced joke, with anyone free to write and publish a Polandball strip. The Sealand character has a similar personality as in the *Hetalia* series, though the strip's humor contains a great deal of the irreverent and surreal comedy characteristic of meme culture.

The Sealand Award Committee conferred annual awards to the principality's favorite movies, athletes, and music, for a brief period in the mid-2000s, including the awarding of the Sealand Peace Prize to Nelson Mandela in 2007. (The committee also bestowed a Lifetime Achievement Award to Homer J. Simpson for being one of the "greatest comedic creations of modern times.") Sealand followers also voted for the 14th Dalai Lama of Tibet to receive honorary Sealandic nobility for his work as a peace activist. "This spells bad news for television personality Suzanne Shaw and ex-Sex Pistols manager Malcolm McLaren, who were also nominated but lost," the announcement stated.

In 2009, Fall Out Boy bassist Pete Wentz said the group would come off its hiatus to play on Sealand, and in 2012 English pop music sensation Ed Sheeran was deemed Baron von Edward Sheeran of Sealand. "A friend of mine owns an oil rig that got made into a country legally, and called Sealand, which made him king of Sealand, which means he can give out titles to people," Sheeran said in a [*sic*] tweet. "So I am a baron. Awesome." Sheeran shares the award with filmmaker Danny Wallace, George Stroumboulopoulos, *Top Gear* host Jeremy Clarkson, and BBC presenters Terry Wogan and Ben Fogle, the latter of whom filmed a few segments on the principality for various news programs over the years.

"It's not every day you get to meet royalty, but when you do, you don't expect to meet them in a port in Harwich," Fogle said.

And while a feature film about Sealand has yet to be made, 2015 brought the first filmed dramatization of the Sealand story for the Travel Channel program *Mysteries of the Museum*. The show highlights strange and interesting artifacts from history and science, and the first segment of episode 7, season 9 recreates the failed coup of 1978. Actors played the Bates family and a British journalist named Andrea Mann provided color commentary on the history of the fort. Michael was contacted to participate in the program and was unable to participate because he was in the midst of negotiations for a Sealand movie adaptation. While the astute historian may notice some errors—Sealand is depicted as a warehouse and the raiders have machine guns, for example—it is cool to see the Bates family and Achenbach on the small screen, the actors recreating the exciting scenes from real life in front of billowing Sealand flags.*

## TRIUMPHANT TONES OF THE SEALANDIC NATIONAL ANTHEM

Basil Simonenko, the man who composed Sealand's national anthem "E Mare Libertas," put his heart and soul into the song. Published in early 2012, the anthem clocks in at 1:21 and is a rousing tug at the patriotic heartstrings. The Bates family was approached by Simonenko about writing an anthem, for up to that point a national anthem was the only thing missing from the repertoire of statehood. The gesture was one of many in which a non-Sealandic national finds himself so inspired by the principality that he undertakes a serious duty on its behalf.

Michael Bates reportedly deemed Simonenko's tune the "greatest national anthem ever written"—and as a YouTube commenter called Red L said, "This is the most BADASS theme, oh my god! It reminds me of the Boston Tea Party, except they're throwing England's music into the sea, and then making their own. Bravo Sealand!" But its sonorous tones not only tell the story of Sealand; they also reflect the triumphs and travails of its composer, a man who has overcome childhood abuse and an eating addiction and who has turned to music as a way to create a positive change in the world.

Simonenko is a music producer and DJ from Yorkshire who has been a lifelong composer, musician, and music enthusiast. He caught a few breaks performing in the early 1990s as an opener for bigger acts, but health concerns formed a roadblock to his career. At one point

---

* Some other enduring myths about Sealand's history involve Joan pretending she was pregnant and whipping out a machine gun from her baby bump to retake the fort from invaders. And retelling of the 1978 coup sometimes includes more machinery than was actually there. "Jet skis. There's always jet skis," James Bates laughed.

in the late 1990s, Simonenko weighed more than five hundred pounds and had serious mobility issues.

Homebound, he developed an alter ego called CP BAZzZMAN and got into the burgeoning cellphone ringtone business, though he found that he was prone to being uncredited and unpaid, so he eventually withdrew from the industry. Simonenko continued to compose music and released an album during this time, and in 2011 he had the biggest brush with fame he'd experienced in years when he was pulled out of the line and selected as a contestant on season 8 of *The X Factor*, a TV singing competition in the UK.

Forty-six years old at the time, Simonenko was not the typical contender, and his appearance got off to a rocky start. He confused the hosts with the specific spelling of his penname and overcompensated for his nervousness by yelling into the mic from backstage, hyping himself up but annoying the audience—a tragicomic bravado not unlike Michael Scott's "Date Mike" persona in season 6 of *The Office*. He was almost booed off stage when he remarked to American judge (and former Destiny's Child star) Kelly Rowland that he couldn't tell what she was saying and then, when she repeated herself, asked to bring back a former British judge.

However, mouths literally dropped open when Simonenko started belting out "House of the Rising Sun" by the Animals. The four judges were taken aback and roundly praised the performance. Simonenko's voice was very, very good, said judge Gary Barlow, a member of UK megahit boyband Take That. "Everybody was immediately put off your character when you came out," Barlow said. "People were shouting out in the audience and we were expecting to see something that was really mediocre. What happened was you started to sing and actually the room lit up."

Simonenko was encouraged to drop the BAZzZMAN character and just be himself. The praise brought him to tears. "I've waited for twenty-eight years for someone to tell me that," he said. Simonenko then progressed to the "Boot Camp" portion of the competition, in which he rehearsed more and sang in an arena in front of 8,000 people. "I'm already experiencing the trappings of fame, I've even had autograph hunters," Simonenko said. However, health problems forced

Simonenko to drop out of *X Factor*, and in 2013 he had to undergo drastic surgery for his weight.

In the meantime, however, Simonenko debuted the Sealandic national anthem to widespread acclaim among micronationalists everywhere. "E Mare Libertas" even appears on Volume 8 of the "Complete National Anthems of the World" collection put out by Marco Polo Records. The anthems on the collection were played by the Slovak Radio Symphony Orchestra, with "E Mare Libertas" appearing on the disc alongside the anthem of another micronation, the Principality of Seborga.

## SEBORGA

The Principality of Seborga is a micronation in northwest Italy, near the French border, whose 2,000 inhabitants claim independence from Italy based partly on a historical administrative error. The fourteen-kilometer territory was autonomous as early as 1079 and was held by a variety of counts and orders for centuries, passing through the hands of Benedictine monks and later becoming the protectorate of a powerful family dynasty. When the discrete kingdoms and territories were united to create the Kingdom of Italy in 1870, Seborga was not mentioned in any of the founding documents. Thus, the argument goes, it is not a part of Italy and remains an independent territory.

The people of Seborga elected florist Giorgio Carbone as Seborga's head of state in 1963, endowing him with the title "His Tremendousness Giorgio I." In 1995, residents voted Seborga independent from Italy, and in 2006, His Tremendousness discussed plans to create insurance and pension plans for residents. The principality has its own stamps and flags, uses its own currency—the "luigino"—in local shops and bars, and has received recognition from San Marino, Andorra, and several African countries. Seborgans do pay taxes to the Italian state, and the village has an Italian mayor. However, the principality's significant tourist traffic convinced the Italy-loyal mayor to allow His Tremendousness to maintain his title.

Seborga, of course, has competing claims to the throne. One contender is one Princess Yasmine von Hohenstaufen Anjou Plantagenet, who claims to be a descendent of a thirteenth-century German family that at one point ruled over the Roman Empire. Seborgans didn't take her claims seriously, as most of the evidence for her lineage came from a website that she herself maintained. The princess formally ceded Seborga to the Italian Republic, but adherents of the real Seborga maintain that she had no authority to do that in the first place. When Giorgio I died in 2009 at age seventy-three, a hosiery heir and former champion sailor Marcello Menegatto was elected as Seborga's new leader. His Tremendousness Marcello I vowed to "create new infrastructure and work for our people," and was reelected to his second tenure in 2017.

Since then, Simonenko helped rehouse a London man who lived in a bus shelter with the proceeds of a song he wrote, became a respected question-answerer on the website Quora, and continues to make music from home with an emphasis on positive lyrics and perspective. "I want global domination, I want to become a musical philosopher," he said. Thanks to the Sealand national anthem, Simonenko got at least a small taste of global domination, for his anthem will surely accompany all of Sealand's achievements on the world stage.

In fact, it already has.

The anthem has rung in the ears of athletes from all over the world who have competed on behalf of the principality in sports mainstream and obscure alike. As Pierre de Coubertin said about the Olympic Games, "The important thing in life is not the triumph but the struggle. The essential thing is not to have conquered but to have fought well." The same could be said about the efforts of the many athletes who have competed on behalf of Sealand, a few of who have been named "*Athleta Principalitas*" in honor of their accomplishments.

# CHAPTER 15

## *ATHLETA PRINCIPALITAS*

---

*"Training was always threatened but it never quite materialized."*

—Derek Sillie

On May 22, 2015, professional mountaineer Kenton Cool carried a Sealandic flag to the top of Mount Everest. It was his eleventh summit of Everest, and the photo of the event shows a beaming Cool holding the Sealandic flag amidst a backdrop of dozens of other nations' flags that have been lugged to the top.

"I'm sure when my parents designed the simple red, white, and black flag back in 1967…they could never have imagined the places it would visit," Michael said. "My father would have considered Kenton a 'Proper bloke.'" The flag, signed by Cool, is framed and hanging in Michael's home.

### MOUNTAINEERING

But while Cool's accomplishment for Sealand is impressive and commendable, another mountain has been summited on behalf of Sealand—this one preempting Cool's ascension by almost ten years and undertaken by a man with little climbing experience. That man was Slader Oviatt, a good-natured Canadian who found himself presented with the opportunity to scale Muztagh Ata, a 24,636-foot mountain in western China near the border with Pakistan. Oviatt said his adventure was inspired almost entirely by the chance to do something for Sealand.

In the summer of 2004, Oviatt was a university student in Edmonton and heard a program on the Canadian Broadcasting Corporation about a fellow Canadian named Darron Blackburn who'd recently run a marathon on behalf of the micronation and was christened *Athleta*

*Principalitas* by the Sealanders in a show of gratitude for his accomplishments.

"That guy is a genius," Oviatt said. "If I was good at anything—which I'm not—then I could offer to do that and be Sealand's guy who does that thing."

A little while later, having mostly forgotten the CBC program, Oviatt got a call from his now-father-in-law about a trip to Muztagh Ata sponsored by the China Mountaineer Association. Muztagh Ata is a popular mountain for climbers, and the Chinese government was changing the management company that oversaw the excursions up and down the face of it. The trip was a sort of publicity stunt to showcase that transition and would be made up of university students from all over China and the world. Participants had to buy a plane ticket and supply their own gear, but China was going to foot the bill for the rest of the expedition. In exchange, the students involved would help clean up the mountain.

Oviatt jumped at the chance to go on the adventure. Then it dawned on him: Like his hero Darron Blackburn, he could be the first person to accomplish another amazing athletic feat on behalf of the principality. He quickly reached out to the micronation, explaining his intention to carry the Sealandic flag to the top of a Chinese mountain. Prince Michael wrote back and told him to go forth.

Muztagh Ata is a monster, Oviatt said, especially to a novice. Part of the challenge was the fact that mountains aren't climbed in a linear fashion. Rather, the team was going to spend a few days acclimating at basecamp before ascending to increasingly higher camps. Oviatt trained for months before the hike in order to get himself in appropriate shape.

"Basecamp was as high as my previous altitude," he said. "It's enormously high. Half the people, myself included, got altitude sickness at basecamp."

But as the trip drew closer, Oviatt realized he couldn't easily acquire a Sealand flag. The flag was the whole point, so he enlisted the help of his mom. They looked up the dimensions of the flag, made sure the fabrics' colors matched those of Sealand's pennant, and ultimately produced a worthy replica. The flag was carefully folded and stashed in his luggage.

Technically beholden to the Chinese Mountaineering Association as a representative of the University of Alberta, Oviatt kept the Sealand reason for the journey quiet. But once the group reached the top of Muztagh Ata, it was time to unfurl the flag and do what he set out to do.

"I get to the summit, we snap a few pictures, and I tell the guys, 'Hold on, I've got to get one more,'" he said. "I take off my down jacket, get one picture of me holding the Sealand flag on the summit. The wind's whipping, I snap it, get the perfect picture."

The trip up and down the mountain took around two weeks. All the while, the participants were in fact cleaning up the mountain. "[We were] going around picking up toilet paper that was just blowing through camps because there were no proper outhouses dug. The mountain was a mess and we were just cleaning it all up," he said. Oviatt was amazed to find how large of a production the excursion was for the Mountaineering Association. At one point, the group of students was treated to a huge parade and performance solely for the climbers, during which they were given gifts and watched singing and dancing and drumming. It was "an absolutely wild adventure," as Oviatt recalled.

Oviatt sent Prince Michael an update from the trip with a photo of him and the Sealand flag at the top. The photo promptly appeared on the front page of Sealand's website. The ascension of Muztagh Ata is mentioned on Sealand's Wikipedia page, and it is a mention that Oviatt fought hard to get.

## FROM KUNG FU TO THE WORLD EGG THROWING CHAMPIONSHIP

In 2007, Sealand's first championship medals were earned by yet another Canadian athlete. Martial artist Michael Martelle represented the Principality of Sealand in the World Cup of Kung Fu, held in Quebec City.*

---

* Kendo, a martial art using bamboo staffs, was practiced on the fort by Sean Hastings and the security guards during the HavenCo years. Hastings said he was really surprised nobody fell over the edge during the intense training bouts.

Like Slader Oviatt, Martelle was inspired by the chance to do something on behalf of the principality and raise awareness of its claims. He was the only micronational athlete competing at the event among macronations, but the flag he was competing under surprisingly didn't raise any eyebrows at the event. He ultimately took two silver medals in the competition and was deemed the *Athleta Principalitas Bellatorius* of Sealand by Prince Michael.

On the more XTREME side of sports, energy drink maven Red Bull hosted a skateboarding event on the principality in 2008. Kris Vile, Lennie Burmeister, Philipp Schuster, and Julien Bachelier—top skaters from around the UK and Europe—were scheduled to fly to the principality and spend a day skating on ramps and quarter-pipes specially built for the occasion.

"I didn't really understand. I was like, 'Sealand, what's that?'" Vile said before the event. "I don't really know what to expect. I suppose it's going to be a different experience. We'll just have to wait and see and see if the weather's good."

The weather wasn't good, and the event was cancelled three times as a result. And then, when the weather finally relented, the wood for the ramps was stolen from the pier before it could be loaded onto the boat. Once everything came together, however, the crew was boated out to the mid-ocean skatepark for a day of shredding.

The skaters rushed back and forth across the "strange aquatic version of a set in a Mad Max movie," a width no wider than if the ramps were set up in someone's garage and literally right up to the edge of the fort. Of course, skating in the garage doesn't carry the same hazards, but that was the point: The event was designed to showcase "the most extreme people in the most extreme place they could find." Two boats circled the principality in the event that someone went flying overboard, and the camera crew making passes in a helicopter got some impressive footage of the feat.

"In the event, we only lost one board," Sealand Events Manager Chris Harrington said. "They are amazing guys. I know they don't have the concept of the word fear. I saw them doing it from one of the boats below and I just wanted to look away—but I had to keep watching."

Sealand was also represented in, of all things, the World Egg Throwing Championship in 2008. Held in Lincolnshire, UK, the Championship featured events such as Egg Throwing and Catching, Egg Russian Roulette, and Egg Trebuchet. The event brought competitors from all over the world, who were, as many wags put it, "egg-cited" to participate.

The principality was represented by Mark Rye and Emma Hagerty, who were able to compete in every event except the Egg Trebuchet, as a design fault scuttled their plans to bring the catapult to the Championship. The team was defeated in the first round of Egg Russian Roulette, in which a competitor is given six eggs to smash on their heads, five of which are hard-boiled and one of which is raw. The loser is, of course, the person who smashes the raw egg first. The two Sealand athletes were joined by a team of Latvian welders for the egg throwing and catching event (which required eleven participants), allowing Sealand to take part in the final event and propel themselves to victory, achieving the Principality of Sealand's first world championship.

## VIVA SEALAND FOOTBALL

In May 2012, a group of around two hundred spectators gathered at a muddy field at Godalming Park in Surrey, UK. They respectfully stood up as the respective national anthems of Sealand and Chagos Islands were played on a tinny loudspeaker. The players—clad in black, red, and white and blue and orange, respectively—stood on the field with looks of solemnity that gave way to good-natured amusement. Basil Simonenko's "E Mare Libertas" echoed throughout the football pitch, and Prince Michael Bates gave a short speech welcoming everyone to the game. It was nice to play somewhere where they didn't keep losing the ball to the ocean, he quipped.

The game was the first official match since Sealand joined the *Nouvelle Fédération-Board*, or N-F Board, a soccer organization for football clubs not recognized by FIFA, the governing body of world soccer. The organization was comprised of around twenty-five teams representing everywhere from Darfur to Chechnya to the Romani people, all vying to compete in the annual VIVA World Cup. The

Sealand–Chagos Islands matchup was to be broadcast by the BBC World Service.

The Sealand team boasted retired professional and semiprofessional soccer players, as well as British actor Ralf Little, star of the sitcom *The Royle Family*, and Prince Liam Bates, who played left back. The group was coached by Scottish journalist Neil Forsyth, who had been trying to get an official Sealand team together for years. Funding and sponsorship issues had kept the idea at bay, but finally the team was playing its first official game. "Training was always threatened but it never quite materialized," professional goalkeeper Derek Sillie laughed.

As one reporter put it, if the story of Sealand's football team is impressive, the story of the Chagos Islands' team was perhaps even more so. The Chagos Islands are a group of around sixty islands in the Indian Ocean colonized by the British, who, starting in 1967, forced the indigenous population to leave to make way for a military base. The islanders were scattered around the world, and in a too little, too late show of attrition, Britain granted Chagossians citizenship. This led to a substantial Chagos population in Sussex, England—hence, the creation of the football team.

"There is an irony that the fixture between Sealand and the Chagos Islands brought together two nations unrecognized by the wider world, one created by the British military and the other destroyed by it," one sportswriter commented.

The match tipped in favor of the more-practiced Chagossians, who remained 2–0 at the half. Sealand's Ryan Moore scored the team's first goal in the second half, but the micronation ultimately fell 3–1. "Watching the match instilled a great sense of national pride," Michael Bates said. "It was absolutely brilliant, but would have been better if we won."

Sealand FA wasn't able to make it to the 2012 VIVA World Cup, hosted in Iraqi Kurdistan, due to lack of funding, but the team did continue to play N-F Board–sanctioned matches in England, including a game against Alderney, from the Channel Island of the same name, and a rematch against Chagos Islands, which Sealand won 4–2. In July 2013, Sealand FA participated in the Tynwald Hill Tournament on the Isle of Man. There the Sealanders took on Alderney, Tamil Eelam (a team comprised of Sri Lanka's Tamil minority), and Occitania (representing a region of the same name between France and Spain with its own culture and language). The Sealanders won 2–1, lost 8–0, and won 5–3, respectively.

The N-F Board ceased to be in 2013, transitioning into the Confederation of International Football Associations (CONIFA), a similar organization but with many more teams stretching all over the world.* CONIFA currently boasts almost fifty teams, including those representing Tibet, the Sami people, Quebecois, and Karpatalya, a Hungarian enclave in the former Czechoslovakia that declared independence and was absorbed by Hungary the next day.

"Countries are often just historic flukes," said CONIFA tournament organizer Paul Watson. "One broad stroke on a map and a peace treaty a hundred years ago. Does that make a country? We don't claim to have the answer but it's worth asking the question."

That being said, so far Sealand FA has not been accepted as a member into CONIFA, but the team continues to play matches when opportunity allows. "Football is international and crosses all borders and language barriers," Michael said.

## MESSENGER'S MARITIME "MARATHON"

Longtime Sealand resident, guard, and historian Mike Barrington, who has spent almost thirty years living part-time on the principality, had his own way of keeping fit on the platform. "I used to have a push-bike on here years ago and I used to pedal all the way down the side here, across the back, then down the other side," he said. "One day I hit a patch of oil on the south deck by the generator out there and nearly went over the side. I chucked the bike after that." With such dangers in mind, Englishman Simon Messenger had to get creative when it came to running a marathon on the fort.

Messenger, an adviser at a climate change think tank with a thin runner's frame, has traveled all over the world to run for his project "80 Runs," which he chronicles on his blog 80runs.co.uk. He has run

---

* CONIFA was formed in part by a German football jersey collector who got all of the FIFA teams and needed more for his collection.

in rain, snow, and scorching temperatures on almost every continent, including a subzero run in Almaty, Kazakhstan, and a half-marathon organized specifically for him in the Seychelles (although he had to pull out halfway through due to what a local newspaper account deemed an "upset tummy").

In April 2015, Messenger recalled daydreaming about Sealand, and it occurred to him that it would be a monumentally cool addition to his 80 Runs itinerary. "Going to Sealand was all about doing something different and traveling towards the unknown. There was something mystical about this fortress, an insignificant significance. So close to England, yet so far," he said.

The *Guardian* had just published an article about Messenger's adventures, and with this apparent boost of legitimacy, he thought he'd email the royal family to see about adding Sealand as one of his destinations. Michael was taken with the idea and agreed to help arrange the encounter. "Initially we thought about organizing it as a [13.1-mile] run around the platform. And then we realized that the platform is only about the size of two tennis courts," Messenger said. The solution was genius in its elegance: set up a treadmill on Sealand.

Messenger reached out to the editor of a British running magazine to see if they'd like to cover the run. The editor was excited by the idea and happened to have some friends who were documentary filmmakers who decided they wanted to make a short film of the event. The magazine editor also reached out to some of his contacts in the running world, ultimately getting Nordic Track to provide a state-of-the-art treadmill for the occasion and a sporting goods store to pay for the cost of getting to Sealand.

Messenger and the filmmakers traveled to Harwich at the end of June to do the run, but the first attempt was scuttled on account of the weather. Messenger got a call from James Bates that the run had to be postponed while he was being interviewed for the documentary.

"As this was caught on camera, [the documentarian] was very excited that we had filmed 'drama' but, other than the good footage, this was a right 'act of god' pain in the arse," Messenger recalled.

Two weeks later, on July 10, the stunt was attempted again. However, Messenger and his crew had about eight hours to get there, complete the marathon, and get back before a storm hit. If they didn't make this timeframe then there was a good chance they would be stuck out there for days. Preparations began at 3:30 a.m.

Messenger could see the platform shrouded by mist. It was "[o] ld, yet brand new; mysterious; rusty, mysterious; huge but also so tiny amongst the endless sea," he wrote. He was winched to the top and the treadmill, still disassembled in its box, followed unsteadily behind him. "It was about to go in the drink. How it missed I do not know," James Bates said. Messenger and the filmmakers got their passports stamped and the crew got to work piecing together the treadmill.

The original plan was of course to set the treadmill on the deck so Messenger could run as he looked out to sea. But a light drizzle started and Messenger was told by Nordic Track that he should treat the treadmill "like a 42inch TV: get it wet and it will die." The team reassembled the treadmill in one of the principality's corridors but realized Messenger would have to stoop to not hit his head on the ceiling. The treadmill was instead put together in the living room where the roof was about an inch from Messenger's noggin.

Messenger ran for about ten miles and noticed that the rain hadn't broken yet, so the treadmill was "remantled" back out on the deck for the completion of the race. The camera crew asked him to keep running beyond the length of a half-marathon for footage's sake, and once he got the go ahead to stop, Messenger jumped off the treadmill and ran onto the helipad and crossed the makeshift finish line at the summit of Sealand. He ended up doing this twice, as the first take was rendered unusable by a bumped camera. Messenger's time was 1:27:02.

"It wasn't the best time I'd ever run, but sod it, it was a national record," he said.

James was on hand for Messenger's feat—"Dad offered me up to race him, but that's not going to happen," he laughed—and contented himself with bestowing on Messenger a laser-engraved medal for being the only person to have completed a half-marathon on Sealand.

Today, Messenger's quest to race all over the world continues. The journey has introduced him to cool people, places, and customs on almost every continent, though Sealand was certainly the most unusual event so far. He's also learned some important lessons along the way. As he writes on his blog, he knows to "always take toilet paper to races; eat sensibly in the morning; forget about fashion when buying running gear; cover your nipples if it rains (ouch); and don't zoom off like an arrow then feel like crap when you get overtaken by a seventy-year-old."

## SWIMMING THE NORTH SEA

It makes sense that Sealand, being a maritime nation, would have representation in the world of competitive swimming. And in 2018, two swimmers inadvertently competed against each other to be the first person to swim from Sealand to the shores of the UK.

On Monday, August 20, 2018, thirty-two-year-old Richard Royal was boated out to the micronation wearing a black wetsuit and Union Jack swim cap. Royal is a competitive long-range swimmer from Hull who had previously undertaken similarly arduous swims—including from Alcatraz to California and a relay across the English Channel—but this was to be the longest swim he'd done in one stretch. Royal's goal was to complete the swim from Sealand in less than six hours, with accreditation by the World Open Water Swimming Association and the British Long Distance Swimming Association.

"It's going to be a really challenging swim. With currents and tides it's bound to be longer than twelve kilometers, and that kind of distance nonstop in the North Sea is tough," he said.

Royal and his crew boated out to Sealand and Royal hopped on the chair to be brought up via winch. But his ascension suddenly stopped, leaving him dangling around fifteen feet above the water. The winch broke and people up top were trying to fix it. Royal didn't mind, though. It was eerily calm, quiet, and quite beautiful, he said, and used the time to gather his thoughts. (Caretaker Joe Hamill said part of the engine sheared off as the winch was moving. He leaned over the side and smiled at Royal. "Slight technical problem!" he said, trying to hide the severity of the issue.)

Once the winch was repaired and after getting his passport stamped, Royal was lowered by crane from the platform, slipped into the sixty-four-degree water, and kicked off toward the mainland at approximately

11:00 a.m. A newspaperman in a boat provided live updates of the feat, keeping track of his progress and his "feedings." By the time Royal had completed 3.5 miles, the reporter noted Royal had eaten a banana, biscuits, and juice.

"[The swim] is as much psychological as it is physical—it can get pretty lonely," Royal said. "The one thing I don't think about is what is or isn't beneath me in the water."

Royal decided he wanted to swim from Sealand after becoming fascinated by the principality in college. It took him about two years to secure the appropriate permissions to conduct the swim and arrange a safety boat to accompany him on the journey. Royal undertook the journey as a way to challenge himself as a swimmer, but he was also swimming on behalf of Aspire, a spinal injury charity.

Though he had budgeted up to six hours to do the swim, Royal found that the mainland was approaching faster than he expected. Soon enough, his hands began hitting sand, and his swim came to an end. Friends and family waving British flags greeted him on the shore. He finished the 12-kilometer (7.2-mile) swim in 3 hours and 29 minutes.

The publicity surrounding Royal's upcoming swim generated on social media prompted fifty-two-year-old Nick Glendinning to take on the challenge himself—and he was going to do it two days before. Glendinning's swim was news to the Sealanders. Hamill was working on the fort when he saw a boat sail up to the fort on August 18. When he came out to greet the boat, he watched a swimmer hop into the water, touch one of the towers, and swim off. Confused, Joe called Richard Royal and asked if the swim had been moved up. Royal said no. Glendinning thus ended up beating Royal to the punch and completed his swim from Sealand in less than five hours. One newspaper likened the competition to the race between Scott and Amundsen to be the first person to reach the South Pole.

"That was hilarious," Hamill said. "You missed it by a day, mate!"

Glendinning maintained it was pure chance that the two swimmers undertook their jaunts from Sealand that close together and that he had been planning the trip for two years. Roy Bates is one of his heroes, he said.

"It's just sod's law," Glendinning said. "I've never spoken to this person, it's an assumption that's occurred and he's made...At the end of the day it's just an old bloke going for a long swim, followed shortly after by a younger man showing him how it should be done."

Royal was unimpressed.

"There's no way in the world this is coincidence," he said.

The Sealanders were asked to discredit the accomplishment-usurper, but the Bateses found it hard to decry the magnitude of such an achievement. "I admire anyone that can swim the distance, even if he wasn't meant to be there," Michael said. In the end, however, though Royal was technically not the first person to complete the swim, his feat was the only swim recognized by the government of Sealand. As a show of appreciation for his effort (and arranging things beforehand with the royal family), Royal was dubbed "Sir Richard Mark Royal" and was welcomed into the Sovereign Military Order of Sealand.

"I'm absolutely delighted to have been awarded a knighthood by Prince Michael of Sealand, it's priceless to me after all the planning and work that went into the swim," he said. "It's important to me to be respectful and courteous of Sealand and its owners, so to have their blessing for the swim in the first instance, and be gifted such an award subsequently is a huge honor."

Sir Richard Royal said the accolade would help encourage him when he competed in the European Masters Swimming Championship in Slovenia the following week. "Whilst I'm representing Great Britain, I'll be taking my Sealand flag along and will make sure it is waved alongside the other nations," he said. Unfortunately, Royal did not end up placing in the championship, but his swimming spirit remains undiminished.

Despite the unprecedented heights of athleticism reached on behalf of the principality—James Bates noted that the Sealand quidditch team is apparently one of the best in the world—the new millennium was not without its sorrows. Even the greatest among us must pass to the next realm, and that sad reality came calling for the Prince and Princess of Sealand.

# CHAPTER 16

# TWO MOMENTS OF PROFOUND SILENCE

---

*"I might die young, I might die old, but I'll never die of boredom."*

—Roy Bates

Over the years, the Principality of Sealand has been called a "quixotic financial sinkhole," a "ramshackle, rusting scrap heap," an "ugly, wind-battered concrete slab," "an industrial-era Stonehenge," a "grotesque marine oasis," an "abandoned, utterly charmless rig," and "the rustiest, creaky, tiny, and precarious country in the world." Every one of these descriptions is superficially accurate, but these descriptions don't do justice to the heart of the place or adequately express its spirit. It is indeed a rusting slab, perhaps, but one that has been tended to with care and many fresh coats of paint. The fort's longevity has surprised even the Bateses, and the contrast between rust and splendor seems almost like the symbolic representation of a man who sensed he was destined for greatness but had to hack his way toward that path.

Over the years, however, reporters began to note the transition of Roy Bates in their accounts of the fort. Once a fiery pirate, Roy was prone to remaining quiet and staring out to sea, his hair swept back and eyes fixed on a distant point on the horizon. Roy would periodically chime in with an exciting recollection of the earlier days as Joan answered a reporter's questions, but then he would lapse back into silence. It was difficult to reconcile the unremitting hardiness of one's early years with the confines of a body that simply isn't up to the same tasks.

In the early 2000s, Roy and Joan retired to Spain—a sunny haven that serves as a Florida for Englanders—on account of Joan's arthritis. They were able to enjoy the splendid weather and the company of fellow retirees, overall leading a much more leisurely and low-key life than that on the fort. Michael and Penny would come and visit when they could, taking a pleasant break from the responsibilities of their two homelands. During this time Michael was named "Prince Regent" of Sealand and took over the running of the fort.

By 2010, when Roy was eighty-eight years old, it was obvious he was in his twilight years. He was forgetful, aloof, exhibiting a more worrisome absentmindedness than the senescence that comes with old age. As it turned out, he was fighting a foe more troublesome than any he'd yet encountered: Alzheimer's, an enemy that couldn't be bested no matter how hard anyone tried.

Michael traveled more and more frequently to Spain to check on his parents. His dad's condition was only getting worse, and finally, after a few years of broaching the topic, they convinced him to return to Leigh-on-Sea to be closer to family. The initial plan was for his parents to live with Michael, and for a while they did share the same home, but the ravages of Roy's illness proved to be too intense. Roy and Joan soon relocated to an assisted living facility where, after a lifetime of maintaining his stubborn kingdom, Roy I, the original Prince of Sealand, passed away peacefully on October 9, 2012. Finally giving in to the inevitable was not a concession of defeat but rather an acknowledgment that he'd wrung as much out of this life that he could. He was ninety-one years old.

News of Roy's death quickly spread. The esteem with which the hardy Sealander was held was a small but welcome comfort to the family in their distress. Roy was a lovable rogue, hard-driving boss, and "absolute legend" that made an impression on everyone he met, employed, fought, and befriended.

Tributes poured in from the DJs of the former Radio Essex, youths who spent their formative years on the fort and were themselves now old men.

"Roy taught us young men a lot in 1966—not just about radio—and I'll miss him," said DJ Gerry Zieler, aka Gerry Zee, a DJ who Roy insisted get his high school diploma before working for the station. "It was impossible not to respect him, though there were times out there that you could have hated him—when your pay didn't arrive, when the boat didn't come, when leave didn't happen—but what he achieved on next to nothing was remarkable. And because of him our colleagues created a damn good little radio station."

Roy was of course best known as the Prince of Sealand, and the rough conditions on the fort were appropriate to a man from a different time. He was a man interested in living as free as he is in his heart, and the durability of the experiment was an affirmation of his victory. As Roy once put it, "There's too much damn bureaucracy in the world right now, too many people doing what they're told, not enough independence, not enough free will in the world."

It was time someone did something about it, he said. And he did.

Roy's obituary appeared in newspapers all over the world. According to the *New York Times*, which published a lengthy encomium on October 14, 2012, Roy was one of the most interesting people that died that year—number two behind Neil Armstrong but ahead of Whitney Houston. A bonus feature commemorating those who had passed included a gorgeous graphic novel spread about Sealand, a huge framed copy of which Michael has hanging in his house.

People are driven by their passions, and Roy made Sealand his life. He was certainly a fantasist, knowingly exaggerating the business prospects of the fort and the ironfistedness of his reign, and he was unapologetic about being a hard bastard of the North Sea. But his legacy was shouted from atop an obscure concrete and metal structure that by all accounts should have disappeared into the sea by now. Think what you will about the sanity of the mission—the winds caught Roy's sails and propelled him across his personal horizon, making for a life journey satisfyingly fulfilled.

"When I made a principality, nobody understood what I was driving at for years and years and years. They thought I was a clown, they thought I was mad. It's taken a bloody long time to achieve my ambition, but I always knew I'd win," Roy said. "I like a bit of adventure. It's the old British tradition. Maybe Britain's changed, but there's a lot of us still about."

From soldier to butcher, swim fin manufacturer to father, pirate radio boss to micronational legend, he had a winning approach to life.

"I might die young, I might die old, but I'll never die of boredom," Roy was known to say.

## "IT'S WHAT YOU ARE THAT'S IMPORTANT, NOT WHAT YOU HAVE"

Following the death of her lifelong companion, Joan Bates soldiered on as best she could. She was chipper and alert, having done most of the talking in the interviews later in their lives and trying to maintain her natural good humor. She could usually be seen decked out in jewels and with her hair pulled up into her trademark blonde bun.

But while Joan was a perpetually social being, she never discussed Roy dying. It was an impossible-to-imagine void. They were never apart aside from the time Roy spent on Sealand, and they had walked hand-in-hand wherever they went for almost sixty years. "I remember them in the summer of 2000, trading memories and smiles about all their close calls, big dreams, and improbable adventures. They seemed to have a kingdom with each other," NPR's Scott Simon said.

The absence of a longtime partner wasn't the only thing to weigh heavily on Joan. She too was on borrowed time, and on March 10, 2016, Joan Bates lay in bed at a nursing home in her beloved Leigh-on-Sea and left this mortal coil to reign as princess in the next realm. She was eighty-six.

"My mother was a stunning woman," Michael Bates said in a statement following her death. "My parents will always be remembered for shaking up the Establishment with pirate radio, declaring Sealand's independence, and confronting the Royal Navy and other foreign governments."

The funeral service was held the following week. Joan's coffin was draped in the Sealandic flag, and Joan herself lay peacefully shrouded in a beloved fur coat with an embroidered tag reading "Princess Joan of Sealand" sewn on the inside. Family and friends from a lifetime in Essex mourned the loss of an elegant, glamorous, and friendly woman. "Grandma was lovely and full of life. I heard so many fascinating things and so many stories as I grew up," James Bates said.

As tough as she was loving, she braved the wretched conditions of the freezing first years on the fort and tried to appreciate the positive side to the experience. "When my husband, my son, and I are all here together, we tend to talk all the time. We're very close. I'm happiest when we're all home," Joan said. Her stature as Princess of Sealand allowed her to do substantial work for various charities, especially the Royal National Lifeboat Institution, which was an abiding cause of hers. The lore surrounding Roy was tremendous, and Penny Bates said she hopes her mother gets the appreciation she was due. Joan was a "vastly underrated woman" and certainly someone without whom Sealand would have not been successful, Penny said.

"I don't have a crown. I think they're a bit outdated," Joan once said. "It's what you are that's important, not what you have."

Joan Bates was eulogized all over the world, and a photo of her radiant, smiling face accompanied accounts of her life. Words of admiration and gratitude poured in from supporters and micronationalists from all over the world.

"On behalf of Viking King Jarsgard and the people of Jarspoole on you to Oden's call," wrote one micronational leader.

"On behalf my myself, Jean-Luc Mauriat, Earl of Sallure, Signeur de la maison du Mauriat, subject of the Principality of Helianthis, and my family, wish to convey our deepest sympathy to your nation on this time of loss," wrote another. "May the principality flowerish [sic] under your guidance."

Everyone in the Bates family admired Roy and Joan's remarkable closeness and made sure to do this companionship justice after they were both gone. Roy and Joan's ashes were mixed together and scattered in front of a home in Southend where they and their kids had spent many years. The rest were scattered in their beloved Spain. "I loved them very dearly. I was heartbroken when they died, just heartbroken. I still miss them. Every day I think about them and miss them," said Lorraine Bates.

Michael once again lives in the apartment building where those ashes were scattered. Now, as it was then, it is perhaps the place in England most imbued with the spirit of his parents. His dad was his hero and a man's man who guided him in business and fatherhood, even if he did things in some untraditional ways, and his mom was a kind soul who instilled responsibility and curiosity with the world.

"Since we've been in existence, I've seen entire other countries come and go, and Sealand is still there," Michael Bates said. "A lot people have been inspired by what it represents—that sense of freedom and adventure." That inspiration came from standout people who created a country—and a family—firmly in their mold.

## PASSING THE TORCH

Roy and Joan's daughter Penny has no regrets about leaving the micro-national life behind. Now age seventy, she is the owner of a bustling clinic in Southend-on-Sea that offers aesthetic services such as lipo-suction and permanent makeup. She works hard managing all aspects of the business, comparing the experience of running the clinic to her time on Sealand: "You're either in or you're out, you can't half do it," she said. Penny is married to David Hawker, formerly an aviation attorney, and the two live in a spacious and modern flat across from a beautiful park with an unbelievable view of the Thames. Their home is not far from their children and grandchildren; it's also within walking distance of her brother Michael. David has a blown-up version of the photo of his wife with pistols hanging above his study in the basement, where he advises on various legal projects and smokes cigarettes.*

Penny loves being a grandmother and great-grandmother. The members of her family grew up with the fort looming in the proverbial horizon, but she never pressed them into service of the family legacy. Sometimes when she is dispensing parenting advice to friends or family, she'll catch herself and recall the circumstances of her own youth. "I grew up in the middle of the North Sea on a bloody fort! Who am I to tell anybody what to do and I take it all back," she said with a laugh.

Penny does appreciate the survival skills that the experience gave her and the fact that she had an adolescence that few can imagine. Friends new and old alike frequently ask her to recount memories and adventures of her youth, even at inopportune times, like when she is in the middle of doing Pilates. The last time Penny went out to Sealand was in 2008. She and David went out in a giant helicopter, thanks to his contacts in the aviation world, and looked with approval at the vastly improved and much more hospitable conditions. The view of

---

* Roy and Joan would phone David to arbitrate disputes between Michael and Roy, and later on he'd even fly to and from Spain and the fort to do so.

the North Sea was one that hadn't changed since she was a girl, and she was filled with nostalgia for a time that was overwhelmingly unique to her family. "The new generation doesn't really know what it was like when we were out there," she reflected.

Nowadays, both Liam and James—tall and handsome—take after Roy. It was James who climbed aboard the wrecked principality via precipitously dangling ladder after a fire engulfed the entire country in flames in 2006, while Liam dons the Sealand red and black to represent the country in international soccer matches. The sense of family pride is there, but the attitudes toward the micronation also differ slightly between generations. Michael, who essentially grew up legitimatizing a fort that has been a part of his life far longer than it hasn't, is more resolute in asserting what Sealand has accomplished and will readily recite the various claims that speak in favor of its sovereignty. His sons seem to consider it with a bit more wryness, however, appreciating its oversized reputation and the patent weirdness of its enduring existence.

"That's something everyone assumes, that you tell all the girls that you're a prince. But no, definitely not," Liam laughed. "It's not really something you open with. People might think you're a bit odd, but eventually you say, 'There's this thing, it's been part of my family for generations now,' and you show them the website and pictures and stuff like that. Funny enough, my girlfriend, when I first told her, she told her parents and her parents' next-door neighbors knew all about it and were big supporters. They basically told her the ins and outs of it before I had to."

Charlotte's interest in Sealand waned over the years as much as her brothers' grew, and she is featured in only a handful of press reports or documentaries about Sealand. Part of the reason, Liam explained, is that she hates boats, and this can be seen in a 2011 feature in which the Sealanders knight BBC presenter Ben Fogle, who would later declare that the "story of Sealand is stranger than fiction, better than Hollywood, and more surreal than Dali." During the broadcast, Charlotte is practically green with seasickness as they boat out to the principality.

Charlotte did take after her Aunt Penny, however, eschewing the fort but adopting some of its national vigor in furthering her own interests. She has run a cat and dog grooming business since she was a teenager and cares for horses on the property she shares with her fiancé. ("She's animal-mad," James summed up.) She also took after her grandmother Joan, as she competed to be Miss Southend 2010, the first round in a pageant that gave "the most stunning, intelligent, and charming young girls" the chance to become Miss England. As part of the competition, Charlotte raised money for Have a Heart Children's Charity by selling raffle tickets for the chance to become a Lord or Lady of Sealand. Charlotte bested former Miss Essexes and a top-20 Miss England finalist at Southend's Rendezvous Casino in May 2010 (and was commended for raising £528 for charity, the most of any contestant) but came in second place.

Fortunately, both Roy and Joan were still around when their grandson James met the love of his life, a nurse from Southend named Charley Rae Holgate who now runs an aesthetics business. The young couple met at a friend's fancy caveman-themed party in May 2009. Charley was dressed up as a cavewoman with a double entendre written on her arm; James was dressed as Fred Flintstone and was immediately smitten. Though they partied enough that they didn't remember meeting until they were tagged in a photo together on Facebook the next day, the pair really hit it off the next time they met. "The second time I met her, I told her I would marry her," he said. He popped the big question in July 2012 on a rowboat during a torrential downpour, and a wedding date was set for September 6, 2013.

Charley hadn't heard of Sealand when she met James, and when he casually brought up the fact that he was a prince one Sunday morning, she thought he might still be a little drunk from the night before. Then he went into the history of the fort and Charley was even more skeptical. "Turns out it was all true, but I had to do my own research to believe it," she said.

Hearing that a Sealander was getting married, reporters were quick to ask Charley how she felt about becoming royalty. "It's still all a bit surreal. Sometimes I stop and think to myself, 'Is this really happening?' It's so strange to think I'll be a princess," she said. "I've always loved Disney films, so it will literally be like a dream come true!"

It wasn't long before Charley went out to survey her new domain firsthand. She liked what she saw. "We go out to Sealand together every couple of months. It's amazing going over there—it's a real adventure, and there's no-one for miles," she said. "After our engagement party, we went out there to hang up a banner, and then caught and cooked our own lobster. It was lovely." Charley said she wants to raise chickens on the fort, but as of yet this idea hasn't been implemented.

The couple honeymooned in Malaysia for almost three weeks, and not long after things took their natural course. The couple had their first son, Freddy Michael Roy, in January 2014, their second son Harry in February 2016, and most recently a set of twins, Matilda and Tabitha, in December 2018. The new generations of Sealandic royalty will grow up to inherit a rusty but endearing and enduring kingdom. But like Michael, who marveled at his laissez-faire upbringing out on the fort once he became a parent, James is pondering the wisdom of raising his kids fifteen meters up in a metal barrel. "My children have inherited the Bateses' strongheaded ways. I can't wait to take them out to Sealand and experience the less-adventurous side of the fort now," Charley said. "No guns or cannons or prisoners."*

But first comes the day-to-day rigors of having four young kids—a full-time job for prince and pauper alike.

"Whenever you're on the phone with [James], there's screaming in the background," Liam Bates said. "Text messaging works better."

And thus the fourth generation of Sealand reigns in greater numbers than ever before.

## HISTORY ONTO PARCHMENT

Joan Bates had been working throughout the years on an autobiography tentatively titled *Seagulls at My Door*, but never got around to finishing it. As his parents got up in years, Michael got more serious about picking up where she left off and set out to pen an everlasting

---

* When asked if the Sealanders would still shoot at any vessel that comes too close, "We cannot confirm or deny this," Liam said with a wry smile. Michael Bates said he would put out the principality's best china and serve a cup of tea if the British military forced their way aboard.

paean to his folks and the life they forged. It took him around twelve years to finally get a manuscript in working order—a project he called *Holding the Fort* that chronicles his family's outrageous story. He plumbed the depths of his memory and that of the friends and family, and he paid a visit to the stately British National Archives in Kew where he was able to get a behind-the-scenes look at what the government was thinking and saying about the fort. Among many thousands of other pages, the archives hold the plans for raids on the fort, original brochures, photos of confiscated broadcasting equipment, and letters and declarations signed by Alexander Achenbach. Michael was both amused and a little shocked at the plans for military-grade helicopter raids, but the documents show just how seriously the family's adventure was taken by the Crown.

*Holding the Fort* was self-published in 2015 and is for sale through the Sealand webpage. Michael and his sons have done copious amounts of publicity for the tome and the sales of the handsome hardcover volume of course help to keep the principality going. Not a professional writer, Michael admits that the punctuation and grammar are not world-class, but as he reminds us, "I always tell people that when you were at school learning how to read and write, I was making a story that people want to read about." The book is a must-have for those interested in micronational history, and it's enough to inspire one to start his or her own country.

But the triumphant story of Sealand has also inspired the machinations of those actively working against it. Johannes W.F. Seiger, successor to the exile government founded by Alexander Achenbach, vociferously claims to be the one true leader of the Principality of Sealand. While Achenbach was a bona fide con artist, Seiger prefers to go a more mystical and revisionist-historical route as head of the dark mirror version of the principality. A lot of unpredictable things have happened to Sealand over the years, but in no way could Roy and Joan Bates have foreseen the strange Seigerian offshoot that maintains its unsettling presence well into the present day.

# CHAPTER 17

# A DARK MIRROR

---

*"It makes no sense to demand from the Gods what one can achieve oneself." – Epicurus."*
—Exile government of the Principality of Sealand

One day in late 1998, two men walked into the administrative offices of the town of Eisleben, Germany, to apply for a digging permit. As the men gruffly explained to Hans-Peter Sommer, a functionary at the offices, they were representatives of the Principality of Sealand, and they wanted official clearance to go after a treasure that had evaded treasure hunters for decades. The men said they were looking for the "Amber Room"—a room supposedly covered entirely in gold and filled with treasures from St. Petersburg that was dismantled and disappeared during the Second World War. The Amber Room was a source of interest primarily to conspiracy theorists, and Sommer hadn't met anyone who took the quest seriously. At a loss about how to proceed, he sent the men on to the administrative offices of the region where the digging was to take place. "I thought that was all bells and whistles, it all seemed so abstruse," he said.

A few months later, police officers were called to a series of caves located on private property in the second town. Crawling through the caves' entrance, the police chief found a large chamber with hoses providing air and equipment suggesting excavations had recently taken place. It turned out the men who applied for a permit in Eisleben had gone forward with the dig, despite not having official permission. Officers could not determine if anything of value was found or taken, though the men certainly didn't appear to have found the Amber Room.

More serious than a dig on private property, however, were the death threats Hans-Peter Sommer began receiving when he didn't issue the digging permit. A few letters had arrived at his office declaring he'd been sentenced to death by the *Kommissarische Reichsregierung* (KRR), or "Provisional Reich Government," for violating a section of the 1933 criminal code against treason. The KRR was one of the putative governing bodies of the *Reichsbürgerbewegung*, or "Reich's Citizens Movement," whose adherents claim that the peace treaty that established the current Federal Republic of Germany (FRG, or Germany as we know it today) is invalid because the Nazi Reich Government did not concede to it at the time of its signing.\* Reichsburgers maintain that the FRG and its various state and municipal subgovernments are puppet governments controlled by Europe and the United States, the latter of which wants to weaken Germany to ensure US global domination.

Similar to the sovereign citizen groups in the US who claim the federal government is unconstitutional, the Reichsburgers are known to issue driver's licenses, documents, and sentences of corporal punishment under the aegis of the KRR (or many similar but competing governments). The Sealandic diggers who appeared in Eisleben had been commissioned for the project by the KRR, who claimed they wanted to return the Amber Room to its rightful owner as a show of goodwill from the Reich government. But because Sommer hadn't issued the digging permit, he had denied the KRR's legitimacy and thus committed treason, an insult that could only be punished with blood. The writ of punishment was issued by the exile government of Sealand run by Johannes W.F. Seiger, who had partnered his version of Sealand with the KRR.

As is readily apparent, the story of the exile government is the seedy underbelly of the Sealand story. Though the activities and ambitions of the exile government don't affect the day-to-day operations of the original Sealand—Seiger has never even been to the principality—they certainly create a remarkably strange side story to the saga of Sealand proper. If you were attending the meeting of a micronational UN, the exile government of Sealand would be the nation in the corner rubbing its hands together and cackling at its diabolic plans.

---

\* The KRR contends it was the German *military* that surrendered to the Allies in 1945 and not the leadership of the Reich Government, which was the only body that could officially concede defeat.

Today, Sealand's government-in-exile operates from behind a great wooden desk at Seiger's home in the western German town of Trebbin on a property that used to be an industrial chicken farm. Seiger is just as tireless and officious as his colleagues were in advocating for the sovereignty of Sealand. He and the exile government's cabinet ministers have maintained a website since the late 1990s whose URL—*www. principality-of-sealand.ch*—might lead one to believe that website is an official organ of the true Principality of Sealand. The website acknowledges that the Bateses founded and ran the principality, but the timeline of official events changes with the coup of 1978. The alternate timeline outlines Roy's "unconstitutional" behavior that necessitated the coup, and the exile government is adamant that the Bates family has had no authority on the principality since then. The website advocates for Sealand's sovereignty and is full of PDFs adorned with official seals and titles that chronicle Seiger's correspondence with branches of government in Germany and abroad. The Leisner and Vitanyi opinions on the principality's sovereignty are readily available, as are scans of Seiger's Sealandic passports, filled with visas from countries all over the world. The exile government even issued silver SX$100 coins with Seiger's bust in 1991.

## A CHECKERED PAST

Johannes Seiger, a portly man with gray hair and a mustache, was born in 1941 to a formerly wealthy family whose factories went bankrupt in an economic downturn. Consequently, Seiger traveled the world looking for investment opportunities. He first came into contact with Alexander Achenbach in the late 1970s while seeking an international lawyer to help him transfer money in a way that his creditors couldn't touch. Although the exact nature of their various dealings remains unknown, the pair bonded over their strange worldviews and hit it off well enough that Seiger was first named Sealand's Minister of Economic Affairs and then Prime Minister in 1989. Based on the prestige of his Sealandic nobility, he was approached by patriots of the former German Democratic Republic (communist East Germany) as the Berlin Wall fell. Seiger says that he was sought out to lead the talks between the reuniting sides of Germany and the remnants of the former Reich-era government. He also says that he and his cabinet were given secret Stasi files, Nazi UFOs, and the whereabouts of cultural assets and looted art, including the Amber Room, from former East German agents, which led to the unauthorized dig in 1999. Seiger says he has attempted to involve the current German government in a partnership with the Sealand authority, but he has also wielded his status as Prime Minister to challenge it—most vociferously the Brandenburg Judiciary, the district government of the area in which Seiger resides.

In 1991, Seiger bought the property in Trebbin and filled the house with decorations befitting a statesman, including oil paintings, the wooden desk, and a large ceremonial sword. For a while Seiger was driven around by a chauffeur and had a butler working for him—an ex-lawyer who said little and refilled candy bowls for guests. The property also contains a half dozen large buildings from its days as a chicken farm, as well as a collection of military surplus, including thousands of gasmasks and tires that only fit obscure Russian military vehicles. Seiger was able to sell off some of the surplus and turned a profit operating a scrap business from the polluted grounds of the old farm, and then entered into an agreement with a group from the Russian Ministry of Trade to salvage and scrap the items they left behind as the Soviets withdrew from East Germany. Some of these agreements were arranged through a company started by Seiger called the Sealand Trade Corporation and nationalized as an official organ of the principality. Written into the contracts was an agreement that any disputes would be settled in the Arbitration Court at the International Chamber of Commerce in Paris, which Seiger points to as affirmation of Sealand's status as an independent state.

Seiger turned a healthy profit scrapping these goods, but banks in at least five nearby towns were said to be after Seiger for not paying back his loans. At one point he received so many letters from debt collectors and legal agencies that his mailbox overflowed. Seiger replied by mailing out stacks of paperwork with elaborate crests and official titles attesting to his authority as the Prime Minister of the Principality of Sealand and to the illegitimacy of the local government. He was able to avoid foreclosure by selling some of the buildings owned by

Sealand Trade Corporation to Johannes Seiger as an individual (a
move that was made more difficult to counter because the question of
who owned the land in the first place was too obscure to get to the
bottom of). When authorities came to tell him there was no way he
could be burning jars of pesticide in the old chimneys on the property,
he issued the customary orders as Prime Minister that the officials
report to an international court to accept their punishment for violating his sovereignty. "He is not crazy. He does that to meander
through the gaps of authorities," said Trebbin's Mayor Thomas Berger.

But the claims in Seiger's belligerent letters eventually caught up
with him, especially after he told authorities he had come into possession of nuclear and chemical weapons along with the other secret
pieces of information given to him by the GDR. "[W]e immediately
contacted the governments of Brandenburg and of Lower Saxony in
order to pass on these materials without any demands on our part,"
Seiger said, but the local government did not consider the offer altru-
istic.

On October 9, 1998, more than sixty police officers and dozens of
officials from the Office for Pollution Control and the Radiation
Protection Office descended on the property in Trebbin to conduct a
raid on the stash of alleged weapons. They dug through the rooms of
the house, the buildings, and the cars on the property, and they ran a
Geiger counter over everything to determine if there were any radioactive components anywhere. Seiger was led away in shackles and a
hood—to be presented in a media spectacle to the world as terrorist,
he said. He challenged the raid by presenting his diplomatic passport
and tax documents attesting STC's incorporation, but he was "stupe-
fied" when he was told that STC was not a valid corporation.

The police told the public that no evidence of nuclear or chemical
weapons was found, but Seiger knows differently.

"The chemical warfare agents contained in a small bottle...were
not returned with the reason given that there was not sufficient room
in the evidence room and that they therefore had 'apparently' been
destroyed," he said. "Our request to issue proof of this [is consistently]
denied by the judiciary, the prosecuting office and the police. I assume
that this material is until today in the possession of these agencies,

because it is absolutely possible to use these materials to terroristic ends." Seiger was ordered to undergo a psychological evaluation, which went ignored.

To Seiger, the struggle for Sealand's sovereignty is a sister struggle to the effort to restore Germany's true sovereignty, and he has aligned himself with various groups working toward this end. As Sealand's purported prime minister, he signed a bilateral contract of recognition with a prominent KRR group led by Wolfgang Gerhard Guenter Ebel. In early 1999, the exile government entered into a "Friendship and Consultation Agreement" to lease an estate and mansion southwest of Berlin called Hakeburg from the Reichsburgers* for the next ninety-nine years.** Hakeburg was once the home of German gentry, but they sold the castle to the Nazi government when they ran into financial difficulties. Because the KRR group considers the Reich government to be Germany's valid government, they argued they were the true owners of the property and had the authority to lease it to Seiger.

At the time of the lease to Seiger, however, Hakeburg was the headquarters of Deutsche Telekom AG, a communications company that owns phone networks all over the world (including T-Mobile in the US). Seiger delivered many lawsuits and legal summonses in an effort to evict them from the property and issued fines of one million Deutschmarks per day for "continued embezzlement." He told one reporter that that the company's lack of response was a good sign, as

---

* Reichsburgers number in the tens of thousands in Germany but there is no single organization or leader. According to one count, there are around sixty separate groups that claim to be the legitimate successor to the government. Though most of the claims can be written off as the rantings of conspiracy theorists, the increasing overlap with militant right-wing groups has Germany's security apparatus on high alert. Such groups can be fairly dangerous—police have confiscated caches of weapons from Reichsburg groups, a former Mr. Germany was wounded in a shootout with police when he and his cohorts refused to be evicted from an apartment, and a member present at the raid later murdered a police officer in a separate incident.

** The agreement also purportedly involves the current German representative of the Supreme Headquarters Allied Expeditionary Force, or SCHAEF, an Allied consortium that oversaw operations in Europe from 1943 until it was disbanded in 1945. Seiger and Reichsburgers maintain that SCHAEF is the only European authority with valid decision-making power today. A copy of the agreement was sent to the Bill Clinton White House; a short reply said that the issue was being forwarded to the embassy in Berlin.

it meant they were deep in thought about the legal predicament they were in. Seiger was eventually banned from the Telekom property and later claimed that the FRG had bankrupted his companies out of spite and were likely behind an assassination attempt in early 2005.

The politics associated with the Reich government make Seiger a bit darker than just a bureaucracy-obsessed con artist. A glance at the exile government's website suggests something is amiss, as there are vaguely fascist symbols and photos of what appear to be Nazi higher-ups in front of a UFO. Looking a little further, the website hosts a lot of anti-Semitic content, including items of Holocaust denial and text from a speech supposedly given by Benjamin Franklin in which he warns countries against allowing Jews to settle within their borders.* Other statements on the exile government's website suggest a desire to establish a world in which all minority rights are respected and everyone is flourishing, but when asked to explain how all of this fits with Sealand and his aims as a head of state, Seiger referred me to the Franklin speech.

Seiger's disdain for the German government does not preclude accepting its acknowledgment of Sealand when it appears to have been granted. In a surreal parallel to the (true) Sealand's historical interactions with the British government, Seiger takes as affirmation the various letters from governmental departments that mention the principality by name (even if they are rebutting Seiger's authority), as well as the fact that the scrap business with the Russian Army necessitated a visit by a representative from the USSR's Ministry of Foreign Trade. He also cites the signature from a mail clerk in the White House who signed for a registered letter from the exile government as proof that the US has taken his claims seriously.

Whether an uber-serious micronationalist or a revisionist Fascist who glorifies one of the greatest evils the world has ever seen, Seiger

---

* The speech, known as "Franklin's Prophecy," was supposedly transcribed from a speech he gave at the 1787 Constitutional Convention and is a complete lie. It appeared for the first time in the 1930s in an anti-Semitic newspaper, and it has been roundly proven to be a forgery by actual historians. (A reference to Palestine a century before its creation is but one of the many historical inaccuracies/impossibilities.) Nevertheless, the speech was widely publicized in Nazi Germany and in the present day by Islamic fundamentalists.

knows that whatever is next for Sealand, it will come thanks in part
to the power of Vril, a mythical Force-like source of infinite energy
whose believers say can provide heat and power to dispossessed people
and nations all over the world.

## SOCIETY VRILIA

According to Seiger, he and Sealand were chosen by secret Thule and
Vril societies to lead the search for Vril, as "only a sovereign state
without power ambitions or lust for enrichment was and is able to
carry out these far-reaching measures correctly." The symbol for Vril,
a *V* with a lightning bolt flourish, is splashed all over the exile government's website. "More than a hundred scientists of international
standing are already working—still unrecognized—under the protection of Sealand" on Vril-related projects, the website states.

Vril first appeared in the 1871 novel *The Coming Race*, written by
a British politician named Sir Edward G. Bulwer-Lytton. The novel's
protagonist finds his way to an underground realm where he encoun-
ters a group of tall and powerful beings who can harness Vril by
concentration. According to the book, Vril is a substance unlike any
on earth, powerful enough that even a child could use it to destroy a
city, but also capable of curing ailments and of invigorating the soul.
It is apparently like liquid energy or gentle lightning, and is concentrated through a staff wielded by the user.* The concept was further
expanded in the novels of authors such as Louis Jacolliot, who connected Vril to the legend of Hyperborea and Thule, ancient civilizations
covered in ice that factor prominently in Aryan mysticism.**

A lot of people took *The Coming Race* to be nonfiction, or at least
a fictionalized account of an actual lost civilization. The concept of
Vril caught on with nineteenth-century mystics, who popularized it,
while Nazi readers determined the advanced subterranean culture that
harnesses it is Aryan based on the author's description of the language

---

* Based on the description, it seems that Marcellus Wallace's briefcase in *Pulp Fiction*
might be full of Vril.

** It should be noted that these legends were co-opted by racist occultists; their actual
histories and the study thereof far precede these ignominious interpretations.

they speak. This association dovetailed nicely with the occult obsession of certain Nazi party members to find Thule and with the alleged formation of a clandestine Vril society associated with a secret Nazi base in Antarctica where the Third Reich elite supposedly escaped to when Germany surrendered. According to this mythos, the Nazis took with them the plans and technology behind the "Reichsflugscheiben," or "Flying Wheel": a hovering craft that would eventually be identified the world over as a flying saucer and that flew by harnessing the same energy attracted by Vril generators. (Hence the picture of the UFO on the website.)

Today, a good bit of the exile government's efforts are dedicated to the sale of Vril generators, which have come in a few different models over the years. One comes with a remote control and looks like a makeup compact with lights and a photo of a Nazi UFO. Various other models have been offered throughout the years that resemble pipe bombs, cigar holders, and, to be crass, golden dildos.

The generators concentrate Vril energy through the "irreversible and self-energizing energization of selected materials." The Sealand Vril generator has no magnets, power cells, or other moving mechanical parts: "[The generator] latches into the cosmic energy field and channels this energy into positive use," the website states. The larger generators should be placed on a shelf in a room, while the smaller generators can be carried in a pocket or bag so that the energy flows directly to the user, though the 2019 generators are said to be powerful enough that they can be placed anywhere. A graphic on the website shows a flashlight powered by Vril that has been continuously turned on for years. "My conclusion: one of the most magical technologies that I have personally tried and whose potential is not yet manageable for me," attests one website user called "F."

All of the exile government's activities are conducted in conjunction with the Sealand Trade Corporation. Though the exile government initially said that priority would be given to select individuals, "especially medium-sized business enterprises in German-speaking countries," Vril generators are now available to anybody who wants to purchase one.

According to the exile government, Vril technology is similarly useful for today's drivers, as the energy helps to boost the power of vehicles and reduce the money spent on fuel. The preferred way of demonstrating the Vril is through combustion engines because the effects of Vril on human biology can't be accurately measured. "The Vril energy demonstrably achieves a markedly better combustion of the respective fuel in explosion engines...which leads to a significant reduction in $CO_2$ emissions," says Seiger.

At one point the exile government contacted Red Bull about using Vril generators to power vehicles in an auto race. The exile Sealanders offered the lease of three generators for a cool million euros, but the organizers of the event didn't respond. A similar offer was made to the president of Formula 1 racing; a response from Formula 1 said the proposal was interesting but that a more appropriate department should be contacted.

The presence of the exile government sometimes rankles the true Sealanders, as people seeking information about the principality can be easily duped by the exile government's website or baffled by the quest for Vril. The Sealanders occasionally get threats purportedly from the exile government* but generally they don't pay this side of the story any mind.

"We don't give it the credit otherwise if you'll draw attention it," James said, "though they do have all those funny little machines."

"I want one!" Michael said.

Of course, the ideology of the exile government is completely incompatible with Roy's own philosophy and experience, and with the history of the fort Sealand is built on. "[T]hese fortresses were put in place by the British government originally to defend Britain from Nazis and fascism, and now these Fascists and Nazis are claiming to be part of Sealand," Michael said. At one point a documentarian tried to arrange for Michael to travel to Germany and knock on Seiger's door, but unfortunately the plan didn't come together. Michael has yet

---

* One threat from 2013 reads: "Your unlawful residency of our land has gone on long enough. We are retaking what is rightfully ours, in the name of the Sealand Rebel Government. If need be, you shall be removed by force. You remember the events of 1978; there is no need for further hostility. Rebel loyalists amongst you are ready. Go peacefully, or on January the first 2015, we are coming. Expect us."

to meet his inverted doppelganger, but the prospect excites him. "I'd be up for that!" Michael laughed. "I'd be well up for that!"

The exile government was initially interested in speaking with me for this book and sent enthusiastic greetings. They were pleased at the prospect that my writing could help add some legitimacy to their claims that ex-Stasi informants had given them information about the whereabouts of chemical and nuclear weapons, and about everything Vril. But our correspondence was brought to an abrupt halt when I couldn't fulfill a request to deliver this data to higher authorities.

"[Since] you have not answered our questions (arranging a credit loan, submitting our information to US President Trump), we have now passed along the information to President Trump through the ambassador in Berlin," Seiger wrote. "Therefore, we are no longer interested in further contact."

Contact was reinitiated, and a few more emails were exchanged, but requests for a visit were denied when I was unable to pay the exile government $10,000 for an exclusive demonstration of Vril technology, possibly using army tanks.

As of the publication of this book, the exile government of Sealand has not yet found the Amber Room or expanded the use of Vril beyond its own adherents, but Seiger is ambitious and speaks of the possibilities of Sealand in rhapsodic, quasi-mythical terms. It is a strange, sketchy dream, but one compelling enough that a man will dedicate his life to Sealand without ever even having to set foot on the fort.

"From the depths of the sea, she rises virginally: [Sealand]—as old as humanity, and yet unborn," Seiger writes. "Sealand could be the flapping of a butterfly's wing; hardly noticeable here, which, however, according to chaos theory, faraway, clandestinely mediated by the formidable chain of cause and effect, may start a hurricane, an earthquake, even the fall of the old and the rise of a new continent."

# CHAPTER 18

# CREW CHANGE

*"For me, there's an awful lot going on in my brain all the time. But I quite enjoy my own company."*
—Mike Barrington

At 6:00 a.m. on a cold day in March 2019, a lone figure could be seen on Harwich's pier in the deep blue of the early morning light. The man in his late fifties wore a taxi driver hat and blue mechanic's jumpsuit over jeans and a sweater. He took a puff from a vape pen and blew a substantial cloud of smoke into the air as he made a pile of boxes and bags at the top of a set of stairs that led straight into the water alongside one of the piers. The man was Joe Hamill, and the pile of luggage was a fortnight's worth of victuals and clothes for his stay on Sealand. Along with Mike Barrington, Hamill is one of Sealand's two caretakers, and the pair alternate two-week stints on Sealand as their full-time jobs.

The Bates family pays the men to keep watch on the fort and attend to its multitudinous repairs and chores. They also pay the expenses the men accrue in supplies and equipment, and it costs a surprising amount to maintain what some might consider an outsized hobby. The caretakers are far removed from the outlying neo-Nazi/Vril aspects of the Sealand story, but their relationship to the micronation is quite personal, as their schedules, well-being, and livelihoods revolve around their duty to the fort.

The night before his shift starts, Hamill drives 150 miles from Basingstoke to Harwich and typically stays in a rented room above a pub. The sleeping arrangement is one from the olden days in a historic place like Harwich. The seaside town full of row houses, stone streets, and ancient churches is juxtaposed with the ports of Felixstowe just across the harbor, which boasts the largest container shipping hub in the UK. With the enormous cranes and shipping facilities surrounding the bay, the area looks like a historical reenactment surrounded by cyborgs.

Hamill piles his bags on the pier in anticipation of hitching a ride on a small fishing vessel from Harwich. Looking across the water to the next dock, he hails Dan Griffin, a Harwich fisherman, crabber, and lobsterman in his thirties with a friendly face and equally pleasant demeanor. Griffin and Pecker, the local fisherman aboard Sealand when it caught fire, are going to pull in that week's haul a few miles beyond Sealand, which they deliver to local restaurants as soon as they get back to shore. Interestingly, Griffin's full-time job is servicing buoys for Trinity House, the agency that drew Michael's fire when it got too close to Sealand.

Pecker, with a grizzled face and two layers of old seaman's sweaters, rushes off with Dan a few hundred feet down the pier to fire up a rickety fishing boat and putter over to where Hamill has stashed his cargo. The boat pulls alongside the pier, green with sea slime and knobby with barnacles, and the three men make quick work of loading the fifteen bags and boxes into the boat. Everything is piled atop a wooden box covering the engine, and Pecker and Dan throw in a few stacks of plastic crates for the crustaceans.

The boat putters along the path outlined by buoys at its top speed of 8 knots (approximately 9.2 mph), steadily leaving the curve of the shore behind and the enormous erector sets that are the cranes of the shipping port. The boat would sail down the narrow channel between sandbanks out into the North Sea and eventually bank right about six miles from the shore for the last leg of its journey toward Sealand. The principality is a little less than seven miles from the shore, but the journey will take approximately an hour and twenty minutes. The group is remarkably efficient at getting ready to go, and that efficiency extends to rolling cigarettes and firing up a rusty stovetop inside the wheelhouse to make the first of endless cups of tea.

The trio shoots the shit and jokes around as they go. Dan and Pecker are the last human beings Hamill will see in at least two weeks. The boat essentially has the sea to itself at that hour, with no fishermen or pleasure cruisers yet hitting the water. One of the only crafts they see is a speedboat that zips by as it ushers a pilot from shore to one of the half a dozen container ships moored far off in the distance. While the pilots of the massive ships no doubt possess tremendous skill, a specialized pilot is necessary to coordinate the ship's passage into Felixstowe's narrow docks. On the way, Dan flips a ten pence coin into the sea.

"It's a bit of superstition—you give something back to the sea that's given you so much," he explained.

Dan leaves the boat on autopilot as he attends to the various chores involved in pulling in the lobster pots while Joe starts unfurling a large nylon construction tote used to hold a ton of rubble. In it he places all of the items he'll be taking to Sealand, and once everything is loaded he joins all of the handles together with a heavy metal clasp that will be attached to a hook at the end of the winch that takes supplies, boats, and visitors up to Sealand.

The principality is visible in the distance for the whole journey. It looks at the same time tiny and gigantic—it's a vulnerable speck in the vastness of the sea, but its legs also seem to extend surprisingly high out of the water. Hamill eyes the centurion with an inscrutable glance and exhales a blast of vapor that smells like Crunch Berries cereal.

## "I'M NOT THE SAME PERSON I USED TO BE"

Joe basically fell into his strange job by mistake, but it was just the opportunity he needed at the time. He worked in the insurance industry for twenty years but was increasingly oppressed by the banal rigors of the nine-to-five lifestyle. A long-term relationship fell apart at the peak of his dissatisfaction, leaving him so fed up with humanity that he wouldn't have minded divorcing himself from society entirely. He was in a pub one evening, and a friend asked him if he was interested in a weekend's work doing security out at sea. Sure, Joe said, what's the gig? It turned out he was to run security for the Red Bull skateboarding expo out on the Principality of Sealand in 2008. Joe had never heard of the micronation, but the price was right and he agreed to the job. A few days later, he packed his bags and went to meet the boat at the pier in Harwich. He was told to wear all black and bring a high-visibility construction vest.

Joe's mouth fell open when saw the bosun's chair being lowered down on the winch for the first time. "I could see it in the distance and I said, 'Do I get strapped into that?'" he said. The skateboarders went right up to the lip on the edge of the fort—stunts that made Joe's stomach drop. "I couldn't even look at them," he laughed. "I was on that platform acting as security and I was the most frightened person aboard." It turned out that the next caretaker the Bateses had lined up didn't have a car and therefore had no way of transporting his stuff to the fort, and so Joe decided to take the job full time.

The first week out on the fort was cold, and the isolation was intense—almost too much for someone who had little experience at sea. But the odd charm of Sealand grew on him, as did the opportunity to have some time to himself. Joe has stayed on as caretaker ever since and is now in the middle of his eleventh year on the job. Now, packing and traveling and sailing out to the fort is as routine to Joe as pulling in lobster pots is to Pecker and Dan. Still, the isolation took some getting used to, and Joe acknowledges the routine isn't for everybody.

"People close to me will say I'm not the same person I used to be," he said. "Before I'd go out there, I'd go quiet, I wouldn't speak to anyone, get very serious. My dear old mother would say, 'you've got to get another job. I'm really worried.' But [the quiet] would only last the night before. Look at me now—I'm fine, and in a way, I'm sort of looking forward to it. Get Mike off, get some stuff done I need to get done on land, do whatever I do."

## A DELICATE MANEUVER

A few cups of tea after they leave Harwich, Sealand looms enormously out of the water in front of the boat, a black silhouette in front of gray skies and gray water and every bit as magnificent, battered, and perplexing as one might imagine. Bits of rebar are visible around the towers, with nubs of metal I-beams still sticking out of the South tower, where the landing stage once attached. Mike Barrington waves from sixty feet in the air, and a generator fires up and hums loudly in the morning quiet. A hook is lowered from the winch as the boat draws alongside, and Dan does a delicate dance of angling the back of the boat under the winch in an impressive maritime parallel park.

Barrington would later say that Dan's skills are unparalleled when it comes to deftly maneuvering around the legs of the fort. The outgoing tide is not only strong, but its suction is complicated by the pillars, making navigation around the fort fairly dangerous, even for skilled pilots. But Dan knows what he is doing, though he has yet to set foot on the principality.

"Oh, no, I've never been up there," he said, shaking his head. "You wouldn't catch me on that chair."

Once Joe's supplies are hovering above the deck, Mike pulls a rope that guides the arm of the winch over the solid ground, and the load is gently set down. He then attaches the bosun's chair to the winch and lowers it back down toward the boat, which by this time has done another lap around the fort and is getting into position again. Joe quickly hops onto the chair and Mike waves to the boat as the winch raises him upward. The efficiency of their work is once again on display, with the boat taking off before Joe is even ten feet in the air. Joe hops out of the bosun's chair onto Sealand hardly more than a minute later.

The work on the fort is never done. "It's a constant battle—it's like having a boat. The rust comes and you have to stay on top of it," Liam Bates said. To that end, piles of steel plates line the deck and oxygen tanks line the perimeter—supplies for the ongoing project of re-steeling the deck. A pallet jack and pallets are parked next to a rusting staircase going up to the helipad with "To be removed" painted on it, and miscellaneous tools sit in piles with no discernible organization.

Inside, the kettle is already boiling on the country's gas stove. Dan and Pecker will be out collecting their bounty for approximately four hours, leaving the two caretakers some overlap where life and work on Sealand can be discussed. The pair drink scalding hot tea as they go over the handwritten list of projects Mike has been working on and Joe's to-do list for the coming two weeks. The kitchen table doubles as Sealand's customs office, as that is where Mike tends to stamp passports with the simple Sealand stamp. A guest book with entries dating back almost fifteen years is an unofficial register of all visitors who've come to the fort.

## THE JOYS OF SOLITUDE

It is approximately forty degrees and windy, with not a hint of sun anywhere in the sky, and one can see their breath in every room of the principality. But Mike, age sixty-four, is comfortable in jeans and a short-sleeved polo shirt. He looks like a combination of Bob Hoskins and Waingro from the movie *Heat*, with the addition of round glasses perched on the end of his nose. He has been on the fort for even longer than Joe, first coming aboard in the late 1980s. He was the perfect man for the job—content being away from society and a jack-of-all-trades. He has been a mechanic, truck driver, builder, and a rabble-rouser with a distaste for delusions of authority both real and imagined.

In fact, Mike used to antagonize the police for fun. He'd zip around the roads that circled the airport, knowing the airport police didn't have jurisdiction beyond its boundaries. He used to blow past them as they frantically waved at him to stop, but one day he whipped around a corner and there was a Sherman tank in the road with its cannon leveled right at his windshield. Another time, he taped together a bunch of camera lenses and was pretending to take pictures of a sensitive government building. Government agents eventually pulled up and grabbed him off the street and took him in for questioning, with Mike having the last laugh because there wasn't even film in the camera. (Interestingly, though, thanks to his abiding interest in photography, he also worked as an agent for the Crown's Health and Social Security Department taking photos of people falsely claiming to have been injured on the job.)

Importantly, Mike also cut his teeth with professional rogues by working aboard Radio Caroline's vessel the *MV Ross Revenge* in the 1970s, a slightly ironic vocation considering Radio Caroline was one of the primary competitors to Roy Bates's Radio Essex. Mike was aboard the Caroline ship fifteen miles out to sea for a year straight during the "Eurosiege" era in the early 1980s, when a British naval vessel relentlessly circled the pirate ship like a hungry shark, attempting to starve the crew into submission. The radio pirates were known to take offensive measures against the blockading government vessels, such as plugging their water outlets with wooden bungs so their toilets wouldn't work, but Mike developed a serious plan if their supplies finally ran out. "We were going to run the engine at full bore, bring her around, and slice you in two," he told the commander later on.

Mike's engineering knowledge has been critical to Sealand staying afloat. Approximately 99 percent of the nation's power comes from wind and solar power—the only such nation that can boast these numbers, as Liam points out—and these systems were designed and built by Barrington.* Mike got thrown out of a hardware superstore for climbing a ladder to get part numbers on a turbine they had for sale; he called the parts maker himself and ordered the parts in order to build turbines that could sustain the conditions on Sealand. The first floor down on the South leg houses the inverters that harness the natural power generated by the wind turbines, a complicated structure that stores the generated power in a bank of high-quality car batteries arranged in rows on the floor. If the solar or wind power fails, one of the original World War II-era diesel generators is still in good working order as a backup to the backup generator. The micronation has also been outfitted with LED lights. "You underestimate the impact that has had, because now that means you can have lights on all the time out there," says James Bates.

Detritus from countless other projects sit in various states of completion on deck and in the workspaces of the North and South towers. The server racks from the HavenCo days are still assembled on the second subfloor of the South tower, looking like a museum showcasing technology from the turn of the millennium. That room was like a spaceship compared to the other rooms on Sealand at the time, Mike recalled, boasting what was at the time top of the line computer equipment. Now, it's showing its age a bit, but the racks of servers are still there, and the wood paneling is still bright white—a time capsule to an especially distinct era of the principality's history. The floor below the server room, which held HavenCo's Network Operations Center, is lined almost all the way around with tables, which in turn hold all of the technical manuals from the various pieces of machinery in use on Sealand.

---

* This is good for two reasons: The fort is a relatively green operation, and the money previously spent on diesel can now be directed to other needs.

There are also great stacks of back issues of at least four different amateur radio magazines, the library for a gearhead such as Mike. Sealand is in essence a big clubhouse where Mike can build and experiment to his heart's delight in peace. He has brewed beer, read dozens of technical journals, spent "millions" of hours playing darts, and devotes a lot of his time to fixing equipment and inventing things.

"Everything is done in the most cack-handed long way so you don't get bored. If you're bored, get a hammer and chisel and start chiseling something or do the washing up," Mike said. "Getting a 45-gallon oil drum, filling it up with oxygen and acetylene, and putting a detonator in there—that's what I call fun." (He eventually stopped with the explosions after he came close to blowing himself up.)

He regularly buys spools of discontinued wallpaper from thrift stores to add a sense of comfort and has brought framed pictures and paintings, one by one, to add some color to Sealand's walls. He even put together a chapel in the fort, replete with an honest-to-God altar and books and reliquaries from many faiths. "It's all bits and pieces that have gradually come together that makes it inhabitable," he said. "It's quite homey."

Barrington put a lot of care into the design of his North tower bedroom, which is one of three partitioned rooms but easily the nicest of the bunch. With its dark carpets and muted lighting, his room looks a lot like a quality hotel room one might see advertised in a travel magazine. There are a few other rooms on Sealand to houseguests and there is also the abundance of mattresses in plastic bags stashed throughout the country for the crews that occasionally come and pitch in *en masse*. His engagement with the fort has kept him physically and mentally active. "When I look at some of the old farts in my village, I think, 'What, you're old men!' I'm just going off and doing stuff and they're just sitting there in their slippers," he said.

Barrington's dedication to the project stems from a deep friendship with Roy Bates, who was both a kindred spirit and mentor. The two met after Mike's stint with Radio Caroline came to an end and he was helping Roy repair his boat. It turned out that Roy needed a full-time deckhand on Sealand, and given that Mike had just spent a year straight living on a radio boat, he was just the guy for the job. As a bonus, he literally had an entire ship of spare parts that could be used for Sealand. With Roy having spent time in a warzone and Mike a year straight on a radio ship, the two could appreciate the need to make one's own adventure in the comparatively dull regular society. The two bonded over the honest hard work of putting Sealand together. They were the kind of people who could be working on Sealand all day, barely speak, and then agree that it had been a really great day. Their friendship grew to the point that Mike would sometimes refer to Roy as "Uncle."

But this isn't to say that the pair's outsized personalities didn't clash in the confines of the kingdom. Mike and Roy had one huge blowout fight whose cause Barrington can't even remember, but it escalated to the point that they were both wielding shotguns and yelling at each other from opposite ends of the hallway up top.

"I'll blow your bollocks off!" Roy yelled.

"I'll blow your brains out!" Mike screamed.

Nobody's bollocks ended up getting blown off, but Mike quit Sealand for a while after that. Wounds eventually healed and Mike reengaged with the fort, and he maintains a lifelong respect for Roy and Joan. They were really good people, he said. Later in their lives they paid off the mortgage to his new house in gratitude for the time years earlier that he had refinanced his house in order to keep Sealand going. Mike says he promised Roy he would look after the fort, even if Michael and his sons lost interest. The caretaker does concede, however, that Roy was pretty good at playing him and Michael against each other when he needed to get something done. "Roy was a lovely man, but he was a hard man," recalls Mike.

## CHALK AND CHEESE

Joe and Mike have different management styles aboard the fort, and they generally have to spend a day or two undoing the other's organizational foibles and getting things back to their liking. Both prefer to be alone, and they butt heads when working together. "We're like chalk and cheese," Joe said, recalling the various explosive arguments they've had over the years.

Whereas Mike holds Sealandic law as the genuine law of the fort when one is aboard—talk about executing invaders was bandied about with apparent seriousness, and he refused to stamp some passports because the passports were out of date—Joe has no interest in engaging with people about Sealand's existential politics. "If you think it is [a state], it is, if you think it's not, it's not," he said. "Leave it to official bodies to decide. That's not what I'm there for." He has, in fact, only met Michael Bates a handful of times, but he is quite committed to the project and feels rewarded by the fort's obscurity as a personal dominion. Occasionally he'll take on a construction project or paint a house with a friend, but this is primarily to help someone out, he said, and not something he has to do to survive. Both men enjoy the solitude. "For me, there's an awful lot going on in my brain all the time," Mike said. "But I quite enjoy my own company."

Still, the prospect of staying on the fort in the middle of winter never gets any easier. It's like wintertime camping indoors, Joe said, with cold so fierce that the coats of paint he's applied won't dry. (Mike says his personal secret weapon is an electric blanket.) And his observations of the conditions on the fort confirm something quite worrisome on a large scale. Overall, the weather has gotten more unpredictable since Joe has been aboard the fort—a change that he attributes to global warming. The seasons were distinctly defined when he started a decade ago, he said, but now everything is much hazier, with odd cold and hot snaps all year. The unpredictable weather has wreaked havoc on his social life, as he has had to miss holidays he had planned because the seas were too rough to get him off the fort in time. The longest he's stayed on the fort at a stretch is over four weeks, and by that point he was worried that even he was succumbing to fort madness. "That's horrible, that's really quite horrible," he said.

Joe, now aboard the fort and settled in, is eager to begin his shift. Mike radios Dan and Pecker, getting word that the boat would be next to the platform within half an hour. He compiles his supplies in a small duffle bag—a much smaller load going back than being brought on. The boat would not have the benefit of walls and windows like Sealand has, so Mike puts on an orange jumpsuit over his jeans and shirt and pulls on a wool hat. The boat would take him to Harwich and to his waiting car (which hopefully hasn't been towed) and then he'd go back to the 120-year-old home he is renovating. Though he didn't take any back with him this time, Mike is known to take a few liters of rainwater home when he leaves Sealand—a taste of his home away from home that is especially good in his whiskey.

The fishing boat putters up to the fort soon enough, with shouts between the fort and the boat much clearer and louder than might be expected. The supplies are lowered down, and then Mike slides easily onto the bosun's chair. Joe just as easily lowers him back onto the boat, and he waves as the boat sails away.

Mike takes pictures constantly on the way back with a semiprofessional digital camera and has built up what is likely the most extensive photographic archives of Sealand possible. The current SD card has more than five thousand photos and is just one of many such cards he has filled and placed in storage at his home. He also takes photos of the boats they pass, the distant horizon, and Dan and Pecker preparing their catches for delivery to local restaurants. The lobsters—humongous creatures colored deep blue, with more appendages than one might expect—sit helplessly in buckets as Pecker cuts strips of an old inner tube to put around their claws. The work is efficient and somewhat sad, with the uninitiated almost certainly anthropomorphizing the creatures soon to be cooked. Pecker doesn't have room for that kind of pathos. "You know what I see when I look at these lobsters?" he asked. "Money." His statement is evidence of the tough attitude necessary for forging a life on the North Sea.

Sure enough, as soon as the boat pulls alongside the dock and is tied up at the pier, the fishermen heave the boxes of lobster and crabs up the grimy steps to the side of the road, where they would be loaded into a truck and delivered to restaurants around town. Once Mike, Pecker, and Dan get everything off the boat and load into the next vehicle, it is time to hit the pub and unwind.

Meanwhile, Joe is just a tiny speck in the distance, and he would do the obverse of this routine fourteen days hence. It was a strange dance with its own rhythm, and a self-contained world that revolves entirely around the mission Roy Bates began more than five decades before. But that's what it takes to keep Sealand afloat.

While the Bateses have devoted substantial amounts of time and money to Sealand, the micronation is only one part of their lives. They have routines and schedules and responsibilities far removed from the principality, and they continue to engage themselves in difficult and dirty work that ensures the livelihood of those they care about. The Bates family is a family of cocklers, and they go about this vocation with characteristic aplomb.

# CHAPTER 19

# PRINCE OF THE COCKLES

---

*"We come from a sensible background with the fishing boats;*
*we're used to looking after ourselves."*

—Michael Bates

Recent research into the common cockle (*Cerastoderma edule*), a small mollusk found all over the world, reveals that the sugars derived from the animal may have some impressive applications.

According to research conducted by the University of Salford and published in February 2018 in the journal *Marine Drugs*, when polysaccharides taken from cockles via a "typical cetylpyridinium chloride extraction procedure" are applied to leukemia, breast, lung, and bowel cancer tumors, the sugars bind to proteins in the cancer and seem to stop it from growing, working in a way similar to chemotherapy.*

---

\* According to the research, the extraction was done thusly: "Polysaccharides were extracted from common cockle (*Cerastoderma edule*), obtained from the Irish Sea, British Isles, using a standard protocol. Shells were removed and the entire soft body tissue was defatted by incubation with acetone for 72 h. Defatted tissue was left to dry for 24–48 h then ground to a fine powder. The powder (4 g) was suspended in 40 mL of 0.05 M of sodium carbonate pH 9.2, and 2 mL of Alcalase enzyme added. Samples were then incubated at 60 °C for 48 h with constant agitation at 200 rpm. The mixture was then cooled at 4 °C and trichloroacetic acid added to a concentration of 5% (w/v) and left for 10 min. Precipitated peptides were removed by centrifugation (5000× $g$ for 10 min). The supernatant was retained and three volumes of 5% (w/v) potassium acetate in ethanol was added to one volume of supernatant and the mixed solution left overnight at 4 °C. Precipitated cockle polysaccharide chains were recovered by centrifugation (5000× $g$ for 30 min) and the pellet washed with absolute alcohol. The recovered precipitate (1 g) was then dissolved in 40 mL of 0.2 M NaCl solution and centrifuged (5000× $g$ for 30 min) to remove any insoluble material. Cetylpyridinium chloride (0.5 mL of a 5% (w/v) solution) was added to the supernatant and the precipitate formed, recovered by centrifugation (8000× $g$ for 30 min). The precipitate was subsequently dissolved in 10 mL of 2.5 M NaCl solution, followed by the addition of 5 volumes of ethanol. The precipitated cockle polysaccharide chains were recovered by centrifugation (8000× $g$ for 30 min) before being dialysed against water for 72 h. The dialysate was lyophilized to obtain a white powder containing approximately 2.0 mg of cockle polysaccharides."

Cockles are abundant—a million per acre off the shores of the UK alone—and they live only centimeters under the mud, making them relatively easy to harvest. For this reason, researchers are cautiously optimistic that a new kind of inexpensive cancer treatment may be on the distant horizon—one that can be given in smaller doses and with much less harsh side effects than radiation.

"Polysaccharides (sugars) derived from mammals have long been a source of experimentation by cancer scientists," lead researcher Dr. David Pye said. "What is really significant about this is not so much the seafood source but that fact that sugars of this chemical structure work effectively at tolerable levels for children."

As it happens, the Bates family harvests the mollusk a dozen tons at a time from the waters of the Thames Estuary under the moniker "Fruits of the Sea."* The family's cockling boats, one of which is called the *Charlotte Joan* ("named after two very important women in my life," Michael noted), launch from the docks of their home borough Leigh-on-Sea in Southend, where the operation has been based since Michael started the business in the 1970s.

Michael was at a party celebrating the Chinese New Year when news broke about the possible cancer-treating qualities of the family's bread and butter. He immediately stepped out of the party and began calling news outlets and inviting reporters to go on a tour of the cockle-processing factory Michael runs with his sons. Cockles are a delicacy in certain parts of the world, and the annual harvest can already yield fairly substantial returns. Use of the mollusk for this additional purpose would be fantastic news to their bank accounts.

"I would hope there's a cure for cancer in cockles!" Michael said with a laugh.

Michael put down the phone after calling a few more reporters and went back into the party. It was too early to tell what this medical discovery meant for his business, and the work was hard enough as it is. Cockling season would begin before he knew it, and

---

* Sealand's first website was a page attached to the website of the cockling business: fruitsofthesea.demon.co.uk/sealand.

he hoped there would be enough of the creatures to fulfill the demand they already had.

## RIVALRIES AND RACKETEERS

The *Charlotte Joan* sits at an angle against the tires lining a concrete dock. The dock marks the edge of a muddy expanse that stretches for about a mile before meeting the waters of a flowing channel of the Thames. At low tide—most dramatic in the morning but similarly substantial in the afternoon—the banks of the Thames are a sodden mudscape with small fields of underwater plants sitting limply in the air. At high tide, the waters extend all the way up the shore, upon which boats float happily and lap just below the patios of old restaurants along the riverfront on down to Southend. But in the meantime the *Charlotte Joan* is completely immobilized, one of many vessels in similarly helpless positions until the tide rises.

Painted bright red, the *Charlotte Joan* bears its name in large white letters, and the wheelhouse bears the lettering "cockle.eu" and "ber-berecho.eu," advertising the bounty pursued by the boat. (*Berberecho* means "cockle" in Spanish.) Behind the boats are rows of shipping containers and pieces of pallets and odd bits of machinery and enormous bags full of thousands of pounds of cockle shells. Huge mounds of shells are piled alongside some of the shipping containers, on which children yip and yell as they play King of the Mountain.

The area is known as "Cockle Row," and among the boats and containers are densely packed green-painted sheds where the day's catches are processed and where fishmongers sell their wares. Cockle Row is set apart from the rest of Leigh by the train tracks that isolate it on a narrow strip of land, which, along with the ancient pubs and historical center, makes up a part of town known as Old Leigh. Inhabitants of the area had been eating the shellfish for thousands of years, but it wasn't until oyster beds were depleted by overfishing around two hundred years ago that fishermen turned to cockles as a cash crop. The trade became lucrative only in the 1960s, thanks to the development of suction-dredging technology that didn't require the cockles to be raked from the muddy sand by hand and transported via heavy baskets dangling from a yoke across a man's back.

The *Charlotte Joan* would look like the average fishing vessel were it not for a strange, drum-like apparatus on board called the suction dredge and a boom arm that helps guide the machinery into the water. The dredge apparatus serves two purposes: one pipe blasts water at the mud to soften it, while another sucks up the cockles like a vacuum. The cockles are then deposited into a metal barrel, with mud, rocks, and other detritus pumped back into the sea. Technology has improved to the point that the 1970s smash rate—that is, the rate at which the cockles are smashed to pieces instead of opened cleanly—of around 20 percent has now mostly been reduced to below 5 percent.

Liam and James are responsible for harvesting the cockles themselves throughout the season that runs from June to October. Liam stepped back from being on the boat after a knee injury required him to take it easy for a summer in the mid-2010s, and it is James who usually pilots the boat and does the harvesting with an additional crewmember. (James was suspicious of the extent of his brother's injuries when Liam happily tooled around in a bouncing dune buggy in Las Vegas.) The actual process of harvesting cockles isn't terribly difficult and is largely automated thanks to the suction dredge, but cockling is a two-man job for safety reasons.

Having grown up with the business, James began cockling full time right after he left high school and began piloting the boat at age twenty. Being in control of the harvest while piloting the boat in unpredictable seas is certainly a challenge. Boats can be sucked far out to sea and tossed heedlessly about the waves. At the very least he could wind up stranded on a sand bank until the tide comes in and eases him off his perch in another twelve hours.*

---

\* Harvesting cockles by hand can be extremely deadly to the itinerant workers from around the world who are paid low wages to do the difficult work. In 2004, twenty-three Chinese laborers harvesting cockles under the table in Morecambe Bay in northwestern England drowned when the tide rushed in, isolating them from the shore.

   Interestingly, Sealand has engendered a very helpful symbiosis between the British government and the cocklers. The Royal Air Force gets permission from the principality to practice rescue maneuvers on the fort, getting men on and off quickly to keep up their chops. "That's pretty daring for us, since it's basically inviting the government onto the fort," Michael said, but the training came in handy when his boat hit a buried anchor and sprung a leak. The RAF flew with a man dangling out of the helicopter to drop off the pump to the beleaguered boat, which by that time had a bucket brigade comprised

After being brought ashore in approximately one-ton loads, the cockles are taken to the family's factory in Shoeburyness, where they are transferred into a hopper and then onto a conveyor belt and into a cooker. After the cooking loosens the clamp of the shell, the cockles are dumped onto a hard, vibrating table that knocks the shell off, sending the cockle meat into a tank of brine and the nacreous dross out the window and onto a skid. The meat floats in the brine, and any lingering bits of shell sink. After a washing process, the meat is sealed in tins with oil and spices and then put into the pressure cooker.

Thames cockles are said to be some of the best in the world and are responsible for 25 percent of the world's edible cockle supply, though the popularity in England is a fraction of what it once was. Cockles have their fans in the UK, but their popularity is unrivaled in countries like Portugal and Spain, who eat them preserved or pickled and use them in cooking. These countries are the primary markets of Fruits of the Sea. Nevertheless, they are readily available to take home from the fishmongers or to eat from the restaurants and stalls along the Leigh shore, alongside other seaside delicacies such as whelks, winkles, and jellied eels (the latter of which preserve themselves in their own excretions, yielding a rather polarizing delicacy).

According to Andrew Lawrence, a Leigh cockler and manager of a fishing operation and restaurant going back to 1881 called Osborne Bros., the best way to eat cockles is boiled right out of the shell and seasoned with white pepper and vinegar. Buyers from Portugal and Spain will come to England and taste fresh cockles and turn up their noses in favor of the canned variety, Lawrence said, which baffles him to no end. Consumers will beg to differ with Lawrence's assessment, James Bates pointed out, as some tins of quality cockles have security apparatuses on them in stores, akin to those securing electronic equipment, and can be opened in fancy restaurants at the table by the waiter like a bottle of nice wine.

There are restrictions on how many cockles each boat can harvest. Fishing limits are determined each spring, with typical regulations

---

of crewmen from neighboring cockle boats who were lending a helping hand. The pump was promptly returned, to the pleasant surprise of the RAF, and the boatmen even included a few bags of frozen shrimp in gratitude.

limiting catches to twelve tons of cockles harvested by each vessel three times per week. According to regulations, skippers are required to keep careful documentation showing the area fished, the quantity taken, and the fishing time. Eight of the estuary cockle licenses are held by Spanish companies, which obviously makes the going price for a license extremely competitive (the last was sold between operators for around $3.5 million). Michael suspects that his success in obtaining a license led to one of his cockle boats being sunk out of spite. However, he also came about his license in a somewhat piratical, Sealandic way, which he admits didn't endear himself to the other Leigh fishermen vying for the same permission.

Back when Michael started, he didn't have permission from the Port of London Health Authority to cockle in the main part of the estuary and could only fish in the less-productive waters outside. It seemed like his father might be right about the unviability of the enterprise, so he began fishing in an area used by the army as a firing range to yield higher returns. He was cited as a result and made himself known to the officials overseeing local fishing for similar offenses. Six months later, when the UK was about to join the European Union, a public enquiry was held in Southend to reassign cockle licenses in accordance with the new regulations, issuing them based on who had been cockling in the area the year before. Michael pointed to his citations for illegal cockling as proof he was fishing in the area. The gambit worked.

"I got the first license," he laughed. "That was a pretty good move for me being an asshole. I suppose I get that from my father."

And this is where Michael Bates's reputation as a real-life, rough-around-the-edges pirate comes into play. At least a few people warned that looking into cockling operations would be wading into a gangster story, and that Michael was known to throw his weight around as if he were Prince of Leigh as well as Prince of Sealand. But such is the history of practically any such operation, where the promise of easy money creates an environment not meant for wimps.*

---

* This is a legacy that dates back to the earliest days of Leigh. Many houses in the town were built literally right up to the edge of the water to facilitate smuggling goods from ships, and the proliferation of ale houses in the past centuries meant that Leigh "became

Cockler Andrew Lawrence said there is some animus between fishermen and cocklers. The latter are perceived to have it easy, since their work season lasts four months while fishermen have to work year-round. "The cockling industry all knows each other, but I wouldn't say we're that well-liked amongst the actual fishing community," he said. "They're on very tight quotas and there's not a lot of money in the soles. It's nothing to do with being overfished, it's just bloody EU regulations. There's a little bit of jealousy, but they don't like that word."

But it's not just the perceived differences of their respective operations that is a cause of stress. The entire area has been hit hard by the development of a humongous port by global shipping concern DP World, which undertook a massive dredging operation in 2010 to enable the river to handle huge container ships at the mouth of the Thames. The dredging moved approximately thirty million cubic feet of riverbed and made the river around forty feet deeper. The excavation also spread silt that wreaked havoc on the local ecosystems, making cockle and fish yields very slim for a number of years.

Michael Bates, like everyone else, eyed his business's returns warily, noting the marked drop in proceeds that corresponded with work on the port. He attended a few meetings among fellow cocklers about filing a class-action lawsuit against DP World and put some of his own money into the effort, but the tendency to butt heads among cocklers made it hard to keep up a unified front, and it was quickly apparent that they simply couldn't match the legal resources of a multibillion dollar company. The cocklers thus bided their time and hoped to tough out whatever lay ahead. Now, with the dredging done and the river settling back down, the cockle beds are making a perceptible recovery. This isn't to say things are particularly abundant, but the industry is not quite as precarious as it was a few years prior.

The fishermen of the estuary haven't been faring so well, however. Visible from Southend are the dozens of inconceivably gigantic

---

notorious for the drunkenness and coarseness of its fishermen," as area historian Judith Lee notes. Heroes were created out of local ruffians, including a man named Snikey Cotgrove who secured his reputation when he and his men beat up a gang of men led by a tough guy named Fisty known to raid area pubs for their alcohol in the mid-1800s.

windmills that supply the area with power, and according to sixth-generation Southend fisherman Paul Gilson, the mechanical noise created by these behemoths, the electrical field emanating from the underwater cables, and the mile-wide artificial reef created by the metal covering these cables have so drastically changed the biodiversity of the area that it is irrecoverably diminishing the numbers of numerous species of fish and driving legions of fishermen out of business. Environmentalists have a different opinion, of course, and there are many more voices that comprise the mandates governing fishing in the area.

All in all, cockling seems to have done well for the Bateses, helping them overcome a slump that, when compounded with the financial responsibility of Sealand, led to some seriously lean times for the family. The enterprise has given Michael and his sons a comfortable living, and the job often requires the trio to fly around Europe negotiating cockle contracts and tracking down the specific kind of machinery they need for the operation. Michael has retired to a well-kept and tastefully decorated apartment with a million-dollar view of the Thames while his sons live in Leigh-on-Sea, which for the past few years has developed a reputation as an up-and-coming town characterized by quiet neighborhoods and thoroughfares full of well-dressed young couples pushing prams. In fact, Leigh-on-Sea was recently voted the happiest place to live in the UK.*

Time will reveal what the cancer-fighting properties of cockles mean for the Bateses and Fruits of the Sea, but if business picks up it will certainly be a boon to Sealand's GDP. "We come from a sensible background with the fishing boats; we're used to looking after ourselves," Michael said. And that's exactly what they do in the estuary of the mighty River Thames.

Nowhere is Sealand's influence more profound, however, than on the community of micronationalists. Leaders from an assortment of

---

* The town's climate seems almost comically assertive in maintaining this appellation. My visit there was characterized by some of the most pronounced and gigantic rainbows I've ever seen, and when nearby Westcliff was characterized by an eerie gray dusk, an absolutely spectacular pink and orange sunset was visible a few miles down the road in Leigh. All that was missing was air that perpetually smelled like freshly baked bread, though the abundance of hip coffee shops did mean that the main drag essentially smelled like java the whole way down.

these proto states come together in a United Nations–like gathering every two years, and in July 2019, presidents, emperors, and generalissimos from around the world gathered outside of Toronto, Canada, to discuss issues concerning the world's smallest states. Sealand is equivalent in renown as the Roman Empire, and a visit to this ministate gala shows just how much is owed to the family Bates.

# CHAPTER 20

# KING OF THE MICRONATIONS

*"I'm not knocking the other micronations, [but our experience] is blood, sweat, and tears and wages and fuel and generators."*
—Michael Bates

In spite of the heat of a sweltering, putridly humid day in July 2019, dignitaries from all over the world donned their finest gowns, tuxedos, and jackets, heavy with sashes and epaulets. It was time for the semiannual micronational summit called MicroCon, and the fancy vestments were important to the United Nations-like solemnity of the event. Microdignitaries came from regions as far flung as Germany, South Korea, and all across the United States to attend a weekend's worth of networking, presentations, and a formal gala dinner with a strict dress code.

MicroCon 2019, the third such meeting since they began in 2017, is the preeminent gathering of its kind in the world and is a real-life meeting place for those who populate the micronational Wiki and various related online forums. It is a cross between a model UN club, live-action role-playing, and a serious meditation on international policy and statehood. Each micronation exhibits a display of its constitution, coinage, history, and governing philosophy. Treaties are signed, conflicts begun and resolved, and lessons are learned that can be taken back to the country of one's own imagination. Diplomacy aside, MicroCon is also a place for friends to get together and inhabit this obscure shared interest to their hearts' content. The 2019 edition brought 110 attendees, the most ever, and the micronations were of varying size, seriousness, and ambition. Everyone there of course readily acknowledges the debt owed to the Principality of Sealand, and the event demonstrates the remarkable reach of Sealand's influence in theory and in practice.

As it happened, MicroCon 2019 was being held fifty years to the day that the Apollo 11 astronauts landed on the moon. As Slabovian Vice Admiral and event emcee Patrick Goddard said in his opening remarks, the moon mission was an extremely influential display of bravery and adventure—the perfect symbolic accompaniment to the aspirations of micronationalists everywhere. "It was an incredible feat of creativity, human ingenuity, and resourcefulness," he said of the moon landing, his voice cracking with emotion. Following a few more inspirational remarks, MicroCon 2019 officially got underway, a gathering carrying the passion of ministates of every shape and size and an inherent homage to the micronation in the North Sea.

## FROM THE AMBULATORY FREE STATES OF OBSIDIA TO THE CONSTITUTIONAL PENTUMVIRATE OF KAZ

MicroCon 2019 was not held in the most cosmopolitan of cities: Hamilton, Ontario, is a large city near Toronto known as "The Hammer" for the abundance of steel mills along the shores of Lake Ontario. The event was in the ballroom of the Courtyard Marriott, a nondescript hotel not far from a highway whose location near strip malls belied the surprisingly upmarket interior. Attendees met at the hotel early on Friday, July 18, to sign in and take tours of Hamilton's castle, battleship, and other landmarks. The tours were led by citizens of the United Slabovian Empire, the micronation who went through an Olympic-style bidding process to host the festival. Slabovia and many of its residents are located in the greater Toronto area, hence MicroCon being in Hamilton.

The Slabovians readily admit that their micronation is not the kind that is serious about independence; rather, it is a sort of running joke that parodies the bureaucratic entanglements of established countries and serves as a way for a group of old friends to bond. Cookouts, camping trips, and role-playing games are official Slabovian outings for the Slabovian population, which is otherwise a group of friends who met in a Canadian high school on a military base in Germany more than thirty years ago. At MicroCon, the Slabovians were readily identifiable in matching uniforms of the Slabovian Navey [sic]: blue pants with white captain's shirts and embroidered shoulder embellishments.

To get to MicroCon, guests walked down a winding hallway to the back of the hotel where a ballroom had been reserved, far away from the lobby and ensconcing the micronationalists in a world of their own. The hotel has substantial banquet facilities and regularly hosts similar events. An unrelated wedding reception was taking place the same weekend, and it was initially difficult to determine which event a well-dressed person belonged to. The sashes, crowns, and medals gave it away, though. According to one desk clerk, MicroCon was significantly less strange than some of the other events the hotel has hosted.

The ballroom was lined with displays and the middle of the room was set with rows of tables facing a podium in front of a wall of flagpoles holding each micronation's flag. Representatives from approximately twenty-six micronations were present, with citizens that ranged in age from grade schoolers to grandparents. The most established attendees were by far the long-standing Republic of Molossia, whose President Kevin Baugh is one of the go-to interviewees for features on micronations, and the Grand Duchy of Westarctica, a territory claimed on an unclaimed piece of land on Antarctica whose Grand Duke Travis McHenry is fundraising for an expedition to the actual Westarctican territory. Representatives from a Seborga-like enclave in France called the Principality of Aigues-Mortes were also present, showing off the currency used among local shops and one of the lynchpins of its tourist draw.

Other attendees were more conceptual in nature. The Kingdom of Pibocip, for example, reflects founder Philip Pillin's interest in political philosophy and the works of John Locke. The Ambulatory Free States of Obsidia, founded by artist Grand Marshal Carolyn Yagjian, is comprised of two pieces of obsidian that she carries in a briefcase. "I don't own a house or any land, so a portable micronation made the most sense," she said, explaining that Obsidia is a vehicle for feminist politics. The "radical centrist" Technocratic Republic of Theodia was founded by linguist Miles Huff, who is constructing an entire theoretical civilization from the ground up. He's given extensive thought to everything from what kind of screws the Theodians use (and the direction they are turned) to the homemade Theodian language.* The Constitutional Pentumvirate of Kaz and the Federal Republic of Caddia were created by separate groups of siblings based on their love for cats (and whose family pets are royalty).

An evening meet and greet was scheduled after the sightseeing tour, bringing together people bedecked in state regalia and others preferring more casual shorts and checkered shirts. The assemblage sipped drinks, meeting new and old friends alike. A large scroll boasting the text of the 1933 Montevideo Convention on the Rights and Duties of States was available to be signed by the parties in attendance, a document that the reader will recall is one of the documents most critical to Sealand's existence.

MicroCon was to be a relatively short affair, beginning with the meet and greet on Friday and ending with a round of laser tag on Sunday morning. Saturday would be the day of heavy-duty diplomacy, with the opening remarks ushering in blocks of fifteen-minute lectures on all things micronational. The Slabovian delegation had been planning the event since October 2017, and went to great lengths to make sure the delegations were impressed by the affair. Everyone was given a gift bag full of information and treats, including a special medal on a ribbon. Coffee breaks between sessions were sponsored by generous micronations, and the formal dinner was scheduled for 8:00 p.m. Saturday.

Attendees could sign up to give a talk, provided it wasn't just an overview of their micronation's history. As passionate as people were about their creations, they had all day to tell the tale of their micronation to those who passed by the displays; more productive would be well-thought-out lectures on more specific topics. All the while, documentarians filmed and interviewed, and the YouTube channel "Not Exactly Normal" recorded their segment.

The first speaker of 2019—aside from the emotional greetings by Slabovia's King George 2.0 and Vice Admiral Goddard—was Minsung Kwon, president of the Justin Republic, who provided an overview of Asian micronations and the state of South Korean counter-countries

---

* Interestingly, traveling to Hamilton for MicroCon was the first time that the multilingual Huff left the United States.

specifically. Asia has been historically underrepresented on the micronational stage, primarily because of the difficulty in organizing Asian micronations online. "I mean South Korea, not North Korea—if you start a micronation there you'll probably get executed," he clarified. Adam Oberstadt of the Kingdom of Überstadt talked about the dilemma of decolonizing micronations—how does one justify claiming territory on land that was stolen from its original inhabitants?—while the history-PhD-pursuing Sôgmô Gaius Soergel Publicola of the State of Sandus planned to refute a talk given at MicroCon two years before claiming that parts of Ancient Rome could be considered micronational.

Kevin Baugh of Molossia, based in Nevada and one of the most well-known and elaborate micronations, organized the original MicroCon and has been a passionate and public advocate for micronations for decades. "While we like to laugh, we consider ourselves a sovereign nation. We would like to have that affirmed," he said. He and his family are used to being in the spotlight, which is why his teenage daughter Alexis gave a talk on what it is like to be a micronationalist's kid. "When I was little I would get really confused when someone asked where I lived," she said with a laugh. Was it the street she lived on? Nevada? Molossia?

Most every micronation showed off its money, stamps, passports, and other appurtenances of citizenship. The Principality of Sealand of course set the standard for this kind of thing and was thus King of the Micronations before micronations even existed. Like many attendees, seventeen-year-old Max Pollack of the Kingdom of Jupiter and Greater Territories credits Sealand and Molossia with introducing him to this larger world.

Despite their prominence and regard, however, a Sealandic delegation was noticeably absent from the MicroCon festivities. The Sealanders don't mean any offense, but Michael Bates has always considered Sealand a different kind of entity that doesn't quite fit in with micronational culture. They have actual territory—territory that was genuinely outside of any nation's waters when they took it over—and the physical, financial, familial, and emotional toll of the endeavor makes Sealand feel like a much more tangible state. "I'm not knocking the other micronations," Michael said, "[but our experience] is blood, sweat, and tears and wages and fuel and generators."

But this is also why some attendees felt a little slighted by Sealand's disinterest in the broader micronational community. The principality's involvement could bring more attention to the idea of micronationality and to those who advocate for it. Exactly what this attention would do isn't clear—Make it a more well known LARPing hobby? Draw more people to a disputed area's struggle for independence?—but an appearance by the Sealanders would be a cool way to acknowledge the tremendous impact they've had on the community and the alternate world atlas that has developed in large part because of their example.

Other attendees don't feel as slighted. Before, Sealand was one of the only known counter-countries, but over the past decade or so the internet has made the example of other micronations just as prominent. The variety even inspires some criticism of the Sealand example. "They're lucky they were in the UK's waters," Theodia's Miles Huff said. "[The UK] was too polite to crush them." Max Pollack of the Kingdom of Jupiter and Greater Territories said he was somewhat unimpressed with Sealand's direction in recent years. "I don't like that they sell honors and titles," he said. Titles should be earned, not bought.

For all the fantasy fun of imagining the complexities of your own micronation, many of those at MicroCon (and many more worldwide) would genuinely like to embark on starting their own nation if given the chance. When there is no new territory to claim as your own, the logical response is to create your own. Sealand's example is of course significantly influential in this regard, but so too is the seasteading movement, largely comprised of free market adherents who have actually attempted to establish floating cities in international waters. Whether climate catastrophe pushes people off parched landmasses or people simply want to escape an increasingly divisive world, the seasteaders have a head start in acting on this new form of nationhood.

## THE SEASTEADERS

In January 2017, a strange but groundbreaking plan was solidified in French Polynesia. A business called Blue Frontiers, an offshoot of a libertarian think-tank in the United States called the Seasteading

Institute (TSI), signed a memorandum of understanding with the government of French Polynesia to establish an experimental community in the waters of the Atimaono lagoon in Tahiti. The community would be built piecemeal on land and then assembled in the lagoon, the first of many theoretical floating cities that would be free to create the society their inhabitants desire.

The government of French Polynesia, which is part of France but largely autonomous, said they would give TSI—which was co-founded in 2008 by Patri Friedman, grandson of Nobel Prize-winning free market enthusiast Milton Friedman, and Wayne Gramlich*—one hundred acres of space on a beach as their home base and would create a special economic zone for the TSI city. The Memorandum of Understanding requires that TSI show the endeavor would be beneficial for the host nation, including positive economic and environmental effects; provided these qualifications were met, the institute was hoping to "break sea" by spring 2018. "I'm confident it'll happen but there are a lot of moving parts," TSI executive director Randolph Hencken said.

The broader seasteading idea is that different waterborne communities would develop in accordance with the political, religious, or social outlooks of their founders and residents, attracting likeminded people to help keep them afloat. Seasteading would democratize nationhood by giving people the power to go from floating state to floating state and work for the betterment of the community most suited to one's own needs. "People would exit by leaving their country of residence and establishing a physical and juridical presence in a new territorial configuration. In this ideal world, numerous such configurations would come into being over time and would compete for citizens, much as companies compete for consumers," explained historian Raymond Craib, who has written extensively about seasteading. Going further, seasteaders envision the communities being a hub for activities typically not allowed by traditional nations, such as medical testing not regulated by a state body, with business conducted in Bitcoin or a cryptocurrency of the community's invention. "If we can solve the

---

* Friedman and Gramlich self-published *Seasteading: How Floating Nations Will Restore the Environment, Enrich the Poor, Cure the Sick and Liberate Humanity from Politicians.*

engineering challenge of seasteading, two-thirds of the Earth's surface becomes open for these political start-ups," says Friedman.

But while Sealand stays afloat with the sale of its titles and merchandise, and Alexander Achenbach and Co. tried to fund their project through fraud, the seasteading venture has some serious backing. For example, the Seasteading Institute was funded in part thanks to the largesse of libertarian billionaire and PayPal founder Peter Thiel, who donated serious money to the institute. These funds helped get the test country started in Tahiti.

Models of seasteading communities show graceful, geometric glass-domed structures on floating green spaces. Seasteaders tout using solar, wind, and wave energy to power the communities, and some theorists posit floating the structures using plastic bottles. Communities could harvest algae on an industrial scale for income, energy, and food. Seasteading communities could even have floating power plants that sell algae-generated power back to land-lubbing nations. The Tahiti project planned to employ local wood, fiber from bamboo and coconut, and recycled metal and plastic in its construction, and the buildings on the platform would have "living" roofs for gardening.

However, even ardent "seavangelists" acknowledge that the idea is not yet practical. Even a simple prototype of a floating city would cost hundreds of millions of dollars and is decades away from reality. Patri Friedman concedes that he underestimated the convoluted and often-conflicting nature of the laws and treaties that govern the sea—and Peter Thiel ultimately left the group due to the insubstantial progress. "I didn't go into it thinking that it would be easy to write the perfect laws or that regulators don't try," Friedman said. "But when I first started out, I kind of naively thought there would be legal hacks." The community in Tahiti would have been the first major test of this concept, but it was ultimately protested for being "tech colonialism" that would have exploited local workers. Tahitian TV host Alexandre Taliercio questioned whether "facilitating the tax evasion of the world's greatest fortunes" would actually be beneficial for the islands.

"It reminds me of the innocent Ewoks of the moon of Endor who saw in the Galactic Empire a providential manna. They let them build what they wanted on earth and in orbit, but that's not to say that the Empire shared the blueprints of the Death Star with them," he said. "These millionaires, lulled by an illusory desire to free themselves from the existing states, seem to have much more to gain than we do." The Tahitian government ultimately withdrew their permission to establish the community.

More recently, some governments have been especially querulous when it comes to challenges to their borders. In April 2019, Thailand came down hard on a couple who inhabited a hilariously small tower thirteen miles from its border in the Andaman Sea. The couple, Chad Elwartowski and Supranee Thepdet, were threatened with execution when Thai authorities discovered their home and declared that the couple was "deteriorating Thailand's independence." The Thai Royal Navy pulled the home back to shore via warship, and the couple went into hiding to avoid the death penalty. Though the ideas are sound among adherents, mainstream society may not yet be ready to permit, let alone embrace, such a concept.*

Nonetheless, TSI hopes to keep moving forward with plans to create these new nation-states that would "unlock an unprecedented level of political innovation [and give] rise to a Cambrian Explosion in government." As TSI President Joe Quirk said, "The more people moving among them, the more choices we'll have and the more likely it is we can have peace, prosperity, and innovation." It is a goal that Roy may not have voiced in the same way but that he certainly respected. Whenever these communities finally come into being, they

---

* Another unorthodox method of claiming territory was attempted in June 2014, when an American man named Jeremiah Heaton tried to claim a disputed piece of land between Sudan and Egypt called Bir Tawil as his own so he could make his daughter a princess. Bir Tawil is an 800-square-mile section of desert that exists thanks to a disparity between the colonial-era maps of the countries that border it. The territory is essentially uninhabitable and is only occupied from time to time by nomads. Heaton contends it is *terra nullius*, as neither border country officially claims it, though they are in constant negotiations about how to resolve the confusion. (Neither will concede it to the other.) Despite the on-paper logic of the experiment and the fact that Heaton made an arduous trek to the territory and planted a flag his children designed on one of its dunes, the governments of both Sudan and Egypt told him there was no way he could claim the area for himself. Heaton's daughter thus remains without a royal title, though there were rumors that Disney had bought the movie rights to the Heatons' story.

will owe a debt to Sealand but will certainly do justice to the founder's dream.

## BACK AT MICROCON

When it was time for her lecture at MicroCon 2019, Queen Carolyn of Ladonia gave an appropriately queenly wrist wave as she walked up to the podium. She gave a rousing speech about making one's micronation about more than just the founder's individual tastes in government and constitutional law. "No one wants to join a micronation just to make you king," she said; a micronation needs to inspire people to call it their homeland.

The sense of inspiration was enormous as MicroCon wound down to a close. Each MicroCon held an awards ceremony, in which the heads of state bestowed honors, medals, and distinctions on fellow micronations. Indeed, many of the medals worn throughout the weekend were earned at previous MicroCons, and the two-hour ceremony was filled with laughter, tears, and a profound sense of comity. (Slabovia's King George 2.0 would give a talk about how to make cool-looking ribbons and medals on the cheap.) The chance to fully indulge fantasies of statehood was uplifting and appreciated beyond belief, even if the diplomacy fantasy lasted only for a weekend.*

Though Michael Bates certainly doesn't mind the renown that comes with being prince, he's not doing it just for the accolades. It has been a lifetime commitment, and the respect and responsibilities that go with it often confound Prince Michael himself. Sealand is a dream that is now in its fourth generation, an endless source of amusement, toil, and bonding for the entire Bates clan. The project has added jaw-dropping stress to their lives and has sent them all over the world as emissaries of the world's preeminent micronation. Michael has been

---

* The author himself was brought to tears numerous times during the event, such as when he overheard a ten-year-old head of state quietly say "I don't really have any" when asked what his friends thought of his micronation, and when another young kid presented his mom with a royal award for organizing the trip and schlepping him to the event. There was also a middle-aged president who had been inhabiting his micronation since he was a kid—a kid probably like the shy kids in attendance whose micronation was a way to help with an otherwise lonely childhood. It was so nice to see the sincere joy of everyone's experience.

beaten up, abandoned, and divorced because of his duties to the principality, and he went broke and bounced back more than once fulfilling the unspoken promise to his father to keep the country afloat. Shimmying down a rope from a helicopter with a shotgun was one of the most exciting moments of his life, and he can recall every detail of those harried days like a star quarterback can recall the night when he threw the championship-winning pass.

Sealand has yet to gain true independence or a resounding scholarly opinion that seriously advances its claims to sovereignty. In fact, arguments of this sort seem to genuinely rankle scholars of international law. As Vincent Cogliati-Bantz of the TC Beirne School of Law in the University of Queensland, Australia, writes, "Since it was established previously that the platform does not qualify as territory, since Bates is a British national, since no occupation took place on behalf of the UK, since 'Sealanders' do not constitute a population and since no recognition by the international community acknowledged Bates's claim anyway, one can only be left with an ineffective claim to statehood."

But abstruse legal arguments are only part of the story, anyway. Sealand exists regardless of how it's officially classified. It is just as real and tangible as Ghana or the Czech Republic is to someone who's never been to those countries. The principality has etched its name unmistakably on the map as we know it and has made an indelible mark across interests, concerns, and disciplines of every kind.

The British government continues to tolerate the presence of Sealand and the occupiers thereon and will only refer to it as "Roughs Tower" when forced to acknowledge its existence. The character of their response remains as it has since the micronation's inception fifty-plus years ago: an amusing mix of exasperation and no-nonsense scolding that occasionally carries a whiff of bemusement or even pride that some of its own are hardy enough to withstand such an undertaking. But the government probably also has bigger fish to fry.

To this day, the Sealanders don't offer a particularly pronounced opinion on why they're continuing the struggle for statehood and what it all means. They are not prone to wistful reflection, preferring instead to recall the exciting history of their stalwart North Sea kingdom.

Once, when asked by a reporter why he did what he did, Roy Bates answered as best he could. "I'll tell you what," he replied. "I've asked myself that question many times and I'm damned if I know the answer. But it was a challenge, and I can't resist a challenge."

This isn't to say the Sealanders aren't serious about their role in setting a precedent for future micronations and seasteading ventures. Sealand posted an impassioned reaction to the aforementioned incident off the coast of Thailand, offering the beleaguered seasteaders safe haven on Sealand and noting that "such a draconian reaction from a national government serves as a stark reminder of why it is important to challenge the status quo." Caretaker Mike Barrington is quite open about his willingness to literally fight and die to protect Sealand. Yes, it is crazy and unbelievable, they'll agree, but it stands for something, and it's certainly been a wild, worthwhile ride.

Prince Roy Bates may have initially taken over Roughs Tower in an act of spite and one-upmanship, without much thought to where it would go five, ten, fifty years hence. But the strange old tower has since become a functioning, self-sustaining operation, bolstered by infamy and renown—a micronation that, say what you will about its legal claims, has had an impact on world affairs far larger than what might be expected from a house-sized platform seven miles out to sea.

Come what may, the Sealanders are content to see where the story goes. They are looking toward the future as they lead lives in two realms. They are fishermen, spouses, and doting parents, and they are also the Princes and Princesses of Sealand, the world's most enduring micronation. There are sure to be many more adventures on the fort in the roiling North Sea, escapades as big as nations that will resonate with those who know they are destined for something bold, exciting, and new.

# EPILOGUE

# ALL HAIL THE STUBBORN KINGDOM

---

*"Sealand is here to stay."*
—Roy Bates

It is an odd thing to be more well-known outside of your town than in it. Michael Bates was born and raised in Southend and was a fixture in area newspapers only a generation before, but he can walk the familiar streets surrounded by people who don't necessarily know anything about what he's accomplished. Those that do know of Sealand have only a vague understanding—*Didn't a man declare himself king or sumfing?* They also tend to be older, from an era where they might have socially known Roy and Joan Bates or listened to the pirate radio phenomenon (in fact, many people in the area can readily recite old pirate station jingles).

It wasn't until Michael published his autobiography *Holding the Fort* in 2015 and the ensuing local publicity that resulted that Southenders realized the character they had in their midst. He got a good bit of ribbing for his royal pretentions after he made the rounds on TV and radio promoting the book, but people also respect the family's gumption and the fact that they've held onto the fort as long as they have. Many locals, who are wary of the meddling of the government in Westminster, can appreciate him sticking it to the Man. "People I lived with and worked with for years didn't know about it. They're quite a cynical lot, they're fishermen and people like that, but they love it now," Michael said.

Sealand has only continued to grow in popularity in recent years, and that's thanks largely to the internet-savviness of millennials James and Liam Bates. Where Roy could play the local press like a fiddle and Michael made a winning impression in interviews like a lovable tough guy from a Guy Ritchie movie, the current generation knows how to work social media to their advantage. The micronation has a professional website, replete with an official history, photos, and legal arguments. Accounts on the requisite social media platforms show Sealand decorated for Halloween and a special delivery of McDonald's being winched up to the fort. The vim and vigor of Sealand on the web has allowed the micronation to emerge from the edge of ruin and reemerge as a more viable nation-state. "The internet has opened Sealand up to the world," James said.

But this also means that the secretarial duties of running Sealand are proportional to the bureaucracy that keeps any macronation afloat. The Sealanders get tons of emails and requests for publicity and interviews, messages of support from all over the world, and offers from people who will send things like their grandmother's recipe for stew to help keep the Sealanders warm and well-fed. Media interest is a constant, to the degree that they have to pick and choose which requests to respond to. Michael says he does have a soft spot for kids from around the world who get in touch for a school project. He makes a point to arrange Skype video chats with them and talk to them about Sealand. "It may sound a bit silly," he said, "but it makes me feel all warm inside."

As anyone with any amount of presence on the internet surely knows, Sealand sometimes attracts the attention of people who seem a little unhinged. There are daily declarations of war against the principality (most in jest), and some of the more harmless episodes include people editing photos of the Bates family and putting them in front of psychedelic backgrounds or superimposing Michael on a Harley-Davidson with flames behind him or in videos with jumping whales.

On the more sinister side, Michael recalls being hounded and stalked for years, receiving twenty to thirty emails a day filled with extreme insults from a man who ended up being a medical salesman from Louisiana. The Bateses sometimes get hate mail about the treatment of whales from concerned activists who confuse Sealand for SeaWorld, and the replies to their posts on social media feature irrational tirades about their claims to sovereignty or crude comments about the Sealand women. But, as Liam notes, "There's a lot more people who support us than who knock the whole idea."

"The best thing about social media is that we don't even have to bother responding and people will defend us," says James.

Sealand has also sent them all over the world. Members of the Bates family have been invited to speak at conferences and art openings in Brazil, Japan, Spain, Finland, and most recently Genoa.* Michael recalls speaking at one event following an artist who had spent three weeks on one of the Maunsell Army Forts and was relaying just how crazy it felt to be there for a mere twenty-one days. When Michael was up to speak, he laughed about the artist's pseudo-predicament and said he wished his father could hear the lament at being stuck on the fort for less than a month at a time.

The upswing in popularity has worked out well for the jovial Michael Bates. A burly man with a shaved head, big laugh, open-necked shirt, and gold chain, Michael is a born storyteller and appreciates the life he's led. His status as prince has led to many drinks bought for him in bars, amenities at events, and even a few chances to hobnob with a British politician coincidentally named Sir Michael Bates. The two Michaels met at a gala, with the politician relating to the Sealander his dismay at Michael of Sealand coming up most often when he's been vain enough to Google himself. Liam and James Bates are somewhat less visible, though recognition is not uncommon. "People don't come up to you but when you start talking to them they might recognize you as the 'Sealand guy,'" Liam said.

The Sealand legacy has also brought Michael into some situations truly befitting a royal. He once found himself being offered the keys to a beach house in Florida for an unlimited stay after chatting with someone at a bar, and there was also the time he was invited to an all-expenses-paid grandiose wedding in La Paz, Mexico, where he was guest of honor alongside Jean-Michel Cousteau. (Highlights included being chauffeured around by an ex-Mossad agent, whale watching, and being sat next to a UN official.)

Perhaps most importantly, however, the growth attributable to the power of the internet has helped Sealand enter a new era of

---

* The organizers of the Genoa event accidentally sent Michael an email intended for another guest, where it was revealed that the guest was going to be paid more than Michael. An astute pirate, he negotiated a better rate for himself.

sustainability. For sale through the Sealand website is merchandise ranging from mugs and T-shirts to its most popular offerings: Sealandic noble titles. The titles are endowed via a certificate that comes framed or in a handsome leather case. Costs increase according to rank: a baroncy will set you back $44.99, a knighthood $146.99, a count or countess $294.99, while one can become a bona fide duke or duchess for the small sum of $734.99. (Also for sale are Sealand ID cards, which resemble driver's licenses, for $36.99.) Sealandic nobles now hail from all over the world, but especially from the United States and Japan. Michael attributes the popularity in the US to Sealand having a frontier-type mythology similar to the Wild West of America.

The sale of Sealand noble titles was an idea that can be traced back to Roy's ambitions for Sealand from the 1960s, but it was difficult to market effectively in those days. At one point Michael scraped together money to run an ad offering the titles in the *New York Times*, but he only got one letter back. Sales are much more brisk today, with Lorraine Bates, Michael's ex-wife, handling much of the behind-the-scenes work of issuing and mailing titles. The family doesn't divulge how many titles they sell each year, but the sales today are enough that maintaining the fort is an operation that is finally breaking even. Not having to bear the financial burden of paying for Sealand yourself is a relief that takes some of the pressure off of keeping the family legacy alive—an achievement Roy and Joan would have loved to have seen. "You think, oh my goodness, there are all these people who are lords and ladies of Sealand all over the world. It's quite remarkable," Lorraine said.

If things keep going well, there are hopes to expand the micronation's footprint by reclaiming land around the territory and to make the fort even more inhabitable, including more solar panels and wind turbines as well as an intercom to communicate between even the most stygian levels of the fort. James and Liam try to get out to the fort for extended stays every few months to pitch in with the necessary upkeep and sometimes take a team of ten friends to help with the project. Further fundraising projects include an "ICO," or "Initial Citizenship Offering," and some kind of digital currency. Much thought is also given to making the country self-sustainable in other ways, such as growing crops for food and other uses. "We really should start growing stuff, and I don't mean weed to all those that keep questioning me on that," Michael Bates said. "A decision has not been made on that but it is not on the top of my priority list."

Just as Sealand has grown and evolved with time, Michael has seen Southend change and grow, and his life with it. He has lived in successively nicer homes as his business and net worth grew, thanks to a lifetime of hard work. The family's base of operations is still in the Southend area and likely will continue to stay that way—a domain just as important to the family as their micronational realm. James Bates's children (and any Bates youngsters that come in the future) will perhaps experience the similarly strange pairing of local anonymity and global renown if Sealand continues to be the phenomenon it is today.

## A ROYAL WEDDING

In March 2019, Michael Bates found himself suddenly thrown into the back of a van. He was heading to Spain on business but had been waylaid in the earliest hours of the morning and did not know where he was going. It was the second time in his life he'd been kidnapped, he pointed out—an activity that nobody wants to become routine.

In this instance, however, Michael knew he wasn't in any danger and was in fact plunging headlong into what would prove to be a whirlwind weekend of fun. Far from a kidnapping orchestrated by followers of Achenbach, the surprise ambuscade was orchestrated by his sons Liam and James, who were going to party with their dad in Riga, Latvia, for his last weekend as a single man.

Michael, Prince Regent of Sealand, was set to marry Mei Shi, his sweetheart of three years, in mid-April in Thailand.

When the plane landed in Latvia a few hours later, the bachelor party proceeded in typical Sealandic fashion: shooting guns, shooting more guns, and ending with Michael parading around dressed like King Henry VIII, accompanied by his laughing sons. Then it was back to Southend, no kidnapping necessary.

Though Michael and Mei didn't meet at any royal function, Mei's bearing is no less impressive. She was formerly a major in the Chinese military, the daughter of a general, and spent thirteen years training, drilling, and working up the ranks. Mei now works as a multilingual Vice President of Customer Relations at the Empire Casino in London, where she acts as a handler to the ultra-wealthy Chinese businessmen. The wedding would be a merger of their respective dynasties. Mei's family was traveling from China for the occasion while the groom's guest list was an eclectic living roster of Sealand's history: radio pirates, HavenCo alumni, deckhands, movie producers, and even Vít Jedlička, leader of the Free Republic of Liberland, a micronation with a claim to a stretch of *terra nullius* between Serbia and Croatia.

After the wedding, Michael and Mei would be relaxing in Thailand for weeks, deliberately distancing themselves from their work lives and the rigors of the micronation. It was a much-needed break that Michael had been thinking about on a larger scale for a while, and during the fourteen-hour flight to Thailand, he gave it further reflection as he looked out at the sea.

The ocean was a vast, forbidding lifeforce and it was crazy to think that so much of his life had been spent on one tiny corner of it. He had made friends, gained enemies, challenged the law and himself, and had led a life of intense adventure. But after all this, it was time to pass the torch, just as his father had with him. Liam and James had long been overseeing the day-to-day of the micronation, and they were poised to transition to full-time heads of state. They were serious and smart enough to keep the dream alive, and Michael could rest easy knowing it was in good hands. He stretched, smiled, and settled in his first-class seat. He would always be Prince of Sealand, but he was walking proudly toward the next chapter of his life.

A little while later, bedecked in flowers and surrounded by friends and family, Michael and Mei had beatific looks on their faces as they exchanged their vows in the warm sun. Michael could hear the voice of his parents as he relished the moment. He was proud of the life he had forged, and he would always be driven by the spirit of the country his parents started. Whatever came next, he would be doing it with his royal counterpart by his side.

"We've had a privileged life even if we have had to invent our own privileges," Roy Bates was known to say. "Sealand is here to stay."

*E Mare Libertas.*

From the sea, freedom.

# APPENDIX

## PRECEDENT, JUSTIFICATION, AND SCHOLARLY OPINION ON SEALAND AS A SOVEREIGN NATION

---

*The "freedom as well as the isolation offered by a maritime location could both inhibit the control exercised by established powers and encourage the formation of alternative political societies, much as Darwin found that separate ecosystems had evolved on different islands."*

—Samuel Pyeatt Menefee

Today, people declare war on the Principality of Sealand almost daily, but the principality also gets voluminous correspondence from people wanting to take advantage of its sovereignty for reasons political and personal alike. A jilted lover asked to fight his rival to the death on the fort, for example, and a pornography company once asked to produce condom-less porn on the micronation because the pornographer's home country required that performers wear protection when filming. "After the vote for Brexit we had several hundred inquiries daily," Michael told the *Daily Mail* in January 2017. "Then following the American vote [to elect Donald Trump as president] it was in excess of 200 daily and we are still getting enquiries as the situation sinks in."* Michael politely declined to host the pornography shoot and duel, and he did not extend asylum to people fed up with the political situation of their own countries. But he is always

---

* Michael didn't think Brexit would be bad for Sealand in the long run, but he hoped the UK got a good trade deal out of it to help his business shipping cockles to Spain.
In 2015, Liam Bates, Michael's son, told a newspaper that he supported the UK staying in the EU, but that Sealand wouldn't be petitioning for membership because to do so wasn't in accordance with its long-term plans. A UK Independence Party spokesperson was unimpressed. "If the EU's so great then why doesn't Mr. Sealand apply to join at the next IGC [intergovernmental conference]?" he said.
Sealand's exit from the UK was deemed "Sexit," by the way.

impressed at how widely people support Sealand's right to govern its own affairs.

That right was of course asserted in major way by the Assize court decision of 1968. That decision had nothing to do with the issue of Sealand's sovereignty *per se*—again, the court ruled Britain hadn't yet extended its reach to the fort, not that it couldn't—but the nature of the ruling did raise many questions about the principality's legal status. If Britain's Firearms Act didn't apply on Roughs Tower, then what exactly was the territory on which the act didn't apply? If the nature of its geography was unclear and it was in international waters, did that mean a disused concrete and steel platform could in fact become an independent state?

It seems worthwhile to explore these questions, not only to assess the situation's standing in international law but to give context to the remarkable events that have taken place on the principality, almost all of which were undertaken with the assumption that Sealand is an independent state. As Foreign Commonwealth Office researcher Grant Hibberd writes, "Rarely have these questions been posed in a more farcical or persistent fashion" than on the Principality of Sealand.

And as it turns out, the questions have some surprising answers.

## DEFINING AND ESTABLISHING TERRITORY

In the days of yore, one group of people would encounter another, overpower them, and claim the vanquished territory as their own. Nowadays, it doesn't quite work like that. All territory ostensibly "belongs" to someone, and it is generally unacceptable for one country to barge in and take another's land. Historically, however, a country could lay claim to a territory by demonstrating "effective occupation" over *terra nullius*, or land not administered by a recognized authority of a territory.

To effectively occupy, an occupier must be able to maintain essential control over the territory, to exercise governmental functions, and to protect its citizens/settlers and the territory itself. Roughs Tower sat abandoned in international waters for at least ten years before it was used by radio pirates. Britain had thus given up effective occupation, arguably leaving the platform open to anyone who wanted to take it and effectively occupy it themselves.

*Terra nullius* and effective occupation are concepts that were used to justify colonization for centuries, as colonial powers didn't consider indigenous groups to have serious claims to the land they wanted for themselves. As steeped in unfortunate colonialism as this may be, this method of acquiring territory creates precedence that backs up Sealand's claim to the platform.

Efforts to decolonize became more mainstream following World War II, and the reigning posture when Sealand was founded was that the aims of small nations striving for independence should be taken seriously. The Atlantic Charter (1941), UN Charter (1945), and the UN Declaration on the Granting of Independence to Colonial Countries and Peoples (1960) enshrine self-determination as an integral right of any emerging state. The effects of colonialism linger today and still inspire tremendous inequity around the world, but on the world stage, leaders at least paid lip service to the idea of genuine self-determination and worked to consecrate these concepts in law.

And so, while a metal naval fort is of course different than a small nation with a longstanding culture, language, and history, Sealand could arguably prove that it met the same qualifications for statehood that these other tiny nations did to be taken seriously as a viable state. Moreover, the Sealanders could cite the Montevideo Convention when making their case.

## THE MONTEVIDEO CONVENTION

The Montevideo Convention on the Rights and Duties of States was signed by sixteen states (and later by three more) at the seventh International Conference of American States in December 1933, in an effort to strengthen interstate relationships following World War I. Britain was not a signatory to this convention*, as the states involved were from the Americas, but the precepts laid out in the Montevideo

---

* The term "convention" refers to an agreement among states that codifies international law.

Convention have long been considered some of the most elegant guidelines for statehood and are accepted as valid on an international scale.

According to the Montevideo Convention, to become a state a territory must have

   a) a permanent population;
   b) a defined territory;
   c) a functioning government;
   d) and the capacity to enter into relations with the other states.

Sealand meets all of these requirements easily. It has always had a permanent *population*, and the Montevideo Convention does not specify how many people are necessary to constitute a population. Michael and Penny and Joan and David Belasco and many others stayed on the fort for weeks at a time throughout the late 1960s (if not always by choice), with the roster of inhabitants expanding greatly in the 1970s. On top of this are Roy's lengthy stays on the fort, which occurred until late in his life.

Colin Simpson, a quiet, somewhat uncomfortable man, lived on Sealand for decades as an armed guard. Simpson was featured in a mini-documentary about Sealand on a British News Program in 1983 and told viewers that "on shore, you have to worry about bills and all that. No worry about that here. It's a lot better out here than in Britain."

"How long can you see yourself staying?" the interviewer asked.

"A while. A long while. The rest of my life," Simpson replied.

Viewers met Simpson again in a 2002 documentary. He still lived on the fort, identified himself as a "Sealander," and said he enjoyed the peace and quiet. He had one lady friend on the coast, he admitted bashfully, who "thinks I'm a bit cracked up."

Other longtime residents are of course caretakers Mike Barrington and Joe Hamill, whose presence ensures there is always someone on the fort and thus a permanent population.*

---

* For those that are wondering, stays on Sealand can be difficult when it comes to certain natural urges. "By the third day though, as I gazed at the hazy UK coastline for probably

In terms of *defined territory*, Sealand obviously has it. The Montevideo Convention contains no stipulation as to what constitutes territory, and there is no language that disqualifies a platform from establishing itself as sovereign. And there are no size requirements when it comes to statehood either, as the recognized nationhood of Vatican City, Monaco, and Nauru, an island nation whose territory is all of eight(!) square miles, demonstrates. Luxembourg, at 999 square miles, is 121 times smaller than the state of New Mexico, yet it is one of the founding members of the United Nations, and its capital Luxembourg City is one of the three capitals of the European Union.

And unlike the territory of some nations that change with storms or global warming, Sealand's 120-by-50-foot perimeter has remained unchanged, and its square footage a steady .004 km² (.002 mi) since it was but a naval fort. Guy Maunsell estimated his forts could stand for two hundred years; according to that estimate, there will be a roughly 5,000-square-foot territory in the North Sea until the year 2142. "Life is much like living in a house in England with a few wind generators thrown in and a terrific view," Michael said.

The *functioning government* aspect is a no-brainer as well: Prince Roy and Princess Joan comprised Sealand's government since its inception. "It is a strange, self-constructed fiefdom, with a class structure unlike that of any other nation in history, comprising as it does only aristocrats," says Adrian Johns, author of *Death of a Pirate*. Sealandic stamps, currency, and passports were issued, and a constitution was written—the staples of a functioning government. The fact that Sealand continues to have a stable government gives it a leg up over many current states. At the time of this writing, Syria is tragically devoid of any effective leadership or infrastructure, but few people would deny the fact that Syria as a country still exists.

As far as the capacity to enter into *relations with other states*, Sealand was ready and willing to enter into relations with friendly nations as soon as such a meeting could take place. The 1970s brought events

the 1,000th time I was naturally feeling exceedingly amorous, to that point that even a passing seagull became attractive," wrote crewmember David Blizzard. "Surely man cannot live on masturbation alone—I've certainly tried," said one documentarian about Sealand's isolation.

that resulted in arguable recognition from other countries of the world, up to and including interactions with an international diplomat.

Moreover, there are many non-state entities that enter into relations with other states all the time. The Central Tibetan Administration, also known as the Tibetan Government in Exile, is not a recognized entity by many states and does not hold any official territory or exercise judicial power, yet it holds embassies all over the world and entertains global diplomats with summits and galas at its headquarters in Dharamshala. Other such entities include the Red Cross, the Sovereign Military Order of Malta, and the United Nations. Fiona McCall et al. argue that the way in which these groups interact with established states, from "loose mimicry that adopts some of diplomacy's trappings to claims of diplomatic equivalence that deny any excess whatsoever," is a form of soft diplomacy that strengthens international relationships of all kinds. In other words, Sealand's interactions with other states help to keep in motion the larger mechanisms of global diplomacy.

The Montevideo Convention conveniently codifies the *declaratory theory* of nationhood as a recognized way for new nations to come about. According to the declaratory theory, a state can declare itself into existence by announcing itself as such, versus the *constitutive theory*, in which nationhood depends on explicit recognition and acceptance by other states. Indeed, the Montevideo Convention states that the "political existence of the state is independent of recognition of other States" provided the burgeoning state can function effectively as a nation.

Of course, it is a fact of life that some amount of recognition is necessary to function as a state in today's world. Obviously, the more powerful a nation you can get to recognize you, the more seriously your claims are going to be taken. So far, no major nation has overtly acknowledged Sealand's claims.* However, Israel, Transnistria, Tibet,

---

\* However, it should be noted that in January 1984, Roy received a note from the Department of Health and Social Security regarding payments he was required to make to the National Health Service. Remarkably, an official with the NHS reported that Roy could deduct from his debts an amount proportional to the time he spent on Sealand. Not having to pay the UK when on Sealand was an affirmation of the principality's claims of sovereignty, but the exact reasons for this startling allowance have apparently been lost to time. A representative of the Department of Work and Pensions, which replaced

and the Republic of Somaliland are states that go unrecognized by more than a few of their global colleagues, but this doesn't preclude their ability to implement the infrastructure of statehood, maintain a population, or develop relationships with territories that do extend them recognition. Volume upon volume has been written exploring which method of becoming a state is "correct," and at this point there is no consensus as to which one is the definitive way to go.

In practicality, an area vying for statehood is decided on a case-by-case basis, as the situations are typically too complicated to have a ready answer available in written law. Areas that might seem perfectly nation-like are not given recognition while states that might otherwise have been stymied by strict interpretations of the rules have become proper countries with little problem. Today there are twenty-five microstates in the world—around 12 percent of all nations—that enjoy status as recognized countries and have voting powers in international organizations. Why shouldn't Sealand be able to follow in their well-established footsteps? After all, it does fulfill all the recognized qualifications and was founded on a territory that was genuinely outside the boundaries of any extant state.

## *IUS GENTIUM* AND UNCLOS I, II, AND III

During the infamous dinner with Lionel Conway in which he broached the idea of statehood, Roy Bates referenced the concept of *ius gentium. Ius gentium* is not an inscribed law but a sort of gentleman's agreement in which nations, though they have differing civil laws, agree to respect international laws and norms. These norms include the rules governing treatment of prisoners of war and the immunity of diplomats, for example, as well as conduct on the "high seas," or the waters beyond the jurisdiction of any national claims.

The spirit of *ius gentium* is reflected in "customary international law." Customary international law is by necessity somewhat vague, as it is impossible to account for every possibility that may arise when

---

the DHSS, said that the records have long since been destroyed; the only publicly accessible document in the National Archives relating to the decision is the 1984 letter itself.

vehicles, people, and installations from all over the world share the same space. However, there are many documents passed between nations that try to set standards for international conduct, and one of the most important and comprehensive of these are the treaties that make up the UNCLOS convention.

In 1956, the United Nations hosted the United Nations Conference on the Laws of the Sea (UNCLOS), the first in a series of conferences whose aim was to facilitate shared access to the world's oceans and clarify certain concepts in maritime law. The conference was prompted by a growing desire to extend territorial waters and (supposedly) to better manage pollution.

One of the biggest UNCLOS developments was to define the territorial waters of coastal states. According to UNCLOS, a state's territorial waters extend twelve nautical miles* from the low-water line along the coast. A state has complete jurisdiction over these waters, below the seabed, and in its airspace. Beyond this twelve-mile limit is the contiguous zone, extending a further twelve nautical miles and similar in scope to the territorial zone, though without air and space rights. Two hundred nautical miles from the shore is the exclusive economic zone, in which a country has the exclusive right to conserve or exploit anything in the oceans and below the seafloor. (UNCLOS also spells out the rights of ships from other countries to pass through these waters.) The UNCLOS convention includes language that specifically addresses the existence of artificial platforms in the ocean.

The regulations governing the emplacement of artificial platforms are fairly vague and deal primarily with not impeding navigation, but the wording of Section 8 of Article 60 of UNCLOS seemingly shuts down any argument that an artificial structure can claim nationhood: "Artificial islands, installations and structures do not possess the status of islands. They have no territorial sea of their own, and their presence does not affect the delimitation of the territorial sea, the exclusive economic zone or the continental shelf."

But the key to applying these standards to Sealand depends on when the treaty took effect.

---

* One nautical mile is approximately 1.15 land miles.

Though UNCLOS says artificial structures can't take on status of islands, if an artificial island became a state in accordance with accepted norms *before* the convention went into effect, then conceivably it would retain the status it had at the time the treaty went into effect, which in this case was that of a sovereign state. There is no "retroactivity" clause in UNCLOS that negates previous agreements or statuses, and so Sealand's sovereignty didn't evaporate when the agreements went into place.

One of the unique things about international law is that it is subject to change based on practice. As Johan Fritz points out, a small amount of practice by a few states can create precedent that leads to law, but the steady contravention of a law can lead to a new legal standard that replaces it. As such, the Sealanders could also simply ignore international dictates, do their own thing, and hope that this practice evolves into practice customarily followed by other nations, therefore becoming as good as law.

In fact, states violate international sea agreements all the time in deliberate attempts to change customary international law, sometimes making it "difficult to determine when an international custom has changed, and at what point, if ever, a state's noncompliance with international custom becomes a new custom or is merely a violation of existing law." It's too bad that other tiny territories and the proto-nations mentioned throughout the book weren't all around at the same time to declare themselves sovereign *en masse*—a flurry of this kind of activity all at once might have been enough to take the issue more seriously and amend practice accordingly.*

At the end of the day, the matter of Sealand's status is a matter of simple logic. Roughs Tower was built by Britain and was considered part of its territory, but then it was abandoned by Britain in international waters and became *terra nullius*. This piece of *terra nullius* was taken over by the Sealanders, who declared a "derelicted" piece of

---

* The inverse of this is true too. UNCLOS didn't take effect until 1994 when the constitution was signed by its sixtieth signatory, but the practice of adhering to the numerous sub-agreements signed over the course of the UNCLOS talks established a precedent that would be firmly in place by the time these laws took effect. They weren't law per se, but they were as treated as the new standard.

(former) British territory as their own. Thus Roughs Tower, which may have begun its life as an artificial island, changed in status from a former British naval fort to official territory belonging to a new country. Customary international law backs up this assertion and there aren't retroactivity clauses that refute it.

"It is a unique case which was possible only here and at that particular time," Roy said. "It was made possible by a strange coincidence of various facts which meanwhile have become history. Nor can such a thing ever be repeated. It was pure chance that all these circumstances coincided here—just like a puzzle, and I just happened to be the one who got the idea."

## ARGUMENTS AGAINST SEALANDIC SOVEREIGNTY

Even though the ruling by Justice Chapman in 1968 set a precedent that was hard to undo, there were at least a few technical legal points that seemed to grant Britain ownership of the fort irrespective of the Assize court's decision. In fact, far from asserting the principality's statehood, some argue that the 1968 decision actually underscores Britain's jurisdiction over the fort: "It is an exercise of its own discretion that legislation may or may not extend to legal transactions on the fort."

It could be argued that just like a lighthouse or an oil rig is definitively owned by a nation, so too were the Maunsell Forts. The fact that Britain continually serviced the buoys around the fort was considered an act of stewardship that showed the UK taking responsibility for its offshore possessions and facilitating navigation in international waters.

In many ways, the formation of the Principality of Sealand was an act of secession, a form of nation-building for which there are no international guidelines and which is generally frowned upon by the international community. Even if the majority of a population votes to secede (a la Catalonia in Spain), the act of secession typically goes unrecognized by other states. Moreover, violence is almost never an acceptable way to build a nation. Article 11 of the Montevideo Convention is against using military force to declare sovereignty, and thus it could be argued that the Bates family, in lobbing bombs at invaders, forged Sealand's independence through illegal violence.

Furthermore, under English law, any territory that is acquired by a British subject is acquired for the UK; thus in claiming Roughs Tower, Roy was actually claiming it for Britain whether he wanted to or not.* Additionally, UNCLOS says that "no State may validly purport to subject any part of the high seas to its sovereignty." This could be taken to mean that Roy Bates couldn't claim Roughs Tower to be his own country, as the platform was in the high seas and belonged to everyone and no one at the same time.

Interestingly, the entire Courts of Assize, whose 1968 opinion is one of the foundational documents of Sealand's existence, was eliminated alongside a number of other British courts in the Courts Act of 1971 as part of a nationwide judicial restructuring. The Courts of Assize and a few other court systems were deemed inefficient and were replaced by centrally organized Crown Courts with a network of some ninety local courts throughout the UK.** The change in the court system doesn't nullify the decisions made before the Assizes were eliminated, but it is a curious aspect to the story that could be exploited by a crafty attorney.

Definitive recognition of the principality could actually cause trouble for Sealand as much as it frees it. If truly sovereign, the tiny ocean statelet would be set adrift to handle its own concerns. If Sealand did something that pisses off another nation enough to act against it, the UK could shrug its shoulders and let Sealand deal with whatever happens to it. The Crown government occasionally adopted the spiteful attitude of leaving Sealand to handle its own affairs as if it were its own state, likely expecting this posture would backfire, but the micronation always managed to make this official indifference work in its favor.

---

* According to English law, "the principle that all conquests made by subjects must belong to the Crown is a general principle pervading the law of both this and other states." As Trevor Dennis writes, international law provides no satisfactory answers as to whether or not individuals can claim territory for themselves because individuals have no legal personality in international law.

** The six Crown Courts are roughly equivalent to District Courts in the US and handle criminal cases, sentencings, and appeals.

## DID THE CROWN BLOW IT?

According to FCO researcher Grant Hibberd, the British government's consistent "prevarication and inaction" blew a chance to nip Sealand in the bud. The hesitation allowed the Sealanders to become further entrenched on the micronation, which complicated Britain's options for the fort. There was always the possibility of some kind of violence if they attacked, but more importantly the prolonged occupation obscured the legal status of the micronation enough that the matter stopped being so black and white.

But Hibberd also affirms that the Crown did the right thing by not coming down too hard on the micronation. Crushing Sealand with serious might would not have made the UK look good.* There had to be a more diplomatic way to deal with the issue and the mission became determining the best angle to make an approach. At the very least, government officials made sure to refer to the fort only as "Roughs Tower," never the "Principality of Sealand," and sent memos back and forth making sure that everyone knew to sternly discourage the notion of its sovereignty. If they gave an inch, Roy would take a mile, and they'd already been in that position before.

Besides, for all the bombastic rhetoric about Sealand's independence, Roy always made a point to emphasize the respect and love he had for the country of his birth. A large color portrait of Queen Elizabeth II hung in the sitting room on Sealand (surrounded by smaller portraits of the Sealandic royalty), and Roy often noted he would fight again in a world war for Britain as soon as he was called. If anything, Roy was a modern incarnation of the wily explorers who expanded Britain's empire and who had no doubt butted heads with the leadership of the time in the same way.

"I'm English, and therefore I was brought up as an Englishman,

---

\* He also points out that it may have been somewhat strategic not to press the issue too intensely, as it may have drawn the Sealanders' attention to the "*Fagernes* Affair of 1926," which would have been very helpful for Roy Bates to reference: A British court ruled that part of the Bristol Channel was outside of its jurisdiction and therefore a British vessel couldn't bring a suit against an Italian ship that caused a collision. As Hibberd writes, the "conclusion Bates would no doubt have drawn from the *Fagernes* Affair would have been if Britain could not even claim full sovereignty over the Bristol Channel, how could it claim to be able to exercise authority over Roughs Tower when it was in the open sea?"

and this demands a great deal of loyalty," Roy said. "I don't see a clash at all—I'm also a Sealander, and I wouldn't permit Sealand to do anything to embarrass or be an unpleasantness in the side of Britain. Nothing will ever happen here that's going to threaten Britain in any way, politically, diplomatically, or in practice."

Britain couldn't be sure that this was definitely the case and a tenuous peace holds between the countries today.

# NOTES

I had the distinct privilege of being invited to meet Prince Michael; his sons, James and Liam; his sister, Penny; Penny's husband, David; and Sealand caretakers Mike Barrington and Joe Hamill in March 2019. Much of the material in this book comes from my personal interviews with the Bates family, conducted from March 20–25, 2019, and with the fort-nation's associates on March 27. I was also fortunate to speak with Prince Michael's first wife, Lozzie Bates, and James's wife, Charley, a few months later. Unless cited otherwise, the quotes attributed to the Sealanders come from these interviews, as does a good amount of background information about the workings of the Principality and the minutiae of its long history.

I am much indebted to Prince Michael's firsthand account of Sealand's history, *Holding the Fort*. Michael's account will make everything you read here seem much more personal in context. Importantly, purchasing the book goes to help the Principality pays its bills and keep its remarkable story going. The handsome hardcover can be ordered through Sealand's website.

On that note, the Sealand website past and present offered a lot to this book, as did the labyrinthine website of Sealand's government in exile. This book relied on information hosted on the websites in the present day but also old versions of the websites accessible through the Wayback Machine.

The book drew extensively from newspapers past and present. Many other news sources from England, Spain, Germany, Slovenia, and the Netherlands were a big help as well. The book also owes a heavy debt to the numerous legal papers dealing with Sealand, micronations, and the broader topics of international, maritime, and internet law. These works are listed in the bibliography that follows.

This book would certainly not have been possible without the files contained in the UK National Archives, whose massive collection of papers related to Sealand from the 1960s to the present day provide fascinating, funny, and eyebrow-raising insight into how the British government handled this perplexing situation. All files quoted in this book are on file with the author, with the only exception being UK National Archive files from the late 1980s to the present. These files are still closed to the public but are quoted extensively by researcher Grant Hibberd, whose work is listed in the bibliography that follows. I would like to reiterate the debt I owe to Professor James Grimmelmann, who provided me access to the files he compiled for the works he's written on Sealand.

When quoting someone like Roy or Joan Bates, who were both unfortunately long-since passed away by the time this book was written, I made every effort to place quotes in the book as true to the timeline in which they were originally made. Occasionally a statement was moved forward or backward in time for narrative purposes, but pains were taken to ensure that the quote was as true to its original context as possible.

## Abbreviations

| | | | |
|---|---|---|---|
| AL | Author interview with Andrew Lawrence | | with Johannes Seiger |
| AP | Associated Press | LB | Author interview with Liam Bates |
| AW | Author interview with Allan Weiner | LE | *Liverpool Echo* |
| BLR | Bob Le-Roi's website | LO | Law Officers' Department, UK National Archives |
| CEG | *Colchester Evening Gazette* | | |
| DE | *Daily Express* | LS | *London Standard* |
| DEFE | Ministry of Defence | LZ | Author interview with Lozzie Bates |
| DM | *Daily Mirror* | | |
| DP | Johns, *Death of a Pirate* | MB | Author interview with Michael Bates |
| DT | *Daily Telegraph* | | |
| EA | *East Anglian Daily Times* | MBR | Author interview with Mike Barrington |
| EG | *Evening Gazette* | | |
| EN | *Evening News* | MW | Sinclair and Le Roi, "Making Waves" |
| EP | *El Pais* | | |
| ES | *Evening Standard* | NYT | *New York Times* |
| FCO | Foreign Commonwealth Office, UK National Archives | PH | Author interview with Penny Hawker |
| FT | *Financial Times* | RBTH | Roy Bates–Ted Haley interview |
| G | *The Guardian* | S | *The Sun* |
| GE | *Grenz Echo* | SEE | *Southend Evening Echo* |
| GTV | "Sealand – a flak tower becomes an economic base in the North Sea" | SG | *Sealandgov.org* |
| | | SN | *Sealandnews.com* |
| | | SHRL | Grimmelmann, "Sealand, HavenCo, and the Rule of Law" |
| HA | *Hamburger Abendblatt* | | |
| HF | *Holding the Fort* | SS | *Southend Standard* |
| HK | Hans Knot, *The Dream of Sealand* | ST | *Sunday Times* |
| | | TG | *The Telegraph* |
| HO | Home Office, UK National Archives | TL | *The Times (of London)* |
| | | TWM | Turner and Watson, *Maunsell* |
| IES | *Ipswich Evening Star* | | |
| IS | *Ipswich Star* | W | *Wired* |
| JB | Author interview with James Bates | WO | *Woman's Own* |
| JH | Author interview with Joe Hamill | WTS | Garfinkel, "Welcome to Sealand, Now Bugger Off" |
| JS | Author correspondence | | |

## Chapter 1

**9. four major attacks and Monte Cassino:** UK Ministry of Defense and Commonwealth Graves Commission, *The Battles for Monte Cassino*; Parker; and Government of India, *The Tiger Triumphs*. **10. a seasoned fighter:** RBTH, Essex Record Office. **"I fought for both sides":** Carol Wallace. **Roy "was a throwback":** MW. **in which the Fusiliers:** "An Extract from the Memoirs of Ex-Fusilier FR Beacham, of the 4th and Final Battle to take Monte Cassino, Italy, 1944, Whilst Serving in 'B' Company, the 1st Battalion, the Royal Regiment of Fusiliers" (hereafter Beacham, "An Extract"). **One of the thousands:** Lt. Col. TA Buchanan, MC, "1st Battalion Royal Fusiliers War Diary, May 1944." **11. The Fusiliers had crossed:** Beacham, "An Extract." **"I rather enjoyed":** HF, p. 12; Amos. **He was born:** Yardley. **lone surviving child:** HF, p. 8. **12. The family moved:** RBTH; Fautley and Garon; Yeardsley; Sherringham; Simper, p. 123-35. **The Bates family settled:** HF, p. 59. **the climate suited:** Lilyan Bates–Ted Haley interview, Essex Record Office. **He was expelled** and quotes/paragraphs about boarding school and Lord Vestey: RBTH. **13. British line infantry:** Griffin. **14. "further up the rank":** HF, p. 12. **German grenade exploded:** Ibid. **caught sight of Joan Collins:** TL, Joan Bates obituary. **15. "It was stunning":** Carol Wallace. **good bit of modeling:** PH. **from a military family:** TL, Joan Bates obituary; Childs. **odd coincidences:** HF, p. 17. **her younger brother:** PH. **three days to propose:** Carol Wallace. **"After all these years":** Ibid. **16. Roy initially embarked and quote:** RBTH; see Alverson for businesses. **friends who sailed:** MB. **In early 1946:** RBTH. **17. willing to try:** SG and obituaries. **"attract me like a madman":** Carol Wallace. **a devoted mother:** PH, MB, HF. **But Michael often witnessed:** SG, "Boyhood memories from the 60s," Oct. 15, 2012. **18. headmaster of Michael's:** RBTH, PH.

## Chapter 2

**20. The fort that would:** Stats and measurements from TWM; Turner sources. Further specifics in SHRL. **"loom drunkenly":** S, "Yo-ho-ho! I board the pop pirates' sea fortress." **Fortifications:** V.T.C. Smith; Claro. **21. a puttering circle:** HF, p. 22; **"like a champagne cork":** Blizzard, "High Tide and Green Grass." **22. 5,920 square feet** and dimensions: TWM; Turner sources. **Michael and Roy walked:** HF, p. 25-27. **23. "a watery bus":** Deeley. Maunsell biography and history of forts: See Turner sources; Monson; *Der Spiegel Online*; "Maunsell Forts," http://whitstablescene.co.uk/forts.htm. **25. "wild cat scheme":** LE. **26. Bad weather caused:** Turner, *The Maunsell Sea Forts*, p. 62-64. **27. "It was successful":** LE. **Each fort was outfitted:** HF, p. 20. **"The room has no windows":** Sellars. Living on the fort: Turner, *The Maunsell Sea Forts*; Lichtenstein, especially p. 175-85 and 253-54. **28. "The story I heard":** Goddard. **The vulnerability to attack:** MBR. **"The four naval forts":** TWM, p. 32-33. **Both sets of Maunsell's forts:** Turner, *The Maunsell Sea Forts*. **29. the forts were all:** TWM; Turner, *The Radio Pirates aboard the Offshore Forts in the Thames Estuary*; BLR; "Maunsell Forts"; for information on wartime action and postwar period, Turner, *The Maunsell Sea Forts*, p. 159-71. **The Red Sands Army Forts:** Shadbolt. **A Swedish**

freighter: "Maunsell Forts" and "Great Nore Towers/Fort," undated note in DEFE 57/55. 30. **Maunsell is known:** TWM, chapters 4-7, 17. **"Engineers have always"**: Ibid, p. 5.

## Chapter 3

33. **The British Broadcasting:** For the BBC's origin and its intended mission, see DP, especially p. 13-34. 34. **Playing fast and loose** and pirate broadcasting history: Ibid., p. 37-41, 45-52; see also "Piracy as a business force." **the territorial claims:** TG, "Prince Roy of Sealand." 35. **"popular with Kent housewives":** *Kent Messenger.* 36. **"The public instantly loved it":** HF, p. 21. **"Pirate broadcasting became definitive":** Johns, "Piracy as a business force." **not foreign to the Bates:** HF, MB. 37. **"tinkering with the idea":** RBTH. **In late October** and descriptions of tussle: *The People*, "Pirates Ahoy! In Battle for Fort"; S, "Pop 'commandos' say We're here to stay"; and *News of the World* undated article. **"The old man was by now":** HF, p. 32. 38. **"We mean to stay":** DT, "Seas Delay Rescue of Radio Pirates." **"A disc jockey"** and Calvert quote: S, "Pop 'commandos' say We're here to stay." **Ads for more DJs:** Henry and von Joel. **"opening a can of beans":** HF, p. 21. 39. **The first transmitter** and life on the fort: Henry and von Joel; HF; MW; BLR. **make jokes on air:** HK. **"pleasantly anarchic tang":** ES, "Element of Farce." 40. **Commercials and call signs:** MW; HF, p. 32-40; **"We're doing a job":** "ITN Reporting 66: Pirate radio stations." **a fledging rock group:** Lucas. 41. **"The only American newsman":** RBTH. **"Between the two":** Ibid. **"I'm not introspective":** "Sealand on Reporting London 1983." 42. **"Bates' continuing source of income":** Alverson. **Bates also had the reputation:** newspaper reports; Henry and von Joel. **"a mythology about Roy Bates":** Ibid. **"We'd long ago eaten"** and quote: *In Living Memory.* **Penny and Michael would often:** PH, MB.

## Chapter 4

45. **Reg Calvert and Oliver Smedley:** for further reading, see DP, p. 1-12; **According to the act:** *Marine, &c., Broadcasting (Offenses) Act*, 1967. **Police also investigated:** HK. 46. **run by an Irishman:** Harris, p. 210. **"I might be sticking":** FT. 47. **Newey, prosecuting:** TL, "Radio Station in the Thames Estuary on Air After Owner is Fined £100." **"hydrographic data":** BLR. **"Sacrificing chickens":** MW. **He was fined:** TL, "Radio Station in the Thames Estuary on Air After Owner is Fined £100." **Southend Carnival Queen:** note in DM, August 2, 1948. **around £200:** "Rough's Tower Fort," letter from C.B. Lovell to E.M. Ross, esq. of the Cabinet Office, November 20, 1967 with Solicitor's Department of the Post Office report (HO 255/1243). **"continue to transmit":** FT; G, "Fined radio 'pirate' says he will go on transmitting"; DT, "Radio Essex will defy court." **"No war is won":** HK. **Solicitor's Department:** "Rough's Tower Fort," letter from C.B. Lovell to E.M. Ross, esq. of the Cabinet Office, November 20, 1967, with accompanying report from Solicitor's Department of the Post Office (HO 255/1243). **seat-of-the-pants:** MB; HK. 48. **Radio Essex moniker:** DP, p. 232-33; DT, "Radio Essex stays on air despite fine." **mushroom farm:** TL, "100GNS Health Trips to Sea Fort." **In August 1965:** MW. **"hard bastards":** Ibid. **Bates**

and his crew: HF, p. 50-52; SHRL 49. "extremely black": HF, p. 50; cut the roast: Brown; came home for Easter: leaving school in HF, p. 54; quote p. 39. 49-50. fortuitous accident: Ibid, p. 55-56; also in HK and MW. 50. "I was mortified": BLR. "the fort's arsenal": Harris, p. 208. "Gravesend Dockers": MW. 51. the first move: HF, p. 64. A barrage of petrol and fight: EN, "Pop pirates in petrol bomb battle"; DM, "Pop for gets switched on to repel boarders." See also HF, p. 64-68; Harris, p. 206-9; Steer, p. 209; and Henry and von Joel. "Mike Thunderstick": DM, "Pop for gets switched on to repel boarders." 52. The *Offshore II* got: Harris, p. 206. "overdid it": DM, "Pop for gets switched on to repel boarders." "We arrived": EN, "Pop pirates in petrol bomb battle." "foreign-looking": TL, "Sea Fort Repels Boarders." 53. "If you're your own": Woodward. "When things are going smoothly": Carol Wallace. Reggie and Ronald Kray: HF, p. 71; statement by Mr. Simser, May 1, 1967 (HO 255/1037); Fogle.

## Chapter 5
55. occupation of Roughs: See letters in UK National Archives; exchange beginning with the Postmaster General, April 14, 1967 (DEFE 13/658) and "Notes of a Meeting held in Sir Burke Trend's Room," July 31, 1967 (HO 255/1037); "Opinion of the Law Officers of the Crown," UK Foreign Office, Fall 1967 (LO 2/1088). Concern about the situation: Post Office to Prime Minister, July 1967 (DEFE 13/658). "The position with regard": Confidential opinion on pirate radio by G.G. Brown, April 24, 1967 (HO 255/1037). 56. "A controlled": Ibid. shout at the occupants: Post Office to Prime Minister, July 1967 (DEFE 13/658). blockading Roughs Tower: Ibid. customs technicalities: C.E. Lovell to D.J. Trevelyan, August 22, 1967 (HO 255/1037). Continental Shelf: H.G. Lillicrap, April 21, 1967 (HO 255/1037); keeping Michael: Notes of a Meeting held in Sir Burke Trend's Room, July 31, 1967 (HO 255/1037). like a lighthouse: W.L. Dale to the Attorney and Solicitor Generals, July 25, 1967 (LO 2/1088 000223). "ponderous move": Unknown to Prime Minister, April 4, 1968 (LO 2/1088); cancelled plans: DP, p. 233. "doubtful privilege": I.H. Lightman to M.A. Coleman, May 23, 1967. "defense budget": C.E. Lovell to Postmaster General, May 11, 1967 (HO 255/1037). 57. "Operation Callow" and plans: "Occupation of Roughs Tower Operation "Callow" Operational Instructions," August 4, 1967 (DEFE 57/55); "Brief for Mr. Sweby, Roughs Tower Fort" (DEFE 57/55). Just before and encounter with Roy Bates: W.A. Sweby's confidential report to the Private Undersecretary of the Army, August 7, 1967 (DEFE 57/55). 59. Bates countered: P.D. Nairne to cabinet departments, August 7, 1967 (DEFE 13/658). "The Ministry hasn't": Alverson. In the late afternoon: Account of HMS *Bembridge* going to fort from Duty Commander of Directorate of Naval Operations and Trade, August 7, 1967 (LO 2/1088); see also HF. Michael recalls with relish: HF, p. 80-1. 60. "His manner": Account of HMS *Bembridge* going to fort from Duty Commander of Directorate of Naval Operations and Trade, August 7, 1967 (LO 2/1088); "preemptive press": Grimmelmann, "Death of a Data Haven." headlines like: TL, "Commandos set to seize fort." Customs and Excise: For more on Customs and

the Bates family, Ibid; HF, p. 90-6; and letter from P.M. Scadden. A letter from C. Bamfield of Customs to H.F. Ellis-Rees, esq. of the Ministry of Defence, February 23, 1968, outlines Customs' approach (LO 2/1088). N.H. Parsons to Mr. Hay, April 4, 1968 (HO 255/1037). **"absurd that Bates":** P.M. Scadden to Mr. Kenway, May 1, 1967 (HO 255/1037). **61. Customs fruitlessly:** TL, "Children not 'marooned.'" **"Children on the Tower":** ES, "Children on fort 'doing fine.'" **scared or lonely:** Ibid; life on the fort, PH and HF, p. 94-6. **Minister of Parliament:** Paul Channon, MP to Harold Lever, esq., March 25, 1968 (LO 2/1088). **62. "Nobody can feel":** Letter to Prime Minister Harold Wilson, April 4, 1968 (LO 2/1088); **"3,200 pounds":** BLR. **explosions sent:** Childs. **Reporters:** MB. **passed into law** and pirate radio closing: DP, p. 225-40 and "Piracy as a business force"; BLR; MW; Harris, p. 212-17.

**Chapter 6**
**65. "I remember":** SG, "Sealand Facebook page reaches 50,000 Likes," July 4, 2012. **late August 1967:** HF, p. 88-91; WTS; **Trickey. "hardly a dream":** Warren. **66. "I wasn't surprised":** WO. **"You might be tossed":** RBTH. **Roy even offered** and quote by Joan: Ibid. **67. "make it a principality":** Ibid. **68. The Indian Stream:** Ferguson. **Guano Islands:** See Underhill and Vergano. **James Mangan:** Richmond. **Outer Baldonia:** Lachlan McKinnon. **69. Rockall situation:** See Bowcot and Duffy. **"a Cuba off":** Warren, and "'Smallest state' seeks new owners." **experiments in nationhood:** Menefee. **70. It happened that** and contemporary UK history: Roberts and Roberts; Marwick. **As Rachel:** Lichtenstein, p. 103-4; **"that difficult":** Gale. **proud Englishman:** HF, p. 53-4. **71. But he was also** and quote: MB. **tax-free** and quotes: Moynihan; SS, "Sealand ex-'Pirate' radio chief claims fort is new state"; Kessler. **72. "It is precisely":** RBTH. **"I'm a Royalist":** Rachel Murphy. **September 2, 1967** and flag-raising ceremony: HF, p. 89-90, Garfinkel, "Welcome to Sealand, Now Bugger Off"; Boudreaux and Miller; Sellars; BLR; MW. **"When we came":** Sellars. **73. "'king of the castle'":** Moynihan. **"She had always":** HF, p. 89. **off-center:** Ibid., p. 89. **"Don't call":** DE, "The Prince even has a captive." **Nowadays residents:** MBR, JH. **74. "On a clear day":** Nizinskyj. **"like hell":** WO. **from food** and early life on the fort: Ibid; PH, MB; HF, p. 72-77, 102-9. **75. catching lobsters:** Warren. **76. "They used to":** WO. **77. "how cold":** Ibid. **rough weather:** BLR. **new dominion** and quotes: Carol Wallace. **78. painted on:** SHRL; IES, "Words in white paint start new takeover rumors." **"being able to do":** Carol Wallace. **"People always":** Moynihan. **Sealand's declaration** and Radio Caroline spokesman's quote: IES, "Fort's independence is 'ludicrous idea.'" **"I had seen":** Carol Wallace. **toilets emptied:** Bates, "Ask Me Anything" (hereafter "Reddit").

**Chapter 7**
**83. within one hundred** and *Egeria* incident: HF p. 97-99, and report with testimony by *Egeria* Lt. Commander C.E.K. Robinson to Sir Norman Skelhorn, Director of Public Prosecution, December 6, 1967 (LO 2/1088). **"suitable case":** Memo quoting Director of Public Prosecution, January 1968 (DEFE 13/658).

**84. On November 2, 1967:** E.H. Palmer to Mr. Sweby, November 2, 1967 (DEFE 57/55). **A fit guy:** Ibid; report on meeting by Sweby, November 17, 1967 (DEFE 57/55); for Belasco and Roy's relationship to him, see HF, p. 54. **"You are not":** E.H. Palmer to Sweby, November 2, 1967 (DEFE 57/55); **The agents were shown:** Report on meeting by Sweby, November 17, 1967 (DEFE 57/55). **85. on the sly:** Sweby to Mr. Belasco, November 17, 1967 (LO 2/1088); **Sweby cut:** Report on meeting by E.H. Palmer, November 17, 1967 (DEFE 57/55); **official clearance:** HF, p. 91. **sworn affidavit** and quotes: DT, "Ministry Planned to Seize Fort," Belasco's affidavit (LO 2/1088). **sold the rights:** Report on meeting by Sweby, November 17, 1967 (DEFE 57/55). **86. "totally unjustified":** Reply to Paul Channon (LO 2/1088); **"incorrect to say":** DT, "Ministry Planned to Seize Fort." **nonviolent takeover:** HF, p. 91 and MB; no suitable boat from DT, "Ministry Planned to Seize Fort." **"I am sure":** Paul Channon to the Rt. Hon. Denis W. Healey, MBE, MP, Secretary of State for Defence, May 30, 1968 (LO 2/1088); **On May 6:** Confidential memo on *Vestal* encounter from H.F. Ellis-Rees, May 17, 1968 (HO 255/1037); **Unbeknownst:** MB. **87. seven hundred feet:** SS, "Why 'Sealand' is free from law"; Hibberd, "The Last Great Adventure of the Twentieth Century." **"I'd like to give":** Hodgkinson. **a .22 pistol** and quote: H.F. Ellis-Rees to E.M. Rose, esq., Cabinet Office, May 17, 1968 (HO 255/1037). **Trinity House quickly:** Memo on *Vestal* encounter from H.F. Ellis-Rees, May 17, 1968 (HO 255/1037); report on follow up to *Vestal* incident, R.L. Waddingham, May 30, 1968 (DEFE 13/658); memo by J.E.D. Street, Head of Home, July 7, 1968. **The escort prompted:** Ibid. **condescension:** "Roughs Tower: the Police Investigation" to cabinet departments, June 1968 (DEFE 13/658). **87-88. "recrudescence":** R.M. Hastie-Smith to D.H. Andrews, esq., May 30, 1968 (DEFE 13/658). **88. officially charged:** HF, p. 115-16; memo on follow up to *Vestal* incident (DEFE 13/658). **police car:** HF, p. 115. **Navy vessels:** HF, p. 121. **Roy's barrister:** Letter to E.M. Rose, esq., Cabinet Office, July 25, 1968 (LO 2/1088). **"We shot":** GTV. **Plans for a raid:** See memos such as "Taking Roughs Tower by Force" and the plans for "Operation Pierrot," "Operation Proclaim," and "Operation Thorough," drawn up by the Ministry of Defence in late May 1968 (DEFE 13/658). **89. On October 21:** HF, p. 114-21. **Boreham argued** and other arguments about status of Roughs Tower: Transcript of *Regina vs. Paddy Roy Bates and Michael Roy Bates*, Friday, October 25, 1968; "Opinion of the Law Officers of the Crown, July 21, 1967 (LO 2/1088). **The debate:** HF, p. 117-21. **When court resumed** and quotes: Transcript of *Regina vs. Paddy Roy Bates and Michael Roy Bates,* Friday, October 25, 1968. **90. "UK's trash":** Lyon. **Scholars:** SHRL; letter from C. Hooten, Assistant Treasury Solicitor to the Ministry of Defence, June 25, 1974 (DEFE 57/55). **According to:** "Minutes of a Meeting held in Conference Room 'D', Cabinet Offices," November 5, 1968 (LO 2/1088). **"some advantage":** Ibid. **"any rights":** Cusik. **"government finally":** Rachel Murphy.

**Chapter 8**
**93. oldest child:** PH. **94. immune:** HF and MB. Quote from Nate Anderson. **95. isolation:** HF, p. 152; BLR. **hitched a ride:** Hodgkinson. **handful of boats:**

On becoming a cockle fisherman, MB. **Penny felt:** PH. **96. Roy turned down:** HF, p. 132; MB. **Things got so bad:** PH. **arbitrary hardships:** Ibid. **"Would you ask":** Woodard. **97. "If you want":** Bohrer, et all. **September 1969** and post office project: HF, p. 130-31; HK. **"our government":** HK. **2 and 50:** Official Sealand websites; HF, p. 131. **98. admitted in court:** Alverson. **Sealand stamps do** and Cinderella stamps: Author correspondence with Derek Watson and Joanne Berkowitz. **99. first Sealand coins** and quotes: HF, p. 133. **minting error:** *Ken Potter's Variety Vault.* **1994 coins:** MB. **100. "Las Vegas":** Baker. **Muammar Gaddafi:** Ibid. **matter of logistics:** HK. **American church:** Deeley. **"a good lunch":** Cusick. **The Bateses:** A. Kruk-Schuster to the Defence Land Headquarters, June 20, 1972 (DEFE 57/55). **Department of Energy:** "Survey of Existing Reinforced Concrete Marine Structures," study proposal with letter from M.S. Igglesden to P. Coombes, esq., July 15, 1976 (DEFE 57/55).

**Chapter 9**
**101. Germans and Dutchmen:** MB. **"coffeeshop":** GTV. **Walter Scheffel** and quotes: Ibid. **Most infamous:** Ibid and Langhans. **102. His title "professor":** SHRL **"great adventure":** GTV. **He told Roy and Joan:** MB. **Achenbach did not speak:** HK. **a volley:** Report from FCO, March 18, 1974 (DEFE 57/55). **Achenbach later estimated:** Hibberd. **Leisner says:** Walter Leisner, "Legal Expert Opinion on the Jus Gentium Situation of the Principality of Sealand," February 5, 1975 (LO 33/2705). **103. "gun platforms":** Baker. **"state on stilts":** Haveman. **German Sealanders:** GTV, Montaigu. For Adrian Oomen's account of the affair, see "The Luxemburg-Story: Primeminister Jean-Claude Juncker Arrogant or Corrupt?" and "Die Principality of Sealand ihre historische und politische Entwicklung bis heute (The Principality of Sealand: their Historical and Political Development Until Today)" at the exile government's website, principality-of-sealand.ch. **"fraudulent business":** J.C. Harrison to D. Broad, esq., April 19, 1978 (FCO 33/3355). **The lawyer was Adrian:** HF, p. 218. **"International Court could":** GTV. **104. Luxembourg was:** J.M. Crosby to F.W. Willis, esq. of FCO's Western European Department, May 20, 1976 (DEFE 57/55). **two years in jail** and release: David Herbert to D. Broad, esq., July 10, 1978 (FCO 33/3355). **August 2, 1976** and account of court proceedings: *In re Duchy of Sealand* 80 I.L.R 683; SHRL; Arenas. **Dutch athlete:** Telex from J.A. Shepherd to A.E. Furness, esq., August 24, 1978 (FCO 33/3355). **105. before the internet:** MB. **Achenbach was accused** and Free Church affair: HA, March 12, 1975, to November 23, 1976; follow-up article on August 9, 1978. **"a commission":** HA, September 14, 1976. **106. pamphlet touting:** Plans explained in GTV and *Hanauer Anzeiger.* **"longer to expand":** Haveman. **107. British official:** A.S. Payne to Mr. Clarke, FCO, February 2, 1978 (FCO 33 33/55). **Scheffel took calls:** *Hanauer Anzeiger.* **plans were bolstered:** Dr. Bela Vitanyi, "Legal Opinion about the International Status of the Principality of Sealand" pamphlet, University of Nijmegen (FCO 33/3355); Analysis in Cogliati-Bantz, Arenas. **90 percent:** GTV. **Guy Hawtin:** H.N.P. Harrison to C.C. Bright, esq., August 21, 1978 (FCO 33/3355). **weren't even shy:** *Frankfurter Allgemeine,* "10 Jahre Sealand

(10 years of Sealand)," ad placed July 8, 1977. **108. Denials from bank officials:** Herr Manke to Mr. Gernot Pütz, April 2, 1976 (FCO 33/3086). **the questions led:** Carolyn Hubbard to F.W. Willis, esq., April 5, 1977 (FCO 33/3086); A. Stephenson to A.S. Payne, esq., August 24, 1977 (FCO 33/3086); C.J. Wright to A. Stephenson, esq., August 8, 1977 (FCO 33/3086); C. Wright to A. Stephenson, esq., August 11, 1977 (DEFE 57/55); Hibberd. **"making money":** *In Living Memory.*

**Chapter 10**
**109. A Mercedes:** *Der Spiegel.* in Salzburg: HF; SHRL; WTS. **Achenbach had proposed:** HK. **110. Soon the chopper:** HF; WTS; Trickey; Boudreaux and Miller. **"oily bastard":** HF, p. 156. **111. "Let's throw":** Ibid, p. 165. **"years spent":** Ibid, p. 166-67. **112. "In this modern":** Stroumboulopoulos. **"Putting things":** *Neue Sealand Journal.* **"We phoned":** WTS. **"throw away our life's work?"** and Roy's quote: HF, p. 172. **113. "sheer disgust":** Ibid. p. 175. John Crewdson: Ibid., MB, PH. **"blow it up":** *Newsweek.* airline pilot: PH. **114. "You don't serve":** Kessler. **"fallen over":** Lichtenstein, p. 172. **"speak English"** exchange: HF, p. 187-89; Trickey. **115. "police ourselves":** "Sealand on the UK Evening News Sept 2002." **Sealanders told** and quote: Gardner, "My four days in captivity at the hands of foreign invaders." **On August 29:** A.C. Furness to Mr. Clarke, August 29, 1978 (FCO 33/3355). **"falsely imprisoned":** R.A. Hibbert to Herr Hans-Heinrich Noebel, September 12, 1978 (FCO 33/3355). **Eck and Boss:** HF, p. 192. **116. Present at his trial:** Ibid., p. 192. **Michael prosecuted:** DE, "The Prince even has a captive." **"Gernot Pütz":** Account of the trial of Gernot Pütz, signed Roy of Sealand on Principality stationary, August 30, 1978 (UK National Archives, FCO 33/3355). **"This Court accepts":** Ibid. **"still be shot":** *Essex Leader.* **"friendly man":** HK. **"killed a lot of Germans":** Simon, "Another Country." **A reporter:** Gardner, "Lonely life of the prisoner of Sealand." **117. At the same time:** *Southend Echo.* **118. "usual chat[s]":** Log Extract 78/47, September 16, 1978 (HO 255/1244). **"your mother":** Ibid. **"couldn't find":** Log Extract 78/50, September 21, 1978 (HO 255/1244). **impressive piece:** Cassell. **enough illegal:** C.F. Bone to Mr. Dredge, "Request for a Search Warrant Authority," September 8, 1978 (HO 255/1246). **Michael Hawkins** and quotes: Cassell; Hawkins. **"I told you":** Ibid. **The equipment:** Ibid.; Ezard. **119. Not long after:** Hawkins. **Bates told** and quotes: Cassell. **Lionel Conway:** Letter from Conway & Conway Solicitors, September 13, 1978 (FCO 33/3355). **due to appear:** SEE, "Sealand 'Prince' faces radio charges." **did not appreciate:** Embassy of the Federal Republic of Germany to the FCO, September 12, 1978 (FCO 33 33/55). **"despairing":** F.D. Berman to Mr. Broad, October 3, 1978 (FCO 33 33/55). **Hannelore:** Bramwell; HF; *Los Angeles Times.* **120. "lost face":** David Broad to Mr. Berman, September 18, 1978 (FCO 33/3355). **"sallow-complexioned":** HF, p. 201. **"early solution":** Bramwell; Wainwright articles; TL, "Attempt to free captive from private 'island' fails." **Joan Bates met Neimoller:** "Sealand after the Invasion 1978 BBC1 News report .mp4." **"Lucky guy":** Reddit. **Not long:** Wainwright, "Sealand keeps its prisoner." **Michael maintains:** HF, p.

194. **addendum:** R.I. Clarke to Mr. Furness and Mr. Goodall, September 1, 1978 (FCO 33/3355). **120-121 more trouble than it was worth:** HF, p. 195-196; Trickey, "Sean of Sealand." **121. "bloody mad":** Trickey. **small crowd** and quote: Sadler; see also Gardner, "My four days in captivity at the hands of foreign invaders" and G, "Lawyer freed from sea fort." **Neimoller even:** SHRL. **Michael maintains:** HF. **"an act of piracy":** *Neue Sealand Journal.* **122. "internationally-established":** *East Essex Gazette.* January 22: HK; SEE, "Jail fear for Prince Roy's boy." **Some scholars:** Cogliati-Bantz. **123. "law society":** Ibid. **Achenbach sent:** HK. **Oomen told:** Ibid. **Michael and Joan weren't sure:** SEE, "Sealand couple sail clear of arrest." **"Any arrest plan":** Ibid. **Michael stood** and quote: HF, p. 218. **Proceedings were:** HK. **Oomen admitted:** Ibid. **The principality:** Sams. **another raid:** HK. **124. temporarily suspended:** Ibid. **pleaded guilty:** IES, "'Ruler of Sealand' fined for radio offences." **the transmissions":** HK. **Roy gave his address:** CEG, "Sealand 'Prince' admits illegal broadcasting." The **1970s:** *Southend and District Standard;* EG, "Church agree to Sealand wedding"; HF, p. 236-39. **125. "traditional wedding":** EG, "Church agree to Sealand wedding." **The Bishop:** Ibid. **Reverend James Chelton:** HK. **"unusual wedding":** Ibid. **hallowed day:** Ibid. **Being hailed:** Ibid. **126. "busy life":** Ibid.

Chapter 11

127. **"There must be":** Lt. Colonel M.D. Legg to Major J.A.B. Salmon, September 3, 1981 (HO 255/1246). **On November 21** and quotes: Roy Bates. **128. "It was during":** Cusick. **129. The proposal was:** HF, p. 224. **The year 1985 and following:** HF, p. 243-44, MB and LZ, October 13, 2019 (all quotes). **In 2016:** AP, "Falkland Islands lie in Argentinian waters, UN commission rules." **130. "very proud":** HF, p. 244. **As James grew:** MB. **131. "I do remember":** Ibid. **"newspaper clippings":** Bohrer, et all. **James one-upped:** Nizinskyj. **132. The pirate stations:** Trueman. **Radio Investigation:** Hibberd; RIS Director Dilys Gane to P.A.C. Baldwin, August 15, 1986 (HO 255/1245); D. Gane to Miss Sladden, August 20, 1986 (HO 255/1246). **"have a team":** Trueman. **HAM radio:** HK; SHRL. **133. 200 million:** EA, "Fort may house radio stations." **"There will":** Comment in newsletter by Now Radio Communications, 1986. **On July 28,** and following, quotes: R.J. Smith; England. **Weiner wept:** Kuipers. **"technical nerds":** AW. **Weiner was arrested:** R.J. Smith. **134. In July 1984:** Ibid.; Kuipers. **summer of 1986:** Ibid. **Transmissions began** and following quotes: Ibid. **135. "always respected":** AW. **Weiner and Michael:** Kuipers. **He noted:** Hibberd, which itself references FCO note, February 1983 (MRD 040/3/83). **136. Roy also submitted:** Hibberd. **"Their arguments":** Ibid. **Territorial Sea Act:** *Territorial Sea Act of 1987 (c. 49) An Act to provide for the extent of the territorial sea adjacent to the British Islands.* **"argument about":** Hibberd, "The Sealand Affair." **Roy bought some time:** SN; HF; Baker. **Australian Governor:** Casley. **137.** *Sarah* **was repaired:** Kuipers. **broadcast for a total:** Ibid. **Based on the cost:** Ibid. **"too carefully":** opinion rendered by Judge Blumenthal, *In re Application of Wiener Broadcasting Company,* January 29, 1992. **James Murphy:** Statement of witness, January 17, 1989. **"incorrigible Weiner":** Blumenthal. **138. Weiner could:** *UPI Wire.* **another group:** England; Gilder and Haggard; Knot,

"De wonderlijke geruchten over Radio London van 1984." **"alternative to the BBC"**: England. **WRLI producer:** Knot, "De wonderlijke geruchten over Radio London van 1984"; Lilburne-Byford. **Weiner allegedly:** England; SHRL. **"blown off"**: Gilder and Haggard. **139. One judge told:** Lilburne-Byford. **"bankrupt for life"** and quotes: Ibid. **An FCC review:** Blumenthal. **Weiner was finally** and quote: AW. **station has aired** and quote: Lathan. **140. In June 1987:** TV brochure with introduction from the station's Director of Advertising D. Newman, National Archives (HO 255/1246). **A brochure** and quotes: Ibid. **1000-foot:** James Murphy to John Laksic, June 8, 1987 (HO 255/1246). **141. Sealand TV would:** Neil Watson. **"diabolical"**: CEG, "Pop and video rival for BBC and ITV." **According to the Colchester:** CEG, "Fortress Sealand TV." **launch this:** *The Mail*; CEG, "Sealand TV 'live in 12 weeks time.'" **Ken Hanlon** and quote: O'Kelly. **Suzanne Mizzi** and quote: *The Mail*. **142. Campaign magazine:** O'Kelly. **UK communications:** D. German to Miss Gane, July 13, 1987; G.J. Spiteri to J. Ketchell, August 3, 1987 (HO 255/1246). **UK government files:** List in National Archives in HO 255/1246. **Wallace Kemper:** CEG, "Sealand TV 'live in 12 weeks time'"; James Murphy to John W. McCaffrey, August 14, 1987 (HO 255/1246); James Murphy to cabinet departments, August 14, 1987. **"Wallace dismissively"**: HF, p. 253-54. **Quoting federal:** Kim Murphy; Gewertz; *Daily News*; Spano; Dawson. **143. Kemper went** and quote: Ibid.; HF, p. 254. **As Michael put it:** Ibid. **Achenbach reappeared:** HK. **intermittently:** Ibid. **arrested and convicted:** Ibid. **144. "many journeys"**: Ibid. **Sealandic constitution:** SHRL; exile government's website, www.principality-of-sealand.ch. **"more optimistic"**: Alverson.

**Chapter 12**
**145. "almost choked"**: Hibberd. **"rifle shots"**: Cusik. **146. discussed in the 1990s:** *Sunday Mirror*. **On July 15**: Orth, *Vulgar Favors*, p. 497-507; *Akron Beacon Journal*; Carpenter and Neubauer; Davidson; Dubocq. **well-spoken:** Scott. **147. under the pseudonym:** Lambiet. **fraud squad:** Author correspondence with Michael Bates. **"more honest"**: WTS. **alias Mattias Ruehl:** Ibid.; Orth, *Vulgar Favors*. **He and Reineck:** Orth, *Vulgar Favors*, p. 501. **Reineck ultimately**: Ibid, p. 503. **Miami Beach Police:** Author interview with Richard Barreto, November 26, 2018. **148. On April 4**: Irujo articles; Ospina; Morcillo; *El Mercurio*; Woodard; Gooch; Boudreaux and Miller. **flamenco club owner:** Morcillo. **boxed him in:** Ibid. **nonplussed:** Ibid. **conspiracies abound:** Orth, "Andrew Cunanan and the Assassination of Gianni Versace, Revisited." **149. "cold and calculating"**: Morcillo. **officially placed:** Ibid. **primary sources:** Boudreaux and Miller. **Ruiz's arrest:** Gooch. **fake diplomatic:** Boudreaux and Miller. **150. Michael wrote:** Ibid. **"what the hell?"**: Woodard. **gang's plans:** Ibid. **Miguel Palacios Massó:** *El Mercurio*. **"Neither I"**: Irujo, "La Guardia Civil detiene en su 'embajada' al regente del falso Principado de Sealand." **Most of the gang's:** Ibid.; Morcillo; Boudreaux and Miller. **151. The gang went:** Morcillo. **came to light:** Boudreaux and Miller. **"stealing our name"**: Ibid. **Ruiz reportedly:** Ibid. **"vegetable"**: Irujo, "Interpol sigue por todo el mundo el rastro del falso principado de Sealand." **shares the same name:** quotes from Morcillo. **152. KH Schrimpf:**

"Memorandum The Matter of Spain/Schrimpf/Ley," signed Seiger and Löwendick, February 14, 1997, principality-of-sealand.ch. **refuted Ley's:** Ibid.; "Press release 2/0400," Diplomatic Mission of the Principality of Sealand, https://principality-of-sealand.ch/html-2017/pressecorner/pm1_span_010420.html. **153. mid-1990s:** Langhans. **Panama Papers:** Ibid. **Using Sealandic documents:** Ropac, "Obresti od zaplenjenega denarja ostanejo dravi." **Slovenian authorities:** *MMC*; Felc; Jakopec; Ropac articles; *Slovenske Novice*; Marin. **"young countries":** Boggan, "Money Laundering." **154. Baiers came:** Ibid. **put a hold:** *MMC*. **In 2005:** *Slovenske Novice*. **money transferred:** Ropac, "Obresti od zaplenjenega denarja ostanejo dravi." **court fees:** Ibid. **"strange philosophical":** Boggan, "Money Laundering." **155. "Every country":** Ibid. **moratorium:** Reddit. **Territory of Poyais:** *The Economist*, "The king of con-men"; Sinclair, *The Land That Never Was*. **157. legitimate and fake:** European Commission.

**Chapter 13**
**161. grim day:** WTS. **162. "$220,000":** Lackey https://www.youtube.com/watch?v=aJ6ByBaTxms&t=9s. **late 1990s:** Platt. **163. "interested in how":** Schafer. **early electronic:** WTS. **Anguilla's ".ai":** Schafer. **twenty-nine:** Trickey. **Vince Cate:** Platt. **164. "toxic barge project"** and quote: Grimmelmann, "Death of a Data Haven." **Anguilla proved:** SHRL. **Cate handed:** Markoff. **overestimate:** Author interview with Erwin Strauss, January 25, 2019. **165. "controversial viewpoints":** Garfinkel, "Covert Catalog." **166. Hastings compiled:** Sean Hastings's offline website, via the Wayback Machine, www.seanhastings.com/datahaven/datahaven_chapter1 (hereafter "Hastings chapters"). **"pirate internet":** Stackpole. **167. "dozens of proposals":** Markoff. **flare-up:** HF, p. 258. **"millions of pounds":** This figure is bandied about quite a bit, though it is of course impossible to verify exactly how much has gone into Sealand. Depending on who is giving the account, some agree that hundreds of thousands of dollars is probably more accurate, but for the mention of millions, see Woodard; Strauss; and Rachel Murphy. **"quixotic financial sinkhole":** Hemphill. **"My father would never":** MB. **Hastings chartered:** Hastings chapters. **"Reading about":** Ibid. **168. HavenCo, Ltd.:** WTS. **first $1:** Ibid. **Parekh thought:** Hastings chapters. **"Until HavenCo":** MB. **"ramping up":** Author correspondence with Joichi Ito. **169. "secure colocation":** WTS. **Lackey's first:** Freedman and Lackey. **Customer costs:** Gilmour. **"break the law":** Ibid. **Client data:** WTS. **170. "three satellite":** Ibid. **Attackers:** Ibid.; SHRL. **"security model":** Freedman and Lackey. **estimated nineteen:** SHRL. **171. "by libertarian":** *Slashdot*. **June 2000:** Markoff. **gambling websites:** Stackpole. **Lackey would wake** and daily life: *Slashdot*; Trickey. **weight bench:** WTS. **"tech journalism":** Grimmelmann, "Death of a Data Haven." **"press inquiry":** Lackey; Trickey. **wind generator:** Sellars. **172. official statements:** *Wired*, "A Data Sanctuary is Born." **tech problems:** Lackey; Grimmelmann articles; HF, p. 276-81; Account of Hastings leaving from Trickey. **"resumes":** Gilmour. **"I have the internet":** Freedman and Lackey. **173. "People that were":** Hastings 2009 talk. **outage and shower:** Lackey; *Slashdot*. **worked out well:** WTS; HF, p. 258; MB.

"reasonably successful": Lackey. vitriolic: Freeborn John. 174. ten-year legal battle: Cornwell, "Roughs Justice." outlining twelve: Ibid.; list of offenses available at Freeborn John. "court ruled": Ibid. newspaper account: Cornwell, "Now it's Sealand of hopes and glories." 175. court threw: Cornwell, "Roughs Justice." Lackey became: Lackey. "It came to": HF, p. 259. In fall 2001: HF; Lackey; Grimmelmann's accounts of HavenCo. 176. streaming video: SHRL; Olsen; McCullagh. "might have been legal": Lackey. "You think": Bohrer, et all. Both the UK: *Regulation of Investigatory Powers Act 2000 (c.23)*, passed by Royal Assent on July 28, 2000; *Copyright Directive*, enacted by the European Union in June 2001 and updated March 2019; Conroy. "They were very good": Lackey. 177. journalists who and following: Ibid. 178. "The venture": Ito. HavenCo briefly: JB, LB; Grimmelmann's articles. Lackey was set: Evans. "After enough": Schafer. 179. "millions of dollars": HF, p. 303.

Chapter 14
182. 11:30 a.m.: EA, "Blaze rages on sea platform"; IS, "Family vows to rebuild Sealand"; IS, "Massive repair bill for Sealand owners"; "Sealand Fort Offshore." Sealand was burning: EA, "Sealand in ruins after blaze." came apart: Ibid.; HF, p. 296. helicopter carrying: Ibid. tarmac: HF, p. 302. 183. rushed off: *Gazette News*; EA, "Sealand blaze causes £500k damage." The firefighters: Ibid. manageable level: Ibid. Michael was: HF, p. 296; MB, JB, LB. "awful lot": EA, "Sealand blaze causes £500k damage." Michael estimated: Ibid.; IS, "Massive repair bill for Sealand owners"; IS, "Vows to repair Sealand." 184. "After the fire" and quote: JB. "It was summer": MBR. fundraiser: IS, "Sealand souvenirs help pay for repairs." exclusion zone: IS, "Sealand will take three months to repair"; IS, "Sealand owners won't foot rescue bill." In November: Ibid. "general practice": Ibid. "entente cordiale": Ibid. 185. informally chatting and following: HF, p. 303-4. "eighty-five": *ABC*. head honcho and quote: Camacho. "Technically": Gómez. 186. potential buyers and quote: Stroumboulopoulos. "Most places": Ibid. Numerous branches and McKinnon: Lindberg; Leyden. 187. "antigravity": Nigel Watson. McKinnon was arrested: Lindberg. potassium chloride: McKinnon. Earlier in 2007 and Pirate Bay: Fernández; SHRL. InmoNaranja was listing: "Sealand Fort Offshore." crowdfunding: Nate Anderson. "not clear": Fernández. 188. campaign only: Nate Anderson. "proprietary": Stroumboulopoulos. sarcastic internet: Van Der Sar. edited and unedited: Nigel Watson; Purba. to distance themselves and quote: IS, "Sealand says no to asylum." Fortunately for McKinnon: Lee. 189. All was quiet: Winter and Kaplan. "There has been": IS, "Could Sealand be a safe haven for Assange's WikiLeaks?" much of a market: *20 Minutos*. until 2003: Dunkley. 190. met Sorensen: MB. most interesting: Lucas. "I first heard": Dunkley. film rights: MB; specific celebrities in Warren; SN, "Sealand: The Movie." Though not a movie: JB, LB, MB. 191. None of the Bates : Ibid. print editions: NYT, "Manga Books Best Sellers." "unbelievable": Reddit. an overview: Hetalia Archives. 192. Sealand Award: SN, "Sealand Awards." "This spells": SN, "The Dalai Lama is now a Baron of the Principality of Sealand." Fall Out Boy: Montgomery. English pop: *BBC*, "Ed Sheeran becomes a 'baron of Sealand'"; Fogle.

Sheeran shares the award: Ibid. "It's not every day": Fogle, "Sealand on the One Show 2011." 193. contacted to participate: MB. approached by: Author correspondence with Michael Bates. reportedly deemed: Attributed to Michael Bates, Simonenko. music producer: Ibid.; *BBC*, "Bus stop tramp song goes online"; *Craven Herald*; *Yorkshire Times*. enduring myths: JB. 194. Forty-six: *The X Factor*, Season 8. "already experiencing": Tate. 195. The Principality of Seborga: *The Economist*, "Castles in the Air"; Ryan, Dunford, and Sellars. 196. "I want global domination": *The X-Factor*, Season 8.

## Chapter 15

197. On May 22: Bates, "Kenton reaches the peak of Everest in record time!" "I'm sure when": Ibid. That man was Slader Oviatt: Author interview with Slader Oviatt, December 5, 2018. 199. Hastings said: Hastings chapters. 200. Like Slader: Author correspondence with Michael Martelle. SN, "Redbull skaters ride Sealand"; "Skateboarding the world's smallest country"; "Red Bull Access All Areas meets Sealand." "I didn't really understand": "Red Bull Access All Areas meets Sealand" video. cancelled three times: EA, "Skaters take it to max on Sealand; SN, "Redbull skaters ride Sealand." 201. at the World Egg: SN, "Sealand wins sporting accolade." In May 2012: Taylor. 202. team boasted: Ibid.; *BBC*, "Ralf Little gets international cap." "always threatened": *Herald*. The Chagos Islands and quote: *Sabotage Times*. match tipped: EA, "Sealand: Ralf Little travels to independent nation for first football match." Sealand FA wasn't and Sealand's games: *World Cups and Beyond*. 203. N-F Board ceased and quote: Engel. "Football is": Chaudhuri. "push-bike": McClure. an adviser: Messenger G articles and "Sealand Half Marathon—The Full Story." 204. "thought about organizing": McClure. "caught on camera" and following, quotes: Messenger, "Sealand Half Marathon—The Full Story." 205. "best time" and quote: McClure. 206. As he writes: Messenger, "Sealand Half Marathon—The Full Story." Monday, August: Kennedy; Moffitt, "Swimmer to attempt 12km Sealand to Felixstowe crossing." "a really challenging swim": Moffitt, "From Sealand to Felixstowe" Royal and his crew: Ibid. Caretaker Joe: JH. 207. newspaperman: Moffitt, "From Sealand to Felixstowe." "psychological as": Barker. Royal decided: Moffitt, "From Sealand to Felixstowe"; Kennedy. 12-kilometer (7.2-mile): Barker. Hamill was working: JH. Glendinning maintained and quotes: Moffitt, "Man finishes record-breaking bid for Sealand glory – but another swimmer beats him to it." 208. "I admire anyone": MB. As a show of: IS, "Arise Sir Richard: Sealand swimmer knighted." "I'm absolutely delighted": Ibid. James Bates noted: JB.

## Chapter 16

209. "quixotic financial sinkhole": Hemphill. "ramshackle": Sellars. "wind-battered concrete slab": Rachel Murphy. "Stonehenge": WTS. "grotesque": Irujo, "Interpol sigue por todo el mundo el rastro del falso principado de Sealand." "charmless": Carol Wallace. "rustiest": Scott, "The Pirate Prince of Sealand, Remembered." early 2000s: HF; WTS; MB; PH. 210. Roy I: See obituaries; HF, p. 307. "absolute" and quote by Zieler: The Pirate Radio Hall of Fame. 211.

"damn bureaucracy": Bates, "Sealand over the years." "When I made": RBTH. "bit of adventure.": Woodard. "die young": Amos; AP, "Self-declared prince of sovereign principality of Sealand dies aged 91"; TG; Yardley; Woo. 212. Following the death: PH. "summer of 2000": Scott, "The Pirate Prince of Sealand, Remembered." March 10: Milmo, "Joan Bates dead: Founder and 'princess' of Sealand dies aged 86"; *Basildon Echo*; Childs; Fitzsimmons; TL, "Joan Bates"; Alexander. "stunning woman": *Basildon Echo*. "Grandma": Ibid. "When my husband": WO. 213. "underrated woman": PH and David Hawker. "I don't have a crown": Carol Wallace. "Viking King" and tribute: Hirschfield and Mauriat. Everyone in: PH. "Since we've been in existence": Milmo, "Sealand's Prince Michael on the future of an off-shore 'outpost of liberty.'" 216. "most stunning": *Miss Southend on Sea*. part of the competition: Ibid. Charlotte bested: MacKenzie. young couple: Courtship, marriage details from JB; correspondence with Charley Rae Bates. "second time" and quote: *Essex County Standard*. "bit surreal" and quote, honeymoon details: Ibid. 217. But like Michael: JB. "Whenever you're": LB. autobiography and Michael writing his memoir: MB.

Chapter 17
219. late 1998 and digging permit, quotes, plus death threat: Bahn; for exile government details see articles such as "Amber Room, Reichspostschatz (Treasure of the Reichspost), and other missing goods." 220. putative governing bodies and "Reich's Citizens Movement": Frigelj; Biermann and Geisler; Hery-Moßmann. Sealandic diggers: Bahn. 221. government-in-exile: For Johannes Seiger's life and businesses, see Reuter; von Flocken; Litz; Reuß; Langhans. even issued: See the exile government's website; *Currency Wiki*. Based on the prestige: For why and how the exile government was chosen for these tasks, see publications on the exile government's website; history and duties further discussed in JS. 222. In 1991, Seiger and business on the property: Litz. For why the exile government is at odds with the local government, see articles such as "The 'Stasi' (State Security of the GDR) a Crime Syndicate!" and letters between the two entities on the exile government's website. Seiger turned and his debts: Reuter. able to avoid: Litz. 223. "not crazy": Ibid. "immediately contacted": JS. October 9 and arrest: Warrant to search Seiger's property, issued by the District Court of Potsdam, September 30, 1998 (on file with author). He challenged: See exile government's website. "chemical warfare": JS. 224. To Seiger and bilateral agreement: The exile government's website, including "Freundschafts- und Konsularvertrag zwischen dem Staat Deutsches Reich und dem Staat Fürstentum Seeland [*sic*] (Friendship and Consular Contract between the State of the German Reich and the Principality of Seeland)." German gentry: von Flocken. time of the lease: Ibid. Seiger delivered: Ibid. tens of thousands: See citations on the KRR government. also purportedly: E.g., "SHAEF Legislator USA in connection with the Commissary Government German Reich" from the exile government's website. 225. Seiger's disdain: See exile government's website. "Franklin's Prophecy": Afsai. 226. he and Sealand: See exile government website; quote from JS. Vril first appeared: See Bulwer-Lytton; concept of Vril and Nazis

coopting these concepts: e.g., Berzin; Goodrick-Clarke. **227. The generators**: See exile government website, documents such as "The Sealand Generator—Vril Technology"; Reuß. **228. "the credit"**: JB. **"I want one!"**: MB. "fortresses": Bohrer, et all. **a documentarian**: MB. **229. "not answered"**: JS. **"depths of the sea"**: Exile government website.

## Chapter 18
Account of crew change, fort visit, life on Sealand, and journey from author's March 27, 2019 visit to the Principality. Details and quotes from author interviews with Mike Barrington, Joe Hamill, Dan Griffin, and Pecker, conducted the evening before and the day of the visit. **237. "You underestimate"**: JB.

## Chapter 19
**243. According to research**: Blanchard. The article references Aldairi, Ogundipe, and Pye. **244. Cockles are abundant**: For more on the estuary cockle industry, see Lichtenstein; Hirst. **"Polysaccharides (sugars)"**: Blanchard. **Bates family harvests**: JB, LB, MB. **245. "Cockle Row"**: Williams; Yeardsley; visit to the Leigh Heritage Center and Museum in Old Leigh. **246. *Charlotte Joan***: Account from JB, LB, MB. **cockles by hand**: Edge. **Interestingly, Sealand**: MB. **247. brought ashore** and cockle factory: JB, LB, MB. **According to Andrew**: AL, March 17, 2019. **There are restrictions**: Kent and Essex Sea Fisheries Committee (http://www.kentandessex-sfc.co.uk/id21.html). **248. Eight of the estuary**: Author interview with Sir David Amess, MP for Southend West, March 15, 2019. **Back when Michael**: MB. **This is a legacy**: Leigh Heritage Center and Museum in Old Leigh. **249. Cockler Andrew**: AL. **The entire area**: Author interviews with the Bates family, AL, and Paul Gilson. **thirty million**: *Land, Sea & Air Magazine*; Crane. **like everyone else**: MB. **250. sixth-generation**: Author interviews with Paul Gilson, March 18 and 23, 2019. **happiest place**: Cornish, quoting a survey by UK real estate agency Right Move. **"sensible background"**: MB.

## Chapter 20
All information about MicroCon 2019 based on the author's firsthand experience; all quotes from interviews conducted by the author at the event, unless otherwise noted. **257. "I'm not knocking"**: MB. **258. In January 2017** and Tahiti seasteading project: Wong; Harten; Gabbatiss. **259. hoping to "break sea"**: Harten. **"I'm confident"**: *BBC*, "French Polynesia signs first 'floating city' deal." **"People would exit"**: Craib. **260. "engineering challenge"**: Abrahamian, "Seasteading." **260. Seasteaders tout**: Harvesting algae and seasteading's other renewable aspects from Friedman and Taylor; Hickman; Mongole. **"I didn't go"**: Denuccio. **Tahitian TV** and quote: Wong; *Radio NZ*; Chapman. **261. querulous**: *BBC*, "US man could face death penalty over Thailand 'sea home'"; Martin; D'Anna. **"an unprecedented level"**: Friedman and Taylor, "Seasteading: Institutional Innovation on the Open Ocean." **"The more people"**: Gelles. **Another unorthodox**: Najaro; Abrahamian, "Princesses Without Borders"; Shenker. **263.**

As Vincent: Cogliati-Bantz. **264. "I'll tell you"**: Simon, "Another Country." **"draconian"**: Statement posted on Sealand's social medias following the Thailand seasteading caper.

## Epilogue
Information about Sealand's current operations, its successes and difficulties, and Michael's wedding and bachelor party from author interview with JB, LB, and MB. **267. Sealand has also:** E.g., see Bates, "Sealand Geopoetics Discussion Part 1." **268. For sale through the Sealand website:** For available titles and merchandise, visit SG. **271. "We've had a privileged life"**: IS, "Flying the flag at Sealand."

## Appendix
**273. people declare war:** Reddit. **jilted lover:** Chaudhuri. **condom-less:** JB, LB, MB. **"After the vote for Brexit"**: Tingle. **Michael didn't think Brexit:** Ibid. **In 2015, Liam:** Ross. **Sealand's exit:** Principality of Sealand [@sealandgov]. **274. As Foreign Commonwealth Office:** Hibberd. **a country could lay claim:** Dennis. **275. Atlantic Charter:** See *United Nations*. **The Montevideo Convention:** Further details about the Convention's content and wording as it applies to Sealand exist in almost every legal discussion of the Principality. E.g., Conroy; SHRL; Cogliati-Bantz. **276. On top of this:** MB; WTS;" HF. **Simpson was:** Addicott. **Viewers met Simpson again:** "Sealand on the UK Evening News Sept 2002." **277. "By the third"**: Blizzard, "High Tide and Green Grass." **999 square miles:** *Grand Duchy of Luxembourg*. **.004 km2:** "Sealand government fact sheet," issued by the Principality of Sealand, 2006. **Maunsell estimated:** BLR. **"Life is much like"**: Chaudhuri. **"strange, self-constructed"**: DP, p. 251. **"Surely man"**: Narrator, "Sealand on Bravo Channel 2001." **278. Central Tibetan** and quote about mimicry: McConnell, Moreau, and Dittmer. **a fact of life:** Arenas. **279. twenty-five microstates:** Conroy. *Ius gentium* **is not:** Almost all legal analyses of Sealand discuss the concept of *ius gentium*. For an overview and context with regard to Sealand, see SHRL and Grimmelmann, "Sealand and HavenCo, Parts I–IV." Sealand's websites tout this concept, as does Michael in HF. **280. In 1956:** Information about UNCLOS was taken from a number of sources. See also "Law of the Sea: A Policy Primer"; Hibberd. **281. As Johan Fritz:** Fritz. **states violate** and quote: "Law of the Sea: A Policy Primer." **282. "unique case"**: GTV. **"an exercise of its own"**: Cogliati-Bantz. **It could be argued:** Hibberd sources; SHRL. **Britain continually:** Report "Continental Shelf Roughs Tower," written by the Treasurer's Department and distributed August 21, 1967 (LO 2/1088); Hibberd; "Law of the Sea: A Policy Primer." **the formation:** See Lyon; Dennis. **283. under English law:** Cogliati-Bantz. **284. According to FCO** and following: Hibberd. **large color portrait:** Alverson. **Roy often noted:** Amos. **285. "I'm English, and therefore"**: Addicott.

# BIBLIOGRAPHY & SOURCES

## Books, Articles, and Websites

*20 Minutos*. "Una inmobiliaria especializada en vender islas, cierra a causa de la crisis (A real estate agency specializing in selling islands closes due to the crisis)." Spain, August 30, 2008.

*ABC*. "Tiny North Sea tax haven for sale." Australia, January 8, 2007.

Abrahamian, Atossa. "Seasteading." *n+1* (June 5, 2013). https://nplusonemag.com/online-only/online-only/seasteading.

———. "Princesses Without Borders." *Foreign Policy*. August 29, 2014.

Afsai, Shai. "Benjamin Franklin and Judaism." *Journal of the American Revolution* (November 2016).

*Akron Beacon Journal*. "Bizarre details emerging in aftermath of Cunanan suspect." July 26, 1997.

Aldairi, Abdullah Faisal, Olanrewaju Dorcas Ogundipe, and David Alexander Pye. "Antiproliferative Activity of Glycosaminoglycan-Like Polysaccharides Derived from Marine Molluscs." *Marine Drugs* 16, no. 2 (February 2018).

Alexander, Michael. "Remembering Sealand's First Sovereign Princess Joan, 1929-2016." *Coin Update*. March 22, 2016.

Alverson, Charles. "A Law Unto its Tiny Self." *The Telegraph Sunday Magazine*. October 1980.

Amos, Thomas. "Prince Roy of Sealand (Passed 9th October 2012): Sealand." Principality of Sealand, Principality of Sealand, Aug 13, 2019, www.sealandgov.org/prince-roy-of-sealand-aka-roy-bates-passed-away-9th-october-2012-obituary/.

Anderson, Nate. "The Pirate Bay hopes to buy its own country: Sealand." *Ars Technica*. January 15, 2007.

Anderson, Ros. "The country we established at sea." *The Guardian*. February 3, 2007.

Arenas, Frank B. "Cyberspace Jurisdiction and the Implications of Sealand." *Iowa Law Review* 88 (2003).

Associated Press. "Falkland Islands lie in Argentinian waters, UN commission rules." *The Guardian*. March 29, 2016.

Associated Press. "Self-declared prince of sovereign principality of Sealand dies aged 91." October 10, 2012.

Atmani, Mehdi. "The Curious Case of Sealand, the Hacker-Friendly Offshore Micronation." *WORLDCRUNCH*. April 27, 2015. https://www.worldcrunch.com/culture-society/the-curious-case-of-sealandthe-hacker-friendly-offshore-micronation.

Bahn, Wolfram. "Suche nach Bernsteinzimmer sorgt bei Wiederstedt für Unruhe (Search for Amber room at Wiederstedt causes unrest)." *Mitteldeutsche Zeitung*. August 21, 2016.

Baker, Sue. "Seized gun platform puzzles Britain." *Newswire*. December 25, 1982.

*Basildon Echo*. "Princess of Sealand, Joan Bates dies." March 15, 2016.

Bates, Michael. *Holding the Fort*. Principality of Sealand, 2015.

———. "Ask Me Anything." *Reddit*. April 16, 2013. https://www.reddit. com/r/IAmA/comments/1cgo6n/iama_im_prince_michael_of_the_ principality_of/.

———. "Kenton reaches the peak of Everest in record time!" January 30, 2015. www.sealandgov.org.

*The Battles for Monte Cassino*. Published by the UK Ministry of Defence and Commonwealth Graves Commission, 2004.

*BBC*. "French Polynesia signs first 'floating city' deal." January 17, 2017. https://www.bbc.com/news/world-asia-38647174.

———. "US man could face death penalty over Thailand 'sea home.'" April 18, 2019. https://www.bbc.com/news/world-asia-47974234?ST hisFB&fbclid=IwAR2LJNb-j7tIpkTj854s9U3SytN9z5msAo_ YEFlwxL9KWdEpzzk2XT3NezA.

———. "Bus stop tramp song goes online." October 29, 2007.

———. "Ralf Little gets international cap." May 7, 2012.

———. "'Smallest state' seeks new owners." January 8, 2007.

———. "Ed Sheeran becomes a 'baron of Sealand.'" December 23, 2012.

Berzin, Alexander. "The Nazi Connection with Shambhala and Tibet." *Study Buddhism*. Berzin Archives. studybuddhism.com/en/advanced-studies/ history-culture/shambhala/the-nazi-connection-with-shambhala-and-tibet.

Biermann, Kai, and Astrid Geisler. "Ein Volk, viele Reiche, noch mehr Führer (One people, many empires, even more leaders)." *Die Zeit*. April 20, 2016.

Binder, Megan. "Taking to the Sea: The Modern Seasteading Movement in the Context of Other Historical Intentional Communities." *Indiana Journal of Global Legal Studies* 23, no. 2 (Summer 2016).

Blanchard, Sam. "Could cancer be fought with 'cockle-chemo'? Sugars from the molluscs are as effective as some chemotherapy drugs, study reveals." *Daily Mail*. September 17, 2018.

Blass, Tom. *The Naked Shore: Of the North Sea*. London: Bloomsbury, 2016.

Blizzard, David. "A Typical Crew Changeover." February 1, 2013. www. sealandgov.org.

———. "High Tide and Green Grass: Parts 1 and 2." January 18, 2013. www.sealandgov.org.

Bob Le-Roi. http://www.bobleroi.co.uk/Home/Home.html.

Boggan, Steve. "Americans turn a tin-pot state off the Essex coast into world capital of computer anarchy." *The Independent*. June 5, 2000.

_____. "Money Laundering: Global fraudsters use sea fortress as passport to riches." *The Independent*. September 23, 1997.

Bonnett, Alastair. *Unruly Places: Lost Spaces, Secret Cities and Other Inscrutable Geographies*. Houghton Mifflin Harcourt, 2014.

Boudreaux, Richard, and Marjorie Miller. "A Nation for Friend and Faux." *Los Angeles Times*. June 7, 2000.

Bowcott, Owen. "Who owns Rockall? A history of legal and diplomatic wrangles." *The Guardian*. May 30, 2013.

Bramwell, Christopher. "German 'held prisoner' on Sealand fort." *Daily Telegraph*. September 5, 1978.

Braun, Adee. "From the Sea, Freedom." *Lapham's Quarterly*. August 30, 2013.

Brown, Louise. "Klar zum Entern! Der Piratenprinz von Sealand (Sure to board! The pirate prince of Sealand)." *Berliner Morgenpost*. September 9, 2007.

Brunton, Finn. *Digital Cash: The Unknown History of the Anarchists, Utopians, and Technologists Who Created Cryptocurrency*. Princeton University Press, 2019.

Bulwer-Lytton, Edward. *The Coming Race*. Blackwood and Sons, 1871; (Project Gutenberg, 2016). https://www.gutenberg.org/files/1951/1951-h/1951-h.htm.

Burgess, Malcolm, and Heather Reyes. *Essex Belongs to Us—Writing About the Real Essex*. The Arts Council (England), 2017.

Camacho, Julia. "Se traspasa microrreino (Transferring the microkingdom)." *El Periodico*. January 4, 2007.

Carpenter, John, and Chuck Neubauer. "Boat owner caught in unwelcome glare." *Sunday News*. July 27, 1997.

Casley, Leonard. "The Formation of the Principality of Hutt River." The Principality of Hutt River (official website). http://www.principality-hutt-river.com/PHR_The_Formation_of_the%20Principality_of_Hutt_River.htm.

Cassell, Raymond. "Investigation into Illicit Radio Transmitters Using Marine Frequencies, and Located in the Borough of Southend." October 3, 1978.

Chapman, Lizette. "A Plan to Build Islands Off the Coast of Tahiti Is on Hold." *Bloomberg*. October 25, 2018. https://www.bloomberg.com/news/articles/2018-10-25/a-plan-to-build-islands-off-the-coast-oftahiti-is-on-hold.

Chaudhuri, Raj Aditya. "Fed up of the UK, one man formed his own country." *Condé Nast Traveler India*. October 25, 2016. https://www.cntraveller.in/story/fed-uk-one-man-formed-country/#s-custtheres-always-timefor-cuddles-on-holiday.

Childs, Martin. "'Princess Joan of Sealand': Former carnival queen who became Princess of Sealand after she and her husband Roy set up the 'micro-nation.'" *The Independent*. March 15, 2016.

*Clacton Gazette*. "Laser quits the airwaves." May 29, 1987.

Clark, Ray. *Radio Caroline: The True Story of the Boat that Rocked.* The History Press, 2014.

Claro, F.Z. "Defense of Thames goes back hundreds of years." Southend Standard. January 10, 1963.

Cogliati-Bantz, Vincent P. "My Platform, My State: The Principality of Sealand in International Law." *The Journal of International Maritime Law* 18, no. 3 (2012).

*Colchester Evening Gazette.* "Dutch police called into Sealand Probe." January 30, 1979.

_____. "Sealand 'Prince' admits illegal broadcasting." June 12, 1979.

_____. "Pop and video rival for BBC and ITV." June 8, 1987.

_____. "Sealand TV 'live in 12 weeks time.'" June 10, 1987.

_____. "Fortress Sealand TV." June 15, 1987.

Connelly, Charlie. *Attention All Shipping: A Journey Round the Shipping Forecast.* Abacus, 2005.

Connor, Steve. "Britain seeks to expand its empire with 77,000 square miles of Atlantic seabed." *The Independent.* August 28, 2008.

Conroy, Matthew. "Sealand—The Next New Haven?" *Suffolk Transnational Law Review* 27, no. 1 (Winter 2003).

Coombe, Derek. *Spiritsail Bargemen.* Bosham: Pennant Books, 2003.

Cornish, Natalie. "Leigh-on-Sea in Essex has been crowned the happiest place to live in the UK for 2018." *Country Living.* November 29, 2018.

Cornwell, Richard. "Now it's Sealand of hopes and glories." *Ipswich Evening Star.* November 27, 2001.

_____. "Roughs Justice." *Ipswich Evening Star.* November 25, 2001.

Cornwell, Richard and Hollie-Rae Merrick. "Could Sealand be a safe haven for Assange's WikiLeaks?" *Ipswich Star.* October 4, 2012.

Cox, Noel. "Tax and Regulatory Avoidance Through Non-Traditional Alternatives to Tax Havens." *New Zealand Business Law Quarterly* 9 (February 2013).

Craib, Raymond B. "Egotopia." *Counter Punch.* August 24, 2018. https://www.counterpunch.org/2018/08/24/egotopia/

Crancher, Steve. *Essex: Sumfing Else! A Cornucopia of Estuary English.* Newbury: Countryside Books, 2005.

Crane, Nicholas. *Coast: Our Island Story: A Journey of Discovery Around Britain's Coastline.* Random House, 2010.

*Craven Herald.* "Sutton man Basil Simon appears on The Extra Factor." September 22, 2011.

Crowe, Ken. *Kursaal Memories: A History of Southend's Amusement Park.* Skelter Publishing, 2003.

*Currency Wiki.* "Sealand 100 dollar coin." https://currencies.fandom.com/wiki/Sealand_100_dollar_coin.

Cusick, James. "Shots fired in Sealand's defence of a small freedom." *The Independent.* February 24, 1990.

D'Anna, Joe. "U.S. bitcoin trader and girlfriend still on the run after Thai authorities dismantle ocean platform home." *Arizona Republic.* May 1, 2019. https://www.azcentral.com/story/news/local/phoenix/2019/05/01/bitcoin-trader-chad-elwartowski-nadiasummergirl-seastead-still-running-from-thai-authorities/3643212002/.

*Daily Express.* "Pop pirate summoned." September 29, 1966.

————. "The Prince even has a captive." September 7, 1978.

*Daily Mail.* "Pop for gets switched on to repel boarders." June 28, 1967.

*Daily Mirror.* "New pop pirate 'in two months.'" September 5, 1966.

————. "Pop for gets switched on to repel borders." Undated.

*Daily News.* "U.S. Indicts 7 In Scheme Promising Low-Interest Loans." Los Angeles (March 27, 1987).

*Daily Telegraph.* "Seas Delay Rescue of Radio Pirates." October 11, 1965.

————. "Radio pirates seek to bury the hatchet." October 12, 1965.

————. "Pirate radio to open off Margate." September 29, 1966.

————. "Radio Essex stays on air despite fine." December 1, 1966.

————. "'Radio Essex will defy court." December 1, 1966.

————. "Pirate radio owner is fined £100." December 1, 1966.

————. "Appeal by Radio Essex dismissed." January 18, 1967.

————. "Radio Caroline plans heliport for supplies." April 12, 1967.

————. "Ministry Planned to Seize Fort." May 30, 1968.

Davison, Phil. "Versace: After the murder, the mystery." *The Independent.* July 27, 1997.

Dawson, Adam. "2 plead guilty in Newport loan fraud - 1 expected to admit role in $2 million case today." *The Orange County Register.* April 5, 1988.

Deeley, Peter. "The Prince and his prisoner." *The Observer.* September 10, 1978.

Dennis, Trevor. "The Principality of Sealand: Nation Building by Individuals." *Tulsa Journal of Comparative and International Law* 10, no. 1 (September 2002).

Denuccio, Kyle. "Silicon Valley is letting go of its techie island fantasies." *Wired.* May 16, 2015. https://www.wired.com/2015/05/silicon-valleyletting-go-techie-island-fantasies.

*Der Spiegel.* "Raum für Roy (Room for Roy)." July 10, 1978.

*Der Spiegel Online.* "'Fort Madness': Britain's Bizarre Sea Defense Against the Germans." November 12, 2010. http://www.spiegel.de/international/zeitgeist/world-war-ii-fort-madness-britain-s-bizarre-sea-defenseagainst-the-germans-a-728754.html.

Drake, Kristina. "New Rochford cockle factory hopes to revolutionise industry." *Southend Echo.* February 16, 2016.

Dubocq, Tom. "Miami houseboat owner passport forgery subject." *Contra Costa Times.* July 28, 1997.

Duffy, Rónán. "Who owns Rockall? The history of the Atlantic dispute between Ireland and the UK." *The Journal* (Ireland). April 17, 2017.

Dunkley, Cathy. "'Sealand' in pic country as Warners catches pitch." *Daily Variety*. October 13, 2003.

*East Anglian Daily Times*. "Boatman takes fuel to Sealand." February 17, 1977.

_____. "Sealand expansion planned." February 28, 1981.

_____. "Fort may house radio stations." August 1, 1986.

_____. "Blaze rages on sea platform." June 23, 2006.

_____. "Sealand in ruins after blaze." June 24, 2006.

_____. "Sealand blaze causes £500k damage." June 26, 2006.

_____. "Skaters take it to max on Sealand." September 17, 2008.

_____. "Sealand: Ralf Little travels to independent nation for first football match." May 8, 2012.

_____. "Sealand, sovereign state off Suffolk coastline, to mark its 50th anniversary with Essex dinner." September 2, 2017.

*East Essex Gazette*. "My Island Kingdom." September 1, 1978.

*The Economist*. "Castles in the Air." Micronations: Special Report. December 20, 2005.

_____. "The King of con-men: the biggest fraud in history is a warning to professional and amateur investors alike." Christmas Specials: Financial Crime. December 22, 2012.

Edge, Simon. "The Deadly Cockle Hunt." *The Express*. October 28, 2011.

Edwards, A.C. *A History of Essex*. Chichester, West Sussex: Phillimore & Co., 1958.

*El Mercurio*. "Sealand y el Tráfico de Armas (Sealand and arms trafficking)." June 17, 2000.

*El Mundo*. "Se vende 'Sealand', el país virtual nacido en una Antigua plataforma sobre el mar (Sealand is for sale, the virtual country born on an old platform on the sea)." January 9, 2007.

Engel, Matthew. "World Football Cup an alternative to Fifa and a lesson in geopolitics." *The Guardian*. June 1, 2018.

England, John. "The Ill-Fated Story of WRLI and WWCR." *Soundscapes*. http://www.icce.rug.nl/~soundscapes/VOLUME05/Ill-fated_WRLI. shtml.

Erlandson, Robert. "In this corner, creating a kingdom." *Baltimore Sun*. March 22, 1983.

*Essex County Standard*. "Today, I become a real-life princess." September 6, 2013.

*Essex Leader*. "Sealand prepares to repel boarders." September 7, 1978.

*European Commission*. ""Information Concerning the Non-Exhaustive List of Known Fantasy and Camouflage Passports, as Stipulated by Article 6 of the Decision No. 1105/2011/EU." May 15, 2017. https://ec.europa.eu/home-affairs/sites/homeaffairs/files/what-we-do/policies/borders-and-visas/document-security/docs/list_of_known_fantasy_and_camouflage_passports_en.pdf.

Evans, Jon. "Wiring the War Zone." *Wired.* September 2005.

*Evening Gazette.* "Rees called on to probe 'piracy' off Essex coast." September 25, 1978.

_____. "Church agree to Sealand wedding." April 9, 1979.

*Evening News.* "Pop pirates in petrol bomb battle." June 28, 1967.

_____. "'They're going to invade my fort.'" May 29, 1968.

*Evening Standard.* "Element of Farce." October 16, 1965.

_____. "Children on fort 'doing fine.'" March 3, 1968.

Ezard, John. "Police raid 'King' of Sealand's home." *The Guardian.* October 4, 1978.

Fautley, M.P.B., and J.H. Garon. *Essex Coastline: Then and Now.* Matthew Fautley, 2004.

Felc, Mitja. "Podjetnik iz virtualne drave toi Slovenijo (An entrepreneur from a virtual country sues Slovenia)." *Delo.* October 16, 2011.

*Felixstowe Times.* "'Pop' Station Planned on Disused Fort?" August 14, 1965.

Ferguson, Bennie Lee. *What is a Nation: the Micronationalist Challenge to Traditional Concepts of the Nation-State.* Graduate thesis, Department of History of the Graduate School of Wichita State University, 2009.

Fernández, Pablo. "Los piratas quieren reino propio (Pirates want their own kingdom)." *El País.* January 17, 2007.

*Financial Times.* "Another Radio 'Pirate' Fined on PO Charge." December 1, 1966.

Fitzsimmons, Sean. "Princess Joan of Sealand." *The Telegraph.* March 28, 2016.

Fogle, Ben. "All hail Baron Ed Sheeran." *The Telegraph.* June 18, 2013.

Fowler, Michael Ross, and Julie Marie Bunck. *Law, Power, and the Sovereign State.* University of Pennsylvania Press, 1995.

Freeborn John. *Rough Sands Gazette.* http://freebornjohn.com/.

Friedman, Patri and Brad Taylor. "Seasteading: Competitive Governments on the Ocean." *Kyklos* 65, no. 2 (2012).

_____. "Seasteading: Institutional Innovation on the Open Ocean." Paper presented at the Australasian Public Choice Society Conference at the University of Canterbury, Christchurch, New Zealand, December 9–10, 2010. seasteading.org.

Frigelj, Kristian. "Was die Reichsbürger wirklich glauben (What the imperial citizens really believe)." *Welt.* May 16, 2015.

Fritz, Johan. "The Creation and Legal Status of States." Master's Thesis, University of Lund Faculty of Law, June 2003.

Gabbatiss, Josh. "World's first floating city to be built off the coast of French Polynesia by 2020." *The Independent.* November 14, 2017.

Gardner, Barry. "Lonely life of the prisoner of Sealand." *Evening News.* September 7, 1978.

_____. "My four days in captivity at the hands of foreign invaders." *Colchester Evening Gazette.* August 30, 1978.

Garfinkel, Simson. "Welcome to Sealand, Now Bugger Off." *Wired.* July 2000.

_____. "Covert Catalog." *Wired*. August 1997.

*Gazette News*. "Harwich: Blaze drama on Sealand." June 26, 2006.

Gelles, David. "Floating Cities, No Longer Science Fiction, Begin to Take Shape." *New York Times*. November 13, 2017.

Geltzer, Jeremy. "The New Pirates of the Caribbean: How data havens can provide safe harbors on the internet beyond governmental reach." *Southwestern Journal of Law & Trade in the Americas* 10 (2004).

Gewertz, Catherine. "Seven Indicted in Fraud Scheme." *UPI Wire*. March 26, 1987.

Gilder, Eric, and Mervyn Haggard. "Of Drugs, Documents, and Pseudo States: the Odd Story of the Missing Broadcasting Ship." *East West Cultural Passage* 9 (2010).

Gilmour, Kim. "Wish You Were Here?" *Internet Magazine*. December 2002.

Goldsmith, Jack, and Lawrence Lessig. "Grounding the Virtual Magistrate." Wayback Machine. http://mantle.sbs.umass.edu/vmag/groundvm.htm.

Gómez, Lourdes. "750 millones por un mini-Estado (750 million for a ministate)." *El País*. January 9, 2007.

Gooch, Adela. "Police Swoop on Sealand Crime Ring." *The Guardian*. April 11, 2000.

Goodrick-Clarke, Nicholas. *Black Sun: Aryan Cults, Esoteric Nazism and the Politics of Identity*. NYU Press, 2002.

*Grand Duchy of Luxembourg*. https://luxembourg.public.lu/en.html.

Gregg, Samuel. "Natural Law and the Law of Nations." *Natural Law, Natural Rights, and American Constitutionalism*, the Witherspoon Institute (2011). http://www.nlnrac.org/earlymodern/law-of-nations.

*Grenz Echo*. "Wird der 'Außenminister' aus Henri-Chapelle das 'Fürstentum Sealand' jetzt zurückerobern (Will the "exterior minister" of Henri-Chapelle reclaim the 'Principality of Sealand' now)?" Belgium, August 19, 1978.

_____. "Jetzt hat das 'Fürstentum Sealand' einen Gefangenen (Now the 'Principality of Sealand' has a prisoner)." September 7, 1978.

Griffin, Charles. "Royal Fusiliers: City of London Regiment." *British Empire*. https://www.britishempire.co.uk/forces/armyunits/britishinfantry/fusiliers.htm.

Grimmelmann, James. "Sealand, HavenCo, and the Rule of Law." *University of Illinois Law Review* 2012, no. 2 (2012).

_____. "Death of a Data Haven: cypherpunks, Wikileaks, and the world's smallest nation." *Ars Technica*. March 27, 2012. http://arstechnica.com/tech-policy/2012/03/sealand-and-havenco/1/.

_____. "Sealand and HavenCo, Parts I–IV." Guest posts on Volokh blog. February 14, 2011. http://volokh.com/2011/02/14/sealand-andhavenco-part-i-the-history-of-sealand/.

*Guardian*. "Fined radio 'pirate' says he will go on transmitting." December 1, 1966.

_____. "Sealand keeps its prisoner." September 6, 1978.

_____. "Lawyer freed from sea fort." September 29, 1978.

*Hamburger Abendblatt.* "Staatsanwalt: Die Sekte war nur auf Betrügereien aus (Prosecutor – the sect was only for scams)." March 12, 1975.

_____. "Nur zwei gaben die falschen Titel zurück (Only two returned the false titles)." March 22, 1975.

_____. "Titelhandel blühte unter dem Zeichen des Kreuzes (Title trade flourished under the sign of the cross)." July 12, 1976.

_____. "'Doktorvater' feilschte mit der Eitelkeit ('Doctoral father' haggled with vanity)." August 21, 1976.

_____. "Ein 'Prof.' kostete bis zu 40000 Mark (A 'professor' cost up to 40,000 marks)." August 24, 1976.

_____. "Ein schmucker Titel ebnete den Weg zum 'großen Geld' (A neat title paved the way to 'big money')." September 9, 1976.

_____. "Wo sind sie geblieben, die vielen Zeugen...? (Where have they stayed, the many witnesses...?)." September 14, 1976.

_____. "Doktor-Titel für 10 000 Mark (Doctor title for 10 000 marks)." November 5, 1976.

_____. "Ankläger: Freiheitsstrafen im Titelhändler-Prozeß (Prosecutor: imprisonment in the Title Trader Trial)." November 21, 1976.

Hammerton, Fred, and Charles Sawyer. "Police Raid on the Prince of Sealand." *Southend Echo.* October 3, 1978.

*Hanauer Anzeiger.* "Ex-Agent wurde der Generalkonsul von Sealand." February 4, 1978.

Harris, Paul. *Broadcasting from the High Seas: The History of Offshore Radio in Europe, 1958-1976.* Edinburgh: Paul Harris Publishing.

Harten, Duke. "Why People Are Building Entire Cities On The Ocean." *Medium.* May 30, 2017. https://medium.com/dose/why-people-arebuilding-entire-cities-on-the-ocean-e8c9376e20be.

*Harwich and Manningtree Standard.* "Happy 50th Birthday Sealand." October 1, 2017.

Haugh, Richard. "Life on Sealand: Firearms, fishing and the Cosmic Sea Cat." *BBC News.* October 17, 2012.

Haveman, Ben. "Sealand: a shadowy little state on stilts." *De Volkskrant.* February 4, 1978.

Hawkins, Michael. "Suspected Illicit Radio Transmitters at 33A Avenue Road, Southend-on-Sea and 14 Wickford Road, Southend-on-Sea." October 3, 1978.

Hawtin, Guy. "'Prince' plans to float a new business empire." *Financial Times.* August 17, 1976.

Hemphill, Paul. "Roy Bates: The Monarch of the Sea." *In That Howling Infinite,* January 28, 2018. https://howlinginfinite.com/2018/01/28/the-monarch-of-the-sea/.

Henry, Stuart, and Mike von Joel. *Pirate Radio: Then and Now.* Blanford Paperbacks, 1984.

*Herald.* "Signed, Sealand, delivered." Glasgow, June 3, 2013.

Hery-Moßmann, Nicole. "Reichsbürger werden – was bedeutet das? (Become Reich citizens – what does that mean?)." *Focus Magazine*. October 23, 2016.

*Hetalia Archives*. "Sealand." *Fandom*. https://hetalia.fandom.com/wiki/Sealand.

Hibberd, Grant. "The Last Great Adventure of the Twentieth Century: The Sealand Affair in British Diplomacy." *Britain and the World*. 2011.

Hickman, Sean. "Flagging Options for Seasteading Projects." The Seasteading Institute. 2012. http://seasteadingorg.wpengine.com/wp-content/uploads/2015/12/Flagging-Options-for-Seastead-Projects-Sean-Hickman.pdf.

Hirschfield, Stu, comment "Princess Joan of Sealand (02 September 1929-10 March 2016)." https://www.facebook.com/PrincipalityOfSealand/photos/a.496490988122/10153530672558123/?type=3.

Hirst, Christopher. "Where are the new cockleshell heroes?" *The Independent*. September 5, 2003.

Hodgkinson, Thomas. "Notes from a small island: Is Sealand an independent 'micronation' or an illegal fortress?" *The Independent*. May 18, 2013.

Howes, John, ed. *My War: Major TC Howes MC, Late 2nd Battalion Royal Fusiliers (City of London Regiment) 1939–1946*. Swansea: Egel Publishing, 2012.

*Ipswich Evening Star*. "Words in white paint start new takeover rumors." May 19, 1967.

_____. "Fort's independence 'ludicrous idea.'" September 4, 1967.

_____. "'Ruler of Sealand' fined for radio offences." June 12, 1979.

_____. "Words in white paint start new takeover rumors." May 19, 1967.

*Ipswich Star*. "Sealand to be England – just for one day." June 20, 2002.

_____. "Family vows to rebuild Sealand." June 25, 2006.

_____. "Massive repair bill for Sealand owners." June 26, 2006.

_____. "Vows to repair Sealand." June 28, 2006.

_____. "Sealand owners won't foot rescue bill." November 9, 2006.

_____. "Sealand will take three months to repair." November 12, 2006.

_____. "Sealand souvenirs help pay for repairs." January 11, 2007.

_____. "There's a bid for Sealand, me hearties." January 16, 2007.

_____. "Sealand says no to asylum." May 21, 2007.

_____. "Sealand – a sovereign state?" June 2, 2011.

_____. "Flying the flag at Sealand." September 21, 2007.

_____. "Secret government Sealand revelations." December 31, 2008.

_____. "£65m price tag for Sealand tenancy." March 2, 2010.

_____. "Could Sealand be a safe haven for Assange's WikiLeaks?" October 4, 2012.

_____. "Arise Sir Richard: Sealand swimmer knighted." August 30, 2018.

Irujo, Jose Maria. "El caso del 'principado' de Sealand pasa a la Audiencia Nacional con 60 implicados (The case of the Principality of Sealand passes to the National Court with 60 implicated)." *El Pais*. April 12, 2000.

_____. "Interpol sigue por todo el mundo el rastro del falso principado de Sealand (Interpol follows the trail of the false principality of Sealand all over the world)." *El Pais*. April 9, 2000.

_____. "La Guardia Civil detiene en su 'embajada' al regente del falso Principado de Sealand (The Civil Guard stops in his 'embassy' the ruler of the false Principality of Sealand)." *El Pais*. April 5, 2000.

Ito, Joichi. "The Practice of Change." PhD. dissertation, Keio University Graduate School of Media and Governance, 2018.

Jacobs, Frank. "All Hail Sealand." *New York Times*. March 20, 2012.

Jakopec, Marko. "Drava povzro ila za 1,6 milijona evrov škode? (The country that caused 1.6 million euro in damages?)." *Delo*. January 23, 2012.

Johns, Adrian. *Death of a Pirate: British Radio and the Making of the Information Age*. New York: W. W. Norton and Company, 2011.

_____. "Piracy as a business force." *Culture Machine* 10 (2009).

Kennedy, Poppy. "Man could be first to swim from 'smallest country.'" *Bridlington Free Press*. August 15, 2018.

*Kent Messenger*. "Its war in the airwaves." October 15, 1965.

Kessler, Felix. "The Rusty Principality of Sealand Relishes Hard-Earned Freedom." *Wall Street Journal*. September 15, 1969.

Khosravi, Hamed. "The Nomos of the Sea: Pirates, DJs, Hackers, and the Architecture of Contingent Labor." *The Avery Review* 29 (2018).

Knot, Hans. *The Dream of Sealand*. Self-published (1987).

Knot, Hans. "De wonderlijke geruchten over Radio London van 1984: De wilde verhalen van John England ("The strange rumors about Radio London from 1984: The Wild Stories of John England")." *Soundscapes*. http://www.icce.rug.nl/~soundscapes/VOLUME05/Radio_Londen1984.shtml.

Kuipers, Dean. "A not so Jolly Roger: the silencing of 'Radio Sarah.'" *The Nation*. April 24, 1989.

Kwiatkowska, Barbara. "200-Mile Exclusive Economic/Fishery Zone and the Continental Shelf – An Inventory of Recent State Practice: Part 1." *The International Journal of Marine and Coastal Law* 2, no. 2 (1994).

Lambiet, Jose. "FBI: No Cunanan-Reineck Tie Yet." *Sun Sentinel*. July 26, 1997.

*Land, Sea & Air Magazine*. "Profiles – London Gateway." No. 4 (2011).

Langhans, Katrin. "Wie ein Ex-Diamantenhändler versuchte, eine Schein-Welt zu erobern (Like an ex-diamond trader trying to conquer a sham world)." *Süeddeutsche Zeitung*. April 25, 2016.

Latham, James. "Behind shortwave hate radio is a group of entrepreneurial station owners who claim they love free speech." *Intelligence Report*. Southern Poverty Law Center, June 18, 2002.

"Law of the Sea: A Policy Primer." Tufts University's Fletcher School of Law and Diplomacy. L.M. Program in International Law and Maritime Studies Program. 2017. https://sites.tufts.edu/lawofthesea/.

Leader. "Swashbuckling saga of seafort struggle." August 24, 1978.

Lee, Timothy B. "UK halts extradition of accused hacker over suicide concerns." *Ars Technica*. October 16, 2012.

Lester, Toby. "The Reinvention of Privacy." *The Atlantic*. March 2001.

Leyden, John. "Sealand dismisses McKinnon asylum offer as 'rumour.'" *The Register*. May 3, 2007.

Lichtenstein, Rachel. *Estuary: Out from London to the Sea*. London: Penguin Books, 2016.

Lilburne-Byford, Paul John. "Occupation: Wonderful Radio London: Open letter to the Insolvency Service of Southend-on-Sea, Essex." *Soundscapes*. http://www.icce.rug.nl/~soundscapes/VOLUME05/ Occupation_WRL.shtml.

Lindberg, Oliver. "Interview with UFO hacker Gary McKinnon." *.netmagazine*. May 2006.

Litz, Christian. "Der Herr Premierminister, fern der Heimat (The Prime Minister, Far From Home)." *Brand Eins*. May 2001.

*Liverpool Daily Post*. "Mersey Estuary Forts – War-Time Structures That Nobody Wants." October 13, 1945.

*Liverpool Echo*. "'Mulberry' Harbor Claim by Designer of Mersey 'Forts.'" October 18, 1948.

*London Standard*. "Invasion of the Pirate Prince." August 5, 1986.

_____. "Have Stereo Will Sail…" August 6, 1986.

*Los Angeles Times*. "Tiny Nation's Capture of German Investigated." September 5, 1978.

Lucas, Mark. "Seven miles off the Suffolk coast, the Principality of Sealand is Europe's smallest self-proclaimed independent state." *The Independent*. November 27, 2004.

Lyon, Andrew H.E. "The Principality of Sealand, and Its Case for Sovereign Recognition." *Emory International Law Review* 29, no. 3 (2015).

MacKenzie, Louise. "Why Southend girls are still happy to be beauty queens." *Southend Echo*. June 7, 2010.

MacKinnon, Lachlan. "Give me fish, not federalism: Outer Baldonia and Performances of Micronationality." *Shima: The International Journal of Research into Island Cultures* 8, no. 2 (2014).

*The Mail*. "Pirate invaders hit British TV." June 7, 1987.

Marin, Robert. "Nemec Slovenijo toi za 6 milijonov evrov (The German is suing Slovenia for six million euros)." *Novice Svet* 24. February 11, 2016.

Markoff, John. "Rebel outpost on the fringes of cyberspace." *New York Times*. June 4, 2000.

Martin, Will. "A bitcoin trader built a floating house off Thailand's coast in pursuit of a Peter Thiel dream, but authorities destroyed his vessel and he could now face the death penalty." *Business Insider*. April 23, 2019. https://www.businessinsider.com/bitcoin-trader-chad-elwartowskithai-navy-destroys-floating-house-2019-4.

Marwick, Arthur. *British Society since 1945*. London: Penguin Books, 1982.

Masnick, Mike. "It's Baaaaaack: HavenCo Trying Once Again To Bring Encrypted Computing To The Masses, But Not Hosted On Sealand." *Tech Dirt*. August 27, 2013. https://www.techdirt.com/articles/20130827/10220724324/its-baaaaaack-havenco-trying-onceagain-to-bring-encrypted-computing-to-masses-not-hosted-sealand.shtml#comments.

Mathieson, Steven. "Prince Michael of Sealand cries freedom." *Vnunet.com*. October 20, 2000.

Mauriat, Jean Luc, comment "Princess Joan of Sealand (02 September 1929 - 10 March 2016)." https://www.facebook.com/PrincipalityOfSealand/photos/a.496490988122/10153530672558123/?type=3.

McConnell, Fiona, Terri Moreau, and Jason Dittmer. "Mimicking state diplomacy: the legitimizing strategies of unofficial diplomacies." *Geoforum* 43 (2012).

McCullagh, Declan. "Has 'haven' for questionable sites sunk?" *CNET News*. August 4, 2003.

McKinnon, Gary. "Theresa May saved my life – now she's the only hope for the Human Rights Act." *The Guardian*. November 15, 2006.

McKinnon, Lachlan. "Give me fish, not federalism: Outer Baldonia and Performances of Micronationality." *Shima: The International Journal of Research into Island Cultures* 9, no. 2 (2014).

Menefee, Samuel Pyeatt. "'Republics of the Reefs:' Nation-Building on the Continental Shelf." *California Western International Law* Journal 25 (1994).

Messenger, Simon. "Around the world in 80 races – the story so far." *The Guardian*. April 14, 2015.

———. "How I ran a half marathon on Sealand, the fortress 'nation' in the middle of the sea." *The Guardian*. September 11, 2015.

———. "Sealand Half Marathon—The Full Story." *Around the world in 80 Runs*, July 31, 2015. https://80runs.co.uk/2015/07/31/sealand-half-marathon-the-full-story/.

Milmo, Cahal. "Joan Bates dead: Founder and 'princess' of Sealand dies aged 86." *The Independent*. March 14, 2016.

———. "Sealand's Prince Michael on the future of an off-shore 'outpost of liberty.'" *The Independent*. March 19, 2016.

*Miss Southend on Sea*. 2010. misssouthendonsea.co.uk.

MMC. "Med ovadenimi tudi Starman? (Starman too?)." December 8, 2006.

Moffitt, Dominic. "Arise Sir Richard: Sealand swimmer knighted." *Ipswich Star*. August 30, 2018.

———. "Brexit vote brings mini-state Sealand population explosion problem." *Ipswich Star*. January 16, 2017.

———. "From Sealand to Felixstowe: Updates as the swimmer sets off on his daring trip today." *Ipswich Star*. August 20, 2018

———. "Man finishes record-breaking bid for Sealand glory – but another swimmer beats him to it." *Ipswich Star*. August 20, 2018.

_____. "Sir Richard Royal: Sealand hero knighted by the micronation."
     *Ipswich Star*. September 5, 2018.

_____. "Swimmer to attempt 12km Sealand to Felixstowe crossing." *Ipswich
     Star*. August 11, 2018.

Mongole, Robert. "Seastead Strategies for Preventing Litigation in the United
     States." *The Seasteading Institute*. 2012.

Monson, Jane. "Guy Maunsell." Engineering Timelines. http://www.
     engineering-timelines.com/who/Maunsell_G/maunsellGuy.asp.

Montaigu. "Tribuinal correctional de Luxembourg—Trois citoyens de la
     'Principauté de Sealand' prévenus d'escroquerie (Luxembourg Criminal
     Court—Three citizens of the 'Principality of Sealand' warned of
     fraud)." *Republican Lorraine*. France, April 19, 1978.

Montgomery, James. "Fall Out Boy are taking a break…unless Sealand calls."
     *MTV.com*. August 13, 2009. http://www.mtv.com/news/1618675/
     fallout-boy-are-taking-a-break-unless-sealand-calls/.

Morcillo, Cruz. "Desmantelada una red de estafadores montada bajo el falso
     'principado de Sealand (Dismantling a network of scammers based on
     the false principality of Sealand)."' *ABC*. April 12, 2000.

Moursi, Manar. "Island Phantasmagoria – Exploring the Political/
     Philosophical Underpinnings of Fictional Islands and Imagining a
     Future of Plastic-Pirate-Island-Utopias." *Thresholds* no. 38 (Fall 2010).

Moynihan, Michael. "Bates family set up the State of Sealand." *The Sunday
     Times*. March 17, 1968.

Murphy, Kim. "3 Orange County Men Among 7 Indicted in Nationwide
     Loan Fraud Case." *Los Angeles Times*. March 27, 1987.

Murphy, Rachel. "Prince of Waves: the Extraordinary Story of How One
     Couple Claimed an Abandoned British Sea Fort and Declared a New
     State." *The Mirror*. May 22, 1999.

Najarro, Ileana. "Virginia man's claim on African land is unlikely to pass test."
     *Washington Post*. September 7, 2014. https://www.washingtonpost.
     com/local/virginia-mans-claim-on-african-landis-unlikely-to-
     passtest/2014/09/07/8bfac456-2ef9-11e4-bb9b-997ae96fad33_story.html.

*Neue Sealand Journal*, no. 2. "Putting things in the right light." September
     1978.

*News of the World*. "Pirates fight for radio fort." October 11, 1965.

*Newsweek*. "Emerging Nations: Prince Valiant." Aug. 28, 1978.

*New York Times*. "Manga Books Best Sellers." October 10, 2010. www.
     nytimes.com/books/best-sellers/2010/10/10/manga/?mtrref=en.
     wikipedia.org&gwh=E4C5F7BE5BF72349FFF1892AAE38BB9E&g
     wt=pay.

Nizinskyj, Paul. "I'm the son and heir to my own principality." *Echo News*.
     January 22, 2015.

O'Brien, Hettie. "The Floating City, Long a Libertarian Dream, Faces
     Rough Seas." *City Lab*. April 27, 2018. https://www.citylab.com/
     design/2018/04/the-unsinkable-dream-of-the-floating-city/559058/.

O'Kelly, Lisa. "Diary: No porn, but Sealand's in the family way." *Campaign.* August 7, 1987.

Olsen, Stefanie. "MPA shuts down video site Film88.com." *CNET News.* June 6, 2002.

Orth, Maureen. *Vulgar Favors: Andrew Cunanan, Gianni Versace, and the Largest Failed Manhunt in US History.* New York: Dell, 1999.

———. "Andrew Cunanan and the Assassination of Gianni Versace, Revisited." *Vanity Fair.* January 11, 2018.

Ospina, Juanita Samper. "Sealand, el país más extraño del mundo (Sealand, the strangest country in the world)." *El Tiempo.* April 9, 2000.

Parker, Matthew. *Monte Cassino: the Hardest-Fought Battle of World War II.* Anchor, 2005.

Payne, Stewart. "Pirates under siege." *Daily Mail.* August 13, 1985.

*The People.* "Pirates Ahoy! In Battle for Fort." October 10, 1965.

Petts, Oliver. "It's war in the air." *Kent Messenger.* October 15, 1965.

Phylactopoulous, Alexis. "Artificial Islands and Installations: a Call for International Legislative Action." *International Relations* 4 (1972).

The Pirate Radio Hall of Fame. www.offshoreradio.co.uk.

Platt, Charles. "Plotting away in Margaritaville." *Wired.* July 1997.

*Practical Wireless.* "Radio Essex." January 13, 1967.

Principality of Sealand [@sealandgov]. "'Sexit' (Sealand Exit) post." Instagram, February 11, 2019. https://www.instagram.com/p/BtvyKh4BUzW/.

*Ken Potter's Variety Vault.* "Principality Of Sealand Dollars and Other Coin Offers." koinpro.tripod.com/WorldCoins/Sealand_Coin_Offers.htm.

Purba, Narinder. "Gary McKinnon reveals detail on NASA data breach and 'extraterrestrial life.'" *WeLiveSecurity,* December 8, 2015. https://www.welivesecurity.com/2015/12/08/gary-mckinnon-reveals-detail-on-nasa-data-breach-and-extraterrestrial-life/.

*Radio NZ.* "Hundreds march in Tahiti against building of floating islands." April 9, 2018. https://www.radionz.co.nz/international/pacificnews/354491/hundreds-march-in-tahiti-against-building-of-floatingislands.

*Reformatorisch Dagblad.* "Hollander zit gevangen (Hollander is caught)." Holland, August 22, 1978.

———. "Hans Lavoo is weer vrij (Hans Lavoo is free again)." Holland, August 24, 1978.

Reuß, Jürgen. "Fürstentum Sealand: Herrscher über eine Seefestung (Principality of Sealand: Ruler of a Naval Fortification)." *Badische Zeitung.* May 27, 2009.

Reuter, Wolfgang. "Glücksritter Honoriger Schwindler (Lucky Knight, Noble Swindler)." *Focus Magazine* no. 10 (March 1994).

Richmond, Ben. "The Outer Space Country that the United Nations Ignored." *Vice Motherboard.* April 15, 2013. http://motherboard.vice.com/blog/the-outer-space-country-that-the-united-nations-ignored

Rincón, Reyes. "Compre una isla a precio de piso (Buy an island at the floor price)." *El País*. September 17, 2006.

Roberts, Clayton and David Roberts. *A History of England*. Vols. 1–3. Englewood Cliffs, New Jersey: Prentice-Hall, Inc., 1985.

Ropac, Iva. "Obresti od zaplenjenega denarja ostanejo dravi (The interest from the seized money remains with the state)." *Delo*. April 3, 2012.

⸻. "Virtualni podjetnik zahteva več kot milijon evrov odškodnine (A virtual entrepreneur requests more than million euros in damages)." *Delo*. January 24, 2013.

Ross, Jamie. "Micronation Of Sealand Officially Backs A Yes Vote In The EU Referendum." *Buzzfeed News*. June 24, 2015. https://www.buzzfeed. com/jamieross/micronation-of-sealand-officially-backs-a-yes-vote-inthe-eu.

Ryan, John, George Dunford, and Simon Sellars. *Micronations: The Lonely Planet Guide to Home-Made Nations*. Victoria, Australia: Lonely Planet Publications, 2006.

*Sabotage Times*. "Sealand FC: The Most Unlikely Story in International Football." February 22, 2015.

Sadler, Richard. "Last Sealand captive freed after weeks in island jail." *Evening Gazette*. September 29, 1978.

Sams, Mike. "Sealanders fear new armed raid." *Evening Gazette*. November 20, 1979.

Schafer, Andrew A. "Q&A with Ryan Lackey." *The Cloudfare Blog*, June 18, 2014. https://blog.cloudflare.com/q-a-with-ryan-lackey/.

Scott, Cathy. "Reineck talks to FBI in Las Vegas." *Las Vegas Sun*. July 25, 1997.

*Sealandnews*. "The Dalai Lama is now a Baron of the Principality of Sealand." May 28, 2008. http://www.sealandnews.com/the-dalai-lama-is-now-a-baron-of-sealand_199.html.

⸻. "Redbull Skaters ride Sealand." May 15, 2009. http://www. sealandnews.com/redbull-skaters-ride-sealand_220.html.

⸻. "Sealand Awards." December 3, 2007. http://www.sealandnews. com/sealand-awards_171.html.

⸻. "Sealand: The Movie." October 12, 2003; February 28, 2007; March 20, 2007; September 14, 2007. http://www.sealandnews.com/category/ sealand-the-movie.

⸻. "Sealand wins sporting accolade." October 30, 2008. http://www. sealandnews.com/date/2008/10/.

Sellars, Simon. "On the Heap." *The Australian*. November 10, 2007.

Shadbolt, Peter. "How UK's Red Sands Sea Forts could become a luxury hotel." *CNN*. December 9, 2015. https://www.cnn.com/travel/article/ red-sands-sea-forts-hotels-uk/index.html.

Shenker, Jack. "Welcome to the land that no country wants." *The Guardian*. March 3, 2016.

Sherringham, Denis. *Growing Up in Southend on Sea (1929–1947 approx.)*. Self-published. 1997.

Simon, Scott. "Another Country." *NPR*. August 11, 2001.

Simonenko, Basil. "Basil Simon." https://www.music2deal.com/gb/music-producer.

Simper, Robert. *Coastal Essex*. Creekside Publishing, 2011.

Sinclair, David. *The Land That Never Was: Sir Gregor MacGregor and the Most Audacious Fraud in History*. De Capo Press, 2004.

Sinclair, David, and Bob Le-Roi. "Making Waves: the Story of Radio Essex on the Knock John Fort." 2005.

Sixties City. http://www.sixtiescity.com/Radio/PirateRadio4.shtm.

*Slashdot*. "Answers from Sealand: CTO Ryan Lackey Responds." https://news.slashdot.org/story/00/07/02/160253/answers-from-sealand-cto-ryan-lackey-responds.

*Slovenia Times*. "Banka Koper changing its name." October 25, 2016

*Slovenske Novice*. "Podjetnik ne bo sluil na ra un Slovenije (An entrepreneur will not serve on behalf of Slovenia)." January 28, 2013.

Smith, Alexander. "A World's Smallest 'Nation' Sealand Grapples with Princess' Death." *NBC News*. March 19, 2006. https://www.nbcnews.com/news/world/world-s-smallest-nation-sealand-grapples-princessdeath-n540621.

Smith, R.J. "Cruisin' for a Bruisin.'" *The Village Voice*. August 11, 1987.

Smith, V.T.C. *Defending London's River: The Story of the Thames Forts 1540–1945*. North Kent Books, 1985.

*Southend and District Standard*. "Armed guard at Sealand's first wedding." May 9, 1979.

*Southend Echo*. "They searched for guns says Cap'n Roy." October 10, 1978.

*Southend Evening Echo*. "Jail fear for Prince Roy's boy." January 22, 1979.

————. "Sealand couple sail clear of arrest." January 25, 1979.

————. "Sealand 'Prince' faces radio charges." March 3, 1979.

*Southend Standard*. "Sealand – ex-'Pirate' radio chief claims fort is new state." September 6, 1967.

————. "Why 'Sealand' is free from law." October 31, 1968.

Spano, John. "Banker Pleads Guilty in Loan Scheme That Cost Victims $2 Million." *Los Angeles Times*. April 5, 1988.

Stackpole, Thomas. "The World's Most Notorious Micronation Has the Secret to Protecting Your Data From the NSA." *Mother Jones*. August 21, 2013.

Steer, John. *Walton and Frinton Lifeboat: A Station History 1184–2005*. Stroud, Gloucestershire: The History Press, 2013.

Strauss, Erwin. *How to Start Your Own Country*. Boulder: Paladin Press, 1979.

Street, Seán. *Historical Dictionary of British Radio*. Scarecrow Press, 2006.

Stubbs, Ed. "Fantasy Football, Micronation Style." *In Bed with Maradona*. August 3, 2011. http://inbedwithmaradona.com/journal/2011/8/3/fantasy-football-micronation-style.html.

Summers, Alexei. "'From the Sea, freedom:' Inside the Principality of Sealand." *The Cascade*. University of the Fraser Valley, February 29, 2012.

*The Sun.* "Pop 'commandos' say We're here to stay." October 11, 1965.

_____. "Yo-ho-ho! I board the pop pirates' sea fortress." October 12, 1965.

_____. "On board pop pirate fort – six shotguns; flame thrower, petrol bombs." June 29, 1967.

*Sunday Mirror.* "How Fort-unate." July 4, 1999.

Tate, Lesley. "Basil Simon compared to Susan Boyle after X Factor appearance." *Craven Herald.* September 1, 2011.

Taylor, Amy. "Sealand and Chagos Island play out football history." *Surrey Live.* May 11, 2012.

*Telegraph.* "Prince Roy of Sealand." October 11, 2012.

Thurlow, David. "Fined Pop Pirate stays defiant." *Daily Express.* December 1, 1966.

*The Tiger Triumphs: The Story of Three Great Divisions in Italy.* His Majesty's Stationary Office for the Government of India, 1946.

*Times.* "Joan Bates; Model who was known as 'princess of Sealand' after her husband turned a North Sea naval tower into a micro-nation." London, March 22, 2016.

_____. "T-shirts and foreign crews are stations' weapons." July 29, 1966.

_____. "Radio Station in the Thames Estuary on Air After Owner is Fined £100." December 1, 1966.

_____. "No rush of disc stations to Isle of Man." March 9, 1967.

_____. "'Pirate' plan to beat law." April 12, 1967.

_____. "100GNS Health Trips to Sea Fort." June 29, 1967.

_____. "Sea Fort Repels Boarders." June 30, 1967.

_____. "Commandos set to seize fort." August 8, 1967.

_____. "Ministry says talks over fort broke down." August 9, 1967.

_____. "Independent Isle 'Ludicrous.'" September 4, 1967.

_____. "Ministry says talks over fort broke down." September 8, 1967.

_____. "Radio man's children 'marooned.'" March 7, 1968.

_____. "Children not 'marooned.'" March 8, 1968.

_____. "Two rescued from estuary fort." March 21, 1968.

_____. "Radio Essex man summonsed." June 29, 1968.

_____. "Sea tower outside court limit." October 22, 1968.

_____. "Attempt to free captive from private 'island' fails." September 5, 1978.

Timothy, Dallen J. "Where on Earth is This Place? The Potential of Non-Nations as Tourist Destinations." *Tourism Recreation Research* 28, no. 1 (2003).

Tingle, Rory. "World's smallest self-proclaimed nation - an old WWII fort the size of two tennis courts - gets 'thousands' of citizenship requests following votes for Brexit and Donald Trump." *Daily Mail.* January 14, 2017.

Treves, Tullio. "Military Installations, Structures, and Devices on the Seabed." *The American Journal of International Law* 74 (1980).

Trickey, Erick. "Sean of Sealand – The incredible saga of a Community High grad, the dot-com bubble, and a 'micronation.'" *Ann Arbor Observer*. December 2001.

Trueman, Matt. "Pirate Radio Turf War, Raids, and Raves: Looking Back at the Early Days of KISS FM." *Vice UK*. May 15, 2015. https://www.vice.com/en_us/article/kwxazm/pirate-radio-ica.

Turner, Frank. *The Radio Pirates aboard the Offshore Forts in the Thames Estuary*. Gravesend: F.R. Turner, 1997.

_____. *The Maunsell Sea Forts, Part 1 : the World War Two Naval Sea Forts of the Thames Estuary*. Gravesend: F.R. Turner, 1994.

Underhill, Kevin. "The Guano Islands Act." *Washington Post*. July 8, 2014.

*United Nations*. "1941: The Atlantic Charter." https://www.un.org/en/sections/history-united-nations-charter/1941-atlantic-charter/index.html.

_____. "Charter of the United Nations and Statute of the International Court of Justice." https://treaties.un.org/Pages/showDetails.aspx?objid=080000028017ebb8&clang=_en.

_____. "Declaration on the granting of independence to colonial countries and peoples." https://undocs.org/A/Res/1514(XV).

*UPI Wire*. "Judge silences pirate radio ship." December 20, 1988.

Van Der Sar, Ernesto. "Aye! The Pirate Bay Anthem is Here." *TorrentFreak*, May 17, 2009. https://torrentfreak.com/aye-the-pirate-bay-anthem-is-here-090517/.

Vergano, Dan. "Bird Droppings Led to U.S. Possession of Newly Protected Pacific Islands." *National Geographic*. September 28, 2014.

von Flocken, Jan. "Vorsicht, Glücksritter! (Beware, lucky knight!)." *Focus Magazine* no. 45 (November 2000).

Wahiche, Jean-Dominique. "Artificial structures and traditional uses of the sea." *Marine Policy*. January 1983.

Wainwright, Martin. "Major defends his minor power." *The Guardian*. September 5, 1978.

_____. "Sealand keeps its prisoner." The Guardian. September 6, 1978.

Wallace, Carol. "It's Sea for Two as Britain's Roy and Joan Bates Rule Their Own Do-It-Yourself Little Island." *People*. June 18, 1984.

Wallace, Neil. "Star ship Enterprise!" *Daily Star*. August 15, 1985.

Warren, Jane. Untitled. *Daily Express*. January 13, 2007.

Watson, Neil. "A TV pirate's platform for debate – Essex Coast may be sailing into deep water." *The Times*. August 19, 1987.

Watson, Nigel. "'UFO Hacker' tells what he found." *Wired*. June 21, 2006.

Watson, Nigel and Frank Turner. *Maunsell: The Firm and its Founder*. AECOM Technology Corp., 2005.

White, Jonathan. *Tides: The Science and Spirit of the Ocean*. San Antonio: Trinity University Press, 2017.

Whitman, Frank. "Joseph invokes Fifth Amendment during Wise Owl hearing." *The Guam Daily Post*. May 23, 2013.

Wild, Jane. "Prince of Sealand who made independent stand." *Financial Times.* October 11, 2012.

Williams, Judith. *Leigh-on-Sea: A History.* Chichester: Phillimore and Co., 2002.

Winter, Jana and Jeremy A. Kaplan. "WikiLeaks to move servers offshore, sources say." *Fox News.* January 31, 2012.

*Wired.* "A Data Sanctuary is Born." June 2000.

_____. "Sealand: Come to Data." June 5, 2000.

Wise, Jeff. "Starting your own country." *Travel and Leisure.* June 2001.

*Woman's Own.* "My Life on Sealand." November 18, 1978.

Wong, Julia Carrie. "Seasteading: tech leaders' plans for floating city trouble French Polynesians." *The Guardian.* January 2, 2017. https://www.theguardian.com/technology/2017/jan/02/seasteading-peter-thielfrench-polynesia.

Woo, Elaine. "'Prince' Roy Bates dies at 91; adventuring monarch of Sealand." *Los Angeles Times.* October 14, 2012.

Woodard, Will. "Storm Warning." *The Guardian.* March 27, 2000.

*World Cups and Beyond.* March 7, 2013. http://nonfifafootball.blogspot.com/2013/03/sealand-set-for-alderney-and-chagos.html.

Yardley, William. "Roy Bates, Founder of Sealand, Dies at 91." *New York Times*, October 13, 2012.

Yearsley, Ian. A History of Southend. Chichester: Phillimore and Co., 2001.

*Yorkshire Post.* "Pirate radios the big topic." June 26, 1967.

*Yorkshire Times.* "X Factor's Basil Simon Preparing Album Release." May 7, 2013.

Zedalis, Rex J. "Military Installations, Structures, and Devices on the Seabed: A Response." *The American Journal of International Law* 75 (1981).

### *Video, Radio, and Podcasts*

Addicott, Graham, rep. "Sealand on Reporting London 1983." BBC's "Reporting London," 1983. https://www.youtube.com/watch?v=zdLFyoXSPKw.

Barker, Rob. "Escape from Sealand." Film. 2018. https://www.youtube.com/watch?v=PsfDcHGSXwk.

Bates, Michael. "Sealand Geopoetics Discussion Part 1." Talk at the Bienal do Mercosul, Porto Alegre, Brazil, September 17, 2011. https://www.youtube.com/watch?v=iNwdjYf1SKs.

Bates, Roy. "ITN Reporting 66: Pirate radio stations." SOT England interviews owner of Radio Essex, aired on *ITN*, May 11, 1966. https://www.gettyimages.co.uk/detail/video/pirate-radio-stations-roy-bates-interview-sot-england-news-footage/828457928.

Bates, Roy. "Sealand over the years." Undated ABC Feature in Facebook video post, February 23, 2009. https://www.facebook.com/PrincipalityOfSealand/videos/143870825480/?v=143870825480.

Bohrer, Robert, Dag Freyer, Jobst Knigge, Niels Negendank, and Matthias Schmidt, dirs. *Ein Leben daneben (A life beside it)*. Episode 5. ZDF Kultur, 2011.

Fogle, Ben, rep. "Sealand on the One Show 2011." BBC's "The One Show," 2011. https://www.youtube.com/watch?v=P_LnPYRSLIc.

Freedman, Avi and Ryan Lackey. "Presentation to H2K2 Hackers on Planet Earth Conference." Talk at the Ultimate Co-Location Site, 2002. http://www.h2k2.net/media/collocation.mp3.

Gale, Benjamin, dir. "Sealand: The Mystery Solved." Commissioned by Sealand's government, 2003. https://www.youtube.com/watch?v=fGb-cIZNdvY.

Goddard, Scott, dir. "Documentary by Scott Goddard." Documentary, 2003 in Facebook video post, 2009. https://www.facebook.com/PrincipalityOfSealand/videos/143936845480/.

Hibberd, Grant. "The Sealand Affair: The Last Great Adventure of the Twentieth Century?" UK Foreign and Commonwealth Office Podcast, November 19, 2011.

*In Living Memory.* Season 16, ep. 1. BBC, 2012. https://www.bbc.co.uk/programmes/b01l7w1p.

Simon, Scott, rep. "The Pirate Prince of Sealand, Remembered." NPR's "Weekend Edition," October 13, 2012.

Stroumboulopoulos, George. "Interview With Prince of Sealand." CBC's "The Hour," January 2007. https://www.youtube.com/watch?v=ZDgg9WjkUdM&t=394s.

Lackey, Ryan. "Def Con 11 – Ryan Lackey – HavenCo: What Really Happened." Talk at Def Con 11, 2003. https://www.youtube.com/watch?v=aJ6ByBaTxms.

McClure, Ross, dir. "No Half Measures." Let It Howl, 2015. https://vimeo.com/154965386.

"Red Bull Access All Areas meets Sealand." RedBull Skateboarding, 2008. https://www.youtube.com/watch?v=jhCVoKZYYNU.

"Sealand – a flak tower becomes an economic base in the North Sea." German TV's Channel 1, January 22, 1978.

"Sealand after the Invasion 1978 BBC1 News report .mp4." Report. BBC 1, September 1978. https://www.youtube.com/watch?v=JgvxgYy10S4&t=3s.

"Sealand Fort Offshore." Report. BBC, 2006. https://www.youtube.com/watch?v=im5G5xYmK0I&t=3s.

"Sealand on Bravo Channel 2001." Bravo's "A-Z of Bad Boys," 2001. https://www.youtube.com/watch?v=4O7NVSocxsU.

"Sealand on the UK Evening News Sept 2002." Report. UK Evening News, September 2002. https://www.youtube.com/watch?v=VeletZa9qQY.

"Skateboarding the world's smallest country." RedBull Skateboarding, 2008. https://www.youtube.com/watch?v=7pHwkbDx_34.

"Sovereign Principality of Sealand." NPR's "Weekend Edition," August 11, 2011.

"Stranger than paradise." NPR's "On the Media," May 20, 2005. www.onthemedia.org/transcripts/2005/05/20/03.

# ACKNOWLEDGMENTS

The principality loomed on the horizon just as I'd been expecting it, exactly as incongruous a thing to come out of the middle of the ocean as I'd imagined. Equally enormous, however, was the soaring joy of my soul as the silhouette came into view. The trip was like stepping into a dream, and almost like a homecoming.

By the time I visited on March 27, 2019, I'd been researching and writing this book for two years and had been a fan of Sealand for over ten. I'd spoken with many, many people knowledgeable about its history or involved with its evolution, and after reading thousands of pages of documents and briefs, I found myself surprisingly knowledgeable about everything from another country's radio pirates to the vagaries of maritime law. But most intensely, I felt like I knew Sealand inside and out. I could picture the towers, hear the winch, smell the diesel; I knew the layout and the contours of the helipad, and I knew there was a makeshift brig down in the bottom of one of the legs. I sometimes even walked the fort in my dreams, and I couldn't believe I was being ferried out there on a fishing boat and hanging out with people who have played a major role in its history.

Meeting Michael inspired a feeling I imagined a historian might feel if given the chance to meet Abraham Lincoln, or a paleontologist who gets to see a real dinosaur. I knew more about this man than I do some of my friends, and yet I was seeing him for the first time. And then I was able to meet James and Liam and Penny Bates, and the feeling of living in an unreal world was compounded intensely. Being invited into your home and being able to ask you all kinds of questions and hear your stories and get some personal insight on this whole adventure was a fantastic treat and I hope that I have done justice to the remarkable lives your family has and continues to lead. The same goes to Dan, Pecker, Joe, and Mike Barrington, who answered countless questions and were such awesome guides. That trip will live in my mind triumphantly forever. Thank you as well to Lorraine Bates and

Charley Bates for the funny and candid insight on what it's like to marry into a royal family.

Cheers and gratitude in no particular order to Slader Oviatt, Erwin Strauss, Michael Martelle, Joichi Ito, Allan Weiner, Thomas Hodgkinson, Roland Teschner, Andrea Mann, Finn Brunton, Hubert Vom Venn, Richard Barreto, Joanne Berkowitz, Derek Watson, Vincent Cogliati-Bantz, Jules Gouvernante and little Shadow, Andrew Lawrence, Andrea Mann, Raymond Craib, and Joyce Lambert for their help and input. Thanks a ton to Minister of Parliament Sir David Amess, Judith Suttling, and Julie Cushion for allowing two Americans to barge in on your constituent surgery, and piratical hails to Brendan Spiegel and Narratively for publishing an amended version of chapter 12 in January 2019. Thanks to Eduard Pagés Riberaygua for the tremendous cache of documents and his serious dedication to micronational concerns, and to Hans Knot for his wildly helpful treasure trove of Sealandic history. Ivy League cheers to James Grimmelmann for providing generous access to his incredible collection of documents, without which I would've had a very hard time getting this off the ground. Huge thanks to Paul Hooten for the enormous help in tracking down information about Roy's company in the Royal Fusiliers and to John Howes for the information and books detailing the same. Thank you immensely to Paul Gilson for the history lesson and guided tour, and for his amazing book, and to the generous, funny, and dedicated organizers and attendees of MicroCon 2019.

Many thanks to the helpful and hard-working staff at the Cornell Library, the Leigh and Westcliffe library branches, the Leigh Heritage Centre and Museum, the UK National Archives, and the Record Offices of Essex and Sussex, and the Forum in Southend-on-Sea.

I am of course enormously indebted to Melanie Madden at Diversion for her expert guidance and answering my millions of questions, and to my agent Amanda Jain at Bookends Literary for taking an interest in the project and helping me navigate the many steps of this sometimes molasses-like process. I really appreciate your guidance and the work you put into this project, and I look forward to embarking on future endeavors together!

And to my mom, dad, and brother: I'm so lucky to be part of this family and to be surrounded by smart, friendly, and good-natured people engaged in their own tremendous pursuits. I love you all very, very much.

Pamela, my love: Traveling with you was so, so fun and I can't wait for the next trip big or small. Your help has been invaluable and your insight spot on—it was always a good sign when you would shoo me away because you were so excited about what you were reading that you didn't want me to interrupt you. I'm glad it wasn't another Fent Noland situation, and I'm glad we got to go on this hilarious and remarkable journey together. You rule the principality of my heart.

# INDEX

## A

Abu Dhabi, 135
Achenbach, Alexander Gottfried, 102, 104–6, 109, 122, 143–44, 152–54, 157, 218, 221, 260
AECOM, 30
Airfern, Ltd., 16
Andersson, Tobias, 187–88
Anglican Free Church, 105
Argentina, 128–29
Armstrong, Neil, 211
Arundel, Russell, 68
Assange, Julian, 189
Ata, Muztagh, 198–99

## B

*Baalbek*, 29
Bachelier, Julien, 200
Baier, Eva, 153–54
Baier, Josef, 153–54
Barbados, 70
Barreto, Richard, 147
Barrington, Mike, 28, 74, 184, 203, 231, 234–41, 264, 276
Baskir, Genie, 138, 173–74
Bates, Charlotte, 131, 215–16
Bates, Freddy Michael Roy, 217
Bates, Harry, 11–12, 217
Bates, James, 74, 130–31, 183–84, 204–5, 208, 215–17, 228, 246, 265–70
Bates, Joan, 3–4, 14–17, 40–41, 47, 49, 59–61, 65–67, 70, 72–74, 76–77, 93, 96, 99, 109, 112–13, 118, 120, 123, 125, 141–42, 147, 151, 157, 209, 212–13, 217, 276
Bates, Liam, 74, 131, 183, 191, 202, 215, 217, 235, 237, 246–47, 265–70
Bates, Lilyan, 11–12, 112
Bates, Lorraine, 213, 268
Bates, Michael Roy, 1–3, 15, 17–18, 20–21, 20–22, 25, 36, 38–43, 42, 49–55, 59–60, 62, 65, 71, 73, 75–78, 83–84, 86–90, 93–97, 99–101, 103, 108, 109–14, 120–21, 123, 127, 129–31, 135, 143, 146, 149–50, 157, 173–76,
183–92, 193–94, 201–2, 208, 210, 212–15, 217–18, 228–29, 240, 243–45, 248–50, 253, 257, 262–63, 265–70, 273–74, 276
Bates, Penelope "Penny," 3, 17, 36, 42, 60–61, 73, 75, 93, 96, 210, 213–15, 276
Bates, Roy, 2–4, 9–21, 30, 33–34, 37–39, 46–48, 52, 55–63, 65–67, 70–74, 77, 79, 83, 86, 88–91, 95–97, 99–100, 107, 109, 112–20, 116–24, 128, 135–37, 140–42, 145–46, 147, 155, 157, 167, 173, 209–11, 238–39, 264–65, 271, 279–82, 285
Baugh, Kevin, 255, 257
B&B Fisheries, 16
Belasco, David, 51–52, 84, 276
Belasco, Marjorie, 84–85
Belgium, 98
*Bembridge*, 59
Berger, Thomas, 223
Berkowitz, Joanne, 99
Black, Kitty, 35
Blackburn, Darron, 197–98
Blue Frontiers, 258–59
Boreham, Mr., 89
Boss, Evert, 110, 114–15
Bridges, Jeff, 138
Brings, Winifred, 110
Brisley, 84
British Army, 9
British Broadcasting Corporation (BBC), 33–34, 63
Bulwer-Lytton, Edward G., 226
Burmeister, Lennie, 200

## C

Calvert, Reg, 35, 37–38, 45
Carbone, Giorgio, 195
Carolyn, Queen, 262
Casley, Leonard George, 135
Cassell, Raymond, 118
Cassino, 9
Chagos Islands, 202
Channon, Paul, 61, 86

Chapman, Judge Justice, 88–91, 282
*Charlotte Joan,* 244–46
Chelton, James, 125
Clarkson, Jeremy, 192
Cockle Row, 245
Cogliati-Bantz, Vincent, 263
*Colchester Evening Gazette,* 121, 141
Collins, Albert, 15
Collins, Elizabeth, 15
Collins, Joan. *see* Bates, Joan
Columbus, Christopher, 97
Conway, Lionel, 65–66, 116, 119, 279
Cook, Captain, 97
Cool, Kenton, 197
Coubertin, Pierre de, 181, 196
Courts of Assize, 283
Cousteau, Jacques, 22
Cousteau, Jean-Michael, 268
Craib, Raymond, 259
Crate, Vince, 163
Crawford, Allan, 35
Crewdson, John, 113, 125
Crowe, Russell, 190
Cunanan, Andrew, 146

**D**
da Gama, Vasco, 97
*Daily Mail,* 61
Doggerland, 19
Drake, Francis, 97

**E**
Ealing, 11
Eastham, Mr., 89
Ebel, Wolfgang Gerhard Guenter, 224
Eck, Helmut, 110, 114–15
*Egeria,* 83
Elbow, Susan, 172
Elizabeth II, Queen, 101, 284
Elwartowski, Chad, 261
Ewing Oil, 141

**F**
Faber Maunsell, 30
Federal Republic of Germany, 220
*Financial Times,* 107
Fogle, Ben, 192, 215
Forsyth, Neil, 202

Fort Knock John, 20, 21, 25, 30, 37–38, 47, 183
Franklin, Benjamin, 225
Freedman, Avi, 168, 179
French Polynesia, 258–59
Friedman, Milton, 259
Friedman, Patri, 259–60
Fritz, Johan, 281
Frobisher, Martin, 97–98
*Fury,* 138

**G**
G. Maunsell & Partners, 30
Gaddafi, Muammar, 100
Gardner, Barry, 116
Garfinkel, Simson, 161–62, 169, 171
Garner, George, 99
George, King, 2.0, 256
Germany, 106–8
Gibson, Mel, 190
Gilder, Eric, 138
Gilson, Paul, 250
Glendinning, Nick, 207–8
Goddard, Patrick, 254
*Golden Eye,* 145
Gramlich, Wayne, 259
Griffing, Dan, 232–35, 241
Gutman (lawyer), 137

**H**
Hache, Christian, 97
Hagerty, Emma, 201
Haggard, Mervyn, 138
Hal Turner Show, 139
Hamill, Joe, 74, 206–7, 231–35, 239–40, 276
Hanlon, Ken, 141
Harcus, Barry, 95, 114
Harrington, Chris, 200
Harrison, George, 48
Hastings, Jo, 163, 172
Hastings, Sean, 161, 163–64, 166–69, 172–73
HavenCo, 161–62, 166–79, 237
Hawker, David, 214
Hawkins, Michael, 118
Hawtin, Guy, 107
Hencken, Randolph, 259
*Hetalia,* 191
Hibberd, Grant, 108, 274, 284

Holgate, Charley Rae, 216–17
Houston, Whitney, 211
Hoy, Michael, 165
Huff, Miles, 255, 258
Huxtable, Karen, 124–26

## I

Indian Infantry Division, 9
Indian Stream Republic, 68
InmoNaranja, 185, 188, 189
*In re Duchy of Sealand* 80 I.L.R 683, 104
Ipswich Post Office, 98
Isle of Sheppey, 12
Ito, Joichi, 168, 178

## J

Jacolliot, Louis, 226
Jagger, Mick, 48
Jamaica, 70
Jarsgard, Viking King, 213
Jedlička, Vít, 269–70
Johns, Adrian, 277
Jones, Tommy Lee, 138

## K

Kammerer, Detlef J., 102
Kemper, Wallace Clegg, 141–43
Kenya, 70
KLM, 123
*Kommissarische Reichsregierung* (KRR), 220
Kwon, Minsung, 256

## L

Lackey, Ryan, 161–64, 166, 168–78
Lavoo, Hans, 115
Lawrence, Andrew, 247, 249
Leisner, Walter, 102–3, 136, 221
Le-Roi, Bob, 10, 39
Ley, Friedbert, 151–52
Lichtenstein, Rachel, 70
Lier, Pim, 143
Lilburne-Byford, Paul John, 138–39, 173–74
Liri Valley, 9
*Litchfield I,* 134
Little, Ralf, 202
Locke, John, 255

Luxembourg, 103–4
Lyon, Andrew, 109

## M

Mac, Gordon, 132
MacGregor, Gregor, 155–56
Magellan, 97
Mandela, Nelson, 192
Mangan, James, 68
Mann, Andrea, 192
Martelle, Michael, 199–200
Martello towers, 24
Martin, Dean, 37
Massó, Miguel Palacios, 150
Maunsell, Guy Anson, 20–25, 23, 26–28, 30, 277
Maunsell Naval Forts, 20–29, 106
Mauriat, Jean-Luc, 213
May, Theresa, 188
*Mayflower,* 74
McCall, Fiona, 278
McHenry, Travis, 255
McKinnon, Gary, 186–89
McLaren, Malcolm, 192
Mei Shi, 269–70
Menefee, Samuel Pyeatt, 273
Menegatto, Marcello, 196
Mersey Estuary, 28
Messenger, Simon, 203–4
*Mi Amigo,* 35–36, 48
MicroCon, 253–56, 262
Mierisch, Walter, 94
Ministry of Defense, 56
Mizzi, Suzanne, 141
*Mizzy Gel,* 16, 19–21, 49, 56, 60, 75
Moffat, Sheriff, 127
Monte Cassino, 9–10
Moore, Ryan, 202
Murphy, James, 137, 138, 174
*MV Ross Revenge,* 236

## N

National Egg Board, 35–36
Nation of Celestial Space, 68
Nazis, 9
Neimoller, Christoph, 120
*Neue Sealand Journal,* 112
Newell, Mike, 190
Newey, John, 47

Nore Army Forts, 29
North Sea, 19

**O**

Oberstadt, Adam, 257
*Offshore II,* 51–52
Olderbug, Mr., 110
Onassis, Aristotle, 96
Oomen, Adrian L.C.M., 103, 111–12, 115, 122–24, 144
O'Rahilly, Ronan, 46
Osborne Bros., 247
Oscar Faber, 30
Oviatt, Slader, 197–99

**P**

Palmer, Dick, 39, 42
Parekh, Sameer, 168
PayPal, 260
"Pecker," 182–83, 240–41
Pillin, Philip, 255
The Pirate Bay, 187
Pollack, Max, 257–58
Post Office, 97–98
Principality of Outer Baldonia, 68–69
Principality of Sealand, 20, 72–73. *see also* Roughs Tower
Principality of Seborga, 195–96
Publicola, Sôgmô Gaius Soergel, 257
Pütz, Gernot Ernst, 109, 111, 114–17, 123
Pütz, Hannelore, 119–21
Pye, David, 244

**Q**

Quirk, Joe, 261

**R**

Radio 390, 35
Radio Atlanta, 35
Radio Caroline, 48–51, 134, 236
Radio City, 37–38
Radio Essex, 39–42, 49, 55, 96
Radio Investigation Service of the Department of Trade and Industry, 132
Radio London, 35
Radio Mercur, 34

Radio Newyork International (RNI), 134, 137
Radio Northsea International, 134
Radio Sutch, 35
Raleigh, Walter, 97
Reagan, Ronald, 127
Reineck, Torsten, 146–48
Republic of Madawaska, 68
Reuhl, Mattias, 147
Roberts, Eric, 190
Rockall, 69
Rolling Stones, 40
Rothstein, Ivan, 133
*Rough Sands Gazette,* 173–74
Roughs Tower, 1–2, 20, 25–26, 30, 48–51, 55–56, 59–60, 72, 78, 85, 181–82, 264, 282–84. *see also* Principality of Sealand
Rowland, Kelly, 194
Royal, Richard, 206–8
Royal Fusiliers, 10–11, 14
Ruiz, Francisco Trujillo, 148–52
Rye, Mark, 201

**S**

*Sarah,* 133–35, 137–38, 174
Sauerbrey, Hans-Jürgen, 152
Schaapveld, Minister, 115
Scheffel, Walter, 101, 107
Schrimpf, KH, 152
Schuster, Philipp, 200
Screamin' Lord Sutch, 35
Sealand Information Gathering and Messaging Agency (SIGMA), 103
The Sealand Trade Development Authority Limited (STDAL), 153–54
Seasteading Institute (TSI), 258–61
Seiger, Johannes W.F., 144, 152, 157, 218, 220–26, 229
Sellars, Simon, 27
Shaw, Suzanne, 192
Sheeran, Ed, 192
Shire Hall, 89
Sillie, Derek, 197, 202
Simon, Scott, 212
Simonenko, Basil, 193–96, 201
Simpson, Colin, 276
Sinatra, Frank, 37
Smedley, Oliver, 35, 45

Sommer, Hans-Peter, 219–20
Sorensen, Sean, 189–90
Starman, Daniel, 154–55
Strauss, Erwin, 164–65
Stroumboulopoulos, George, 192
Sunk Head, 20, 30, 62
Sweby, William, 57–59, 84–86

**T**

Taliercio, Alexandre, 260
Tan, Alex, 176
Territory of Poyais, 156
Teschner, Roland, 94
Thames Estuary, 19, 20, 24, 29, 70, 244
Thames Estuary Special Defense Units
    (TESDUs), 25
Thatcher, Margaret, 127
Thepdet, Supranee, 261
Thiel, Pete, 260
Thorpe Bay, 18
Tongue Sands, 20, 30
Trinity House, 87
Trump, Donald, 229
Turner, Frank, 30

**U**

United Kingdom, 98
United Nations, 103, 280
University of Salford, 243

**V**

Versace, Gianni, 146–47
*Vestal,* 86–87
Vestey, Edmund, 13
Vilchez, Gabriel Medina, 185–86
Vile, Kris, 200
Vitanyi, Bela, 107, 136, 221
von Hohenstaufen Anjou Plantagenet,
    Yasmine, 196

**W**

Wakering, 15
Wallace, Danny, 192
Watson, Emma, 190
Watson, Nigel, 30
Weiner, Allan, 133–35, 137–38, 139, 174
Wentz, Pete, 192
Wesley, Mark, 42
Westcliff, 17

Wheeler, Lorraine "Lozzie," 129–30, 132
WikiLeaks, 189
Wilkinson, Gordon "Willy," 95, 113–14,
    124–26
Wilson, Harold, 55, 57
*Wired,* 161–62
Wogan, Terry, 192
Wonderful Radio London (WRLI),
    138–39
Wylde, Captain, 95

**Y**

Yagjian, Carolyn, 255

**Z**

Zieler, Gerry, 210

CPSIA information can be obtained
at www.ICGtesting.com
Printed in the USA
BVHW080746040720
582857BV00002B/4